he Popular Guide to Suf

. P. Mortlock: Former County
ibrarian of Norfolk was born at
'ixoe, Suffolk—100 yards from the
)unty boundary so it was a close run
ing! Spent most of his childhood at
ildenhall where he was a choirboy
: St Mary's, one of the finest churches
the county. Grammar school was
•llowed by service in the Indian
rmy. His library career began in 1947
'ith the old West Suffolk County. By
is time 'church bagging' was a
)mpulsive habit, continuing in the
'est Riding and Derbyshire before he
ime back to East Anglia in 1960. He
arted making notes on Norfolk
urches at that time and in partner-
iip with C. V. Roberts, produced the
iree-volume *Popular Guide to*
orfolk Churches between 1981 and
)85. In doing so, he completed the
)und of all the county's medieval
urches and is looking forward to
)ing the same in Suffolk.

ront cover: Great Finborough, St Andrew

ack cover: Hengrave, Church of the Reconciliation

Walk about Sion, and go round about her:
and tell the towers thereof,
Mark well her bulwarks, set up her houses:
that ye may tell them that come after.

Psalm XLVIII

D. P. Mortlock

The Popular Guide
to Suffolk Churches
: West Suffolk

With an encyclopaedic Glossary

ACORN EDITIONS

To the fragrant memory of my Suffolk forebears

Acknowledgements

The photographs are reproduced by permission of Mr D. P. Mortlock. The elevation and ground plan is reproduced by permission of Ms C. Mortlock.

Acorn Editions
P.O. Box 60
Cambridge
CB1 2NT

British Library Cataloguing in Publication Data

Mortlock, D.P.
    A popular guide to Suffolk churches.
    1: West Suffolk
    1. Suffolk. Churches. Visitors' guides
    I. Title
    914.26'404858

    ISBN 0-906554-10-1

Copyright © D. P. Mortlock 1988

First published 1988

Printed in Great Britain by,
Richard Clay Ltd, Bungay, Suffolk

All rights reserved. No part of this publication may be reproduced, stored in retrieval system, or transmitted in any form or by any means, electronic, mechanical, photocopying, recording, or otherwise, without the prior permission in writing of the publisher.

Contents

Front cover: Mildenhall, St Mary

The Styles of Architecture

An instant check-list – but see 'Styles of Architecture' in the glossary (p.159) for detailed background.
All dates are approximate only.

Saxon – C7 to the Conquest (1066)

Norman – 1066 to about 1200

Transitional/Early English – 1200 to 1300

Decorated – 1300 to 1350

Perpendicular – 1350 to 1500

Tudor – 1500 to 1600

The Monarchs

William I, 1066-1087
William II, 1087-1100
Henry I, 1100-35
Stephen, 1135-54
Henry II, 1154-89
Richard I, 1189-99

John, 1199-1216
Henry III, 1216-72
Edward I, 1272-1307

Edward II, 1307-27
Edward III, 1327-77
Richard II, 1377-99

Henry IV, 1399-1413
Henry V, 1413-22
Henry VI, 1422-71
Edward IV, 1461-83
Richard II, 1483-5

Henry VII, 1485-1509
Henry VIII, 1509-47
Edward VI, 1547-53
Mary I, 1553-8
Elizabeth I, 1558-1603

Map references in brackets after church names refer to map on p. ix.
Glossary entries appear in **bold** type.

ntroduction

he churches of Suffolk are among its
iiding treasures, and to study them
l in depth demands a lifetime.
onetheless, a short visit to any one of
iem can be an adventure of discovery
id delight, and this volume, the first
 three, provides a concise guide in
indy form to each. Because I am an
ithusiast rather than an expert or a
iecialist, technical terms are avoided
here possible but, when used, they
e printed in **bold** and an explanation
ill be found in the encyclopaedic
lossary. There are entries, too, for
iints, famous persons, artists,
ichitects and craftsmen, as well as
storical notes for background
formation. The series covers all
nglican churches currently in use,
id those cared for by the **Redundant
hurches Fund** which are used for
casional services. Modern churches
ive their own fascination and sur-
rises and do not deserve to be
nored, and I cannot recall a visit that
d not provide something of interest.
 The parish church is sometimes the
ily building in a village with any
aim to architectural distinction, and
 often an intriguing amalgam of
terations, additions, oddities and
iigmas. More than that, it bears the
ipress of centuries of social, political
d religious change, and has become
e silent witness of its community.
iere is peace, a sense of continuity,
id an invitation to take the long view.
 it seems neglected, remember that
is is nothing new. In 1562, The

Second Book of Homilies talks of
'... the sin and shame to see so many
churches so ruinous and so foully
decayed in almost every corner...
Suffer them not to be defiled with rain
and weather, with dung of doves,
owls, choughs...and other filthiness'.
The Victorians in their turn inherited
a legacy of neglect, and while many a
restoration or rebuilding can be
criticised, we owe them a debt that is
not always acknowledged. In general,
our churches are in better state than
they have been for centuries, thanks to
the energies and faith of local
communities, the stirling work of the
Suffolk Historic Churches Trust, and a
growing national awareness of the
scale of the problem.
 For the casual visitor, access is
sometimes difficult, but it was
heartening to find that, of the 168
churches covered in this volume, 57%
were open, 23% were locked but
displayed a contact address, and only
17% were locked with no suggestion as
to what to do about it. The remaining
3% had keys ingeniously hidden—
convenient for those in the know but
infuriating if you have spent half an
hour scouring the village for help.
History repeats itself even in this, for
an 1846 guide to some Norfolk
churches remarked:
　It is very tiresome when one has
　travelled so far—in our case 12
　miles—to see a church, to find that
　the parish clerk lives a mile off: and
　on reaching his cottage to hear that

he has gone out, and has taken the key in his pocket...

If conditions demand that the church be locked, I would plead for a legible and up-to-date notice in the porch or on the outer door, giving an unambiguous address (Mrs Smith, The Street, is not always enough for strangers).

To appreciate the beauty of roofs and stained glass, binoculars are a great help.

I have read assiduously preparing these guides—my debt previous writers on the subject massive. Many people have als helped me that to particularise seem invidious. However, I must record m grateful thanks to Birkin Haward, Ro Tricker, Peter Hollingham, Andre Anderson and the Suffolk Herald Society. The host of kind people that met by chance along the way hav treasure in store.

West Suffolk

NORFOLK

N

A B C D E F G

1

2

Santon Downham

Brandon

Lakenheath • Wangford

3

Elveden

Barnham • Euston

Market Weston • Hopton • Thelnetham

Coney Weston

Redgrave

Palgrave

Wortham

Hinderclay

Fakenham • Sapiston Barningham Rickinghall Inferior

Mildenhall, Eriswell Honington Bardwell Hepworth **Botesdale**

Beck Row Stanton Wattisfield Rickinghall Superior

Mildenhall, West Row **Mildenhall** Troston Ixworth Langham Walsham-

Worlington Ampton Thorpe Stowlangtoft le-Willow Westhorpe

Freckenham Barton Mills Icklingham Wordwell Great Badwell Ash Finningham

Herringswell Tuddenham West Stow Ingham Livermere Stanton Hunston Great Ashfield Wyverstone Bacton

Lackford Culford Timworth Pakenham

Cavenham Flempton Fornham Great Barton Thurston Norton Elmswell

Kentford Hengrave St Martin Beyton Tostock Wetherden

Exning Risby Fornham **Bury St Edmunds** Rougham Hessett Woolpit Drinkstone Shelland Haughley Harleston

• Higham All Saints Rattlesden Onehouse

Moulton Gazeley Barrow Westley Rushbrooke Lit Welnetham Bradfield Gedding Buxhall Great Finborough

Newmarket Dalham Little Saxham Nowton Great St George

Hargrave Great Saxham Welnetham Bradfield Felsham

Denham Horringer Hawstead Bradfield St Clare

Ickworth Whepstead Combust

Ousden Chevington Rede Stanningfield Lawshall Cockfield Thorpe Morieux

Lidgate Chedburgh Brockley Somerton Preston Kettlebaston

Cowlinge Depden Wickhambrook Hawkedon Hartest Shimpling Brettenham

Great Denston Boxted Alpheton **Lavenham** Chelsworth

Bradley Stradishall Stansfield Stanstead Monks Eleigh

Little Bradley Hundon Poslingford Glemsford Brent Eleigh

Great Thurlow Bamardiston Kedington Cavendish Long Brent Eleigh

Little Thurlow Melford

Great Wratting Withersfield Little Wratting **Clare** Acton

Haverhill Wixoe

Stoke-by-Clare

Sudbury

ESSEX

8

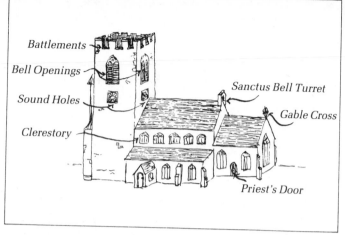

Battlements

Bell Openings

Sound Holes

Clerestory

Sanctus Bell Turret

Gable Cross

Priest's Door

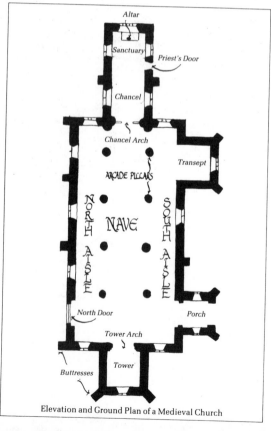

Altar

Sanctuary

Priest's Door

Chancel

Chancel Arch

Transept

ARCADE PILLARS

NORTH AISLE

NAVE

SOUTH AISLE

North Door

Porch

Tower Arch

Buttresses

Tower

Elevation and Ground Plan of a Medieval Church

Foreword by the Duke of Grafton

As chairman of Trustees both of national and local bodies concerned with historic churches, I welcome this book and believe that it will prove to be an invaluable companion for all who visit Suffolk's churches. As more and more people discover the richness of our heritage, there is a need for guides that are authoritative but not boring, comprehensive yet pocketable, and this is what Mr Mortlock has provided.

It is not only in the grand churches of Lavenham and Long Melford that things of interest and beauty may be found. Virtually every village church has something to offer and this book will encourage its readers to go and see for themselves. When they do they will realise the tremendous efforts being made by hundreds of small parishes to maintain their churches, not only as places of worship, but as havens of rest and quiet refreshment for all who visit them. And having done so I hope that they too will lend their support.

Alphabetical Guide to Churches

Acton, All Saints (D7): Placed on the western edge of the village, a long avenue of tall limes leads up to the church. The base of the tower dates from about 1300 but it became unsafe and was partly demolished in 1885 when there was an extensive restoration by W.M. Fawcett. The roofs were entirely replaced, using oak from Acton Place, the **chancel** was raised, and the e. window was restored following the style of the original. It was not until 1923 that the tower was rebuilt. The walls of the **porch** and s. **aisle** are rendered and there is an attractive **string course** decorated with a selection of tiny masks and animals. The s. aisle chapel goes beyond the chancel and the windows are blocked by the large tomb within, for which the chapel was built. The n. aisle chapel finishes level with the chancel and has a handsome C19 e. window. Its n.e. window has a late example of the four-petalled flower motif in the **tracery**. There is a **priest's door** on that side and a plain early C14 n. door with signs above it of a vanished porch. There is a **stoup** by the s. door under a **cusped** arch and the remains of a **hood mould**. Within the tower, a strange relic of the more recent past is a small bomb dropped on the village by a Zeppelin in 1916. Above the tower arch is a **sanctus-bell window** and over the n. door is an exquisite set of **Hanoverian Royal Arms**, pierced and beautifully carved in limewood. They are smaller than the set at Long Melford but are so

similar that the same craftsman may have been responsible. The **font** is C19 but in the s. aisle at the e. end stands the bowl of the late C13 original which was recovered from the vicarage garden. Also at that end is an interesting C19 **bier** which, unlike most of that period, was made by a wheelwright in the fashion of a miniature waggon. The **nave** benches have a fine selection of **poppyheads**, including an unusual subject on the third bench-end from the w. in the s. aisle - a pair of moorhens. The s. aisle chapel doubles now as a **vestry** but was built to contain an excellent monument installed in 1761 for Robert Jennens, the Duke of Marlborough's aide-de-camp who died in 1725. He lies on a pillowed couch in long wig and sumptuous coat whose lace edgings and buttons are beautifully modelled. His wife's figure, seated pensively at his feet, was placed there at her death. The background is in pale, mottled marble, with three urns on the **pediment** and a **cartouche** of arms behind the figures. Also buried here is Jennens' son, William, who died in 1798 at the age of 98. He had been a page to George I, a life-long bachelor, and an inveterate miser who died a millionaire and intestate. The interminable case in Chancery had all the trappings of false claimants, fake family bibles, and an unsigned will, and has been taken to be the basis for 'Jarndyce v. Jarndyce' in *Bleak House*, although Dickens did not admit it. The chancel roof is attractive in red and white, with star shapes over the **sanctuary** as a **canopy of honour**. Below are late C17 **communion rails** with well turned **balusters**, and the two-bay **arcade** to the s. has a good bearded **headstop** in the centre. Opposite is a lovely **ogee** arch which opens into the n. aisle chapel over a tomb. It is **cusped** and **crocketted** on both sides, and the large angel terminals to all the cusps have sadly lost their heads. There are **paterae** in the mouldings, tall side pinnacles, and two shields hang from heads above. Whose it was is not known but its magnificence and position point to an important benefactor, and it is highly likely that it was used as a base for the **Easter sepulchre**. A small doorway at the side connects with the chapel. The e. window glass is a Last Supper by **Heaton, Butler & Bayne**, with the painted faces showing signs of deterioration. The n. chapel contains the church's treasure - the finest military **brass** in the country of its period. By the n. wall, it commemorates Sir Robert de Bures who died in 1331 and it is the oldest brass in Suffolk. It is also, at 79 in, one of the largest, and is in beautiful condition. The style of armour is that of the 1300s and it may conceivably have been made for another knight. The shield is engraved as a separate plate which is most unusual. Sir Robert is dressed entirely in mail except for the elaborate knee guards and wears a surcoat over the armour. He was a distinguished servant of his country and further over is the effigy of the last of his line to live at Acton, Henry de Bures who died in 1528. Henry wears a good example of **Tudor** armour, with a long sword hung in front of him. Also on the n. side is the brass of Alyce, widow of Sir Edmund Bryan, who probably died about 1435; she wears widows' weeds with a veil head-dress, and portions of the canopy and two shields have survived. Another Dame Alyce, widow of Sir Guy Bryan, priest, endowed a **chantry** here before the **Reformation**.

There are two smaller brasses in th s.e. corner of the chapel: for Edmur and Margaret Daniel (1569 and 158! and John Daniel (1590)replica of th famous de Bures brass is mounted c a table for the convenience of bra rubbers.

Alpheton, St Peter and St Paul (D€
The church is a good half mile to th w. of the village and the main roa but it is clearly signposted. The **Pe pendicular** tower has a wide w. wi dow, renewed bell openings, and pa of the battlements retain some **flus work**. The C14 **priest's door** in the wall of the **chancel** has slim, partial renewed attached columns and the are two ranks of **paterae** in the moul ings above worn **headstops**. The ba of the chancel walls is decorated wi chequer flushwork and the e. windo has renewed intersected 'Y' **tracer** There is a blocked n. door to the **na** and on that side the windows hav interesting headstops - grotesque three crouching animals and tv human heads. The wooden s. **porc** was extensively restored in 1911 ar given new doors, but the door fran and main timbers are the original C ones and there are exposed timbers the sides within, some of which a moulded. The handsome inner doc way has three bands of **fleurons** in th mouldings and large king and quee headstops; over the years the so stone has accumulated lots of graffi To the r. is a **stoup** under a **trefoil** ar and the oblong shape of the bowl su gests that it may once have been a **re quary** The nave lies under single-framed open **roof** with **cast€ lated wall plates**. At the w. end, th plain octagonal C14 **font** rests on base of **purbeck marble** whi belonged to its C13 predecessor. T the w. of the n. door are the very fai remains of a large **St Christopher** ar opposite hangs a set of Charles II **Ro al Arms** painted on board in mut€ colours, with naive supporters. At th

. end of the nave there are three
nges of plain and solid **box pews**.
he **rood loft** stair was on the n. side
nd there are niches either side of the
hancel arch. For some unknown rea-
on an aperture was cut in the wall to
e l. in the C19 and the niche moved
igher up. It has paterae in the mould-
ng, a **groined** canopy, and a grinning
acchus mask at the top. The other
iche has lost its canopy but there are
ear little painted heads carved as
orbels to the miniature **groining**;
aces of gold and blue remain and
ere is the outline of a figure. The
cobean pulpit is decorated with
onventional lozenge patterns in the
wer panels and shallow carving
nder the rim; the base and stairs are
odern, as is the low **screen**. The stall
the l. within the chancel has carved
bows, and a pair of **misericords**,
ith their lips chopped off, have been
sed very eccentrically to form a
ck. To the s. of the **sanctuary** a Per-
endicular window was inserted in
e C15, thereby mutilating what
ust have been a beautiful combined
ite of **piscina** and **sedilia**. As it is,
e piscina has a heavily **cusped ogee**
rch with side pinnacles and of the
epped sedilia, only the w. stall for
e sub-deacon is intact. Its canopy
as an ogee arch with large **crockets**
sing to a **finial** in the form of a
owned figure. There is a crouched
on in the parapet moulding, flank-
g pinnacles, and a triple range of
aterae in the arch mouldings. The
all behind the altar was faced in the
19 with large unglazed tiles
pressed with diaper work and col-
ured in soft pastel shades, and as a
redos it is quietly attractive. On the
all to the l. is a memorial to John
hepherd who, as a Royal Marines
ptain served 'under the immortal
elson in an attack on the harbour of
oulogne' in 1805 and died of his
ounds ten years later. When I vis-
ed the church it was decked for the
arvest Festival and that, combined
ith oil lamps and honest brick
oors, made it memorable, calling to
mind Betjeman's lines:

> Light's abode celestial Salem!
> Lamps of evening,
> smelling strong...

Ampton, St Peter (D4): This compact
little church stands across the village
street from the door in the high brick
wall guarding the grounds of the Hall.
It was extensively restored in the
early 1840s by **Samuel Saunders Teulon**, one of the rogue architects of the
period whose characteristic was com-
plication rather than simplicity, but
here he was quite restrained. The
unbuttressed C14 tower has **Decorated** bell openings, large **gargoyles** at
the corners, and a stair turret on the s.
side that continues the line of the
nave wall. Blocked **put-log holes**, outlined in red brick, show up clearly. A
vestry was added in the C19 against
the old n. door and beyond the projecting **chantry chapel** on that side
there is a bricked-up portion of a window with intersecting **tracery**. The e.
window is pure Teulon and on the s.
side of the **chancel** is a large **lancet**
with the remains of **cusping** in the
head and the outline of another window. The hopper of the drain pipe at
the corner is dated 1888. The s. nave
windows are C19 and the **porch** has
Decorated windows with deep **labels**.
Within it, the steep medieval roof
timbers are enhanced by small **paterae** in the mouldings and the **wall
plates** have two bands of embattling.
There is quite a lot of graffiti on the
window **jambs**, including the date
'1589' on the w. side. Through the
plain and small C14 doorway is an
interior that is attractive and interesting. The door to the tower stair is
medieval and on the walls overhead
there are two **hatchments**, the paint
on the canvas now flaking, unfortunately. That on the n. wall is for Henry, 1st Baron Calthorpe (1797), and
the other is for his widow Frances
(1827). A small C19 **font** stands in
front of the tower arch and there is a

consecration cross on the wall to the l. and part of another on the other side of the opening. Nearby, on the n. wall, is an unusual set of **Stuart Royal Arms** cut in thick fretwork, with exuberant mantling and faded colour. They were originally tenoned into the top of the now vanished **rood screen**, and the emblems of rose and thistle that stood with them are now hung upside down at the bottom. Further along the n. wall is a memorial to James Calthorpe designed by **John Bacon**. It is an excellent bas relief portrait head in an oval medallion set on a grey obelisk, with a shield and crest above. To the e. is a marble tablet that reminds us that Jeremy Collier - divine, contraversialist and non-juring bishop, was rector here from 1679 to 1684. His *Short View of the Immorality and Profaneness of the English Stage*, which attacked Congreve and Vanbrugh, made a great stir a few years later. On the s. side of the nave, are the remains of a **stoup** by the door and a memorial to Dorothy Calthorpe, founder of the village almshouses, who died in 1693. There is a sweetly worded epitaph and her graceful little statue kneels within an arched niche flanked by **pilasters**, with her shield of arms above. In 1479, John Coket obtained a licence to found a perpetual chantry here, and the first chantry priest was Valentine Stabler who was given a house opposite the church. The chantry chapel is on the n. side of the nave and is entered through a late **Perpendicular** arch which has blank shields within **quatrefoils** in the **spandrels**; the cornice is **castellated** and below it, carved in relief, is the legend: 'Capella perpetue cantarie - Joh'is Coket'. Beneath the blind tracery within the arch, there are fine mosaics each side. To the w. is **St Christopher**, commemorating the use of Ampton Hall as a hospital in the 1914-18 war, when over 6000 sick and wounded were cared for then. Opposite is the figure of **St George** below the badge of the South Staffordshire Regiment, in memory of the

rector's only son, Lieut Bernar Wickham, killed at Ypres in 1917 Within the chapel there is an uprigh C13 grave slab against the e. wall, an on the n. wall, an oval tablet to Si James Calthorpe and Dorothy his wif who died in 1702 - marble drapes a the sides, a profusion of richly carve flowers at the top, and a coat of arm tucked in at the bottom. There ar fragments of medieval glass in the w window and the arms of the Calth orpe, Gough, Reynolds and Yelverto families in the other windows. Th square recess in the s.e. corner wa probably a **piscina** for the chantr **altar**. There are a number of **brasse** in the church, and the most easil seen is that of a lady of about 149 which is now fixed to the nave wa by the chapel entrance. At the e. en of the nave floor there are the 18 in fig ures of members of the Coket famil the wife wearing a veil head-dres The brass dates from about 1480 an includes a plate showing their seve daughters, all in **butterfly head dresses**, although the complementar group of sons is missing. Half Coket's merchant mark survives. Ha way down the nave is a very wor brass which probably depicts Alic the wife of John Coket, who died i 1480. She too wears a butterfly head dress and, although the inscriptio has gone, her shield of arms remain The plain, panelled pulpit is late C1 and the underside of the **tester** is de orated with a marquetry star. Above is the blocked entry to the old **roo loft**, and the bottom doorway can b seen to the r. of the pulpit. The nav was re-roofed in the 1888 restoratio and it was then that the C17 **arc braced** chancel roof was uncovere and the boarded panels, with the painted **bosses**, recoloured. There a two important monuments on the side, the largest of which is for Henr Calthorpe, signed and dated in small oval below, **John and Matthia Christmas**, 1638. The half-length fig ures of Calthorpe and his wife ho hands; he in massive ruff and sma

Van Dyke beard looking pompous, while she seems distinctly bored. Between the epitaph and the main figures, there is a panel containing little figures of their family (those that died young hold skulls), an infant and three boys on one side and a **chrysom child** and the girls on the other. There are seven coats of arms in all, and the parents are flanked by black marble columns with a broken **pediment** above. To the e. is one of the best mural monuments carved by **Nicholas Stone** - an excellent portrait of William Whettall, Henry Calthorpe's father-in-law, who died in 1630. He wears an enormous ruff over a furred gown and the bust stands within a dished oval and finely moulded frame. Above is a cherub and a pair of swags, a curved pediment enclosing a small coat of arms, and a full **achievement** on top. The late C18 **communion rails** have very slender **balusters** and in the **sanctuary** there is an early and very time-worn piscina. An iron-bound chest with complicated locks stands in the n.e. corner, and just above it is a brass inscription for Edmund Coket; it is undated and the shield has gone. The e. window is filled with glass by **Burlison & Grylls**, with large figures of **Saints Edmund**, **Peter**, **Paul** and **Etheldreda**, with Christ in the centre; there is very little flesh colour but there are deep tints in the robes, and musical angels fill the tracery. The interest centres on the panel beneath the figure of Christ. There, 'In grateful memory of January 3rd, 1885' we have Shadrach, Meshach and Abed-nego in the rich, dark red and purple flames of the fiery furnace, commemorating the destruction of Ampton Hall by fire when all within were saved.

Bacton, St Mary (F4): There are not many churches in the county with spires and so it is rather a pity that Bacton's had to be removed in 1935 (although it was but a modest C18 affair). The church stands back from the street behind a line of elms noisy with rooks. The C14 tower has 'Y' **tracery** bell openings e. and w., and less usual **Decorated** tracery in the others. An early C16 brick stair turret rises on the s. side to a conical cap at **nave** roof level. **William Butterfield** was in charge of extensive restorations in the 1860s and may have been responsible for the **Norman** shape of the w. door arch. Under the **aisle** eaves there are inscriptions cut on blocks of **ashlar** that are interesting but now very difficult to read. On the n. side, over the blocked door, one is asked to pray for the souls of Robert Goche, a C15 chaplain, and his wife, and on the s., the same request for Sir James Hobart, Margaret his wife, and their parents. Hobart was Henry VII's Attorney General. The nave has ten tall **clerestory** windows on each side and there are two ranks of **flushwork** panels between them, with a wide range of symbols. They include the **sacred monogram**, Catherine wheel, mitre, triangle for the **Trinity**, and the venerable Christian sign of the fish (4th from the w. on the n. side). A **sanctus-bell turret** crowns the nave gable, and the e. windows of the aisles have **reticulated** tracery. Passing through a heavily restored s. **porch**, one reaches a fine interior with many points of interest. There is no tower arch into the nave but merely a low door, and the tower stair, with its medieval door, rises from the w. end of the s. aisle. The early C16 **font** has **paterae** and blank shields in the stem panels, with angels spreading their wings under the bowl. The bowl is carved with alternate **Tudor roses** and angels bearing shields, and the fact that one face is blank suggests that it originally stood against an **arcade** pillar. The fine pair of benches at the w. end of the nave have varied tracery on the ends and backs, as well as good carvings on the elbows; an eagle and a monk in a pulpit on the n. side, a dog and a fierce lion on the s. The two arcade pillars here carry

*Bacton, St Mary: double hammerbeam
roof and Doom*

lovely **cartouche** memorials for George Pretyman (d.1732) on the n., and Jane Pretyman (d.1738) on the s. The lovely C15 double **hammerbeam** roof has cresting on the hammers, the **collarbeams** below the ridge, and on the **wall plates**, and there are large flowers at the intersections. Unfortunately, all the angels have gone, together with the figures that once stood under delicate canopies at the base of the **wall posts**. It is worth using binoculars to study the carvings in the **spandrels** over the clerestory windows where, with a little patience, one can find dogs fighting over a joint of meat and another seizing a rat. Butterfield found the roof in a dangerous state in the 1860s and a great deal of new timber was inserted. At the same time, the **celure** at the e. end over the **rood** was recoloured, following the original design. The work was done by a local artist by the name of Osborne and it still looks beautiful. In 1968, the **Doom** over the **chancel** arch was excellently restored and now much of it can be seen. Wearing the papal tiara and bearing his keys, **St Peter** receives the righteous as they rise from the tomb on the l., while devils consign the rest to hell fire opposite. The centre section will have shown Christ in Majesty but this did not survive. Behind the C19 pulpit is a painted memorial for Thomas Smyth and Dorothy his wife who died in 1702 and 1728 respectively and on the other side of the nave is the entrance to the **rood loft stairs**. The s. aisle chapel has the simplest form of **piscina** set in the window ledge, and it is worth noting that some of the aisle roof **bosses** incorporate figures. In the early 1500s, Richard Nix was the last Bishop of Norwich to be Lord of the Manor of Bacton, and his shield of arms is in the e. window of the s. aisle. This was once the **chantry chapel** of the Pretyman family, Lords of the Manor from 1587, and its **parclose screen** was moved (probably in the C19) to take the place of the destroyed **rood screen**, which explains the awk-

ward joins in the tracery and absence of panels. The low-pitched chancel roof is **arch-braced** and was effectively recoloured by Butterfield, with extra decoration forming a celure over the **high altar**. At that time, the whole chancel was refurbished, complete with **encaustic tiles**, **reredos**, and glass in the s. windows by Alexander Gibbs. The piscina was re-set in a square recess. The e. window is a 1914-18 war memorial and the glass is by **Morris & Co**. The arrangement of figures in two ranks is typical of the firm and shows how the designs of Morris and **Burne-Jones** continued to be used long after their deaths. In the upper tier, the angels with long trumpets are adapted from a Burne-Jones design, and the figures of St Peter holding a book and **St John** are both by him. His too are the **Evangelists** in the bottom rank: from the l., **Saints Matthew, Mark, Luke** and John. The Christ as saviour of the world in the top centre is by Dearle (see Glossary under Morris & Co) and the Virgin and Child below is also his - a repeat of a design he used at Bloxham near Banbury. The backgrounds are alternating blue and red drapery and the Evangelists have their symbols behind their heads; the eagle of St John pecks at his shoulder and St Matthew's foot rests on a casket containing money as a sign that he was a customs officer. It is a fine window.

Badwell Ash, St Mary (E4): In the centre of the village it is a good looking church which resembles Ixworth, Walsham le Willows and Bacton in many points of detail, particularly in the use of **flushwork** monograms. The handsome C15 tower has three **drip courses** with intermediate **set-offs** on the diagonal buttresses, and the stepped battlements with flushwork panelling carry the inscription: 'Pray for the good estate of John Fincham and Marget hys wyf'. There are emblems set in the **base course**, and there are little foliage shapes backing the letter 'R' on the s.w. buttress. Big **gargoyles** punctuate the s. **aisle** parapet and the **clerestory**, where the window arches are relieved by thin red bricks. There are tall **Decorated** windows and a **priest's door** on the s. side of the **chancel**, and beyond the C19 **vestry** on the n. side, the absence of an aisle gives the **nave** a leggy appearance. The doorway on that side is blocked and entry is via an attractive C15 s. **porch**. Like the tower, there are emblems in the base course, and on the s.e. buttress, a panel displays blacksmith's tools (like the bench end at nearby Great Ashfield). The battlements are stepped above a central canopied niche, the frontage is faced with thin panels of flushwork, and **St George** fights the dragon in the **spandrels** of the arch. Quite deep steps lead down into the church. The cream-washed interior is light and open and the tall **arcade** rests on octagonal **piers**. Overhead is a good C15 **roof**, with alternating **tie-beams** and **hammerbeams** that have large angels in good condition except that some of their emblems have been hacked away; a range of smaller figures in equally good condition adorns the **wall posts**. There are early C18 churchwardens' names carved on the end tie-beams and, although it does not look like it, **Cautley** thought that the beams might have been inserted then to prevent the roof from spreading. The shields on the stem of the late C14 **font** were once carved with coats of arms or emblems, and there is a Sacred Heart on the s. side of the bowl which has **cusped** and **crocketted ogee** arches in the panels, heads (possibly re-cut) underneath, and a **castellated** rim. A **Jacobean** chest with a carved front stands at the w. end of the s. aisle and the glass of the e. window is a war memorial which includes regimental badges in the **tracery**. The early C14 angle **piscina** nearby has an arch within an arch and pretty, pierced tracery, with a blind **trefoil** above the side opening. The

rood stairs rise to the s. of the chancel arch, with a little **quatrefoil** window in the segment that bulges out into the aisle chapel. The church was restored in the 1860s when the chancel roof was replaced and the choir stalls date from then. They are excellently done, with **poppyheads** and **Evangelistic symbols** on the elbows. The late C13 piscina in the **sanctuary** lies within a deep trefoil arch, the cusps of which terminate in leaves. The e. window glass of 1920 is probably by the **Powells**. It has Christ the King flanked by the **Blessed Virgin** and **St Peter**, against a blue background and within interlaced tendrils of vine - the whole set off by clear glass. There are three tablets in the chancel by Matthew Wharton Johnson, a prolific but not exciting C19 statuary. All are for members of the Norgate family and the best, in white marble on black, is for Thomas Norgate who died in 1818 - a draped urn above, coat of arms below, and frontal **acanthus** leaves as scrolls each side of the tablet.

Bardwell, St Peter and St Paul (E3): The tall tower with its centre spike can be seen from some way off, and one climbs what amounts to a little hill in these parts to reach the churchyard. The **nave** windows have **tracery** which shows how the **ogee** arch came back into favour in the early part of the C15. The **chancel** was virtually rebuilt as part of an extensive restoration in 1853. The tower, built about 1420, has a chequer **base course**, **Perpendicular** windows, and a stair turret on the s. side. As was often the case, considerable care was lavished on the s. **porch**, and the front is decorated with **flushwork** panelling. There is a chequer base course and there are three niches around the entrance, occupied by modern figures of **St Peter** and **St Paul**, with the **Blessed Virgin** in the centre. The arch **spandrels** contain shields of arms of the de Bardwell and de Pakenham families. The arch mouldings are decorated with two ranks of **fleurons** and the tall Perpendicular windows, with **transoms** cutting through the tracery, have deep **labels**. The interior of the early C15 nave is brightened by a colourful blaze of embroidered hassocks resting on the C19 pews, and there is a lovely **hammerbeam** and **arch-braced roof** overhead which has the unusual distinction of being dated. Only four of the angels in the hammerbeams remain, but one of them on the n. side holds a book which bears the date 1421. The two on the s. side carry **Passion emblems**, and the 30 or so painted **bosses** are carved with a lovely variety of forms; binoculars are a great help here. Much of the painted decoration still shows, including very attractive leaf trails on the rafters, coloured red on pale yellow. There is a plain octagonal **font** which probably dates from the C14, and over the tower arch is a **hatchment**, with emblems on the frame, for Charles Reade who died in 1720. The **Royal Arms** over the blocked n. door are **Hanoverian** for George II. Four **consecration crosses** may be seen on the s. wall, and one on the n., where there are fragments of what was an extensive series of wall paintings. They are C15 and show the 'Descent from the cross'; one can see part of a ladder and Christ's body, with a face (possibly **St Mary Magdalene**) on the l. Of the medieval paintings on the s. wall, only a single head can now be recognised. Sir William de Bardwell lived from 1367 to 1434 and was a great benefactor of this church, probably paying for the tower and the s. porch. A professional soldier from his youth, he entered the service of the Duke of Suffolk in 1400, was Henry V's standard bearer in the French wars, and probably served at Agincourt. The church's great treasure is the stained glass collected in the windows at the e. end of the nave on the n. side; there you will find Sir William's portrait at the bottom of the easternmost **light** and it is one of the most interesting in

Suffolk. Some small parts have been replaced by mutilated remains of other figures, but it is a fine piece. He kneels in armour, bareheaded on a stool, with a small shield hung round his neck, wearing a long broadsword and with his helmet beside him. Above are his arms with helm and crest, together with the arms of de Pakenham (his wife's family) in the other light. All trace of her effigy has gone. Above him, a panel of fragments includes the **Trinity** shield on a dark red ground, one of the five flags carried by the English at Agincourt. Sir William, known as 'The great warrior', and his wife were buried in the chancel. Before the **Reformation** there was a shrine dedicated to Our Lady of Pity, and the **Pietà** in the bottom of the l. hand light (moved from the w. window) may have been associated with it, although the glass is continental rather than English. In the bottom of the window to the w. are two more figures which probably represent Sir Roger Drury and his wife Margery who died in 1405. His head is a modern replacement, but she wears a beautifully ornamented coif and, and apart from her purple robe, the whole design is carried out in white and yellow stain. The **rood stairs** rise on the s. side of the chancel arch, and there is a **trefoil**-headed **piscina** in the corner below. There were undoubtedly **altars** on both sides of the nave because there are **squints** either side of the chancel arch which give a view of the **high altar**. Leaning against the wall on the n. side are two sections of the old **rood screen** which were rescued from the rectory attic in the 1890s. They are now a beautifully pale colour and the quality of the carving is excellent. There are some interesting memorials to members of the Crofts Reade family in the chancel. During the 1853 restoration, a tomb chest was rather eccentrically cut in half and a portion erected on each side of the **sanctuary**. On the n. side it commemorates Sir Charles Crofts who died in 1660, and on the s., his grandson, another Sir Charles; both have coloured bas relief shields of arms in the panels. On the s. wall of the chancel is a large wall monument which still has a good deal of the original colour. The alabaster figures of Thomas Reade and his wife Bridget (daughter of the first Sir Charles Crofts) kneel facing each other across a desk. He died in 1651 and she lived a widow for over 40 years. Tiny figures of their children occupy the panel below. Those who died young hold skulls and those that survived their infancy, a red rose. The blocked doorway on the n. side of the chancel was either a **priest's door** or led to a **vestry**. To its l. is an **aumbry** hewn from a solid block of stone. Above is a tablet by Cushing of Norwich with rounded reeded sides and a sarcophagus on top for the Rev James Whelton who died in 1772. On the s. wall of the sanctuary is a large monument for Thomas Reade who died in 1678. The **touchstone** panel has marbled Doric columns each side and the heavy cornice is a broken scroll with a **cartouche** of arms in the centre. The side windows have matching glass of 1869 by **O'Connor**. On the s. side, the theme is 'Feed my sheep', with Christ and two disciples against a background of a fence with flowers; on the n. side the text is 'Abide with us'. (One of the disciples wears a very Victorian hat.) The 1863 glass in the e. window also looks like O'Connor's work - six scenes in two ranks, illustrating the Virtues.

Barnardiston, All Saints (B6): The church stands high and can be seen from some distance from the w. The early C14 tower has a heavy belfry stair turret to the s. and on that side there are deep **nave** buttresses. On the one e. of the small s. door there are two **scratch dials** which, unlike most, have Roman numerals marking the radiating lines. **Septaria** show in the walls and thin tiles, particularly in

the **chancel**. The **priest's door** is on the n. side facing the rectory and there is a massive square turret for the **rood stairs**, with a battlemented top. The mansard shape of the nave **roof** appears rather strangely above the parapet and there is a very tall C15 n. **porch**. The lovely C14 inner doorway, with deeply moulded arch, has pairs of slim shafts and vestiges of large **headstops**. There are pairs of **crocketted** pinnacles above, and a straight **castellated** cornice that fitted snugly within the old roof line. To the r. is a square-headed **Decorated** niche with the remains of headstops but no trace of a bowl, although it was presumably a **stoup**. Entry is by an ogee-headed wicket gate within the medieval door , and see how the step has been worn away just below, showing the preference of countless generations of worshippers. The nave roof with its cambered **tie-beams** and false **hammerbeams** is modern, and the recumbent figures bear shields carved with **Passion emblems**. The low C15 benches have simple **tracery** in the ends, with shallow buttresses and there is a door to the tower stair in the s.w. corner. Close by, the large C14 **font** was badly cracked a long time ago and an iron band was clamped round the bowl. The floors are a homely mixture of bricks and **pamments**, and opposite the door stands a plain **Jacobean** chest. There are fragments of medieval glass in the top of a s. nave window, and the simple **Stuart** pulpit has a decided lean to starboard. There are very shallow blind arches in the top panels, and in the C19 the two sections that formed the door were removed and built into the reading desk that stands along side. A C17 **hour-glass stand** juts from the wall and there is a **piscina** below, marking the site of a medieval nave **altar**. The door to the **rood loft** stairs opposite is blocked by panelling and the C15 chancel **screen** has tall double-ogee arches, **cusped** and crocketted. It was well repaired in the 1920s and fitted with a new cornice

There is Jacobean panelling behind the choir stalls on the n. side, and in the window sill opposite there is a fascinating piece of graffiti. It has been lime-washed over but is clearly a drawing of a windmill and part of another. Looking out on the rolling countryside one can imagine a bored medieval priest or idle clerk sketching the familiar mill across the valley. The C17 **communion rails**, with their close-set **balusters**, were drilled in the C19 to hold triple-branched candelabra on rods - the only instance that I can recall. Beyond **dropped-sill sedilia** there is a C15 piscina under a wide arch and castellated top. It still has its wooden **credence shelf** and the little side recess that was often provided. The hole drilled in the top left-hand corner is a mystery, however. What was it for?

combination of **trefoils**. The e. window, with intersecting 'Y' tracery, has glass of about 1912 in **Arts and Crafts** style by Archibald Keithley Nicholson. This is a fine design which portrays Christ crucified on a living tree, flanked by the **Blessed Virgin** and **St John**, with **St Mary Magdalene** kneeling below and a medieval-style concept of Jerusalem beyond. Good glass too, probably by the same artist, is in a s. nave window, with **St Gregory the Great** in papal tiara holding a missal open at the Gloria, paired with **St Genevieve** with her candle. Two roundels below illustrate episodes in their lives. The link between the two saints is the fact that the Graftons' own church at Euston is dedicated to St Genevieve. As you go, you will pass a rather coarsely painted set of William III's **Royal Arms** by the door.

Barnham, St Gregory (D3): In 1864, the Duke of Grafton of the day added a n. **aisle** and **transept** and made sundry other improvements, so that is is now difficult to identify much of the old church with any certainty. The early C14 buttressed tower has 'Y' **tracery** bell openings, **lancet** belfry windows, and a later **Perpendicular** w. window below. There is an outside door to the stair on the n. side and all round the tower one can see where the square **put-log holes** have been filled in and left. The **priest's door** in the s. wall of the **chancel** is C13 and part of the e. window tracery looks original. Inside, by the door, is a plain octagonal C13 **font** with a spiky little Victorian cover. All around, the 1864 work is plain to see: plastered ceilings to **nave** and transept, simplistic **arcade**, and all the furnishings in pitchpine except for the reading desk. However, the chancel arch was undisturbed and there is a plain C17 **Holy table**. The nice C13 **piscina** has a multi-foil drain, the **hood mould** has small, worn **headstops**, and the arch is filled with tracery in a graceful

Barningham, St Andrew (E3): This is one of the few medieval churches in East Anglia that sensibly enjoys joint use by Anglicans and Methodists. The tower has **Decorated** bell openings, but according to local wills it was being called the 'new tower' in 1440 and so it is likely that, as in many other cases, it is the product of more than one period. It has a plain panelled **base course**, diagonal buttresses to the w., and a heavy stair turret on the s. side. There are prominent **put-log holes** on the w. and the battlements are stepped. The pattern of the base course recurs on the **nave** buttresses, and they stand between tall **Perpendicular** windows. There is a **priest's door** in the s. wall of the early C14 **chancel**, and to its r. the two-**light** window has a **castellated transom**, forming a **low side window** at the bottom which has one section closed by a wooden panel. There is attractive flowing **tracery** in the e. window, and on the n. side, two large sloping buttresses shore up the wall. The **sacred monogram** appears in **flushwork** on the **porch** parapet and the remains of a **stoup** can be seen to the r. of the C14 doorway within. Just inside the door is an octagonal early C14 **font**. Many others in the area have window tracery patterns carved on the bowl, but on this one there are woodcarvers's designs in the small panels, rather than those of the mason. The small wooden cover is C15 or early C16 and has radiating **crocketted** braces with a turned **finial**. On the s. wall behind the font is a section of board painted white and lettered in black Gothic script with red capitals. It reads: 'Flagellatus est (sacred monogram) Sancta Trinitas unus Deus. Sepultus est'. In referring to Christ's Passion and Entombment it is likely to be a rare survival - part of a moveable wooden **Easter sepulchre**. There is no tower arch as such - only a plain deeply recessed doorway. The **roofs** of nave and chancel are **arch-braced** and the latter has pendant **bosses** at the ridge, as well as demi-figures bearing shields at the bottom of the **wall posts**. One of the delights of this church is the lovely set of C15 benches in the nave. They are low, with large **poppyheads** and they stand on deep sills. The ends are carved with an extraordinary variety of blind tracery, and although the backs are not pierced, they are moulded and carved, some with leaf trails. Many of the animals and birds on the elbows are crudely carved but there is a nice camel at the e. end on the s. side next to the wall, and a sweet little owl next but one to the w. The range at the w. end on the n. side are good C19 copies. Equally fine is the C15 **rood screen**, despite having been heavily varnished 50 years ago. The **ogees** of the main lights are crocketted and **cusped**, and over the centre opening is a graceful compound ogee arch. Judging by the painted decoration on all the uprights and arches, and the remains of gilt **gesso** on the leading edges of the buttresses, it must have been magnificent in its youth. **Cautley** reported traces of figures on the lower panels (where one would

expect to see them) but I could detect none. Above the buttresses there are slots which housed the brackets supporting the floor of the loft that is no longer there. The stairs leading to it rise within the window embrasure on the r. to a very narrow entrance at the top. The stump of the main beam of the loft can be seen in the wall close by and there is a **piscina** below the steps. On the n. side, the late C17 oak pulpit has plain panels with a deep **acanthus** moulding at step level; its **tester** is **Jacobean**, with scrollwork, and turned pendants at the angles. Entry to the chancel is through a pair of doors added to the screen in the **Stuart** period. There are turned **balusters** in the top sections and panels carved with shallow strapwork beneath them. The **altar** is of the same date, with a carved top rail and a rather odd reversed baluster shape to the turned legs. One section of the **communion rails** that went with it can now be found in front of the nave benches on the n. side. The angle piscina in the **sanctuary** is very simple and there are **dropped-sill sedilia** alongside. There is an **aumbry** in the n. wall and, above it, a **brass** in good condition for Rector William Goche who died in 1499. The 13 in figure shows him in academical dress and the inscription asks us to pray for his soul. Metal-painted **decalogue boards** flank the altar and the 1870s oak **reredos** frames a painting of the Last Supper (more or less after Leonardo da Vinci) by the rector's sister Eliza Evelyn Edwards. The s. sanctuary window contains attractive glass probably 1870s work by **Clayton & Bell**. It has four panels of the **Seven Works of Mercy**, with groups of figures in medieval dress and uses lots of deep red and good blue. The only medieval glass in the church consists of C15 fragments in the nave window tracery. Over the n. door, a boldly painted set of **Royal Arms**; they were **Hanoverian** painted before 1801 (but later given the initials 'VR' for Victoria).

Barrow, All Saints (C4): The church is the best part of a mile n. of the village centre and was extensively restored in the 1840s and 1850s. The unbuttressed tower, with its small C19 w. door, has **Decorated** bell openings and there are numerous **gargoyles** spaced out below the battlements. In the e. wall above the nave roof there is part of a **Norman** window showing, within which is a small slit opening. The early C14 s. **aisle** windows have **trefoiled lights** with a **quatrefoil** above them and there is **ogee tracery** in the aisle e. window within a **label** which has **headstops**. Below the window is a curious little opening leading into a shaft behind the **altar** which possibly ventilated a small charnel chamber where bones from old burials were laid. Nearby is a selection of well carved C18 headstones. The three-stepped **lancets** of the e. window were apparently unchanged by the 1848 restoration and the **Perpendicular** windows on the n. side have worn male and female headstops. Entry is by the s. **porch** and although this has been renewed, there are small C14 quatrefoil openings in the walls. The s. aisle has a lancet to the w. and the Decorated **arcade** rises from octagonal **piers**. The large tower arch of the same period is blocked and a small doorway has been set within it. The **chancel** arch may have matched it before it was widened to the extent that nave and chancel are virtually one. The late C14 **font** has an attractively panelled shaft and the bowl panels are bright with a very interesting series of shields which were repainted in 1969. Clockwise from the e. they are: the See of Canterbury, the Royal Arms of France and England, **Passion emblems, St Andrew**, le Despencer, Ely (or East Anglia), **St George**, and France (modern?). The Despencer shield is charged with a five-point label and this suggests that the font is a memorial to Elizabeth, widow of Hugh, Lord le Despencer and daughter of the

Earl of Gloucester. By the side of the entrance a small bell has been hung in a frame on the wall, complete with all the fittings for change ringing - wheel, stay, slider and rope. This provides an opportunity to study the mechanics of that subtle art. Beyond the doorway, the **brass** for John Crosyer has been mounted on a board. There is the bottom half of his effigy and a verse about this benefactor of the poor and 'late parson of this towne' who died in 1569 and was buried in front of the **high altar**. Next to it are replica sections of a brass now in the British Museum. The front benches in the s. aisle have roughly traceried ends and deeply cut leaf trails on the backs. This chapel was once dedicated to **St Michael** and the **piscina** (in the e. rather than the s. wall) was uncovered during the 1852 restoration. It consists of two plain lancets with trefoil heads below a pierced quatrefoil and although there are two compartments there is only one drain. To the r. in the corner is a C14 tomb recess with a pointed canopy decorated with flat **crockets** on the chamfer. Restored **sedilia** join on, and because all the levels in the church were raised two or three ft in the C19 they are now close to the floor. Another C19 discovery was the Norman lancet in the n. wall and the deep splays are painted with two lively little figures. The reading desk has panels of medieval tracery and only the bottom boards of the **rood screen** survive, together with the centre rail. The tall bench ends of the chancel stalls have **paterae** on the chamfers and some of the **finials** have masks with their tongues hanging out. Two others sport a jolly pair of heads in medieval billycock hats and there are birds and faces carved in the **spandrels** of the stall fronts. A C15 carver of Bury, called Richard Aleyn, left money for the high altar here and could conceivably have done this work. In the **sanctuary** the mid-C13 double piscina stands next to reconstructed sedilia and both of them are now at floor level. In the e.

wall there are two large **aumbries** rebated for doors and the C19 **reredos** is in **Early English**-style blind arcading. The e. window lancets are filled with glass by R.I. Colson of 1848. Roundels painted with episodes in Christ's life are effectively married with patterns and borders in which a bright green figures. The large tomb in the sanctuary n. wall may well have been used as an **Easter sepulchre**. Of **purbeck marble**, the front of the chest is decorated with **cusped** lozenges enclosing shields, the recess is panelled, and there is a frieze cornice with a line of **quatrefoils** below. All the shields now have brightly coloured arms applied to them, painted on hardboard. The style of the monument is early C16 but on the back wall is a brass for Sir Clement Heigham who died in 1570. MP and Governor of Lincoln's Inn, he was Queen Mary's Chief Baron of the Exchequer and one of the few knighted by Philip of Spain. His little kneeling figure wears **Tudor** armour and his gauntlets hang neatly on the prayer desk with his helm in front. His two wives are shown with him, each with her brood of daughters, and one dead son in a shroud is shown behind his father. All the shields were once inlaid with colour and the long verse epitaph is worth studying, for while Heigham's dismissal by Elizabeth is not mentioned, the reason for it is:

> ... the feare of God he alwaies had,
> fast fixte in holy hearts,
> And from his prince in loyaltye
> noe iote would he departe.

On the s. wall of the sanctuary is the monument to Sir John Heigham who died in 1626. This is by John Stone and very like his father's work - a black and white marble tablet under a broken **pediment** with urn, and a **cartouche** of arms below. On the chancel s. wall is a tablet for Susan Heigham (1695); painted white, with the detail in rather startling green and purple. There are fat side scrolls and two bas relief skulls in drapes at the bottom corners. Her husband, Clement, sup-

plied the long epitaph and admonition to the reader. Another Clement Heigham, who died in 1634, has his monument in shocking pink and black further along with a bold inscription, arms in strapwork above and three coloured shields of arms below.

Barton Mills, St Mary (B3): The pollarded limes which front the churchyard were planted in 1845 but they are still vigorous and do not betray their age. The base of the tower, with its w. door, is late C12 but the upper stages date from around 1300. The simple 'Y' **tracery** of the bell openings was altered in the C19 and the **clerestory** renewed in a debased style at the same time. Walking round, you will find human **headstops** on the s. side and animal ones on the n. The tall n.e. **vestry** has a blank window shape large enough for a **transept**. Entry is via the C14 **porch**, with a modern Virgin and Child in a niche overhead. There is a **scratch dial** to the l. of the inner door, showing that it was in use before the porch was built and just inside are the remains of a **stoup**. The bright and shining interior is beautifully kept. The C14 **arcades** have mutilated headstops - male on the n. side, female on the s. Above the tower arch, note the 'Y' tracery belfry window that will have been above and outside the line of the original roof. The present **nave** roof dates from 1886 and that in the **chancel**, with its red and green panels, is modern too. The C14 **font**, on a modern shaft, provides good examples of window tracery designs adapted to suit the panels and is similar to the one at Icklingham All Saints. The long C14 oak chest bound with iron is not joined work but is hollowed out of a solid trunk. The **Decorated** tracery in the **aisle** windows is particularly pleasing, with **mouchettes** springing from the centre **mullion** and curving over in a flowing line. On a stone base, the early C17 pulpit is country work, with very coarse and poorly laid out panels of shallow carving. There is a brass lectern of 1903, and above the chancel arch, a mural of the Good Shepherd set against a stencilled background, designed by the firm (if not the hand) of **Sir George Gilbert Scott** and painted by Powells of Whitefriars. The chancel has some interesting things: look first for two **consecration crosses**, one just inside the arch on the s. side and the other w. of the blocked door on the n. that led to the original vestry. The arch and organ chamber alongside are C19. Close to the first consecration cross is a pair of **low side windows**, rebated for shutters with the hinges still in place. To the e. there is a stylish C18 **cartouche** with heraldic **achievement** above and cherub below for William Glasscock. Beyond that are **dropped-sill sedilia** and an eroded but still attractive late C13 or early C14 **piscina**. It has twin drains and the centre shaft supports **cusped ogee** arches with a **quatrefoil** above, all contained within an outer arch. There is an **aumbry**in the n. wall. **G.F. Bodley** was in charge of restoration work in the early years of this century and all the seating is to his design. The chancel stalls with **poppyheads** are a very solid no-nonsense design. The church must have been rich in C14 glass at one time, and when the **nave** was re-paved in 1904, innumerable fragments were found below the brick floor. Most of what is left is in the s. aisle and in the e. window there are two figures, one of **St Edmund** on the l., with the three arrows symbolising his martyrdom and the other one of **St John the Baptist**. In their haste, the C17 image breakers thought it enough to destroy the heads only of the saints, but it is interesting that they also smashed the heads of the winged dragons in the tops of the aisle windows. Seek out the one they missed at the w. end of the s. aisle! There is, incidentally, a family likeness in the stylised churches to be seen in three

of the windows. There are some C14 fragments in the chancel too but most of the glass is C19 and early C20. The 1866 e. window by **Clayton & Bell** has lots of small scale figures - Nativity, Transfiguration, Calvary, the women at the tomb, Ascension - with the five best-known miracles in panels below, of bright colour but little feeling. The 1867 window over the sedilia by **Ward & Hughes** is a vapid piece of sentimentalism but the 1907 **Heaton, Butler & Bayne** opposite is much better - two panels in **Arts and Crafts** style on the theme of charity, with cool colour and sound modelling. As you go, have a look at the two half-ends of benches by the tower arch, part of what must have been a fine C15 set.

Beck Row: See Mildenhall, Beck Row (B3)

Beyton, All Saints (E5): The thing one remembers about Beyton is that the tower (probably **Saxon**) is oval rather than round and that two heavy C15 buttresses rise almost to the top. The narrow top section was rebuilt in 1780 and there may have been a more imposing bell stage at one time. By the 1850s the rest of the church was in a parlous state and the **nave** was rebuilt to the designs of John Johnson of Bury, with the addition of a n. **aisle**. The old **Norman** doorway with its simply carved arch was re-set in the new outer wall. In 1884 the **chancel** was restored, lengthened, and given a new e. window by **Sir Arthur Blomfield** - all good quality work. The large **vestry** annexe, in flint and white brick that looms on the s. side of the chancel, was added in 1973. It has a fussy triangular oriole window jutting out of the w. wall that does nothing for it. The **porch** is at least part C15 with an earlier inner doorway, and contains a C17 plain chest. For those with an appetite for the curious there is a doorstop formed from a pony's hoof, complete with shoe. Within, all is fresh and neat as a pin. The tower arch is C15 and above and beyond it is a ceiling of the same period supported by a heavy **arch-braced tie-beam**. The nave **roof** is **scissors-braced** and the 1850s benches have some good carving, including a **pelican** on the n. side which is the first realistic interpretation that I have seen in a church. The C19 oak pulpit has triple columns at the angles and delicate leaf forms carved in relief on the upper panels, but the lower panels are a quiet surprise. They are formed of strips of walnut, tongued and grooved, with tiny dovetail keys at intervals across the joints, and then they are pierced by narrow slit crosses - very odd. In the n. aisle the centre window has beautiful 1960s glass from the Goddard & Gibb Studio on the theme of the Sower; he is shown in medieval dress within one circle of a Celtic scroll that links him with a harvest vignette. Pigeons, chaffinches, larks and linnets perch about and it is very diverting. To the e. is a war memorial window with excellent glass designed by Morris Meredith Williams and probably made by **Lowndes & Drury** - a kneeling soldier bows his head over his rifle and Christ stands in the other **light**. Blomfield designed a handsome waggon roof in oak for the chancel, with arch-braces resting on stone **corbels** and demi-angels on the **wall plates**. The stalls incorporate a good deal of C15 work, notably bench ends with replacement figures and a bench back on the n. side decorated with shields carved with initials in **quatrefoils**. The **reredos** panel is a mosaic of the Last Supper, with a gold chalice on the table and a bowl and towel in front for the washing of the feet. It came from **Powells** who also provided the e. window glass - but that is poor work. For collectors of epitaphs I found an unusual quotation on Rosa Wright's stone to the w. of the n. aisle outside: 'he brought down my strength in my journey and shortened my days'. She died at 39 in 1882.

Botesdale, St Botolph (F3): At the top of the village street, this little church has an interesting pedigree. It was founded as a chapel of ease for Redgrave (and gave the village its name - Botolph's Dale) about the year 1500. Later, it was restored and endowed as a **chantry** chapel by John Herife, his wife, Juliana, and Bridget Wykys. Above the door is a large **flushwork** inscription (interrupted by a later window) asking us to pray for their souls. Chantries were abolished and their endowments plundered in 1547 and so this one had a relatively short life. Then, in 1576, Sir Nicholas Bacon of Redgrave took over the building as Lord of the Manor, and used it to found a Free School. He added the house to the r. which shares the same roof. So it continued until it reverted to being a church in 1884. There are **Perpendicular** windows under flint and red brick arches, and a single bell is perched on the roof ridge without any cover. Pass through the original door to an interior lobby which is divided from the chapel proper by a simple screen, such as would be found in substantial houses of the period. The **gallery** above was constructed at the same time and now houses a chamber organ; below is a small C19 **font**. The chapel has a plain **arch-braced** roof, with plastered ceiling between the principals and no division marking the **chancel**. There are C19 pitchpine pews and a plain, angled, set of **altar** rails. The C19 glass in the e. window, by **Heaton, Butler & Bayne** is rather good. The centre panels depict the visit of the Magi, and on either side there are scenes of Christ's baptism, His teaching in the temple, the Last Supper (with Judas turning away from the table with his purse), and Gethsemane. Musical angels inhabit the top **tracery**.

Boxted, All Saints (C6): *now Holy Trinity* A little church that is sweetly situated in rolling meadowland above the village in the valley. The unbuttressed C14 tower has a modern short three-**light** window beneath the **Perpendicular** w. window and there are **gargoyles** below the parapet. Although there is no s. **aisle** the **nave** has large, late Perpendicular **clerestory** windows and those below are C19 replacements. The **chancel**, with its **priest's door**, is plastered and the s.e. window projects between buttresses under a little tiled cap. On the other side of the chancel stands the C18 brick chapel of the Poley family and the brick battlements continue along the n. aisle whose C14 door is blocked. Oddly, a little round brick chimney is perched on the n.w. corner. The C19 timber **porch**, with heavy barge boards and openwork sides, is very pleasing and it leads to a charming interior. A modern wooden **gallery** and screen have been inserted in the tower and there are C19 benches with **poppyheads** in the nave (with two C16 examples enclosed at the w. end); two ranges of **box pews** at the front are matching and are presumably a late example of that comfortable form. The cambered **tie-beams** of the roof are carved with a folded leaf pattern and the angel supporters are dated 1885 - one of the signs of the lavish restorations of the C19. The narrow n. aisle lies beyond a low C14 **arcade** on octagonal **piers** and at the w. end is a plain C14 **font**. The other two bays were formed into private pews by the insertion of **Jacobean** screens with turned uprights, and one of them now houses the organ. In the other you will find the remains of a **piscina** near the floor which shows that there was an altar in the aisle long before the pews were made and the Poley chapel built. There is a recess to the l. of the chancel arch which shows where the stair to the **rood loft** emerged, and above the chancel arch is an open arcade of three wooden arches - a modern insertion that seems extraordinarily eccentric. The **Stuart** pulpit has shallow carved arches in the lower panels with rose roundels above, and over the backboard the **tester** has turned pendants and is dated 1618. The chancel roof is early C17 and therefore a late example of a **hammerbeam** construction and is very similar to the nave roof at Wickhambrook; there are openwork panels above the hammers and pierced pendants below. The **sanctuary** has a very nice set of late C17 three-sided **communion rails** with twisted **balusters**, while all around are reminders of the Poleys. **Hatchments** hang overhead dating from 1756 to 1849, and to the r. of the **altar** is a most interesting tomb. It is entirely black, with no inscription or decoration, and on the chest lie the oaken figures of William Poley and his wife Alice who died in 1587 and 1579 respectively. Wooden effigies were out of fashion by about 1350 but there was a revival in the C16 and these, black like the tomb, are very good examples in beautiful condition. He wears armour over embroidered breeches and his head, with its long moustache and beard, rests on a helm. She wears a French cap, with three chains round her neck and the prayer book suspended from her girdle is carved with their joint arms. As I said, there is no inscription but round her pillow is carved 'Beati mortui qui in Domino moriuntur' (Blessed are the dead who die in the Lord) and 'A.P. 1579 Mar 7'. There are good **ledger-stones** in the chancel, including one for John Worsley of 1625 with a fine epitaph. In the n.e. corner is a **brass** inscription for Richard Poley of 1546 and the e. window is a memorial for Hugh Thomas Weller-Poley, killed at 20 in the RAF in 1942. The design is by William Aikman - the figure of Christ in bright middle-eastern robes, with rays of light springing from Him; below are vignettes of the church and Boxted Hall, with rabbits on the greensward. Through an arch is the Poley chapel which contains two excellent and important statues, both standing in arched niches. Sir John Poley died in 1638; in pink-veined alabaster, he poses hand on hip, while his helm and gloves lie behind his feet. The modelling is crisp and lively, the pose taut and convincing. Coloured arms in a **cartouche** are above the alcove, with swags of fruit picked out in gilt, and putti draw aside the drapes each side. A finely lettered epitaph is set within an **acanthus** frame below while wreathed skulls adorn the corners of the base. All was meticulously restored in 1986. The monument was probably not erected until 1680 and its quality has suggested to some that it is the work of John Bushnell, that eccentric C17 genius. Sir John served in France under Henry IV and in Denmark, and he wears a small golden frog in his left ear that may be the badge of a continental order of chivalry. It has been said that it denotes the Danish order of the Elephant but the Royal College of Arms in Copenhagen refute this. It does, however, provide an intriguing link with the rhyme:

'The frog he would a wooing go,
With a Roley Poley Gammon and
Spinach'

- a probable reference to the local families, the Roleys, Poleys, Bacons and Greens. Dame Abigail died in 1652 but her statue was not installed until 1725; London work and roughly matching her husband's effigy, but the architectural frame is simpler. It is perhaps the latest work in English alabaster until the C19. On the w. wall is an omnibus epitaph for the family lettered on an open book with an urn at the top, and below it the descent of the Poleys from the C14 to the C20 is displayed on two marble scrolls. In front lies a C13 coffin lid and a stone child's coffin of the same period, while the shaft of a **pillar piscina** can be found on the window sill. The window contains some medieval glass, including a king's head, and the 1930s heraldic glass is again by William Aikman.

Bradfield Combust, All Saints (D5) The church stands by the side of the busy Bury to Sudbury road and there is a venerable cedar in the churchyard. Although you may not fee. inclined to obey the charge: 'Let every real patriot shed a tear, for genius tal ents worth lies here', pause at the tomb of Arthur Young just e. of the **chancel**. He was not a successfu farmer himself but at a time when the mould of medieval practice was being broken in agriculture, his writings played a vital part in assisting the change. In 1768 he began publishing series of *Tours* that gave accurate accounts of farming in England, Ire land and France, and his *Farmer's Calendar* went through many edi tions. Young became secretary to Pitt's Board of Agriculture in 179: and organised the publication of county surveys (writing some him self) which have never been equalled in their comprehensiveness. His las years were sadly clouded by blind ness and melancholia and he died in 1820. The walls of the stubby chancel are in banded red brick and flint and there is a tiny **priest's door** in the cor ner. The C19 e. window has a beauti ful **tracery** design based on three **trefoils** and could conceivably repea the original. The s. **aisle** is C14 and the w. end of the nave was remod elled in the C19 when it received new window below a quirky bellcot for three bells. Within the wooden **porch** of 1861 is a plain C14 doorwa but note that the arch was re-cut and given a moulding 200 years later. Th interior is rather dark but the first things that catch the eye are the earl C15 paintings on the n. wall. In th corner there is a large and lovely **S George** wearing black armour and wielding both sword and lance. Lon red mantling flows from his crested helm and he wears his emblem o breast and shoulders; his caparisone charger rears over the head of th dragon. Alongside is an equally fine **St Christopher** - a huge figure in re tunic, with the Christ child wearing 'ed robe seated on his right shoulder. The saint holds a massive, sprouting staff; there are fishes in the river and the hermit stands by his hut on the r. Below the painting is a tall, blocked **Norman** archway and you may have noticed outside that a C14 doorway was inserted within it. The Norman **font** stands on a short drum shaft and the underside of the square bowl is scalloped; the e. face was later carved with a **quatrefoil** within an arch flanked by side panels. The C14 **arcade** has three unequal bays and in the aisle chapel there is a double **piscina** under a pair of trefoil arches and a pierced quatrefoil; there are **dropped-sill sedilia** alongside. The C19 glass in this aisle is good. The 1899 w. window is likely to be by the **Powells** Christ the King with grouped female saints); the pair of 1850s windows in the side wall are by **Lavers & Barraud** (an early **Westlake** design), in C13 style and glowing with deep, rich colour. It is worth noting that the figure of the risen Christ displays no wounds. There is a Victorian stone pulpit and although there is no **rood screen** now, the old stair turret shows outside to the n. The aisle and chancel **roofs** are C19 but the **nave** retains the medieval **tie-beams** and **arch-braces**. The glass in the chancel e. window is a memorial to Arthur Young, put in by public subscription in 1869, long after his death. By Lavers, Barraud & Westlake, it is a Crucifixion displaying unusually good colour and composition; witness the varying attitudes of the angels above the mourners, the centurion, and the weeping **St Mary Magdalene** at the foot of the cross. On the n. wall is a marble tablet below a pyramid and **cartouche** of arms for Arthur Young senior, who was 40 years rector here and died in 1759. There are more Young memorials in the little **vestry** and perhaps the most affecting is for Martha, Arthur's 14-year-old daughter: ' "Pray for me papa - Now! Amen" Her last words'.

Bradfield St Clare, St Clare (D5): Set in the midst of fields with only a thatched farmhouse for company this little church, bearing a unique dedication, is ringed about by oak, Scots pine, and horse chestnuts that hang low over the churchyard gates. A great deal of careful restoration was done in the 1870s and 100 years later an ambitious programme of renewal has left the fabric in good heart. The C14 tower has strong diagonal buttresses to the w. and the other pair continues the line of the e. face. There is a flint panelled **base course** and the w. window and bell openings all have **Decorated tracery**. The **nave** and **chancel** have renewed **Perpendicular** windows and the s. **porch** was 'thoroughly restored' in 1921. There is, in addition, a blocked late C12 n. door and a **Tudor priest's door** in the s. wall of the chancel. By one of those odd accidents of history, a small piece of a C13 grave slab is embedded under the eaves in the s.w. corner of the chancel, with a portion of the double omega sign showing. Inside, all is freshly lime-washed and beautifully neat. A small **stoup** is set in the wall to the r. of the door and to the l. is a C19 octagonal **font**. The tower arch is blocked with a modern door inserted, and the C19 nave **roof** is a copy of the C14 original; it has tall **king posts** resting on the **tie-beams**, with **scissors bracing** under the ridge. In a s. window tracery are some pieces of C15 glass. Beyond the wide, plain chancel arch the light coloured C15 roof has fragments of tracery above the collars of the **arch-braces** and the **wall plates** have a double **castellation**. The stalls incorporate three medieval **poppyheads** carved with leaf forms and in the **sanctuary** is a small **piscina** under a **trefoil** arch. The **decalogue**, Creed and Lord's Prayer are painted on canvas within oak frames on the e. wall and the three kneelers in front of the rails are quite special. They have the village name writ large and a panorama of the countryside from the s.w. of the church - all embroidered by George Insley in 1976. On the n. wall is a plain marble tablet by de Carle of Bury for Robert Davers, a C19 vicar. Over the priest's door is a small **touchstone** tablet in an alabaster frame for Richard Grandorge and his family. He was priest here for 41 years, dying in 1619, and his epitaph is worth quoting:

> Greatness sounds in his name, his hart was lowly,
> His soule was faithful, and his life was holy.
> Here lies the man who longe this flock did feed,
> I know not whether more, by tonge or deed...

Bradfield St George, St George (D5): This is rather a coy church that hides itself w. of the village and at the end of a lane a little curving avenue of limes crosses the churchyard to the s. **porch**. The tower is C15 although the w. window and bell openings have **Decorated tracery**. There is an inscription shared between two panels at the bottom of the buttresses which reads: 'Her begynnyth John(n) Baco(n) owthe / of the fun(n)dacyon Jhu p(re)serve hym'. So John Bacon presumably paid for the beginning of the work. There is a stair turret on the s. side up to the bell stage and the battlements have been renewed. There are C13 **lancets** in the **chancel** and a variety of **Perpendicular** windows in the **nave** and n. **aisle**, but the **Norman** origin of the church is betrayed by a lancet in the s. wall of the nave. When the n. aisle was added, the walls were raised and a **clerestory** inserted. There are fine **gargoyles** in the parapets. A large C19 **vestry** abuts the chancel on the n. side and there is a **priest's door** to the s. Over the porch entrance is a handsome C18 sundial with its reminder 'Come in time'. There are lots of graffiti on the simple arch **jambs**. A curious feature of the window embrasure on the e. side is

the carving of a hand raised in blessing. This was normally a symbol of the Deity and may conceivably have been associated with a **stoup**. The delightful late C14 inner doorway has shafts with carved **capitals** and an **ogee** arch whose deep mouldings were once beautifully enriched, although mere fragments of the decoration now remain. On the inside there is a C16 **hood mould** resting on what appear to be C19 head **corbels**. The capitals of the tall and narrow tower arch are decorated with **paterae**, and at the e. end of the Perpendicular **arcade**, with its **quatrefoil piers**, there is an additional small arch through to the n. chapel - probably inserted in the C19. There, the **altar** is a **Stuart** table with a simply carved top rail and sturdy legs. The late C14 **font** has pairs of **trefoil** arches in the bowl panels and a Victorian **bier** stands in the n. aisle. Nearby are four medieval benches with varied tracery backs and **poppyheads**, one of them well carved in the form of a winged lion. The C16 nave **roof** has **arch-braced** cambered **tie-beams** and two of the **spandrels** are appropriately carved with dragons in acknowledgement of the church's dedication. The **Jacobean** pulpit on a new base has two tiers of the usual blind arches, with strapwork panels above them. Jutting from the wall by the window is the iron frame that once held the C17 **hour-glass** which timed the sermon. To the l. of the chancel arch there is a niche with trefoil head and **castellated** canopy which houses a figure of the patron saint sculpted by C. Blakeman and installed in 1949. The C19 chancel roof is plain and white except for the e. bay which is picked out effectively in red to form a **canopy of honour**. Beneath it is a handsome wooden **reredos**, gilded and coloured, with carved panels of the Shepherds and the Magi, with the Holy Family in the centre. The e. window glass of 1913 was designed by Edward Prynne and painted by John Jennings. Christ crucified is flanked by the **Blessed Virgin** and **St John**; there are attendant angels and a group of cherub heads encircle the Saviour's head - good colour and composition. The only medieval glass is now in the s. chancel window - parts of an early C16 figure of **St George** which was originally in one of the clerestory windows.

Brandon, St Peter (C2): Set apart to the w. of the little town centre but now lapped around by new housing, the church stands in a generous churchyard fringed with limes. It is made memorable by the pair of heavy octagonal turrets, complete with spirelets, that rise above the **roof** line of the early C14 **chancel**, flanking an e. window which has **Decorated tracery**. Very worn **gargoyles** jut out well below the parapets and the outline of **rood loft** staircases can be seen built into the buttresses on both sides of the church. The profile of the C14 tower is punctuated by prominent **string courses** and it has two-**light** Decorated bell openings, with a later w. window. The early C16 n. **porch** has heavily **transomed** unglazed side windows and the original door is enlivened by worn carving of folded leaves round its edge. To the r., a substantial **stoup** is set on a traceried shaft. The interior is bright and fresh but has that rather bare feeling so often left as a legacy of heavy-handed C19 restorations which in this case spared not a single memorial from the many that were here. Behind the high **altar** is an indigestible C19 stone and marble **reredos**, but the inset roundels of Gethsemane, Entombment and the risen Christ are good. Note that there is an **aumbry** set in the n.e. turret and a door leads to the stair in its opposite number. The n. chancel windows have lovely glass of 1898 by Leonard Walker - remarkable work for a 19-year-old craftsman. They portray **Saints Paul, Peter, John** and **Luke** in **Arts and Crafts** style; the

faces are boldly blocked and there is a lot of movement and vivid colour in the design. Vignettes from their lives occupy the lower panels and it is interesting that St John's, unlike the others, anticipates C20 design trends. The original C16 stalls, with **poppyheads**, and the remains of winged beasts on the front buttresses, have been remade into two ranges for the choir. Apart from recolouring, the bases of the C15 **rood screens** are intact, with **ogee** tracery and twin **quatrefoils** containing shields in each panel. The panels of the s. **aisle** section retain their stencil decoration in gold on alternate red and green backgrounds. Both ranges have modern tops and the tracery and cornice in the aisle section are very attractive. Note the blocked C16 door on the s. side which led to the **rood stairs**. The World War I memorial in the s. aisle is a **Heaton, Butler & Bayne** window of **St George** and **St Michael**, with the crowning of a knight in the centre - all in 'William Morris medieval' style. Below, in a glass case, is a fine copy of a bible printed by Robert Barker the year after Shakespeare died. There are some bench ends in the nave to match those in the chancel and they too have the remains of grotesques on the elbows; mixed in with them are C19 replicas in pine. The C13 **arcade** between **nave** and s. aisle has elegant quatrefoil **piers**, with bases typical of the period. The chancel arch has male and female **headstops**. Below it, on the n. side, is a C19 wooden pulpit with a very nice pair of **Ecclesiological Society** design brass candelabra. The simple octagonal bowl of the C13 **font** stands on a central column, with a ring of shafts whose caps and bases intersect cleverly. The cover carries a modern baptismal group in blond wood by Reeve of Lawshall. The church had some more bench ends made in the C17 and their strangely clumsy poppyheads can be seen against the wall w. of the n. door. Some advertisements are timeless they say, and to prove the point, look at the lockplate of the n. porch gates - an enduring reminder that they were made by Burrells of Thetford, the firm once famous for its steam traction engines.

Brent Eleigh, St Mary (E6): To the n. of the main road and the River Brett, the church lies quiet and secluded by the Hall. Entering the churchyard from the e., one of the first things that catches the eye is the **reticulated tracery** in the **aisle**e. window. The n. windows of the **nave** also have attractive **Decorated** tracery. The **chancel** e. window dates from 1860 and a window on the n. side was blocked when a large monument was installed within. Further along is a C19 brick and flint **vestry** in lieu of a n. **porch**. The w. doorway is well-recessed and note that the placing of the tower stair forced the w. window off-centre. It is likely that the door in the s. chancel wall was originally the **priest's door** but it was altered in the C18 or early C19 for use as a private entrance for the family at the Hall. Close by it stands the table tomb of Robert and Dionesse Colman (1730 and 1697), boldly carved with the emblems of mortality. There is a number of good late C18 and early C19 headstones and one, (1813) s. of the porch, has an age-old theme:

> We daily see Death spares no son nor age,
> Sooner or later all do quit the stage.
> The old, the young, the strong, the rich, the wise,
> Must all to him become a sacrifice.

The porch windows, with their Decorated tracery, are unglazed and there is a **scratch dial** to the r. of the entrance. A modern statue of the **Blessed Virgin** stands in a niche over the inner doorway and the C14 door has lovely reticulated tracery in the head and retains all its original ironwork. Now we come to a charming interior in which a medley of architectural styles and furnishings dwell comfortably together and which were not harshly disturbed by the Victorians. The s. **arcade** and the tower arch confirm that the church has not changed significantly since it was built in the late C13 or early C14. The C13 **font** stands by an arcade **pier** and has a shallow octagonal purbeck **marble** bowl, with canted sides each carved with a pair of typical blank arches. The early C17 cover is an unusual design - a solid pyramid with a flat top from which rise turned spindles to support a **finial**. On either side of the tall tower arch hang charity boards bearing the names of rector and churchwardens for 1830, and over the n. door is a set of dark and yet vivid **Royal Arms** painted on board. They have the post-1707 arms and motto for Queen Anne but the initials were later changed to mark the accession of one of the Georges. The church's remaining **hatchment** on the nave s. wall is for Dr Thomas Brown who died in 1852 and whose wife inherited the manor. There are solid **box pews** of two periods in the aisle and nave; those at the e. end have C17 shallow carved top panels and the original butterfly hinges, and some further w. enclose C17 benches with rudimentary **poppyheads**, of which there are more at the w. end of the aisle. The single remnant of the C15 seating is a bench end at the e. end of the box pews on the s. side of the nave and it has a bird and an animal carved on the poppyhead. Above the homely brick and **pamment** floors the nave **roof** is plastered with only the single framed wall strips showing. On the n. wall is a faint trace of one of the improving texts beloved of the Elizabethan church. It was probably one of a series and consists of the first two verses of psalm 72 followed by a contemporary prayer. The stairs leading to the old **rood loft** are in the n. wall and the fine **Stuart** pulpit stands on a very tall turned post, with heavy carved brackets and skirt below the

Brent Eleigh, St Mary: Edward Colman
monument

body. The lower panels have quite unusual patterns within ovals and the whole of the underside of the canted book ledge is intricately carved. Across the nave stands the oak lectern given in memory of William Baldry, killed in action in 1915. The s. aisle chapel is enclosed by a fine C14 **parclose screen** which displays Decorated tracery above turned uprights and the doors to nave and aisle still have their original hinges with incised decoration. Although it has been covered over on one side, from within the chapel you can see a trefoil **elevation squint** cut in one of the boards of the w. side of the screen. It was not usual for C14 screens to be coloured but here we have a rare example which is probably the earliest in Suffolk and likely to be the only one from the C14. On the door to the aisle there is a painting of the eagle of **St John** bearing a scroll; the predominant colours are red and green and it is enclosed in a twisted wreath of thorns. On the side facing the nave there are three shields - a lily symbol of the Blessed Virgin, a cross and crown of thorns, and a coat of arms. The chapel became the Hall pew in time and a box pew was set within it. There are a few medieval tiles in the floor and a **piscina** in the corner. The panelled chancel ceiling dates from 1684 and the three-sided **communion rails** are of that period or a little earlier; they have twisted **balusters** which are grouped in fours at the corners and the gate posts. The tomb against the n. wall dominates the chancel and is an impressive and important piece by Thomas Dunn, who as a builder-mason was employed by Hawksmoor to build Spitalfields Christ's Church and St Mary Woolnoth in the City. It commemorates Edward Colman who died in 1743 and the pensive, reclining figure in flowing drapery is set against a striated grey marble backing arch between **Corinthian** columns. A large **putto** offers a crown overhead and two of his chubby fellows gesture either side of the shields of arms on the **pediment**. The C18 panelling on the s. wall was fitted round the old priest's door and the **sanctuary** piscina had its canopy cut away to give a straight run to the corner. The e. window glass of 1860 is by the **O'Connors** and is a good example of their better work. It is a Crucifixion with stylised medieval figures and lots of busy ornament; the colour is sharp and well-handled. They probably also provided the s.e. window, with its patterned **quarries** and arms of the Brown family. In 1960 a very important and significant group of paintings was uncovered on the e. wall. They date from between 1270 and 1330, indicating that the chancel pre-dates most of the rest of the building. The centre **reredos** panel of the Crucifixion, in red against a pale green background, portrays the twisted figure of Christ with overlarge feet flanked by the Blessed Virgin and **S John** in the gawky attitudes so often seen in medieval manuscripts. They remind one of the figures on the Thornham Parva **retable**. To the l. are two kneeling angels (one of which is complete) censing the space originally occupied by a statue, probably of the Virgin. The blue background has blackened with the years and is dappled with stars. On the s. side of the altar is the remnant of a life-size figure of Christ bearing the banner of the Resurrection. The painting was originally a version of the 'Harrowing of Hell' in which Christ rescues Adam from the pit. Parts of Adam can still be made out and the figure of the priest donor is plain in the bottom corner with the inscription +RICA above him and a wine jar by his side. The modern choir stalls have panels carved to match the C17 box pew and there are some excellent **ledger stones** with the coats of arms cut deeply enough to trip the unwary. As you leave, ponder the fact that the humble C19 building by the gate once contained a fine parochial library of some 1500 volumes bequeathed in 1715 by the squire Dr Henry Colman rector of Harpley and Foulsham in Norfolk. Sadly now dispersed, these volumes were originally housed in a library built onto the e. end of the chancel which was demolished in 1859.

Brettenham, St Mary (E6): The church is basically a C14 building and there is an interesting variety of **Decorated** window **tracery** in the **nave**, with early **Perpendicular** forms on the n. side of the **chancel**. The e. window appears to be C19 and below it are three shields of arms - Stafford, Buckingham and Sampson. The Earl of Stafford's son, Humphrey, was patron here in the 1430s and later became Duke of Buckingham. The tower doubles as a s. **porch**, with a flint panelled **base course**, a decayed niche above the entrance, and worn **headstops** to the arch of the inner doorway. There is a **stoup** to the r. and the doors themselves are medieval, with an attractively carved border of leaves. The late C14 **font**stands on two high steps and is similar to that at Rattlesden. It has a **castellated** rim marked with incised crosses all the way round and the panels are carved with **cusped** and **crocketted ogee** arches; the heads at the angles below have been defaced. During the invasion scare of 1940, all signposts were uprooted and names of villages obliterated so that the Germans would have to rely on map and compass. In an excess of zeal the village name was painted out on the benefaction boards here, but had the visiting 'herrenvolk' looked carefully they would have found that one example had been overlooked to give the game away. The nave **roof**is **arch-braced** and below are C19 benches - apart from two pairs of mutilated bench ends by the pulpit. The easternmost window on the s. side has stained glass of 1866 by **Henry Hughes** of **Ward & Hughes** illustrating the miracle of the loaves and fishes - heavy colour and precious little animation for such a

theme. There is a plain **piscina**, indicating that a nave **altar** stood here. Nearby is a bronze plaque for Lieut. Cornwallis John Warner who was killed in 1915; it has his arms in enamelled colour with replicas of his four medals and there is a duplicate at Thorpe Morieux. The prayer desk incorporates a pair of medieval bench ends and tracery panels. On the n. side, the blocked door and little **quatrefoil** window mark the position of the stair to the now vanished **rood loft**. The first window on the n. side of the chancel has some fragments of C15 glass and they include a good **Trinity** shield in a roundel. There are C15 **poppyheads** and some panel tracery built into the C19 stalls and two more old bench ends that match those in the nave. The late C17 **altar rails** have vigorously twisted **balusters**, with gates that, when closed, complete the clusters of four balusters at each side - an uncommonly clever little piece of joinery design. The late C14 angle piscina has a cusped and crocketted ogee arch, with Buckingham and Stafford shields in the **spandrels** repeating those outside; to the r. are the **dropped-sill sedilia**. The 1882 Ward & Hughes glass on this side portrays doubting **St Thomas** and Christ with **Peter** and **Andrew** but it is not memorable and the rest of the chancel glass is poor. On the e. wall there are two C19 or early C20 murals painted on metal - he Wise Men, and Christ with two disciples on the road to Emmaus. The figures stand under canopies and are reminiscent of Walter Crane's work. In the n.e. corner of the **sanctuary** is an interesting **brass** inscription as well as verses for Thomas Weniffe who died in 1611:

A gentle and modest young man who leavinge this life lefte also this verse touching the vanity thereof.

Short was his life yet liveth he ever, Death hath his dewe yet dyeth he never.

Ledger-stones are seldom signed, but under the stalls on the n. side Elizabeth Wenyede's stone shows that it was cut by Charles Bottomley of Bury in 1751. Before you go, have a look at the bible by the door. Published by John Basket in 1716, it is known as the 'Vinegar Bible' because the heading for the parable of the vineyard was misprinted.

Brockley, St Andrew (C5): The church is picturesquely placed among open fields n. of the present village. A path runs alongside the moat of Brockley Hall farm through a meadow to the base of the late C15 tower. This has handsome diagonal buttresses bearing **flushwork** emblems, including 'MR' for the **Blessed Virgin** and **St Andrew's** cross. The **base course** is flint panelled to the w. and on the s. side it incorporates a fine and bold inscription, 'In Mg Ricardus Coppynge'. In his will of 1521, Richard Copping of Brockley left money for the completion of the tower roof and the inscription shows that he probably financed the whole work. The w. window is a later **Perpendicular** insertion and the battlements are modern. Variations in the structure show that the **chancel** was originally much shorter and may indeed have been **Norman**, but there is a window with 'Y' tracery on the n. side pointing to a rebuilding at the end of the C13, and others in both **nave** and chancel have early C14 tracery. There was a wholesale restoration 1866-1871 when the church was re-roofed, and the **reticulated** tracery in the e. window no doubt dates from then (although it probably copied the original). There is a small **priest's door** to the s. and a large **scratch dial** can be seen high on the s.e. nave buttress. There are some particularly good C18 headstones in the churchyard and s. of the chancel is the base of a **preaching cross** that an early C19 rector moved from the nearby meadow. The s. **porch** is simple C15 timber on a brick and flint base and the entrance door is medieval, bearing exceptionally good ironwork which is probably early C14. The closing ring is pierced and there are four lizards cast on the rim - ancient emblems of good fortune that were favoured for handles. The keyhole escutcheon, in the form of a pierced crown, is of equal quality. In front of the lofty tower arch stands a plain C13 octagonal **font** on a circle of renewed shafts and base and, like the entrance, the stair to the tower still has its medieval door. The roofs and benches were part of the 1860s restoration and the C19 pulpit was remodelled in 1986. In the s. wall there is a large tomb recess under a **cusped ogee** arch rising to an excellent **finial** and if, as has been suggested, the C14 rebuilding was by Alexander de Walsham, this might be his tomb. As at nearby Whepstead, there are simple **piscinas** cut in the **dropped-sills** of the windows each side of the nave at the e. end to serve subsidiary **altars,** and on the n. side the whole sill shows traces of colour. There is now no **rood screen** or loft but the stone **corbels** that carried the **rood beam** remain high in the wall each side of the chancel arch. The chancel stalls are Victorian but they make use of C15 bench ends. In the **sanctuary** there is a small, late C13 double piscina under two plain arches, and you will see that the centre shaft is notched at the back to house a **credence shelf**. The C19 lays heavily on this part of the church; there are Minton tiles with a particularly dense pattern in the sanctuary and the e. wall is panelled in metal and painted with stiff figures of the **Evangelists**. The vapid e. window glass of 1869 (the Good Shepherd with Faith on the l and Hope on the r.) is by **Ward & Hughes** and shows how much their standards fell as the result of mass production. Rector James Sprigge's 1846 memorial on the n. wall is a slightly unusual plain marble shield on grey background by Reed of Bury -

Brockley, St Andrew: C14 ironwork

one of the less well-known local masons. Before leaving, have a look at the sweet little chamber organ in a plain pine case with decorative cornice. It was built in Rutland in the 1880s and brought here 100 years later.

Bury St Edmunds, All Saints (D4): On Park Road, in an urban situation, the church was designed by Cecil Beadsmore Smith and built in 1962 to cater for the extensive development on the w. side of town. Utilitarian and built for economy, it has faintly bizarre echoes of older things - cosmetic buttresses on the w. porch and a C14-style arch to the **sanctuary** within. In plain, mottled red brick, its only distinguishing features are a large cross in relief on the e. end and an octagonal turret sheathed in copper on the **roof** above, ringed with sharply pointed buttresses and carrying a cross. The building consists of a large hall, with three flat-topped dormers each

side and a n.e. **vestry** block balanced by a Lady chapel - both with flat roofs. There is a flat roof too for the large w. **porch** enclosed by iron gates. The inner doors have attractive dolphin handles and lead to a plain, open hall with a ceiling that follows the line of the sanctuary arch and has chunks bitten out to admit light from the dormers. There are tall side windows, all with frosted glass, and doors midway down the **nave** are fitted with crash bars. Beyond the Gothic arch, the sanctuary has a blank e. wall and is lit by pairs of glass brick windows each side; a **consecration cross**, flanked by alpha and omega signs, is cut in the centre of the step before the **altar**. The stark whiteness of the interior is relieved only by the broad swathe of plum-coloured carpet up the centre. The fittings are unadventurous but of good quality - a small octagonal **font** with alternate panels traceried, and a solid pulpit in C18 style, with split **baluster** decoration that matches the prayer desks and **communion rails**. The small oak lectern has some character. It consists of an eagle on a tapering octagonal shaft, with a Greek inscription round the base and signed 'C.J.C. 1939'. The low-ceilinged Lady chapel has nicely detailed curved rails before the altar, and as an altar piece there is a coloured plaster Nativity panel set in a carved pine frame. A boy shepherd kneels to the side of the Virgin and Child and there are three young angels to the r., with an ox beyond. This attractive design in muted colours is the work of Ellen Mary Rope (1855-1934). She was the aunt of the two **Margaret Ropes** whose stained glass can be seen at Leiston and elsewhere in the county. Ellen studied at the Slade School, exhibited at the Royal Academy from 1885, and lived at Tunstall.

Bury St Edmunds, St Edmundsbury Cathedral (D4): In the C17, Thomas Fuller wrote in his *Worthies of England*:

> This county hath no cathedral therein... but formerly it had so magnificent an abbey church in Bury, the sun shined not on a fairer, with three lesser churches waiting thereon in the same churchyard. Of these but two are extant at this day, and those right stately structures.

One was the parish church of St James, built by Abbot Anselm in the C12 and the stone shafts on the outside n. face of the present building are all that remain of that beginning. By the C16, the parishioners were looking enviously at the other far grander church of St Mary's across the churchyard, and began to rebuild St James' to keep pace. It is almost certain that the new work was designed by John Wastell, king's mason and one of the great architects of the Middle Ages. He lived in Bury and was probably the abbey's master mason, but he ranged widely, designing part of King's College Chapel at Cambridge (the w. window here is a small-

er version of the one at King's) and was master at Canterbury where he built the Bell Harry tower. Beginning in 1503 by extending the w. end to the street, the work moved eastwards, giving us a superbly proportioned **nave** which relies on simplicity rather than surface decoration for its effect. Wastell died in 1515 and the work was probably continued under Henry Semark, to be completed around 1550. In the 1860s there was a major restoration by **Sir George Gilbert Scott** under **J.D. Wyatt**. A new **chancel** was built, the nave **roof** replaced and the w. gable rebuilt. In 1913, the new diocese of St Edmundsbury and Ipswich was established and St James' became the new cathedral, although it was recognised at the time that it would need to be enlarged to match its new role. However, it was not until the 1960s that the new concept began to take shape under the direction of Stephen Dykes Bower. The n.w. entrance porch came first, and then Scott's chancel was replaced by a larger e. end, **crossing tower** and stub **transepts**, completing the main phase of the work in 1970. Plans exist for a large new building on the n. side to contain a refectory, song school and other facilities, as well as the completion of the cloister, crossing tower and n. transept. The s. frontage gives the best view of the way in which the new has been combined with the old. The walls are faced with **ashlar** and there is fine **flushwork** decoration in East Anglian style framing the arches of the tall choir windows with their **Decorated tracery**. More flushwork exists on the battlements at the e. end, and on the upper range of the s. transept, with its octagonal **sanctus- bell turret** crowned with a shapely spirelet and weathervane. Another matches it on the n. side of the building. A bronze figure of the boy martyr, King **Edmund**, by Elizabeth Frink stands in the centre of the green, and to the w. is the C12 **Norman** tower, built by Abbot Anselm as the main entrance to the abbey. It is a splendidly massive structure and has served as the bell tower for St James' since the Middle Ages. From the new cathedral entrance, steps lead down into the first section of the glazed cloister - very plain with a flat-boarded ceiling. Memorials on the r. hand wall include a good portrait silhouette, by J.C. Lough, of Benjamin Malkin, master of the local grammar school, who died in 1843. Arms of the province of Canterbury and of the diocese flank the entrance to the nave, and above the door inside are the carved and gilded **Royal Arms** of Charles II. Above them, a fine gilded cherub blowing a trumpet once decorated the original organ case and was discovered in a Belgian antique shop before being returned to its home. With the new crossing and e. end, the interior is notably light and spacious and the **aisles** still have their C16 roofs. In the C18, Wastell's low-pitched roof was replaced by a poor thing of deal, as well as a **stucco** ceiling, and so it is not surprising that Scott decided to do better with a steep double **hammerbeam** design. Harsh things have been said of it and while it may not equal St Mary's, its modern colouring of green and red enlivened by gold, contrives to be extraordinarily jolly. The **font** was designed by Scott in 1870 and it has a splendid traceried cover in East Anglian style which rises over 20 ft to a corona and **crocketted** spire. It was made by F.E. Howard of Oxford as a 1914-18 war memorial and, with the font, was richly coloured and gilt in 1960. The pulpit is another Scott piece of the 1870s. There are few notable memorials in the cathedral but by the w. door is the figure of James Reynolds, Chief Baron of the Exchequer and MP for the town who died in 1738. He sits, squat and rather lumpish, facing the nave, flanked by standing cherubs, one carrying a skull and wiping his eye, while another trumpets from the **pediment** above a shield of arms. Although the lantern over the cross-

ing is unfinished and the n. transept arches blocked, the transepts have attractive panelled roofs, densely painted and gilded. The e. end is light and airy, with tall high-level windows. The good, early **Kempe** glass in the e. window came from the C19 chancel. The choir has a painted roof matching the transepts and a line of narrow arches runs below the side windows and across the bottom of the e. window, forming a narrow passageway. The bishop's throne on the n. side of the **sanctuary** was, like the font cover, made by F.E. Howard. It is an example of quality C20 woodwork in the medieval style, with buttresses capped by wolves guarding St Edmund's head and was a memorial to the first bishop of the diocese. The top of the arched recess behind the high altar is filled with a design in wrought-iron surmounted by a gilded sunburst designed by Stephen Dykes Bower. The chapel on the n. side of the choir is dedicated to St Edmund and the double-arched entrance has a handsome wrought-iron screen of silver filigree lozenges set in a framework of blue and gold. The **reredos** and **Hardman** glass of 1869 (above it) came from the old choir. The n. wall is unadorned stock brick, showing where the proposed extension will (hopefully) join on, but good use has been made of the space to display a tapestry of the life of St Edmund, commemorating the 1100th anniversary of his martyrdom. Designed by David Orchard, a Suffolk teacher, the nine framed and glazed panels contain scenes of the Liberty of St Edmundsbury embroidered by pupils of secondary schools (the Liberty was the area adminstered by the abbey). The Lady chapel on the s. side of the choir was completed in 1970 and is entered through a wrought-iron screen in red and gold. In 1828, such ancient glass as remained was collected together and arranged in the westernmost window of the s. aisle, opposite the entrance door. The central upper **light** contains the figure of

St John with the chalice and on either side are figures, each with its label, from a Jesse Tree design. In an upper **tracery**light on the r. is a rare portrayal of the Blessed Virgin's father, **St Joachim**, carrying a lamb. The lower panels are filled with Flemish C15 glass illustrating the story of Susannah and the Elders, with the heroine in a very compact tub in the centre. The r. hand scene has some excellent figures robed in purple and reminiscent of Holbein's drawings of Sir Thomas More. The cathedral has a splendid array of C19 glass - look first at the s. aisle w. window, a **Clayton & Bell** Jesse window of 1899. This is a solid composition in very rich colouring, with meticulously detailed fur robes, brocades and curly beards, reminiscent of Kempe's work. The Hardman 1869 w. window is one of their best being solid Victorian quality, using clear colours and confident lines. The theme is the Last Judgement, and while the archangel weighs the souls in the bottom centre panel, the blessed and the damned gather on either side, with Christ in majesty over all. There is another bright and lively Clayton & Bell design at the w. end of the n. aisle on the theme of the Creation. Lines from Genesis run along the bottoms of the two ranks of panels, Adam and Eve are in the garden at the centre and there is a nice diversity of creatures, including a spouting whale. The glass in the rest of the nave windows is mainly by the same firm, with themes from the Old Testament on the n. and the New Testament on the s.

Bury St Edmunds, St George (D4): Sited on Anselm Road, this church serves the Mildenhall Road Estate and is used by Roman Catholics as well as Anglicans. It was originally built as a community hall and was converted by Waring & Hastings in 1967. In the 1970s the Whitworth Partnership designed the extension at what I will call the w. end (the back of the church). Remembering its beginnings it is, as one would expect, a conservative building in grey brick, with sash windows and pantile roofs; the main hall has two **transept**-like projections just short of the (nominal) e. end, with a matching pair at the w. end, one of which forms the entrance lobby. A slim spirelet sheathed in lead with a cross **finial** above the **sanctuary** confirms its new role to the passer-by. The interior is calm and simple and has a very nice atmosphere. There was originally a stage at the w. end and this space, combined with the extension, forms a large activities and meeting area separated by partitioned doors from the church proper. The sanctuary is defined by a simple arch and the obscured glass of the neo-Georgian e. window has a cross and border in pale yellow. The **altar**, which is placed at the front of the sanctuary, is a slightly unhappy combination of boxy, angled pedestals and a top with a deep curved apron, all in sycamore and mahogany veneers. The sturdy **communion rails** form a half circle around it and there is a small octagonal mahogany **font** to match which was the gift of the St George and Stonham Aspal Sunday Schools in 1969. The reading desk has a very lively **St George** and the dragon frontal and there is a collage on the same theme framed by the entrance which was produced by the Holiday Club children in 1985. The **chancel** arch has a **consecration cross** inset on the s. side and a door leads through to the Lady chapel which is quietly impressive in its simplicity. The plain, oak-veneered altar has an incised cross centre front, and an oil painting, of the head of the sorrowing Christ with a heavy crown of thorns, hangs on the wall.

Bury St Edmunds, St John (D4): With the development of the railway and the gas works, the town grew in that direction and St John's was built in

1841 to meet a need. This was before the influence of the **Ecclesiologists** had really taken hold and William Ranger's design cannot have pleased them. The building, in local Woolpit bricks that have darkened to a greenish grey, is gaunt. Its tower is four-square to the level of the **nave** roof where large octagonal corner turrets, with conical caps, sprout short flying buttresses into a second stage. This has pairs of very tall latticed windows with sharp gables and then comes another set of corner turrets with flying buttresses to support the spire which rises to 160 ft. The whole thing is a restless and uneasy affair. The base of the tower now has recessed doors and windows set in red brick and they provide effective relief to the overall drabness of the building. The interior was originally packed with pews to achieve maximum accomodation but, as rearranged, it is now light and airy, with an engaging colour scheme - mouldings and attached columns of the **arcades**, w. arch and **clerestory** all picked out in egg-yolk yellow, with the **groined** wooden roof of the continuous nave and **chancel** in dark brown. The **aisle** ceilings are flat and there are open-back benches, pulpit and choir stalls in oak, all probably designed by **J.D. Wyatt**, the architect in charge of the 1870s refitting. The three large **lancets** of the e. window were originally filled with glass by Forrest & Bromley of Liverpool in 1858, but it had become decayed and a reglazing in 1960 retained only the shaped panels, now set in antique glass. In early C19 painterly style, the centre panel is a Crucifixion, with the Last Supper and Ascension on either side. Below, the carved stone **reredos** of 1876 was coloured in 1947 and statues of **Saints Peter, John, Michael** and **George** were inserted in the panels. The lancet at the e. end of the s. aisle contains **Heaton, Butler & Bayne** glass, with a seated St John writing the Gospel. He has a haunting face and the style of the layered background makes it look

later than its 1863 date. There is later glass by the same firm in the n. aisle - a 1902 window depicting **St Mary Magdalene** meeting the risen Christ. Next to it, a heavy **Kempe** design of 1900 - the visit of the Magi in two panels. The tower arch was fitted with an elegant glass screen to its full height in 1974 and this allows a good view of the 1903 w. window, with its tall figures of Christ as the Good Shepherd (with curiously green flesh tints). The crucifix over the pulpit is Oberammergau work and so is the figure of St Michael in the n. aisle.

Bury St Edmunds, St Mary (D4): A previous church dedicated to St Mary was demolished in the early C12 to make way for the s. **transept** of the abbey and the sacrist Godfrey sited its replacement in the s.w. corner of the cemetery. The building was designed, like St James', to serve the needs of a town parish. The late C14 tower is offset on the n. side, aligning with the old precinct wall. The **chancel**, built in the early C14, has a later **sanctuary** projecting one bay to the e., with a crypt beneath. The main body of the church was magnificently rebuilt between about 1424 and 1446 and is a proud example of C15 work, drawing upon the riches of the burgeoning local wool trade. Most of the work was completed in the first decade and it is likely that the architect was William Layer, a local mason who was also concerned with the vanished great w. tower of the abbey. The rebuilding brought the w. front forward to the street line and the w. face of the **nave** is almost all window - **transomed Perpendicular tracery** that is matched in the great range of windows down the s. frontage to the e. end. Above is a **clerestory** with pairs of window to each bay, and **crocketted** spirelets rise from the twin **rood stair** turrets at the e. end of the nave. The n. side is interrupted by a **porch** nearly halfway down its length - an unusual position, but the siting of the tower prevented a more conventional arrangement and it aligns conveniently with the s. door of St James' across the churchyard. This fine porch was bequeathed by John Notyngham, a wealthy grocer who died in 1437. An inscription over the door invites prayers for his soul and that of his wife Isabelle. There are **stoups** in the buttresses on either side of the door, three canopied niches above and a crocketted gable. The stone ceiling within is beautifully panelled with a circle of blank arches, and the centre hub is carved and pierced as a pendant, within which is a carving of God the Father attended by angels. Entry to the church this way is via an early C14 doorway which, like the flanking windows, has been re-used.

The interior of this, one of the largest parish churches in the country, is very impressive. The pillars of the nave **arcade** of ten bays are lozenge-shaped with broad, hollow mouldings and are slim for their height. Above them and the glass wall of the clerestory, is one of the finest C15 **roofs** in England. **Hammerbeams** alternate with **arch-braced** trusses that have, themselves, nascent hammerbeams carved as grotesques and clamped to the sides. The main timbers rise from 42 splendidly carved **wall posts** representing mainly apostles and prophets, but you will find **St Michael St Margaret** and **St Walstan** on the n. side towards the w. end. The double depth cornice is carved with demi-angels and the **spandrels** beneath the hammerbeams are pierced and carved with all manner of beasts and birds. At the e. end there is a **celure** that honoured the original rood below and the figures of the **Annunciation** are against the wall posts - the archangel **Gabriel** on the n. and the **Blessed Virgin** on the s. The hammerbeams are carved as recumbent angels, with wings partly unfurled, and they form a fascinating sequence. They are in pairs, a series of eleven each side and, instead of dis-

playing the usual **Passion emblems** or musical instruments, they are clergy vested for mass, followed by an archangel, a queen and a king. Beginning from the e. end, there are the angels of the celure (with C19 colouring), incense bearers with boat in one hand and spoon in the other, thurifers with **censers**, candlebearers with spiked candlesticks (the one on the s. may hold a box for flint and steel in his right hand), sub-deacons holding the Gospel book, deacons with the chalice, celebrants wearing chasubles, choirmasters (clearly conducting), archangels feathered overall with double wings, young women holding crowns, and crowned kings. The features of the king, particularly the version on the n. side, remind one of the National Portrait Gallery's Henry VI as a young man, and the woman could well represent Margaret of Anjou, betrothed to Henry in 1444 and crowned in May 1445. It is tempting to suppose that the roof was finished in time for Henry to see it when he held his parliament in the abbey refectory in February 1447. Apart from the nave roof, there are dozens of superb carvings in the **aisles**, in spandrels and on **bosses**, a number of which relate to medicine and disease (reflecting the importance of Bury as a medieval centre for infirmaries). All the roofs are dark and it is well worth the small fee to have the lights switched on and to go armed with binoculars.

John Baret was a wealthy clothier and official of the abbey who died in 1467 and his **chantry chapel**, at the e. end of the s. aisle, was originally the Lady chapel. The roof is splendidly decorated and has been restored so that the small convex mirrors in the centre of the painted stars gleam and twinkle. Henry VI honoured Baret with the **collar of SS** and this figures in the decoration, together with his monogram and motto in bold gothic letters: 'Grace me governe'. He had his tomb made in his lifetime as a reminder or mortality, and when the present Lady chapel was built it was moved to its present position against the wall. The hand of the emaciated cadaver on top rests on a scroll with traces of original colouring: 'He that wil sadly beholde one with his ie, May se hys owyn merowr and lerne for to die'. A **piscina** under a **cinque-foil** arch and **dropped-sill sedilia** remain behind the tomb from the time when the Lady chapel was here. Jan-kyn (John) Smyth was another wealthy Bury merchant and both chapels flanking the chancel were built at his expense; the Jesus chapel on the n. about 1460 and the Lady chapel on the s. a little later. The architect was probably Simon Clerk or John Forster, a pupil of William Layer. Smyth's chantry was at the e. end of the n. aisle, matching the posi-tion of the Baret chantry and he was buried there. The Jesus chapel has become better known as the Suffolk chapel and houses many memorials and colours of the county regiment. Entered through wrought-iron gates, it was furnished and decorated under the direction of **J.N. Comper**. One of the best **brasses** in the church may be found under the sanctuary carpet here - a 36 in figure of John Fyners vested in cassock, surplice and amice, with a Latin inscription. He died in 1509 and was Archdeacon of Sudbury. The Lady chapel, too, has a number of brasses and although Jan-kyn Smyth was buried in his chantry in the n. aisle, his memorial seems to have migrated here, within the sanc-tuary on the n. side. He wears a Yor-kist collar with the lion of March as a pendant over his tunic, and his wife Anne has a **butterfly head-dress** and mantle. The brass for Henry and Edmund Lucas, a fine shield with mantling and a verse, has been taken from the floor and fixed to the wall on the l. of the chapel entrance. Henry Lucas was a cousin of Henry VII, his father being the king's solicitor gener-al. The grave of Thomas and Elizabeth Heigham (1542) lies in the centre of the chapel but the effigies and

inscription have gone, leaving three shields only. The painting over the **altar** here is 'The Incarnation' by John Williams - the young Virgin crouched in a swirl of cloud and light, with vignettes of Christ's birth, teaching, Crucifixion and Ascension in the cor-ners. There are other brass inscrip-tions in the nave; at the w. end, Matthew and Margaret Lancaster (1634 and 1661) set on a later stone, and one for George Boldero (1609) with shield and inscription in front of the chancel screen on the n. side. The original **rood screen** is no longer here and the present one is a 1913 memo-rial to members of the Suffolk regiment. Note that the old **rood loft** had access stairs on both sides and that the doors remain at ground and first floor level. It is particularly inter-esting that the top door on the n. side is much larger than its opposite num-ber, pointing to the fact that the dea-con would enter from that side to read the Gospel during the mass. The chancel roof, excellently restored, is panelled with intricate **cusping** and carved bosses, and here again binoc-ulars are a great help in appreciating the quality and diversity of the carv-ings, many of which illustrate favou-rite medieval themes, such as the fox preaching to chickens. The cornice is painted with angels carrying scrolls inscribed with the 'Te Deum'. The stalls below incorporate sections of tracery from the old rood screen and there are some fine and large gro-tesques on the arm rests. An interest-ing brass is to be found on the s. arcade pillar at the e. end of the choir stalls. It is for George Estye, the minis-ter here who died in 1601. The inscription was composed by Joseph Hall, then a young Cambridge don but later to become the much harried bishop of Norwich under the Com-monwealth. His initials are engraved on the plate and the guttering candle in the top corner has the words: 'Luceo et absumor' ('I give light and am consumed'). There are two large tombs at the e. end and the one on the

n. side is for Sir William Carewe who died in 1501, and his wife Margaret, who followed him in 1525. The effigies are large and stiff, he in coat armour with his head on a helm and his feet on a sizable lion, she in kirtle and mantle with a pair of small dogs at her skirts. The tomb was originally canopied and there is a funeral helm placed above. Coats of arms in **quatrefoils** decorate the front of the tomb. Opposite is the tomb of Sir Robert and Lady Anne Drury. He died in 1536 and the effigies have much in common with those on the Carewe tomb, although his feet rest on a large greyhound. The brass inscription round the top is a replacement; again, a helm hangs overhead. The projecting sanctuary was another bequest of Jankyn Smyth and matches the style of the side chapels. Traces of a coloured celure can still be seen and the pulleys for the **Lenten veil** are still in position. John Reeve (or Melford), the last abbot, lies buried before the high altar, having been deprived of office in 1540, but his grave was stripped of the brass and even the stone itself was removed and used for a time as a doorstep in the C18. In the n.e. corner of the sanctuary lies a **mensa** still bearing the **consecration crosses**, and on it is cut: 'Mary, Queen of France, 1533'. This is the last resting place of the younger daughter of Henry VII, sister of Henry VIII and, briefly, wife of the old and ailing king of France, Louis XII. Charles Brandon, Duke of Suffolk, was sent to bring the widow home but married her in secret and paid heavily for the privilege when her brother found out. Wolsey conciliated and, after a court marriage ceremony at Greenwich, the couple came to live at Westhorpe. Mary Tudor was buried in the abbey in great state and at the Dissolution hers was the only body to be removed and reburied. In 1881, Queen Victoria gave the **Clayton & Bell** window in her memory, to be seen on the s. side of the sanctuary in the Lady chapel. Not great art perhaps, but it portrays six scenes in

Mary's life, including the meeting with Henry VIII and her burial service.
Although the church has no medieval glass, it is extraordinarily rich in C19 windows. There was a restoration by L.N. Cottingham in 1844 when the shape of the window over the chancel arch was altered, and **Thomas Willement** supplied a Martyrdom of **St Edmund** design for it. The w. window was reconstructed at the same time, and in thanksgiving for the harvest of 1867, glass by **Heaton, Butler & Bayne** was installed. It has a harvest theme in the top centre panel, a Crucifixion below, and medallions on either side in three ranks depicting scenes from the life of Christ. Looking down the lovely vista from the chancel, the colours of the window are very reminiscent of a Victorian kaleidoscope, and there is a fine selection of Heaton, Butler & Bayne 1880s glass in the s. aisle windows. The C15 chapel of **St Walstan** is tucked in the n.w. corner of the church and there one finds, among memorials and colours of the county regiments, a **Ward & Hughes** w. window of 1869. It is rather sentimental in feeling, with lush colouring - the Last Supper across the lower panels and the Magi, the flight into Egypt, and 'no room at the inn' above. The relatively small size of the e. window, set high in the wall of the Lady chapel, indicates that it was moved from its old position in the Baret chantry and used again when the new chapel was built; in 1856 it was filled with stained glass by Alfred Gérente of Paris. The three shaped medallions depict incidents in the life of Christ and the colours, particularly the blue, are akin to **Hardman** glass of the same period. There is another Ward & Hughes window of 1884 towards the e. end of the n. aisle - a Transfiguration scene in the upper panels, with **Saints James the Great**, **Peter** and **John** below, all in pictorial style using soft colour. Next to it, a window of 1894, probably by **Kempe**. The great surge of church building and restora-

tion in the 1850s created a great demand for stained glass, and one artist who turned painter-glazier was Charles Clutterbuck. He is represented here with a window over the s. door of 1854 - David, Samuel and Solomon in the main **lights**, with scenes from their lives in the smaller panels beneath - the colours creamy and soft. There are two more of his windows in the chancel and the e. window there has glass of 1914 - the four archangels vividly outlined against clear panes, with angels in the bottom centre panels holding the shields of St Edmund and the Sacred Heart. This glass is unsigned but could be **Lavers & Westlake**. The great windows of this church allow very little wall space for memorials and monuments, but advantage has been taken of the interior tower wall, and there tablets are ranged almost to the roof. By the door is a memorial to those men of the Suffolk regiment who went down in the HMS Birkenhead disaster off South Africa in 1852. Round the corner is a tablet in memory of Peter Gedge, publisher of the first local newspaper, the *Bury & Norwich Post*. He died in 1818, and his epitaph reads: 'Like a worn out type he is returned to the Founder in hopes of being recast in a better and more perfect mould'. The medieval sacrist was lodged in the first floor of the tower and his watching window can be seen above the door. On the interior w. porch there is a set of post-1837 **Royal Arms** and there are two interesting pictures on the w. wall of the s. aisle. One is a view of the church interior as it was in the early C18 and the other is a lovely C19 or early C20 painting by Rose Mead entitled, 'Friday morning at St Mary's Bury St Edmunds'. It was the custom for bread to be given every Friday to the aged poor and they gathered in the Lady chapel to receive it. The picture shows that at that time the **font** was there and not at the w. end.

Bury St Edmunds, St Peter (D4): This church, in Hospital Road, is one of the many built in the mid-C19 to cater for the needs of a growing population. Designed by **J.H. Hakewill** and consecrated in 1858, it is a useful example of the small town church of the period, economical in design but with little trace of local feeling. Set against the s. wall of the **nave** one bay from the w. end, the tower has stone latticed bell openings and a shingled broach spire. The nave windows have simple **Early English tracery** and the **chancel** is only marked off by the use of a pair of **lancets**. The e. window has three lancets with **quatrefoil plate** tracery over, and the wall below has a stark banding of **knapped** flints. These are also used on the side walls below the windows, with random flint and stone work above. The arch of the w. door is picked out in stone and flint and lines of dressed flints cross the w. wall, lifting over the doorway as a **label**, with a two-**light** window above. The interior is 'plain Jane' indeed but attractively neat and bright. The nave **roof** is simple boarding, with a false chancel arch in wood coming down to **colonnettes** which rest on stone angels holding the chalice on one side and the paten, piled with bread, on the other. Beyond, the barrel roof of the chancel is painted a deep blue, with small **bosses** picked out in gold. Beyond an archway at the e. end of the nave on the n. side there is a stub **transept**, and the panels that used to flank the **altar** have been fixed to the walls there. Of metal with moulded wooden frames, they have the Lord's Prayer, **decalogue** and Creed. The **font** is typical of the period - **quatrefoils** in the bowl panels carved with cross, star of David, **Agnus Dei** and the dove of the Holy Spirit. There are four coupled shafts beneath and heavy foliage carved under the bowl. Plain pitchpine pews and a stone pulpit-cum-reading desk unit which incorporates a small stone and marble lectern supported by an angel are also to be found. The choir-stalls are pitchpine with **poppyheads** and there are plain recessed stone panels across the e. wall of the **sanctuary**, backing the plain oak **reredos**. The glass of the 1902 e. window is probably by **Kempe** and has figures of **St Peter** flanked by **St James the Great** and **St John** - florid, with intricate canopy work. There is a most attractive **Annunciation** window at the e. end of the nave on the s. side of 1955, designed by Hugh Easton. The archangel **Gabriel** has brilliant red and gold wings, wears a scarlet robe and holds a sceptre, while the dove of the Holy Spirit hovers over the **Blessed Virgin**; in the background is a view of Bury's **Norman** tower.

Buxhall, St Mary (E5): This is a fine church in a secluded setting, with a long walk up to the s. **porch**. It was rebuilt about 1320 and the tall two-**light** windows have **Decorated tracery**. There is a **scratch dial** on one of the s. **nave** buttresses and on the other is a **flushwork** flint cross which might be the first of the external **consecration crosses**. The **chancel** gable carries tall pinnacles and the **crockets** terminate in human heads and grotesques. The e. window is large and handsome, with good flowing tracery and the nave battlements are in later brick. The tower followed the main building at the end of the C14 and its base is flint panelled, with chequer work on the buttresses. The **string courses** are bold and there is a stair turret on the s. side up to the ringing chamber. The large porch has a chequered parapet and the niche, with its crocketted **finial**, was provided with a small figure of the **Blessed Virgin** in 1984. The inner door has rosette stops to the arch, and in 1956 workmen discovered the **stoup** to the r., with its **trefoil** arch and half of the bowl hacked away. The tower arch within is very tall and the **jambs** have a mass of C16 and C17 graffiti. The **Royal Arms** of George I, painted on canvas, were well restored in 1982 and now

hang over the n. door; by the entrance, a light with a time switch has been thoughtfully provided so that they may be the better seen. The early C14 **font** with its **castellated** rim stands on a low shaft and there are crocketted gables backed by tracery in the bowl panels. The church was restored in the 1870s by the rector and the pews of oak from the Buxhall estate were carved by a daughter of the rectory, Agnes Emily Hill. She repeated the w. window tracery design in the panels of the pulpit. The nave **roof** was replaced in 1923 but that in the chancel is C17 and one of the **arch- braced** principals is dated 1656 with initials of the churchwardens. There was a chapel dedicated to **St Margaret** on the s. side of the nave and its **piscina** remains under a flat **ogee**arch with trefoil **cusping**. On the other side, the guild of **St John the Baptist** had its **chantry** and although there is now no screen, the stairs to the **rood loft** survive in the n. wall. Before the restoration the nave was above the level of the chancel but now steps rise to the **sanctuary** where there is a lovely C14 double piscina - two tall and narrow compartments under steep, crocketted gables with finials, and three pinnacles reaching to the full height. There are tracery **mouchettes** above the ogee arches and the springing of the **sedilia**canopy alongside shows that it once matched the piscina. On the sill of the sedilia is a C13 grave slab carved with a discoid cross and the familiar double omega sign of the period. The stalls incorporate four medieval bench ends with **poppyheads** and one of them is carved as a double head, with a tongue-out mask on top. The s.w. window in the chancel contains some C15 glass, including two angels, and look for the hand holding the poisoned chalice of **St John** which has a little grey beast crouching on top instead of the more usual devil. The next window has two cocks on red shields in the tracery, and in the sanctuary s. window is a C14 armorial shield which illus-

Buxhall, St Mary: double piscina

trates the care with which the artists of the day designed such things. There are more jumbled C15 fragments in the window above the n. **vestry** door and in the tracery of the s.e. nave window but the glass in the tower window is modern.

Cavendish, St Mary (C7): There is no more pleasant a prospect than the broad expanse of village green rising to the harmonious grouping of cottages and church beyond. The C14 tower has a massive s.e. stair turret rising well above the battlements and capped by an openwork bell frame, giving it an unmistakable silhouette; the ringing chamber served originally as living quarters and the fireplace chimney still emerges at the top. There are **lancets** at ground floor level, two-**light** belfry windows and **Tudor** bell openings. Unlike Clare, it measures up to the body of the church that was rebuilt in the C15. The whole of the **clerestory** and battlements of the **nave** are beautifully finished in **flushwork** and one of the lead rainwater hoppers carries the Tudor device of a rose between leopards' heads. It is likely that the s. **aisle** was designed by Reginald Ely, Henry VI's architect who began King's College Chapel, Cambridge. Built about 1471, the window **tracery** shows how the four-petalled flower motif survived well into the **Perpendicular** period. The **chancel** was rebuilt under the will of Sir John Cavendish, Edward III's Lord Chief Justice who was put to death with the Prior of Bury in 1381. There is flushwork chequer along the base of the walls and the windows combine the **ogee** shape with pure Perpendicular tracery in the heads. The **priest's door** is original and niches curve over the whole of the archway. The seven-light e. window is vast and virtually fills the whole wall. The C19 **vestry** stands on the site of an earlier chapel and the C14 n. aisle retains its modest doorway and unaltered buttresses; the blocked door at the e. end was probably used as the entrance to a private pew. The low s. **porch** is early C14 and the outer arch has been varied above the pairs of **Early English** shafts. There are side **arcades** resting on clustered shafts above the stone seats, and pairs of 'Y' tracery windows, one of which is cusped. The C14 door still has its original closing ring but only the rivets remain to show that it once had lizards attached - those ancient emblems of good fortune that can be seen at Withersfield and Great Thurlow.

Within, the nave is tall and wide in relation to its length and light floods in from the **transomed** clerestory windows and through the wall of glass at the e. end; this, together with

he delicacy of the arcade **piers** imparts a delicious sense of space and airiness. There are the remains of a **toup** to the r. of the entrance and to he l. stands a C15 **font** with nicely raceried shaft and the remains of **Evangelistic symbols** in the bowl panels. The low and sharply pointed ower arch has been re-cut and is fitted with a modern glazed **screen**. It is unusual to find a vaulted ceiling in he ground floor of a tower and this one has the added distinction of a large **green man** centre **boss**. Overhead there is a **sanctus-bell window** and the dark, cambered **tie- beam** nave **roof** springs from **wall-posts** hat bear the mutilated remains of canopied figures. The carvings in the **spandrels** are very similar to those at Stansfield, and with binoculars one can see a fierce dragon at the w. end on the n. side and a man with a spear at the e. end to the s. There are two fine windows in the s. aisle; the first of 1922 in memory of Emmeline Edmonds has the **Blessed Virgin** and Child within a niche frame, flanked by angels bearing shields of the Sacred Heart and **St Edmund** against a background of slightly tinted quarries; the second, by Cox & Sons of 1873, displays the **Agnus Dei** and Evangelistic symbols, set in attractive, heavily patterned glass. Nearby is a **piscina** within a wide, cusped arch with a small recess off to the l., and the **altar** is a good **Stuart** table. Behind it stands a gorgeous **reredos** ablaze with gilding and colour. On a relatively small scale, it is a C16 Flemish bas relief of the Crucifixion in painted alabaster which came from the private chapel of Athelstan Riley in London. The three crosses of Calvary rise above a crowd of animated figures carved with infinite delicacy and feeling; the rounded enclosing arch of gilded wood, deeply niched and intricately canopied, contains figures of Jonah emerging from the

Cavendish, St Mary: Flemish reredos

jaws of the whale, **St Veronica** offering Christ her kerchief, and a **pietà**. Below the main panel stands the Virgin and Child, with **St Anthony** on the l. and (probably) **St Roche** on the r. The early C15 n. aisle roof is interesting because it was obviously designed to fit the old building, and when the new arcades were built in the 1480s some of the spandrels had to be cut back for it to fit. Some fashionable pendants were added later and dated at each end - 1625 and 1626 (the colouring of the bosses and pendants is modern). In the n.w. window of the aisle there is a late C14 shield of arms which probably represents the marriage of Margaret Clifton of Buckenham in Norfolk and Roger, eldest son and heir of Sir Thomas de Grey. The monument on the wall further along is an oddity of retrospective family duty. A flat obelisk with side drapes, set on mottled marble, it was made by John Soward in 1810 but commemorates Shadrach Brise who died in 1699, his widow and various children up to 1752. There is another piece by this rather mundane sculptor at Thorpe Morieux. William White carried out a wholesale restoration and rebuilding here in the 1860s and it was then that the n. aisle was extended eastwards along the side of the chancel and the vestry built. The C15 eagle lectern is like the one at Woolpit except that in this case it has lost its base and stands on a stone plinth. The church's other lectern is in the chancel and is an interesting early C16 design in wood; the double slope is carried on a turned stem and the cross bars and feet of the base are also turned work. The late C14 windows of the chancel have slim **jamb shafts** and the hollowed embrasures are worked with shallow canopies. There is a C19 boarded waggon roof with bosses, and the bays over the **sanctuary** are painted to form a **celure**. The piscina, with its **crocketted** arch and large **finial**, has been sharply restored but within there are exceptionally delicate shafts that rise to **groining** which has a centre lion boss. There is a small portion of medieval glass canopy work in the centre light of the e. window and the door to the vestry is original. When it was a chapel, the small **quatrefoil squint** to the r. enabled the celebrant to see the **high altar**. Below the squint stands the tomb of Sir George Colt who died in 1570. There are three large shields carved in the side panels which retain traces of colour and an inscription is carried on the bevel of the worn **purbeck marble** top. Beyond it, to the l. of the window, is a canopied niche with two crocketted finials; below, two demi-angels support a cloth in which there is the tiny figure of a soul. They would appear to have been re-cut and the niche now contains a modern statue of the Virgin and Child.

Cavenham, St Andrew (B4): There is an 'S' bend at the end of the village street by the entrance to the Hall and the church lies just beyond. There are one or two interesting features on the outside - look first at the ancient slab of stone, possibly C12, under the gable at the s.w. corner. The carving is of two animals rather like rabbits and at the s.e. corner of the **nave** there is another, this time of a pair of human heads. The C13 **chancel** has a pair of matching **lancets** with **Decorated tracery**, although the fine mouldings are now partly obscured by plaster. The one to the w. had a **low side window** below but the opening has been bricked up. On the l. hand **jamb** you will find two **scratch dials** and there is another further up. Between these windows is a simple C13 **priest's door** and an earlier lancet. The e. window dates from the restoration of 1870. On the n. side of the chancel are two **Early English** lancets (one blocked) and a **trefoil**-headed C13 window. Both the w. gables of the nave have very broad caps, and there is a short length of **dogtooth** moulding under the one on the n. side. The

unbuttressed tower probably dates from the late C13, its w. door blocked at the bottom and glazed at the top to form a window. The bell opening on that side has 'Y' tracery but those on the n. and s. sides are late C14. The interesting item here is the weather mould high on the w. face. It can only mean that at one time there was a two-storied extension, presumably a **gali-lee porch** with a chamber above it like the one at Lakenheath. The s. porch has developed a decided lean outwards and the Early English doorway to the church shows traces of colour on the stonework. Within, note that the archway to the tower is hardly larger than a door and in front of it stands a large **font** with a tub bowl that is likely to be C12, standing on a later stem - the whole piece heavily plastered over. The restored nave **roof** is lightly **scissors-braced** and the windows form an interesting selection of Decorated and **Perpendicular** designs from the C13 to the C15. At the e. end, the irregularities in the walls and window embrasures show that steps went up to the **rood loft** on both sides of the chancel arch, and not only are there image brackets on the s. side but a **piscina** in the window sill behind the pulpit. It is a reminder that before the **Reformation** there were guilds in the church dedicated to **St Andrew**, **St John the Baptist**, **St Mary**, and the **Holy Trinity** - all of which would have had their individual altars. There is a fragment of C15 wall painting just w. of the lancet in the n. wall by the pulpit; suppliant figures kneel before a king who holds sceptre and scythe and wears a cloak secured at the top with a band of round brooches. There are traces of colour but the subject is unidentified. The 1914-18 memorial window at the e. end of the nave on the s. side is by Jones & Willis - **St George**, with the dragon writhing from behind him with teeth bared, and a background of dark sky and hills; two vivid red roses peep over the brocade that backs the figure. At the e. end of the nave floor is the only **brass** now in the church, an inscription for John Symunt who died in 1588. The late C14 chancel arch has grooves above the capitals where the **tympanum** fitted behind the rood and there are plenty of graffiti in the mouldings low down on the e. side. The **screen** is a simple late C16 example, square-headed, with **fleurons** in the top moulding. The stencilled decoration on the panels is likely to be a later addition and the curious tracery in the centre arch is modern. Note the lowered sill of the low side window on the s. side of the chancel just beyond the arch, and also a narrow band of yellow stained glass masked by a glazing bar at the top of the window. It is difficult to get at, but it has a medieval inscription in French asking us to pray for Adam the vicar. This window also has a border of C14 glass in yellow stain and a roundel at the bottom. In the **sanctuary** there is a good early C14 angle **piscina**; the corner pillar has a foliaged **capital** and the gable is **crocketted** with a **finial**. The e. window is filled with glass of the 1870s by William Wailes of Newcastle. Christ stands with children in the centre **light** and there are groups of figures on either side. The background is a hard blue and the painted faces have faded. The tracery lights are taken up with figures of the **Evangelists** with their symbols, together with two angels. C19 **commandment boards** flank the window and there is a tiny **aumbry** lurking behind the tortoise stove on the n. side which bears faint colour on the stone surround. The same colour appears again on the low arched recess on the other side of the chancel and round the priest's door. On the n. wall is a memorial to Sir William Webb - a marble tablet with reversed scrolls each side, a **pediment** above and a **cartouche** of arms against a pyramid. To the l. is a pair of tablets one above the other, combined in one classical design, with restrained swags at the sides and made by Jackman of Bury, dated

1865. Interestingly, the design was duplicated 46 years later by Hanchet of Bury on the far side of the Webb tablet. As you leave, note the medieval wrought-iron closing ring on the centre of the door.

Chedburgh, All Saints (C5): The church stands by the Bury - Haverhill road. The **nave** was rebuilt in 1842 using the old windows. There are C13 **lancets** with tilted **headstops** and one two-**light** window with 'Y' **tracery** of about 1300 on the s. side. This has two in-filled panels below and one wonders whether it came from the old **chancel** and was originally a **low side window**. The chancel and small s. **vestry** were built in 1842 but the early C14 e. window, with **reticulated** tracery, was salvaged from the old building. At the same time the old n. **porch** was removed to make way for a grey brick tower and spire. There is a pleasing C14 **quatrefoil** window in the w. gable which has small headstops on the **dripstone**. Through the small wooden s. porch lies a very simple interior, with a Victorian w. **gallery** housing a small organ and deal pews in the nave. The **font** is the same vintage and the floors are paved with East Anglian **pamments** - much less common in churches than bricks or glazed tiles. The inner arch of the re-set window with 'Y' tracery has attached **jamb shafts** with ring **capitals**, and they match those flanking the e. window of the short chancel. There you will see fragments of medieval glass in the tracery, including two little suns in splendour and two sets of lions which were probably part of a shield of **Royal Arms**. The stylised 1920s glass in pale colour depicts an angel catching the fluid from the side of the crucified Christ while two floating angels mask their faces above the **Blessed Virgin** and **St John**. The **sanctuary** is bounded by a delicate little set of Gothick **communion rails** with pierced **spandrels** to the arches, turned shafts, and scrolly wrought-iron supports (made no doubt for the new chancel). On your way out you will step over a **ledger-stone** in the nave that shows how varied C18 and early C19 pluralities could be. Thomas Knowles was not only rector of Ickworth and Chedburgh, he was a prebendary of Ely and 'Preacher' of St Mary's, Bury, as well.

Chelsworth, All Saints (E6): Attractively sited, the church stands s. of the street in one of Suffolk's prettiest villages. The walls are rendered and the C14 tower has a flint panelled **base course**, with 'Y' **tracery** bell openings. The w. window is a small **cusped lancet** and there is a narrow slit to light the belfry above. A major C15 rebuilding followed, with spacious **clerestoried nave** and wide **aisles**. The s. **porch** dates from the same period and is set flush with the w. end of the aisle; a carved lion and **griffin** stand at the corners of the battlements and the **dripstones** of the side windows have **headstops**. The glass in them was restored in 1966 and displays an interesting variety of mainly continental glass, including a selection of small heads, a group of men rowing a boat, and a figure of **St Nicholas**; one of the panels is dated 1637. The porch was adapted as a **vestry** in 1843 by Peter Gage, a local builder, and it was he who made the outer doors, using the inner C15 door as a model. The windows, of about 1300 with 'Y' tracery in the s. aisle, were apparently re-used at the time of the rebuilding. Round the corner, on the e. wall a sheet of roofing lead is fixed bearing the names of the churchwardens of 1838 and of the plumber who did the work. The **chancel** is C14 but was extensively restored in 1866 when a new e. window was inserted, although a fragment of the wider original is embedded in the wall to the r. There was evidently a chapel n. of the chancel at one time and a roof **corbel** juts from the wall; below it is the sweet little **ogee**- headed connecting doorway, still with its medieval door. The large tomb that you will see inside was re-sited in the wall of the n. aisle during the rebuilding and projects slightly. There is **ball flower** under its parapet and below the battlements of the small circular corner turrets. This re-arrangement was evidently an afterthought because 'Y' traceried windows had been re-used (as on the s. side) and then they were cut into by the tomb, leaving a lancet shape visible each side. The n. porch was repaired in 1852, again by Peter Gage, and he also lettered the arch of the plain C14 doorway. Just inside stands a C14 **font** and the bowl panels are carved with attractive **crocketted** gables, each rising to a **finial** enclosing **trefoils**. The painted shields on the stem cannot now be identified. A set of George IV's **Royal Arms** hangs above the tower arch within which stands the organ, and on either side there are cut-out painted metal lilies with scroll texts - a favourite form of Victorian decoration. The tall nave **arcades** have **quatrefoil piers** and above them runs a prominent **string course** carved with **paterae** and demi- angels bearing shields. The **wall posts** of the cambered **tie-beam** roof rest on corbels shaped as demi-angels, two of which hold stringed instruments. The feature of the n. aisle is the magnificent early C14 tomb - probably free-standing before it was re-sited. It is likely to have been made for Sir John de St Philibert who died in 1334. The main gable is heavily crocketted up to a large finial and the area within the main arch is covered with diaper work. Marks on the background suggest that there were once statues in the centre trefoils, and the pairs of short **purbeck marble** columns either side of the recess have stiff-leaf **capitals**. The recess has a **groined** ceiling with a centre **boss** and the tall, elegant side pinnacles are closely crocketted. Apart from the

Chelsworth, All Saints: early C14 tomb

original move, the tomb was restored in 1850. To the r. is a large trefoil **piscina** arch and it is unusual to find another close by to the r. of the e. window - a later design which belongs to the rebuilding. The 1890s glass in the aisle e. window is an Ascension by **Lavers, Barraud & Westlake**. The colours are **pre-Raphaelite** and there is a lowering sky behind the figure of Christ. It is competent without having the quality of the firm's work in the middle of the century. The e. and w. windows of the s. aisle contain C19 heraldic shields of successive Lords of the Manor which are all named and dated, and the other aisle windows have 1850s glass by a little-known Ipswich glazier, R.B. King. Text **labels** are in pink and brown against coarsely patterned **quarries** of an insipid green - not very nice. The s. aisle has a shapeless piscina recess uncovered in 1953, and below stands a heavily banded C14 waggon chest. The deep **rood loft** stair rises from the s. aisle and there are medieval tiles within the doorway, some painted heraldically. Although there is now no **screen** the upper opening of the rood stair shows that it was lofty, and the iron hook that supported the rood itself remains embedded in the top of the chancel arch. Above are extensive remains of a painted **Doom**. Re-discovered in 1849, it was ignorantly restored, particularly the central figure of Christ on the rainbow. To his l. is the large and flaming mouth of hell, with the souls of the damned chained and held captive by a demon. To the r. of **St Peter** stands a sooty devil with a long tail but beyond the figure of the **Blessed Virgin** little survives of Paradise. The **hatchment** over the n. door is for Pleasance, wife of Samuel Pocklington who died in 1774, and over the s. door is the slightly damaged hatchment for Robert Pocklington who died in 1767. The last and most interesting is the one to the l. of the s. door. It is for Sir Robert Pocklington who died in 1840 and who was made a knight of the military order of Maria

Theresa in 1794 by Francis II, last emperor of the Holy Roman Empire. Serving with the 15th Dragoons, Pocklington had saved the emperor from the French near Cambrai. The star of the order is painted on the hatchment and also figures on his memorial further along, together with plumed helmet and martial trophies. The chancel has a panelled waggon ceiling and the e. window is filled with excellent glass of 1875 by **Hardman**. It is a Crucifixion in three panels - all medieval in feeling; the figure of Christ is set against a deep red pointed oval, and the blue of the patterned backgrounds is typical of the firm; there is attractive leafwork and **Passion emblems** in the tracery. The **sanctuary** piscina lies within a simple C14 lancet, and on the s. wall of the chancel is a plain but elegant tablet for Elizabeth Fowke (1820) by Henry Rouw.

Chevington, All Saints (C5): At the end of a cul-de-sac and in a large churchyard, the church has a decidedly gawky look. This is brought on by an almost flat **chancel roof** combining with prominent brick battlements on the tall **nave** and an oddly proportioned tower. The latter was well built, conventional late C15 until Frederick Augustus, 4th Earl of Bristol and Bishop of Derry, decided to make it an object of view from Ickworth Park and added another stage - open to the sky and complete with pseudo-Gothic **lancets**, battlement and pinnacles. The lower stages of the w. buttresses have pairs of flint-filled panels with **trefoil** heads, there is a **flushwork base course**, and the angular w. window has small **headstops** to the **dripstone**. The belfry stair turret is on the s. side but there is another access door to the tower on the n. side - probably C19. The nave shows signs of its **Norman** origin with a very plain C12 n. door and a small single lancet. Another window has **plate tracery** and a large brick buttress was added

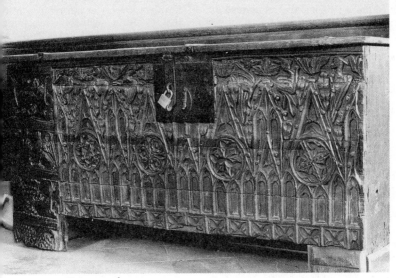

Chevington, All Saints: chest

on that side in the C16 or C17. There are **Early English** lancets in the chancel, one of which is masked by a later buttress, and the e. window set high in the wall is a relatively modern insertion. There is a lancet **low side window** on the s. side and another late C13 window with plate tracery on that side of the nave. The s. **porch** is largely a reconstruction but the outer arch of the early C14 original survives, with **jambs** and curves cut from single pieces of timber. Three steps lead down to the late C12 **Transitional** doorway - **dogtooth** ornament enclosing the arch and down the sides, and pairs of unequal shafts with coarse foliage **capitals**. Within, there is a modern ringers' **gallery** and the early C15 **font** looks out of proportion without its step. The shaft has fin buttresses and the decoration of the bowl is unconventional, with narrow tracery panels offsetting the **quatrefoils** and shields. Some of the benches at the w. end have wide traceried ends and there is a very interesting

collection of **finials**. There are five praying women by the n. wall (one with a rosary) and another on the s. side; nearest the door is a bearded man back to back with a lute player, the third from the w. on the n. side plays a double pipe, followed to the e. by players of trumpet, bagpipe and cymbals. The westernmost figure on the s. side plays a stringed instrument and next to him is a possible harp player. Thus, with a little licence, we have the full orchestral complement for psalm 150. One of the bench backs is traceried and it may once have formed part of the old **rood loft**. By the n. door is an excellent C14 chest; the front is intricately carved with **Decorated** tracery and on the l. there are panels containing pairs of monkeys and birds, with a dragon below. The matching panels to the r. have disappeared and a later end has been grafted on. Over the s. door is a rather nice set of George I **Royal Arms** painted on board, within a square frame, and at the e. end on that side there is a **piscina** under a trefoil arch marking the site of a nave **altar**. The roof of cambered **tie-beams** has pierced and traceried **spandrels** and additional tie-beams were inserted later. Dated 1590 and 1638 they bear the names and initials of churchwardens, and have leaf trails carved on the chamfers. The chancel arch is tall and narrow and comes down to half-round ring capitals which have curly pendants rather like pigs' tails. At each side there are subsidiary arches with plain chamfers which would have given a view of the **high altar** from the nave altars. The original chancel was much shorter than the one built in the C13 and then that was cut back in 1697 to the present dimensions. It has recently been provided with an unadorned stone altar placed centrally and a black metal tabernacle for the reserved sacrament stands on a stone column in the n.e. corner. The simplicity of this arrangement against the stark whiteness of the walls is a potent combination. Beams in the low-pitched roof overhead are carved 'Edward Grove' and 'Soli Deo' and there are some more medieval bench ends - a figure holding a shield, another trumpeter, a bird picking berries, and a woman with a fine headdress. Nearby is an epitaph in stately periods for Elizabeth White, the rector's wife, on a **ledger-stone** cut by William Steggles of Bury in 1834 - he probably provided the one for the husband in 1818 as well. Don't overlook the exceptionally attractive rococo C18 tablet for Ann Burch on the **sanctuary**s. wall - in white marble with a coloured **cartouche** of arms.

Clare, St Peter and St Paul (C7): A large and handsome church, it stands within a spacious churchyard in the centre of one of Suffolk's nicest small towns. The walls of the old priest's house to the s. are decorated with some of the best pargetting to be seen anywhere. The base of the tower is C13 and the w. door has pairs of shafts, with two bands of small **dog-**

tooth in the deep moulding. In 1899 however, the tower was rebuilt abov that level re-using the majority of th old material. The **nave** was rebuilt i the 1640s and the **chancel** in 1478 and they are very tall for their length making one wish that the tower ha been altered in scale. By the beginning of the C17 the chancel was ruin ous and it was effectively rebuil again in 1617. It seems that the e. win dow **tracery** was used again, but i doing so the pointed arch wa smoothed out to an even curve. A study of the window emphasises how the same **Perpendicular** style was i vogue with very little variation ove two centuries. Prominent **rood stai** turrets are placed on each side of th nave gable and their **crocketted** spire are reminiscent of the singleton a Lavenham. There is a **Tudor priest'** **door** on the s. side of the chancel with an unusually good original traceried door. The n. **porch** was built aroun 1400 but still has **Decorated** tracery i the side windows; it now houses th C19 **bier**. The outer arch of the C14 s porch is decayed, and above it th 1790 sundial bears the peremptory instruction 'Go about your business' apt, when one considers how much o it was traditionally transacted in th porch. Within, the ceiling is **groine** and the centre **boss** is a fine carve head (possibly Christ's). The inne doorway is decorated with three bands of **paterae** and masks, and th traceried panels of the wicket matcl the rest of the C16 door. Note that on of the effects of the C15 rebuilding was to reduce the length of the porcl by a quarter. Built on to it is a C14 chapel whose interior arch was re used at the rebuilding. It was convert ed later by inserting a **Jacobean gal-** **lery** with nicely turned newel post and **balusters** to the rear staircase This was discarded in the 1880s bu providentially there were second thoughts later and it was replaced. On the wall overhead are two **hatch-** **ments**: on the l. for Lieut. Col. John Barker who died in 1804, and on the r or his widow Caroline who died in 848. An iron-bound chest stands below and by the s. door is the early C15 **font** with **quatrefoils** and shields in the bowl panels (except one which is blank and shows that it may originally have stood against a pillar). The church is airy and spacious, full of light, and the nave **arcade** is particularly interesting because the quatrefoil **piers** of the old C14 arcade were retained by the C15 builders. They were mounted on high bases and given new **capitals**; their slimness accentuates the sense of space. There is a **sanctus-bell window** over the tower arch and a very decorative **string course** runs below the **clerestory**; it is carved with paterae and masks, and there are demi-angels where the slim shafts cross it that rise to the **wall posts** of the **roof**. There are widely spaced crockets and **finials** on the arcade arches and the wide chancel arch is similarly decorated. The **rood screen** must have been unusually tall (see the doorways either side of the arch) and a section of it now stands in front of the organ at the end of the s. aisle. To the r. is the C15 **screen** of a **chantry** chapel and the beautiful cresting above the tracery incorporates a series of crowned 'M.R.'s for the **Blessed Virgin**, with **griffins** as supporters. To the l. a glass case contains the ringers' gotch or beer jug of 1729, and it is a fine specimen with a bell inscribed 'campana sonant canore' ('Let the bells resound with song'). The 1880s **aisle** window, in memory of town benefactors John and Betsy Isaacson, is by **W.G. Taylor** of **O' Connors** - figures of Faith, Hope and Charity, with the rest of the window filled with amber-coloured squares. On the wall by the n. door is a very good example of a C19 **brass** and a royal one at that. It commemorates Queen Victoria's 4th son Prince Leopold, Duke of Albany and Earl of Clarence, who died in 1884 and was at that time Master of the local masonic lodge. Further along the n. aisle is a fine window by Frederick C. Eden,

architect and stained glass designer. It has a Calvary flanked by the Blessed Virgin and **St John**, with **St Mary Magdalene** kneeling below. There are figures of **St Michael** and **St George** in the side **lights**, with God the Father and the dove of the Holy Spirit above. The figures are outlined against clear glass, with green as the dominant colour and the whole effect is cool and calm more of his work can be found at Hengrave and Whepstead. In front of the chancel arch is an outstanding late C15 lectern of the type that can be seen at Redenhall and King's Lynn, St

Clare, St Peter & Paul: lectern

Margaret's, in Norfolk. Like them, it has that lovely buttery texture that brass acquires when it has been scoured and polished for centuries, but this model has three dogs as feet rather than the lions of the others. In the chancel, the arcades and the string course match those in the nave and below is a very handsome suite of **Jacobean** stalls. There are blind arches in the front, strapwork panels, and heavier carving in the seat backs. The scroll-sided **poppyheads** are carved with varied leaf forms and are so like those at Little Thurlow that they may have been carved by the same man. Some of the stalls incorporate C15 tracery that probably came from the rood screen. The late C17 **communion rails** with twisted balusters are an excellent set and there are signs that they were originally three-sided. There is a plain **piscina** in the **sanctuary** and on the n. wall, an early C18 tablet for Susanna Johnson and two of her children with naive carving and lopsided lettering. Unless he was exaggerating with his 'We brake down 1,000 picture superstitions', in January 1643 **Dowsing** smashed more glass and other things here than in any other single church that he mentions. But although he ordered that 'the Sun and Moon in the East window' should be destroyed, they are still there. Below them is an attractive series of shields commemorating the benefactors of 1617 - local magnates Sir George le Hunt, Sir John Higham, Sir Thomas Barnardiston, Sir Steven Sonnes, Sir William Storton, as well as the Haberdashers' Company. Underneath, a lot of continental glass fragments have been formed into roundels. There is a very narrow **squint** giving a view of the **high altar** from the s.e. chapel. Across in the n.e. chapel there is a piscina and on the floor the greater part of a C13 grave slab with an elaborate cross on top. The 1823 monument to Mary Sayer on the wall is by Charles Smith, the sculptor of the great fountain on the s. front at Holkham, but with this minor

work his attention wandered and a spelling mistake had to be corrected plumb in the middle.

Cockfield, St Peter (D6): Many parishes had church houses which were used for **guild** feasts, church ales and other community activities and Cockfield's stands by the churchyard gate - most attractive, in herringbone red brick and timber. The church's C14 tower has flint chequerwork on buttresses and battlements, and the s. bell opening was offset to make room for the stair turret. An C18 rector was keen on astronomy and made extra windows for his telescope below the parapet on n. and s. The outlines can still be seen, and so can the **put-log holes** which were used when the tower was built. There are **headstops** to the **dripstones** of the windows in the C14 n. **aisle** and on that side is a **vestry** which was at one time a chapel with a room above it. The early C14 **chancel** has wonderfully fierce devil **gargoyles** and the buttresses to e. and s. contain large niches which are lavish in a quiet way. Their **crocketted ogee** dripstones bear little headstops and rest on shafts with ring **capitals**. There is a **priest's door** with worn headstops on the s. side and the **rood stair** turret nestles between chancel and s. aisle - of brick and obviously a later addition. All the windows to the s. are **Perpendicular** and the s. aisle battlements are quite showy, with crocketted pinnacles. The **porch** is in the same grand manner. Dating from the 1460s, it is panelled in **flushwork**, with three decayed niches above the entrance whose arch is decorated with **paterae**. There are more gargoyles and the blind **tracery** of the battlements differs from the pattern of the s. aisle. The inner door is C14 and there is a **stoup** to the r. Within, the tower has buttresses which jut out brutally alongside the beginning of the nave **arcades**, and above the **clerestory** there is a C15 **tie-beam roof** with **king posts** that are braced four vays. There are decorative stops on he tie-beam chamfers and until 1879 he roof was coloured. The carved tone **corbels** of earlier aisle roofs can ie seen above the arcade pillars and wo principals of the C16 s. aisle roof lave remnants of **wall post** figures. iome of the main timbers of the roof tself are carved with a leaf trail and here are lines of paterae under the vindow sills on that side. There is a square **piscina** recess in the s. aisle :hapel and the **rood loft** stair goes up o the l. of the **altar** - a long and thin ituart **Holy table** which has been estored. The s. aisle windows conain some good examples of C14 tained glass borders and in the winlow to the s. of the altar there is a nice C15 panel of **St Anne** teaching the **Blessed Virgin** to read. A plain octaonal C14 **font** stands in front of the blocked n. door and at the e. end of he n. aisle there is another - a Victorian reproduction of C15 style. Nearby n the e. wall is an intriguing C12 niche which pre-dates the rest of the aisle. It has a moulded **trefoil** arch with an ogee top and the **spandrels** are shallow carved with tendrils bearng leaves and flowers. The shaft of a contemporary **pillar piscina** is set against the adjoining pillar. The aisle e. window contains a panel of modern stained glass (possibly by Maile & Son of Canterbury); a swirling composition of irregular outline and vivid colour, with the figures of **St George** and **St Michael**. Resting on an earlier coved pedestal, the early C17 pulpit has blind arches crudely carved in shallow relief on the panels and a broad, canted bookledge. One side is blank and shows that it originally backed against one of the arcade pillars. The wooden lectern appears to be modern but it does incorporate a cluster of four C17 twisted **balusters** that probably formed part of a set of altar rails somewhere. The chancel stalls are largely C19 but they make use of medieval remnants and the w. ends are delicately traceried and feature crocketted pinnacles (note how

the designs differ). There are **poppy-heads**, old tracery in four of the front panels, and four mutilated **misericords** at the back. On the n. side of the chancel is a large and splendid monument to James Harvey who died of smallpox while an undergraduate at Cambridge in 1723. It is signed by N. Royce of Bury, about whom nothing is known but who was, on this evidence, extremely skilled. A central black sarcophagus supports a bust of the young man, dressed in coat and scarf and wearing his own hair, and there are coupled **Corinthian** columns and **pilasters** each side in mottled marble. A **cartouche** of arms, supported by swags, rests on the **pediment** and the tripartite base is elegantly lettered with Latin epitaphs - the last dated 1767. Styles changed - witness one of Robert de Carle of Bury's 'plain Jane' tablets opposite for the Rev George Belgrave and his wife, 1831. The medieval door to the old chapel is in the n. wall and beyond is a sumptuous C14 **Easter sepulchre**. Much of the detail was replaced as part of a C19 restoration but the effect is impressive. The base is a recessed tomb in roughly textured **purbeck marble**, with four blank shield recesses. Above it there is a very tall and steeply gabled triple canopy, crocketted and topped by **finials**. Tall, thin pinnacles divide the frontage and within the gables there are **quatrefoils** enclosing leaf forms. On the other side of the **sanctuary** there is a matching piscina and to its r. a fragment shows that the **sedilia** were originally canopied, before the Perpendicular window was inserted. The **communion rails** have modern tops and supports but the twisted balusters are late C17; it is said that they were once three-sided but I could detect no evidence of this. The 1889 glass in the e. window is by **Kempe** - an uncharacteristic design, with twelve small panels in very dark colours of post-Crucifixion scenes. It is a memorial for Churchill Babington, kinsman of Macaulay, Cambridge professor of archaeology, authority on local natural history, and vicar here for over 20 years. An earlier Cockfield parson also has his place in history, for John Knewstub convened the first large Puritan conference, when 60 ministers met here in 1582 to discuss the prayer book and to forge the basis for English Presbyterianism.

Coney Weston, St Mary (E3): This is one of those churches that can prove illusive; it lies a mile or so to the e. of the village on the Hopton road and, not having a tower, it cannot be seen from a distance. With a background of trees and standing above the lane, it is an attractive C14 building with a thatched **nave**. As was often the case, the frontage was given more attention than the rest and a panelled **base course** links the tall **porch** with the nave, the walls being faced with carefully dressed flints. The **dripstones** of the three s. **chancel** windows are linked and there are remains of **corbel** heads at the outer ends, thus forming a complete unit. The **Decorated tracery** is badly decayed and in one case it has been repaired in a simpler form, possibly at the time of the restorations in 1887 and 1891. Below is an arched tomb recess. At one time there was a chapel n. of the chancel and two large arches remain embedded in the wall, with fragments of two smaller ones further e. A square-headed **Perpendicular** window was inserted within one of these arches and shows that the chapel or **chantry** cannot have lasted long. The nave originally had a n. door as well but this has been blocked up. The tower fell in the early C19. By the s. door is a **stoup** under a **cinquefoiled** arch. Within is a C13 **font** with a slightly odd selection of designs in the panels of the octagonal bowl; there are window tracery patterns, a **crocketted** canopy, large square leaves, and one panel has 12 rosettes set out like cakes on a tray. On either side of the chancel arch there are pairs of niches, one set taller than the other

and retaining the **hood moulds**. There will have been nave **altars** under both originally, and one small **piscina** survives in the s. wall. The niches were re-used in the C19 to house a painted **decalogue** on the n. and two quite ambitious angels on the s. - all painted on tin. The brass lectern is a good example of mid-C19 design as influenced by the **Ecclesiological Society** and above the openwork pulpit of the same period is a graceful oval tablet. Set on a grey obelisk with a coloured shield of arms hung from a ribbon, it tells of the misfortunes of Maurice Dreyer, a London merchant who died in 1786:

> a man of warm feelings, but of strict integrity, reduced from affluence in the prime of life by the fraudulent conduct of a partner in the foreign trade, he bore the total wreck of his property with fortitude and resignation.

The chancel e. window has truncated tracery at the top, probably another part of the C19 restoration, and across the s.e. corner of the **sanctuary** are the remains of a massive image niche which rises above the spring of the window arch, still with traces of colour. Below is a fine C14 **angle piscina** with steep crocketted gables over **trefoil cusping**. The corbel heads are broken off at the angle but the hood mould continues round to form a sill for the e. window. Alongside are stepped **dropped-sill sedilia**. The C19 altar has intricately traceried panels, painted and gilded with figures of saints and even enriched with some **gesso** work, all most competently done in the manner of a C15 **screen**. The saints, l. to r., are: **Edward the Confessor**, **Paul**, **Barbara**, the **Blessed Virgin**, **Bartholomew**, **John**, **Margaret**, **Helen**, **Hugh** and **Apollonia of Alexandria**.

Cowlinge, St Margaret (B6): The body of the church is early C14 and there is attractive **tracery** in the **aisle** win-lows, with late **Perpendicular** designs at the e. end of the s. aisle and **chancel**. A modern door has been inserted in the s. aisle and a **scratch dial** has been replaced upside-down in the centre buttress. In the C18, heavy brick buttresses were introduced to shore up the chancel, and note that under the e. window there is a small grilled opening that probably ventilated a charnel chamber. Churchyards were re-used in the Middle Ages and bones from earlier burials were removed to charnels for safe keeping. The splays of the doorway in the chancel n. wall show that it once led into a chapel or **sacristy** and there is more evidence of this within. The C18 brick tower is severely plain - round arches to door and bell openings, with a circular belfry window to the w. The little brick and stone n. porch is homely and there is a lot of C17 and C18 graffiti on the C14 inner arch, with its medieval door of lapped boards. The w. **gallery** is contemporary with the tower and one must climb the stairs to see the tablet which records the munificence of Francis Dickins who built the tower in 1733. It is large with well cut lettering, and his arms are in a **cartouche** within a broken **pediment**. Overhead, the fine set of George II **Royal Arms** painted on canvas is unfortunately decayed in places; it has the royal cipher, baroque scrolls above and below, and flanking **Corinthian** columns, all painted on a board surround, with the names of the churchwardens of 1731. Also on the tower wall is a set of boards painted with the **decalogue**, Creed and Lord's Prayer. Seating was strictly regulated from the C17 onwards and at the w. end of the n. aisle is a most interesting local arrangement. Four plain, backless forms are stepped one above the other and the tablet on the wall above explains their purpose. They were installed by special permission in 1618 to accommodate the keeper of the Cowlinge House of Correction and his prisoners in what was no

doubt the coldest and draughtiest corner. The **font** dates from about 1400, its bowl decorated with **quatrefoils** and roundels and there is window tracery in the panels of the short stem. The octagonal **piers** of the C14 **arcades** have masses of medieval graffiti, but individual items are not all that easy to find or decipher. Just below the **capital** of the pillar near the n. door there is a Latin inscription which translates:

Whensoever you go by me,
Whether man, woman or boy you be,
Bear in mind you do not fail,
To say in passing 'Mary Hail'.

Its position suggests that the stone was re-used and was originally at eye-level somewhere. There are many interlaced plait-work and geometric designs, as well as hands, feet, a ship, and the crude profile of a man, possibly a bishop. The C14 **nave** and chancel **roofs** are **tie-beam** and **king post** construction, with coved and plastered ceilings. Until about 1400, the design of woodwork followed that of masonry but the **rood screen** here shows the parting of the ways. Although the tracery is still carved in the solid, the **mullions** are moulded and the main structure is more logical in relation to the material. The doors rise to the full height and three of the original hinges are intact, with decoration on the plates. There are quatrefoil and single hole **elevation squints** like those at Dalham. At the time of my visit there were three varied but uniformly hideous electric lights fixed to the top of the **screen**, but perhaps this was a temporary expedient. The C14 **parclose screen** in the s. aisle is also interesting because, although the workmanship is crude, the bottom panels are the earliest Suffolk example of tracery which is applied rather than being carved in the solid. The main **lights** are wide but they were originally divided into three and four compartments by mullions which were later removed. The principal uprights have little tracery shapes carved at the top and the cresting is virtually complete - the design similar to that on the parclose at Dalham. On the wall nearby is a medieval painting, mainly in pale red, of the top half of a saint against a patterned background. There are the remains of a **piscina** in the chapel and on the l., a rough arch that will have led to the **rood loft**. Next to it is a long **squint** through to the chancel and in the n. aisle there is another like it behind the organ. Instead of a window the n. chapel has a tall niche in the e. wall and, although the canopy has been cut away, traces of the vaulting remain. The chancel arch is decorated in barber's pole fashion and above it there is a fascinating variation on the traditional **Doom** theme. To the r. **St Michael** holds the scales, with an orange-coloured evil spirit being weighed against the little figure representing the souls of the righteous. On the l. of the arch the **Blessed Virgin** holds a long wand, the tip of which tilts the balance against the devil and neatly illustrates her power of intercession. All is very faint and binoculars are essential to catch the detail. Beyond the modern **communion rails** in the **sanctuary** the **high altar** is a massively solid block with a bevelled **mensa** 8 ft long and 4 ft wide. The C14 piscina and **sedilia** are as simple as can be, and in the n. wall is the door that must have led to a chapel or sacristy. The puzzling thing here is the small doorway above and to the r. It shows that the annexe was two-storied as at Hessett, but an entrance in this position is most unusual and I can only suppose that it might have afforded security for the storage of valuables. On the s. wall is a tablet for Henry Usborne who died in 1840 and his **hatchment** hangs close by. The chancel is, however, dominated by the memorial for Francis Dickins. He died in 1747 and his flowery epitaph tells us that he 'repaired and ornamented this church and built the steeple at his

own expense'. The monument is th only Suffolk example of the work o Peter Scheemakers, whose bust o Shakespeare in Westminster Abbe established his reputation. The fig ures of Dickins and his wife in Roma dress sit either side of an urn, belov which there are reversed torches wit a wreath of oak leaves (a popula snippet of classical symbolism). Bot base and backdrop are massive. I front of the organ in the centre of th nave is a **brass** for Robert and Marga ret Higham (1571 and 1599). It is i good condition, with 18 in figures o the couple - he in ruff and gown an she wearing a Paris cap. There ar groups of five sons and five daugh ters, a shield and an inscription. Hal way down the nave is a bras inscription and verse for Thomas Der sley who died in 1614:

> Here underneath this ston interred, rest
> A while deare freind, so God ha thought it best...

Culford, St Mary (C4): The churc lies close to the hall (Culford School within grounds laid out by Hum phrey Repton in the C18; the setting i superb. Except for the base of the tow er, it was rebuilt by **Sir Arthur Blom field** from 1856 to 1865, with a n. aisl added in 1908. All the work was car ried out by estate craftsmen. Th architect used flint pebbles through out for facing material, except fo **flushwork** battlements on the towe and dressed flint panels on the but tresses. Some interesting Blomfielc touches are the **chancel** buttresses **dogtooth** and **paterae** decoration under the eaves, and the quite eccen tric placement of a clock in the e. bel opening. The general form is **Early English**, with geometric **tracery** and one feels that this is what the avant garde thought a country churc

Cowlinge, St Margaret: Dickins' tomb by Scheemakers

should look like. Through the small s. **porch** into a High Victorian interior dominated by dark and heavy **roofs** with **arch-braces** in the nave, coming down to half-octagonal **corbels** encrusted with foliage underneath, and open tracery between the top of the braces and the ridge. A four-bay **arcade** on **quatrefoil piers** separates the **nave** and aisle. There is a small wooden w. **gallery** and, within the tower, a Blomfield **font**. Above it on the s. wall is a 1668 Cornwallis family memorial - two **touchstone** panels (only one of which was used) separated and flanked by polished black marble **Corinthian** columns, the twin **pediments** topped by skulls crowned with wreaths of laurel, and alabaster swags at the bottom. On the opposite wall is an excellent portrait bust of Nathaniel Bacon, the amateur painter who died in 1627. It stands within a scooped-out oval set on a black marble lozenge garnished with a pair of palettes and coats of arms. On the w. wall of the nave is a plain marble tablet topped by a draped urn commemorating Charles, 2nd and last Marquess Cornwallis who died in 1823. Considering the European reputation of its sculptor Edward Hodges Bailey, it is disappointingly ordinary. Within the rails at the e. end of the n. aisle is the large tomb chest of Beatrix Jane Craven, Countess Cadogan, who died in 1907. The life-size figure in white marble was sculpted by Feodora, Countess Gleichen, and lies with crucifix to breast, the head with its Edwardian hair style resting on a pillow. The front of the tomb has two bas relief cherubs plucking harps and the wall behind carries a shallow design in plaster - cherubs supporting a scroll below a crucifix framed in leaf tendrils. The aisle windows are filled with fine glass by J. Dudley Forsyth (one of **Henry Holiday's** apprentices, whose work includes windows in Westminster Abbey); at the w., for Henry Arthur, Viscount Chelsea (d. 1908); at centre, for Edward George Henry, Viscount Chelsea (d. 1878), in

which a portrait figure kneels by a sick bed, with an angel in the other **light**; at e. end, for the Countess Cadogan, including a woman bearing a slung bowl apparently full of potatoes! The tops of all the windows are filled with canopy work and the colours of the robes are particularly rich. The nave windows are by **Lavers & Barraud** and illustrate the life of **St Peter**. On the l. side of the chancel is the delightful monument of Dame Jane, the widow of Sir Nathaniel Bacon whose bust we saw in the tower. It was ordered in 1654 during the Commonwealth and it shows a fine disregard for the contemporary belief that all such things were idolatrous. The finest work of Thomas Stanton (uncle of the more famous William), it was to be carried out 'according to the best skill of a stone-cutter, alle in whit and black marble without the addition of any other ston whatsoever', at a cost of £300 (no mean sum at the time). It sems that the chancel was rebuilt around it, leaving its base well below the present floor level, and it stands within a new arch. A stiff composition, with a stern Dame Jane sitting facing front, wearing a wide Puritan collar and coif; a little girl sits on her lap, faintly smiling, and her other grandchildren are lined up each side. To the l. are the girls, with the youngest holding a fan and her sister clasping a handkerchief; to the r., three boys, with the smallest holding a stoolball toy. Below the group, Lady Bacon's first husband, Sir William Cornwallis, lies with legs very uncomfortably one on top of the other, resting his head on his elbow, prayer book in hand with a finger keeping the place. The family is framed within a low arch and Ionic columns, with a pediment and coloured **achievement of arms** above. Only when it was finished and 'the draft compared with the monument' did Stanton receive the balance of his fee. The portrait does not belie the character of a lady who knew what she wanted and ensured that she got it. The chancel roof is a compact **hammerbeam** design, with angels on the hammers and **wall posts** resting on kingly head **corbels**. There is a 1909 **reredos** and the recesses each side contain mosaics of the **Annunciation** - the archangel on the n. and the **Blessed Virgin** on the s. The e. window glass is in memory of Emily Julia Cadogan, Baroness Lurgan, and is, I think, also by Forsyth. It depicts Christ crucified, with the Virgin below supported by **St John** and **St Mary Magdalene**; the Roman soldier and followers of Christ stand each side, and there are two gorgeous attendant angels. Christ on the cross is enclosed in a pointed oval beautifully painted with a series of small cherub heads in salmon and pale yellow. Returning to the w. end, you will see that the tower window contains a colourful array of modern heraldic glass.

Dalham, St Mary (B5): A delightful sunken lane leads up from the village and the church stands on a hillock next to the Hall, with grand views across the rolling country to the s. There was a complete rebuilding in the C14 - two **Decorated** windows remain in the s. **aisle** and the **tracery** of another can be seen on the outside of the e. end of the n. aisle. In the C15 the n. aisle and **clerestory** were added, and some of the **chancel** and s. aisle windows were replaced. By the 1620s the tower had become unsafe and was rebuilt, with a newly stair on the n. side. There is a door in the e. wall giving on to the **nave** roof. The w. window has **Perpendicular** tracery but the bell openings are re-used C14 windows. The parapet has bold **flushwork** lettering: 'Keepe my Sabbaths', 'Reverence my Sanctuary', 'Deo Trin Uni Sacrum', and 'Anno Domini 1625'. The w. buttresses carry **consecration crosses** in flint and there are two more flanking the plain C14 **porch** entrance. In walking round you will find an interesting series of C19

tablets on the n. and e. walls for servants of the squire: Francis Watts, a dairy and poultry woman; Washington Andrews, the butler; John Keates and Joseph Brett, aged labourers whose epitaph concludes:

> Who change their places often change with loss,
> 'Tis not the Rolling Stone that gathers Moss.

The **vestry** abuts the n. wall of the chancel and to the w. is a roofless C17 compartment used in the C18 as a mausoleum for the Affleck family, whose weathered and largely illegible tablets now line the n. churchyard wall.

At the rebuilding, the old inner arch of the tower was retained and there is a medieval drawing of a post mill scratched on each **respond**. The story goes that there was such rivalry between the two later village mills that their sails were made to turn in opposite directions, C19 **decalogue** panels flank the arch and matching Creed and Lord's Prayer boards are on the n. aisle wall. Within the tower there is an interesting C17 **bier** with the same type of sliding handles as the one at Little Saxham. Above the arch is a huge and boldly lettered inscription setting out all the details of the tower rebuilding by the squire, the rector and their friends, with coloured shields in the **spandrels**. Dalham's **font** is one of the few C17 examples and has pleasing **ogee** curves to the bowl. There is a fine set of **Hanoverian Royal Arms** over the n. door - three- dimensional coloured and gilt. The nave and chancel roofs are modern reconstructions and the 1860s benches are excellently carved - all with **poppyheads** and, on the s. range, birds and animals on the elbows, including squirrel, sheep, lion and eagle. The s. aisle chapel has a C14 **piscina** with **trefoil** arch and stone **credence shelf** and image brackets flank the **altar**. The 1850s e. window glass here is a fine example of **Thomas Willement's** work - Christ with groups of children and disciples against a bright blue patterned sky. The tracery is filled with **tabernacle work** and the Affleck family arms figure at the bottom. There are extensive remains of wall paintings in the nave above the n. **arcade**. The westernmost section is a tree of the **Seven Deadly Sins** which is very similar to the Hessett painting but not, unfortunately, as complete. The trunk sprouts branches which become snarling dragons' heads, three of which remain, and the figures of the individual sins would have issued from them. To the r. was a **Seven Works of Mercy** sequence but the central angel has faded away. However, on the l., the faint outline remains of a figure handing clothing to the naked, and high on the r. a woman is giving bread to the hungry. Instead of the more usual **Doom** over the chancel arch there were paintings of **Passion emblems** and scenes, but all that is left of the flagellation is a pair of feet on the l. and a scattering of 'M's and **sacred monograms**. Although much has gone, binoculars do pick up a surprising amount of detail in all these sequences.

The base of the C15 **rood screen** remains. The panels are decorated with highly individual flower patterns, and the gilt and coloured carvings in the spandrels include a dragon, birds, and grotesques. Note the three **quatrefoil elevation squints**. Just beyond the arch on the s. side is a tall blank arch of indeterminate age with a recess beyond it. Outside, it has its own little lean-to roof but its origin and purpose are obscure. In the **sanctuary** is a simple C14 piscina with an original wooden credence shelf, and to the r. is the tomb of Thomas Stutevyle who died in 1571. The chest is decorated with three shields in strapwork **cartouches** and on top is a large standing tablet bearing his epitaph in front of the window. The line of defaced shields behind probably remain from the tomb of an earlier Thomas Stutvyle who died in 1468.

Across the sanctuary is the memorial to Sir Martin Stutvyle, Thomas' grandson, who died in 1631. He was knighted by James I but was essentially an Elizabethan who in his youth had sailed with Drake to the Americas. The design is compact, with marble bas relief busts of Sir Martin and his two wives set in ovals. There are **touchstone Corinthian** columns each side with gilded **capitals**, three shields under an arch on which rests a coloured **achievement of arms**, and the figures of eight little children kneel in a panel below. A funeral helm rests on a bracket overhead. The C15 s. window was replaced by **Sir Arthur Blomfield** with an awkward design but the early C20 glass is very good. The central figure of the **Blessed Virgin** with the Christ child in a cradle is flanked by an adoring angel and a king, and surrounding panels have angels bearing symbolic disks and scrolls. In the top **lights** there are demi-figures from the Old Testament and **Saints George, Etheldreda, Jerome** and **Ambrose**. The glass is by **Kempe & Co** and is much warmer in tone than their earlier work. You will have seen a large obelisk outside by the porch commemorating General Sir James Affleck who died in 1833; on the s. wall of the chancel he has a second memorial - a tablet cut by Robert de Carle the younger of Bury. The epitaph cleverly paraphrases a redundancy: '. . . having attained to a rank exempt from ordinary services, he retired to his estate...' On the opposite wall is a pink veined alabaster tablet in C17 style for Col. Frank Rhodes, brother of Cecil Rhodes and a distinguished veteran of many campaigns who was wounded at Omdurman and beseiged at Ladysmith.

Denham, St Mary (B5): Extensively C19 restorations have left the tower and the s. side of the church looking like new work, with a regular flint pebble finish, but the n. wall of the nave was left alone and there the blocked door has an unadorned **Norman** arch. The **chancel** e. window has simple **Decorated tracery**, matching windows in the nave and tower, while within the largely restored s. **porch** there is a C14 doorway. In the C17 a large mortuary chapel in red brick was added to the n. of the chancel and its roof is as high as the rest. Within, there is a large, plain C14 **font** and the tower arch has a tall C19 wooden **screen**. The modern roofs rest on stone head **corbels** which are varied and appear to be original. There is no screen in the wide chancel arch and the **sanctuary** walls are clad with C17 panelling which was decorated with coloured stencil patterns in the C19 or a little later. Three plain arches take up the whole of the chancel n. wall and give access to the side chapel containing two tombs of considerable interest. In 1605 Sir Edward Lewkenor and his wife Susan died within two days of each other of the smallpox, that C17 scourge, and the size of the chapel was probably dictated by their enormous tomb. The chest stands below a heavy canopy supported on six **Corinthian** columns rising from tall plinths decorated with strapwork. There are four **cartouches** of arms in the cornice and a full **achievement** above is supported by a pyramid of strapwork between tall obelisks. Figures of the family kneel in pairs on the chest - Sir Edward and his two sons bareheaded in armour, his wife and three of her daughters wearing caps with long black flaps at the back; the three younger daughters have close bonnets. All the figures are stiff, with little individual character. Much of the original colour survives but the paint of the long Latin epitaph on the bottom panels has partially worn away. In contrast, the nearby tomb of Sir Edward's grandson is beautiful. He was another Sir Edward, falling victim to smallpox in 1635 as the last of his line, and the monument was sculpted three years later by **John and**

Matthias Christmas. The side panels of the alabaster tomb chest are carved with shields set within a combination of wings and scrolls, with cherub heads over each. The heavy black slab is supported by coloured marble columns, and on it, the recumbent 5 ft effigy in gleaming, polished marble is in almost perfect condition. It is dressed in full armour with a wide lace collar and lies on a straw mat. The features are finely modelled and one hand rests limply on the breast. Behind his head is an oval **touchstone** tablet between black marble columns, his coat of arms, and two **putti** reclining on the curving **pediment** above, with a skull between them.

Denston, St Nicholas (B6): This is one of the finest of the smaller village churches in the county, a noble building, full of interest. The late C14 tower, with its chequered **base course**, is rather overwhelmed by the magnificence of the rest - rebuilt on a larger scale in the last half of the C15. It displays the full flowering of the **Perpendicular** style, with great **transomed** windows letting the light flood in, **aisles** that match the unbroken length of **nave** and **chancel**, and buttresses of **ashlar**. There are **priest's doors** n. and s. below truncated windows, and two **scratch dials** can be found on the buttress to the w. Another is found high on the central nave buttress still with the remains of its original pointer. On the n. side, an octagonal **rood stair** with battlemented top, complete with its own **gargoyle**, rises to the level of the aisle **roof**. It is sited two bays from the e. end, but once inside you will see that the **screen** is one bay further w. A bridge along the wall once connected the stair with the **rood loft**. For a building of such quality this would seem to be a surprising gaffe but it is probably because circumstances changed just before or just after the main structure was completed. In 1475 a **chantry** college was founded under the will of John Denston, with three priests living in a house, part of which is now the cottage to the w. of the church. Although the status of the parish church was not changed, the building had to be adapted so that the master of the college and his two brethren could celebrate 'for ever the divine offices day by day' for the souls of John Denston and Katherine his wife. Thus a choir of two bays was needed, arranged in collegiate fashion, and the screen separating it from the parish church proper was placed to the w. of it. This may well have been chosen by the executors as a way of avoiding an eastward extension. There are echoes of Long Melford's opulence here - understandable because Katherine was a Clopton before her marriage, and portraits of the couple can be found in the n. aisle there. The chantry survived until 1547 when, like the rest, its assets were seized by the Crown. The **porch** is not so grand as the rest and was perhaps adapted from the old building, although its roof is beautifully **fan vaulted**, an uncommon distinction in Suffolk. To the r. of the door there is a fine **stoup** with a **castellated** top, set in the buttress angle like the one at Hawkesdon.

Passing through the original **trace-ried** double doors one steps into an interior where all the virtues of Perpendicular architecture are displayed, but on an intimate scale. It impresses but does not overwhelm, and stands unchanged to all intents and purposes. Tall **arcades**, their mouldings flowing uninterrupted from base to peak, march from end to end, and the wall above them is broken only by the widely spaced **clerestory** windows and a plain **string course**. The cambered **tie-beams** and heavy timbers of the low pitched roof are beautifully pale, enhancing the sense of space and light below. There is foliage on the **spandrels** and large lions, hounds and hares prance on the **wall plates**. Of all the **Seven Sacrament Fonts** in East Anglia this is the only one carved in an oatmeal-col-

oured stone (imported from Aubigny in Normandy, according to **Cautley**) the bowl panels are compressed within plain roll mouldings. As at Woodbridge and Great Glemham, the scenes are set against rayed backgrounds, and they are of particular interest despite their harsh mutilation. From the e. clockwise, the sacraments are: mass, penance (note the C15 practice of the confessor sitting in the special shriving pew, with an attendant holding a book), confirmation, extreme unction (with the sick bed tilted so that one can look down on it), Crucifixion (Christ's figure obliterated), ordination, matrimony, and baptism (priest behind the **font** and parents to the l., the mother wearing a **butterfly head-dress** which dates the font between 1450 and 1485). There is a medieval screen in the tower arch and above, the **Royal Arms** of Queen Anne are well painted on board. Note that the arcade pillars stand on rubble bases that probably formed part of the old nave walls, and then turn your attention to the fine set of low C15 benches standing on substantial sills designed to keep the foot-warming straw or rushes in place. The two ranges at the front of the n. side are C19 copies but there are 60 grotesques sitting on the castellated caps and elbows of the bench ends. Seek out the **unicorn**, the **cockatrice** the fox and goose, and particularly the elephant, whose fan-shaped ears and long nose demonstrate a brave attempt at imagining the unbelievable. The relatively narrow aisles were designed for processions but there are now C18 **box pews** on the s. side. Beyond them is part of a set of **altar rails** with another section in the n. aisle, near a plain **Stuart Holy table**.

The high-silled **rood screen** stretches the whole width of the church, with excellent tracery and an attractive leaf trail along the top. There would have been **altars** at each side, and overhead the massive moulded and castellated **rood beam** remains, on which stood the Calvary

Denston, St Nicholas: misericord

flanked by figures of the **Blessed Virgin** and **St John**. The pulpit is C17 and beyond the screen the s. side is a raised pew behind a **parclose screen**, with C17 panelling on the outer wall. Strangely, the gates for the priest's door are a C17 wooden imitation of wrought-iron. At the time of my visit all the glass in the e. window was away for restoration and the Robinson tabard, helmet and sword, that normally hang in the s. chapel, had also been removed; hopefully they will return. The lovely stalls in the chancel are arranged so that four face e. backing on to the screen, and these have **misericords**. Three of them are carved with flowers but the fourth, on the n. side, is a rare and excellent carving of a crane, recognised by the stone that it holds with one foot. The **bestiary** taught that cranes always slept with one of their number standing sentinel, with a stone clutched in its raised claw which would fall and wake it should it inadvertently drop off. The chamfers of the stalls are decorated with **paterae** and there are large **fleurons** beneath the lip of the sloping book ledge; a low and narrow ledge for boys runs along the fronts, pierced with **quatrefoils** below. The late C17 **communion rails** have nice, twisted **balusters**, with sets of four as gate posts, and beyond them on the n. side is a large tomb with a **purbeck marble** top from which the **brasses** have been reaved. Within the open arches lie two figures as in death, their shrouds gathered in a topknot and held by heavily tasselled cords. The man's emaciated chest is bared and although the identity of both figures has vanished with the brasses it is possible that this key position in the church was reserved for Joan and Katherine Denston, the founders of the chantry. Across on the s. side, Robert de Carle the younger made a tomb to match in 1822 (except that it is solid and has no grisly cadavers) for the Robinson family. It has a polished black marble top and side panels with epitaphs and a shield of arms in an oval. There is a very good and important brass in the centre of the chancel, with 26 in figures, for Henry Everard who died in 1524 and his wife Margaret. This is the only heraldic pair on separate brasses that survives in Suffolk. Henry Everard wears an heraldic tabard or coat over his armour, and a helm with a large head as a crest lies tilted behind his head; his wife wears a **kennel head- dress** and an heraldic mantle displaying her husband's and her father's arms. Two of the four shields remain and, like the tabard, they were once inlaid with enamel. In the n. chapel there is an inscription for William Bird (1591) and his wife Mirable. Note that this is fixed to a stone which still bears two of its five **consecration crosses**, showing that it was the original **high altar mensa**. There is a third brass in the centre of the nave, with an 18 in figure of a late C15 lady in a kennel head-dress (probably Felice, the wife of Roger Drury of Hawstead who died in 1481). There is some attractive modern glass in the s. aisle; in the e. window is a **St Nicholas** theme by Martin Travers of 1932. In the centre St Nicholas cradles Denston church, on the r. is a medieval ship with sailors in modern sou'westers, and on the l. the cook flees in alarm as the saint blesses the boys in the tub. The 1914 window of Christ in glory, with the Blessed Virgin and the two Maries, is by **Heaton, Butler & Bayne.** As you leave you will see two **hatchments** on the aisle w. walls - the n. aisle for John (or possibly William) Robinson 1818 or 1826, the s. aisle for Rebecca, the wife of Lieut. General John Robinson who died in 1795.

Depden, St Mary (C5): There is no road to this church and the footpath takes off somewhat obscurely from the section of superceded main road by the junction to Depden Green. Then follows a pleasant ten-minute walk through copses and by fields but, for this reason, preliminary enquiries about the key are advised. The building was badly damaged by fire in June 1984, when the **nave** was gutted and lost its roof. Fortunately neither the **chancel** nor the tower were seriously affected and it was not long before restoration was put in hand. Under the direction of the Whitworth partnership the work was

excellently done by Valient & Sons, who received a well-earned award from the Suffolk Association of Architects. The church was re-consecrated by the diocesan bishop in October 1985 and it is now a beautiful little building in a delectable setting. The body of the church is late C13 or early C14 and the chancel corner buttresses have steep ledges and oddly restored pinnacles. The plain C15 tower has a flint chequer **base course** and a stair turret to the s. Entry is by way of a wooden C17 n. **porch** whose **balustrated** sides have been boarded over. The door is medieval with close-set mouldings. Within are tiled floors and modern chairs, and the new roof is carried on pairs of clamped trusses which sweep in a Gothic curve up to the ridge, their apricot colour showing up well against the white ceilings. The s. door is **Norman**, with scallop **capitals** to the thick shafts and a zig-zag bobbin mould in the arch. You will find a **consecration cross** incised halfway up the e. **jamb**. The porch has been rebuilt as a **vestry** and is separated from the nave by a plate glass door, which is effective and attractive. Beyond the tall tower arch there are nicely restored **Hanoverian Royal Arms** of 1836 lettered with the rector's and warden's names. A charity board signed by the same warden hangs opposite. Below is a plain **Stuart Holy table** and there are a few of the old benches that were saved from the fire at the w. end, some with broad **traceried** ends. The octagonal **font** is a rare early C18 model, and the shaped bowl has four carved **cartouches** painted with arms. The nave windows have 'Y' tracery and there is now no screen in the wide chancel arch. To the l. is a tall **Decorated** niche, **groined** and embellished with **paterae** on the chamfers but the canopy and pinnacles have been cut away. It now contains a framed engraved portrait of Anthony Sparrow, the late C17 bishop of Norwich, who was born here. Nearby is a fine **brass** set within a pair of shallow arches and framed by a crested panel on the wall. There are two pairs of figures kneeling at faldstools, each with a shield above, and it is an interesting composite memorial for Anne Drury and her two husbands. The first was George Waldegrave (on the l.) who is shown with their five sons, the eldest of whom was active in Queen Mary's cause. Waldegrave died in 1528 and his widow married Sir Thomas Jermyn, High Sheriff of Norfolk and Suffolk and rebuilder of Rushbrooke church where he was buried. The Lady Anne died in 1572 and her two effigies are similar but not identical; there is a long Gothic lettered inscription and the brass is in perfect condition. The early C14 **piscina** in the **sanctuary** is exceptionally nice. It has a pair of tall **trefoiled lancets** with pierced **spandrels**, and a **quatrefoil** over two layers of mouldings. Although there are two compartments there is only one drain. The e. window is tall and thin, and within the **reticulated** tracery there are two fine coats of Royal Arms of Henry VII and Victoria, enamel painted in C16 style. Just below there are large C14 canopies and then two German or Flemish C16 panels in the centre. Look for the little man trudging off with the ladder in the background of the scene where Christ is lowered from the cross, and for **St Veronica** in the bottom r. of the painting of Christ carrying the cross. There are four more contemporary panels of confused fragments and some Flemish roundels. On the s. wall is a memorial by de Carle of Bury for Sarah Lloyd, the rector's wide, who died in 1838 - a sarcophagus on which a drape falls realistically over the epitaph cut below. The panels of the modern oak **altar** are pierced with C15-style tracery which is very handsome.

Drinkstone, All Saints (E5): The brick tower peeps over surrounding trees from a distance and it is a replacement dating from 1694 with round-headed bell openings and stepped battlements. There is a tablet on the w. face that says the minister, Thomas Cambourne, left money for its building and for the bells. Below is a tall C19 **lancet** that was probably part of the extensive 1860s restoration by **Edward Hakewill**. He re- roofed the **nave** and provided a new e. window in the C14 **chancel**. The large three-**light** window in its s. wall with flowing **tracery** and worn **headstops** may have been in the e. wall originally. The other chancel windows have single **reticulation** tracery shapes and there are **Perpendicular** windows in the **aisles**. Hakewill provided three new **quatrefoil**, **clerestory** windows on each side (which possibly repeated an original arrangement). There is a little C14 **priest's door** on the n. side and in the r. hand **jamb** of the aisle door a section of a **churchyard cross** shaft has been inserted upside down. Under the eaves of the s. aisle wall is a late example of a **rebus**. Simon Cocksedge died in 1751 and a small cockerel struts on the top of the tablet. Beside it is an enterprising **cartouche** with arms, drapes and cherubs, but the inscription is worn away. The **porch** was rebuilt in 1872 and to the r. of the C14 inner doorway there is a small **stoup** under a **cusped** and **crocketted** ogee arch. The door itself is medieval, although the plain lapped boards have been backed and repaired at the bottom. Just inside to the l. is a single **hatchment** and the C13 **font** stands on a step against the first pillar of the s. **arcade**. Its **purbeck marble** bowl is a worn octagon with canted sides and pairs of shallow blind arches in the panels; it rests on a central shaft within a ring of columns. The **Decorated** arcades have tall, pointed arches rising from octagonal shafts and to the l. of the wide chancel arch is the **rood stair**, with narrow doorways and a stone newel rising to the full height within. There is a **Jacobean** chest at the w. end with a simple carving and a panelled top. Nearby are some medieval benches with **traceried** backs and battered **poppyheads**, one with the vestige of an angel holding a crown. The centre range of 1860s nave benches looks like the work of **Henry Ringham**. It contains some traceried ends and fine carvings on the arm rests (including a **pelican** in her piety, the dove of the ark with its olive branch, and a crowned eagle). The openwork C19 reading desk stands on an intriguing stone platform found beneath the floor of the old pews. Its edges are carved with **mouchettes** in circles and it has been variously described as part of a tomb chest, an **Easter sepulchre** moved from the chancel, and a preaching stone. I think the last is the most likely. A section of the floor here is paved with medieval tiles; two have lion designs, one has an heraldic shield, and four are placed to form a circle with an interlaced design. Behind the C19 pulpit there is a **squint** through to the e. end of the s. aisle, with **trefoil** ogees at each end, and although there is no **piscina** now there must originally have been an **altar** there. It was flanked originally by statues and the mutilated remains of the C14 pedestals are on either side. The church's outstanding piece is the C15 **screen** which was at one time relegated to the w. end. The ogee arches of the main lights are double cusped and the tall crocketted **finials** reach to the top, backed by close panelled trtacery; the centre arch is heavily cusped and crocketted and the stubby ogees above it are backed by roundels. The coved underside of the **rood loft** once sprang from the miniature pillars at the top of the buttresses, which themselves retain some stencil decoration. Much of the colour survives and is a clear example of how the artists followed the heraldic rules of alternating tinctures and metals (gold and silver). A link with the screen is to be found in the **sanctuary** where a narrow band of flowing tracery which may well have formed part of the rood

loft has been fixed in the back of the **sedilia**. The piscina is C19 and the sanctuary floor is banded with Minton tiles. There is a contemporary oak **reredos** with heavy vine and wheat borders to the panels and a central oil painting depicts the sorrowing Christ. The rest of the wall panelling is C17 style but looks a good deal less than 300 years old. The e. window is filled with **Lavers & Barraud** glass of 1865. There are bright figures of Christ as Saviour of the world, the **Blessed Virgin**, **St John the Baptist**, and an old man with a raven (Elias?). There is some medieval glass too. On the s. side of the chancel is a C14 Christ in Majesty with four **censing** angels and three other figures. Opposite is a much restored figure of the Virgin, in the n. aisle e. window are C14 leaf forms and in the s. aisle are some fragments. While in the chancel, have a look at the pretty pair of late C18 tablets flanking the priest's door. For Joshua and Jane Grigby, they have concave sides rising to large bas relief urns, with coloured coats of arms within fronds at the bottom. Nearby, Elizabeth Motham's C17 **ledger-stone** uses the old form 'Burnt Eleigh' for Brent Eleigh. On the n. wall near the screen, a sone of the rectory, with the resounding name of John Peloquin Cosserat, has his memorial. Shot in the mouth by a musket ball while leading the 1st Punjab Cavalry in the Indian Mutiny, he died at Lucknow in 1858. A similar penchant for detail crops up in the s. aisle where a small sarcophagus tablet by Joseph Kendrick for Capt George Grigby records that he perished with 233 others en route for Cadiz when his trooper was run down by the frigate 'Franchise' in 1811.

Elmswell, St John the Divine (E4): Seen from the w., the church stands commandingly on a rise at the very edge of the village. It was built by the Benedictines of Bury and the abbot entertained Henry VI here at his grange in 1433. The beautifully pro-portioned C15 tower was restored in 1980 and it has a lovely selection of flint and stone **flushwork** panels in the **base course** and on the buttresses, with binoculars one can identify the arms of Bury abbey between two chal-ices on the s.e. buttress and on the panel above that, the inscription 'Syr Wyllm Maundevyl'. The upper stages of the buttresses have canopied nich-es and the one on the s.e. corner is embellished with a **crocketted** pin-nacle. There is a band of intricate flushwork beneath the stepped battlements and the bell openings are unusually large, with pairs of two-**light** windows under a single **drip-stone**. The **clerestory** walls are made up of an attractive mixture of flint and freestone, with red bricks spaced over the window arches. The bold pattern of flushwork on the e. wall of the s. aisle probably dates from the early C17 when a large tomb was placed against it within. High on the buttress to the l. of the **priest's door** in the **chancel** is a **scratch dial** and, unlike most, it has the remains of the metal spike (the gnomen) in the centre. Near the **porch** is a fine example of a **chur-chyard cross**. Although parts of it have been renewed, there are well carved panels on the square base.

Within the church, a damaged stone head **corbel** has been re-set above the s. door and the C14 **font** stands nearby. Its bowl panels are carved with multi-**cusped** circles containing shields; one is blank but the others carry initials spelling out I (or J) HEDGE (probably the donor's name) and the three scallop shells on the last shield may have been his arms. There are angels below the bowl, and at the corners of the shaft there are three eagles, on wickerwork nests, and a horned beast. A series of C19 restorations was begun by **E.C. Hakewill** in 1862 when the s. **aisle** was rebuilt, and the chancel was thor-oughly restored by R.J. Withers two years later. In 1867, **J.D. Wyatt** added the n. aisle, copying the **Perpendic-**

ular s. **arcade** with its concave- faced octagonal **piers**. There are medieval benches in both aisles, with one carved back in each set. The ends, with their large **poppyheads**, have varied **tracery** cut in the solid but the square **castellated** elbows have had their carved figures chopped off. **Wil-liam Dowsing** was here in 1643 and this may have been part of his work. A **string course** decorated with closely set **fleurons** runs below the clerestory and the shafts with rounded **capitals** that supported the former roof stand between the windows. One wonders why the C19 architect did not make use of them to carry **wall posts** for his replacement. Bold Victorian texts adorn the arches of the chancel tower and n. door. The e. end of the s. aisle is enclosed by a **parclose screen**, the n. section of which is original, with sub-tle variations in the tracery (including a mask in the head of one of the **ogees**). The w. range is a good C19 copy which repeats the carvings of birds and leaves in the **spandrels** of the panel tracery. The paintings of saints and martyrs on the n. side are modern. The chapel e. wall is taken up with a large and imposing monu-ment to Sir Robert Gardener who was for 18 years Queen Elizabeth's Chief Justice in Ireland and her Viceroy there for two years. The epitaph men-tions his valiant action against rebel-lious Tyron and the Spanish at Kinsale; King James I subsequently sent him to sort out the islands of Jer-sey and Guernsey before he retired here. He died at a good age in 1619 and founded the almshouses e. of the church. The monument was sculpted by James I's master carver, Maximi-lian Colt, and the figure of Sir Robert reclines on an elbow, gloves in one hand and prayer book in the other. His heavily bradied, ermine-edged gown falls open to reveal a short coat and blue waistcoat. A lovely little ala-baster rhinoceros (his crest) stands at his feet, and beyond kneels his son William. Rather oddly, his splendid robes lie bundled on a ledge below, mixed up with oddments of armour. All the colour is good and the tomb is contained within a coffered arch in black and white with flanking pink marble **Corinthian** columns. To the r. is a **piscina** with a cusped arch that will have served the **altar** displaced by the tomb. There is a C19 low stone chancel **screen** with a wrought-iron framework above, and a fine pair of matching gates designed by J.D. Wyatt. In the **sanctuary** is a **piscina** under an ogee **trefoil** arch, and an angular C19 stone **reredos** of simple tracery shapes. The window on the s. side of the sanctuary has 1860s glass by Alexander Gibbs - a resurrection panel, and the three Maries at the tomb. The e. window glass is by **Lavers & Barraud**, and the main panels depict Christ's baptism, Gethsemane, the Crucifixion and the Entombment. The stylised figures are set against a dark blue background and the tracery above contains heads in roundels against heavily patterened backgrounds.

Elveden, St Andrew and St Patrick (C2): The grounds of the hall provides a gracious, leafy backdrop to the church, compensating for the relentless traffic surging along the A11. Walking round the outside, the only visible remnant of the original **Norman** church is the small slit window low in the centre of the s. **aisle** wall (which was then the **nave**). A tower was added in the early C14 and rebuilt in its present form about 1420, using the old materials. It has **flushwork** panelling at the base and the standing figures at the battlement corners are said to represent the four shepherds who gave them. There is a 'Y' **tracery** window of about 1300 w. of the cloister walk and, beyond it to the e., the C14 **chancel** (now the s. chapel) with flowing **Decorated** tracery in both s. and e. windows. The old nave was altered again when late changes, things remained as they were until the 1860s when the Mah-

arajah Duleep Singh came on the scene. Heir to the Sikh Punjab, he had been forced to resign at the age of 11 and, having become a Christian, he had come to England to be made much of by Queen Victoria, given princely status and encouraged to take his place among the aristocracy. *Queen Victoria's Maharajah*, by Michael Alexander and Sushila Anand tells his extraordinary and rather sad story. Having taken Elveden, he set a careful restoration of church in hand in 1869. By 1904, the wholesale rejuvenation of the estate by the new owner, the Earl of Iveagh, demanded a larger church for his workers and it was then that the conjunction of the Guinness fortunes with the talents of the 'rogue' architect W.D. Caröe produced an astonishing building in which lushness and wilful eccentricity combine. A new nave and chancel were added to the n. dedicated to **St Patrick**, in a style which **Pevsner** labelled with some acuteness 'Art Nouveau Gothic'. The feeling is medieval but much of the detail decoration, particularly in tracery and **finials**, has the smooth sinuous lines of the late C19. Long, reptile-like, water sprouts keep company with the rich cresting and seated figures of the chancel parapet, and beyond the small rose window of the n. **vestry**, a slimly buttressed chimney stack rises as though from a country house of the period. One of the angels on the vestry parapet has unfortunately lost his copper trumpet. A medieval stone coffin lies within a low arch in the n. chancel wall and the nave windows on that side are deeply recessed, with high sails. The w. front has a small corner turret and the low doorway is flanked by squat, angled buttresses topped by angels. The small figure of a bishop occupies a niche below the gable end. The medieval octagonal **font** has been relegated to the churchyard by the s. **porch** and beyond is the most satisfying of the new work - a bell tower built in 1922 as a memorial to Viscountess Iveagh, connected by a cloister walk to the s. chapel. Here, Caröe's design is closer to the traditional East Anglian style, with an octagonal stair turret rising above the batlements, pinnacled buttresses, paired bell openings and flushwork of a very high quality.

Entrance to the church is by the s. chapel door and to the r. is a C14 **angle piscina** with a new stone **credence shelf** next to **dropped-sill sedilia**. The chapel e. window, a memorial to the Maharajah and his wife, has 1894 glass by **Kempe** - the Adoration of the Magi with lots of luxurious fur-trimmed robes, attendants with banners, and the outlines of a medieval city beyond. Below is a **Jacobean altar** table, and to the l., a tablet with full armourial **achievement** for Prince Frederick Duleep Singh. Below that is a severe black tablet for his elder brother, Prince Victor Albert Jay Duleep Singh, for whom Queen Victoria stood godmother in 1866. Note the head of a small Decorated niche in the embrasure of the chapel s. window and then go through the fine modern oak **screen** into the fecundity of Caröe's interior. The round-headed arches of the **arcade** have chunky enrichments in the mouldings and the deep **capitals** are carved with a weird mixture of designs in layers, none of which are alike. The octagonal **piers** have shafts separated by deeply recessed traceried panels of a quite eccentric design. The s. aisle **roof** is overbearingly massive for the space covered and two of the **wall posts** spring from limply shaped transverse stone arches set in the embrasure of the Perpendicular windows that Duleep Singh had carefully restored - a most unhappy arrangement. The window by the screen is a memorial to Arthur, Viscount Elveden, and has a bright **St George** design by Hugh Easton who also designed the glass in the window to the w. - a memorial to men of the USAAF 3rd Division. A serviceman kneels below an angel with mighty

wings in vivid blue and the scene beyond encapsulates the transitory feeling of a wartime air base - Flying Fortresses at dispersal and the odd tent here and there. The other window on this side, a memorial of 1971 to the 2nd Earl and Countess, is by Lawrence Lee - an attractive patchwork of colour and plant stems overlaying an C18 man-of-war. Also on the s. wall is a 1786 portrait medallion of Augustus, Viscount Keppel, and there are plain early niches flanking the Norman slit window. The **font** dates from the Duleep Singh restoration and is in Sicilian-Norman style, with eight slim barley-sugar columns under a bowl whose panels contain demi-figures and shields. The nave w. window of 1937 commemorates Edward Cecil, 1st Earl of Iveagh. It was designed by Sir Frank Brangwyn, the most successful artist of his generation and, possibly, least appreciated in this country. He did little stained glass work but was anxious to commemorate Lord Iveagh who was both his patron and his friend. Brangwyn was commissioned to provide a window for the Protestant cathedral in Dublin and this one. In it, children crowd round a father who reads to them and a mother who comforts them, while the two dedicatory saints look benignly down from among a host of baby faces. Squirrel, hare and doves are worked into the base of this dense design, with everything in fresh pastel colours. As with all that Brangwyn did, it is lively and vibrant. Below it, the war memorial designed by **Cautley** is stiff and early Victorian in feeling, as though in quiet protest at all around. The nave roof is a massive double **hammerbeam**, embellished with a multitude of angels and richly carved on every available surface. The effect is slightly oppresive, possibly because roofs of this stature are normally higher. Beyond the chancel arch, itself enriched with carving, is a closely panelled barrel roof with **bosses** at every intersection; the eastern ranges of panels are decorated to form a **celure**. With no chancel screen the eye is taken forward to the **reredos** which rises on both sides of the altar to the spring of the w. window arch. Sumptuously carved in alabaster and heightened with gilding, the supper at Emmaus at its centre, it has 14 statues of saints and East Anglian monarchs, together with a host of minor figures. The effect is extraordinarily rich. The vestry door in the n. wall of the chancel is a prime example of Caröe at his most wilful and least effective. The choir stalls are relatively conventional but the nave pews are more interesting, with smooth scrolly tops to the bench ends and low relief carving in panels. The wolf guarding **St Edmund's** head, in a style reminiscent of Walter Crane, can be found both in the nave s. side and in the s. aisle. All the woodwork is of very high quality, the organ case and pulpit in particular. A visit here is an experience that one should not lightly forgo.

Eriswell, St Laurence (B3): This church has a very neat and tidy churchyard, with a little avenue of cherry trees leading to the n. **porch**. There has been some confusion over the dedication here because Eriswell's church was St Peter's over a mile away to the n., but when it became derelict this dependant chapel of St Laurence was taken over and was called St Peter's for some time. Outside in the s. wall there is a low tomb recess and this C13 **aisle** is the earliest part of the building, although re-used stones from a **Norman** predecessor can be found in the walls. In the mid-C14, a tower, porch, **nave** and **chancel** were added and what had been the old chancel at the e. end of the s. aisle became a **guild** chapel dedicated to **St John the Baptist**. Once inside, the details of this rearrangement can be seen. In the corner of the s. chapel is an **angle piscina** with a **cusped, cinquefoiled** arch and **dropped-sill sedilia**. When the wall **screen** was put in

to divide the chapel from the s. aisle, an **altar** dedicated to the **Blessed Virgin** was placed against it, and a small square window was added to give it light. This has medieval glass in the centre **quatrefoil** - a C13 figure with a C14 head. Below is a ledge piscina (the simplest form used), and on the dropped-sill beside it is a stone quern that may have begun life as a **stoup**. The chancel e. window has tiny **head-stops** and **Decorated tracery** with an oval above **ogee** arches. Across the n.e. corner of the **sanctuary** is a large niche for a statue which, at some later date, has had a pair of small cupboards inserted at the bottom. The original **aumbrey** is the other side of the altar, by the C14 piscina under its cusped **trefoil** arch, with stepped dropped-sill sedilia beyond. There is a medley of medieval glass fragments in the heads of the chancel n. windows, and before moving down into the nave, look for Martha Turk's grave slab below them: 'She lived in the late Earl of Orford's family 41 years greatly respected by all that knew her'. Well yes, that is a kindly and charitable sentiment, but this was 'Patty', the young maid at Houghton with whom George, 3rd Earl of Orford fell in love and set up house in Eriswell rectory - so convenient for Newmarket. His famous Uncle, Horace Walpole, who eventually succeeded him in 1791, was perpetually irritated by the unorthodox arrangement. The stone plays safe and says 'spinster', but the register is a shade closer with 'wife and companion of the Earl of Orford'. They say that George died of a broken heart three weeks after losing his Patty. The chancel screen appears to have modern base panels. They carry armorial shields: from l. to r., de Rochester, de Tudenham, the sees of Norwich and Ely, Bedingfield and Chamberlain. Although the shafts on the s. side are replacements, those on the n. are original C14, as is most of the Decorated tracery. From this point you can see the **sanctus-bell window** high in the tower wall, with its ogee trefoiled head. The wrought-iron lectern and openwork pulpit in pitchpine and wrought-iron date, like the nave roof, from the 1874 restoration. The **arcade** between the chancel and the s. chapel has a quatrefoil **pier** with rounded **capitals**, but the nave pillars and capitals are octagonal. Unfortunately, very little survives of the carved figures on the medieval bench ends that remain, but there are some telling graffitti cut into two seats in the s. aisle (second from w. and third from e.). They show crude gibbets and were no doubt a child's reaction to the drama of having two men hanging in chains at the village and for the 1782 murder of old Frances Philips, a miserly spinster who lies buried in the s. chapel. The solid C14 **font** has cusped quatrefoils in the bowl panels and attached shafts around the stem. On going out, you will find a modern figure of a saint in the niche over the door which, if it is meant to be **St Laurence**, does not have the traditional gridiron emblem. The original did, no doubt, bought with ten sheep under the will of shepherd John de Scherlokke who was buried in the porch. In 1649, 'The Society for the propagation of the faith in New England', known as 'The New England Company', bought the manor of Eriswell. It was the first missionary society in this country and the members later experimented by bringing back a 14-year-old boy and apprenticing him to the village carpenter. Alas, in 1820 he died after only two years in the alien land, and on his tombstone just in from the path by the porch door can still be read 'James Paul, a North American Indian'.

Euston, St Genevieve (D3): A charming setting deep in the park; the track to the church passes in front of the Hall to continue under a line of lime trees, some of which are huge and ancient. Henry Bennet, Earl of Arlington, was secretary of State from 1662 to 1674, a member of the Cabal ministry and close friend of Charles II. His much loved and only daughter Arabella was the child bride of Henry Fitzroy, 1st Duke of Grafton, the most attractive and able of the king's natural sons. Arlington kept great state at Euston, but in his retirement he told his friend John Evelyn that 'his heart smote him that, after he had bestowed so much on his magnificent palace, he should see God's house in the ruins it lay'. And so, in 1676, he rebuilt this church which is one of only two classical designs in the county. The core of the building is medieval, and the tower retains w. buttresses up to the second stage, but the entire conceptis **Stuart**. **Nave** and **chancel** are of equal length and the ample **transepts** make this a cruciform building. The nave has circular **clerestory** windows and the **aisles** have simple window **tracery** - two round-headed **lights** with a circle over. The e. window also is round-headed and so are the bell openings in the tower, which has an openwork parapet with corner pinnacles. The aisles have doors (now blocked), approached by a semi-circle of broad steps and, having seen inside, one wonders whether they were ever open.

Entry is by the matching w. door, and once through the tower vestibule, the richness of the interior opens up. Over the w. door is a fine and large three-dimensional set of the arms of the 1st Duke of Grafton. As he was illegitimate, the **Royal Arms** are surmounted by a baton sinister; they impale the Bennet arms of his wife and the shield is contained within the ribbon of the Garter. The **achievement** is fully coloured and gilt and is, I suspect, plaster rather than wood. Nearby is an 1880s **font**, typical of the period. The ceilings of nave, chancel, and transepts are cross vaults of plaster, with the moulded ribs picked out in tan to match the walls, and they have gilded monograms and shields for **bosses** at the intersections. One of the features here is the use of **stucco**, and the arches of the centre crossing are inset with large flowers, with **acanthus** leaves on the chancel arch and on the cornices - all in tan against a dark brown background. The aisles have unadorned flat ceilings, except for the family pew in the s. aisle. There you will see stucco work of very high quality, with coronets over blank shields at the corners of a heavy garland of flowers. This is reminiscent of similar work in the great houses of the period. The walls are panelled and the nave pews have panelled ends and doors, while those fronting the crossing are enriched with carving. The six- sided pulpit has canted floral trophies over panels with deeply moulded acanthus frames; cherubs and swags of flowers adorn the angles, with scrolls and fruit on the base. (It has a large **tester**, too, prior to 1875). Beyond, a low chancel **screen** rises in elegant curves at the sides, with oblong openwork panels of acanthus foliage on either side of the opening. The **reredos** is a panel of the Last Supper carved in bas relief; surrounding swags of fruit and flowers link with a cherub's head within folded wings at the top. This finely modelled work is deeply undercut and is reminiscent of work produced by the **Grining Gibbons'** workshop. The rest of the e. wall has enriched panelling on either side of **Corinthian pilasters**. Although the architect is unknown, there seems little doubt that he was well aware of Wren's work in London, and the excellence of the detailing, particularly of the woodwork and stucco, points to craftsmen who were well above the standard to be found in the provinces.

The church has a number of **brasses**: 1.nave: a man with his wife who wears a **butterfly head-dress**, late C15, 2. nave: a lady in a **kennel head-dress** (inscription missing), about 1520; 3. nave: inscription for Gerard Sothil, 1528; 4. chancel, n. side: the top half of a man and his wife (minus

Euston, St Genevieve: pulpit

her head), about 1520; 5. chancel, s. side: a late brass inscription with his arms in a roundel for George Feilding, Earl of Desmond, 1665; 6. chancel, s. side: inscription for William Foster (effigy lost), 1524; 7. sanctuary, n. side: top half of a man in Yorkist armour with his head on a helm. His wife, with her head on a cushion, is wearing a kennel head-dress caught up with two clasps, and has a purse and rosary hanging from her girdle. This is probably Edmund Rokewood who died in 1530, and Alice his wife. He was Lord of the Manor and his arms are below the figures with those of his two wives above, all originally inlaid with colour. At the back of the family pew there is a large but restrained memorial in white marble to Lord Arlington, the builder of the church. It has an heraldic achievement between scrolls at the top, twin cherub heads within folded wings at the sides, and acanthus supporting scrolls below. To the r. is a Venetian Gothic memorial in a variety of marbles to the 6th Duke of Grafton, and on a nave s. pillar, a **St George** panel in enamelled mosiac for Lieut Edward Fitzroy RN, who died in 1917. One seldom has the opportunity to examine coffin plates, but there are many C18 and C19 examples here, mounted on the panelling good examples of changing fashion and taste. Before you leave, do not overlook the many fine C18 gravestones in the churchyard.

Exning, St Martin (A4): The land falls away on two sides of the large churchyard, giving St Martin's a commanding position in the centre of the village, easily visible from the bypass. **St Etheldreda** was born here in AD 630, and both Roman and **Norman** masonry have been identified in the tower, so one can assume that there has been a church here since very early days. Of the present building, the earliest part is the **chancel**, where you will see two blocked slit windows in the s. walll which date from the late C12. The tower has two bell stages, one above the other, showing that the work of about 1300 up to the first set of bell openings, with their 'Y' **tracery**, was extended within the next 50 years or so up to the present battlements. A new w. window was installed at the same time, its tracery matching those in the **transepts**. The wooden cupola containing the clock bell was added in the C18. The C19 saw extensive restorations; **nave** walls heightened and new roofs in the 1820s, **aisle** windows and much of the chancel replaced in the 1860s, and a new e. window quite different in style from its predecessor. However, part of the **Decorated** tracery in the n. aisle windows is original and both C14 transepts have large end windows with fine **reticulated** tracery.

There is a C15 **priest's door** with **trefoils** in the **spandrels** in the s. chancel wall.

Entry is by the s. **porch**, where all is restored except the **headstops** of the outer arch. Going through the C14 inner door, note the large holes in the **jambs** where the heavy beam was set for security. The interior is well kept and spacious, with attractive splashes of colour here and there, particularly the use of blue wall hangings in the n. transept. There are C14 **arcades** with octagonal **piers**, and a **font** of the same period with foliated crosses and shields in the bowl panels. All the ceilings are plastered. The C17 **gallery** in the tower arch originally accommodated the singers, but it now houses the organ which was moved from the n. transept in 1965. Look above it for the **sanctus-bell window**, opening from the ringing chamber. There are two sets of **Royal Arms** here: a large and dark **achievement** of George II painted on board just by the s. door, and a good example of George III's dated 1817 painted on canvas and displayed on the front of the gallery. Over by the n. door is a large, badly mutilated niche, with **Perpendicular** tracery behind what was a **crocketted** canopy. It may have housed a **St Christopher** statue or one of the church's patron saint, **St Martin**. The nave benches have C16 **linenfold** panelled ends and there are a few more in the s. aisle; these are a century later than the majority of pews in East Anglia and may have replaced a very early set. One bench, with very slim **poppyheads**, remains in the n. transept from a late C14 or early C15 chancel set. It has a line of **quatrefoil** sound holes under the plinth and there are vestiges of animals on the front buttresses. The **altar** here is a simple but satisfying late C16 table, and it carries a fine cross and candlesticks adorned with the emblems of **St Edmund**. On the w. wall of this transept is a most interesting early C17 memorial for Francis Robertson. It is a framed wooden square painted with a full achievement of his arms, and may have been used as a **hatchment** at his funeral, although the verse beneath makes me doubt this:

> Stay passenger, not ev'ry Calverie
> Can tell thee of such Reliques as here lie,
> Here lies one, that besides Coat-armorie,
> And other Monumentall braverie,
> T'adorne his Tombe hath left, ye memorie...
> Of Worth and Virtue Heavens heraldrie

The s. transept was restored in 1971 when some very interesting things came to light including the **aumbry** in the e. wall, a C13 **piscina** in the s. wall, with **dogtooth** ornament in the moulding of the trefoil arch, and a rare example of a C14 double **heart burial**, also in the s. wall. This is under a defaced **ogee** canopy and is divided into two compartments, each containing a pair of hands holding a heart. The C18 pulpit is tall, with a very high backboard and **tester**. It is plainly panelled in oak and would be vastly improved if the dark and muddy varnish could be removed. A small, typically **Jacobean** chest stands in front. There is now no chancel **screen**, but the stairs of the **rood loft** remain on the n. side, and an opening on the s. side shows that the loft probably extended over a **parclose screen** in the s. transept originally, rather like the arrangement at Dennington. In the chancel there are deeply-set **Early English lancets** and you will see that one on the s. side has been cut into to make room for the C15 priest's door. The C17 **communion rails** have nicely turned **balusters** but have had the same varnish treatment as the pulpit. In the n.e. corner of the **sanctuary** is a **purbeck marble** tomb which may, from its position, have been used to mount the **Easter sepulchre**. The late C13 double piscina is now a pair of short lancets devoid of ornament, with the original centre shaft. The altar **reredos** consists of the **decalogue**, Lord's Prayer and Creed painted on tin (a common and rather nasty C19 habit). The altar **Ecclesiological** candlesticks are those discarded from the pulpit when it was demoted from two-decker status in 1909, and have happily found their way back to the church. They were possibly purchased originally by Thomas Frognall Dibdin, the memorable, if slightly zany bibliophile who was vicar here from 1823 and who is remembered both for the pioneering and beautifully produced catalogue of the Spencer library at Althorp and for his own 'Bibliomania'.

Fakenham, St Peter (D3): It is important to walk round the outside of this church. Only by so doing can one see that it was begun before the Conquest. At the junction between **nave** and **chancel** on both sides there are typical **Saxon long and short quoins**. The original chancel will have been narrower than the present one. There is a blocked **Norman** slit window high in the n. wall and another is partly concealed by the **porch** roof. The doorways and the **lancets** in the chancel are C13, but apart from a modern e. window the rest are C14. So too is the tower, which has a chequerwork **base course** and angled, stepped buttresses up to the belfry stage where there are **Decorated** windows on three sides with a lancet to the e. The porch was rebuilt in 1859, re-using the old windows and restoring the **stoup** in the angle by the door. The n. door was blocked up at the same time and the church was fitted out with new roofs, floors, pews and a **vestry**, with the organ coming in ten years later. The **font** is apparently medieval, with **paterae** on the base, stem and under the bowl, but the cross carved on one side of the bowl looks like C19 work. There is now no chancel arch, except for an **arch-braced** roof member which rests on **colonnettes** with angels below. The pulpit is C19 and the lectern of 1926 date. The **screen**

incorporates some C15 work, notably the **cusping** in the main **lights** retaining a little colour, and the **mullions** which have shafts and **capitals** on the front side. The top coving, centre arch and the base panels are modern, but the blending is good and the total effect very pleasing. The C19 arch to the organ chamber- cum-vestry has stiff musical angels. The restorers dealt with the **piscina** and added **sedilia** alongside. Fragments of C15 glass, including angels' and devils' heads, have been collected together and arranged on patterns in the windows on the s. side of the chancel. In the n. wall of the **sanctuary** is a reconsituted arch over a table tomb for Reynolds Taylor (d. 1692). The front panels recount a lengthy genealogy and there are seven shields of arms, with swags and drapes on the **pilasters**. Have a look at the four C13 grave slabs, with their elaborate floriated crosses, set in the w. wall of the tower, and as you close the modern s. door, admire the C14 ring handle with its mask **boss**.

Felsham, St Peter (E5): Fronting the village street opposite the Six Bells public house, with tall limes along the frontage, this church received fairly drastic treatment in the C19. Its **chancel** was rebuilt in 1873 and there was a heavy **nave** restoration in 1899. The low w. doorway of the tower has worn **headstops**, with flowing **Decorated tracery** in the window above. The bell openings have **Perpendicular** tracery and the strong **string courses**, combined with a staff on the s. side, make it very attractive. The nave is tall, with elegant C14 windows and **flushwork** battlements and beyond the plain little s. **porch** is a faint **scratch dial** on the first buttress. The main entrance from the street is much more impressive and the C15 porch is large and lavish. The whole front and the buttresses are embellished with flushwork and the large side windows have **transomes** within

the tracery. The mouldings of the entrance arch are decorated with three ranks of **paterae** and the **dripstone** rests on carved lions accompanied (and this is unusual) by birds. There are shields in the **spandrels** and a canopied niche over the entrance is matched by a pair in the buttresses. The old staircase to the **rood loft** juts out of the nave wall on this side and there is a **priest's door** further along in the chancel. Entry is via a plain C14 doorway and over the C19 doorway opposite is a set of George III **Royal Arms** dated 1820 and painted on board. The C15 **font** is excellent, its panels filled with intricate tracery which incorporates shields on four sides. There are demiangels below the bowl and the shaft rests on a large octagonal base. This has all the appearance of being the bowl of a C14 **font** which was cut down and filled in to carry its successor. Its side panels are carved with **cusped ogee** tracery, within which are halves of **green men's** heads, sea monsters, and one half of a standing figure. All the church's fittings and **roofs** are C19, as is the **bier** that stands at the w. end. There are fragments of C15 glass in the tracery of two nave windows and the **reredos** in the chancel is a copy of Raphael's 'Charge to St Peter'. All is neat and well cared for, but much of the interior's character has been restored away.

Finningham, St Bartholomew (F4): Entry is now across the n. side of the churchyard, but the emphasis originally was on the s. and the lavish C15 **porch** there is very attractive. It has three fine niches around the outer arch, one with an elaborate canopy, and the arch **spandrels** contain a merchant's mark and a **Trinity** shield. The front has **flushwork** panelling overall and there is a line of **quatrefoils** under the gable, with **crocketted** pinnacles at the corners. When walking round, look for a **scratch dial** on the l. of the s. **nave** buttress about 6 ft from the ground. All the side windows of the nave and **chancel** are **Perpendicular**; but the **priest's door** on the s. side is early C14. The e. window was renewed in the C19 and there is a niche of the same period above it. The red brick, late Perpendicular n. porch has virtually no ornament and (the door having been blocked) it is now a **vestry**. The unbuttressed early C14 tower has 'Y' **tracery** bell openings on three sides and a quatrefoil to the e.

Entering by the s. porch, note that the C19 restoration included a new **roof** on stone **corbels** and that three **consecration crosses** cut in the **jamb** of the early C14 inner doorway. The door itself is medieval and still has its original closing ring. **Sanctus-bell windows** are generally small affairs, but here there is one nearly as large as a door, and in view of the date of the tower, it is possible that it might have been designed as a secure access to the upper chamber. Below is an attractive C19 **gallery**, in front of which stands the late C15 **font**, raised on two steps in Maltese cross form. The bowl panels are deeply carved with tracery and, instead of a flower at the centre, the n.w. panel has a mask. The contemporary cover is a beautifully compact version of the tabernacle type, and the radiating ribs are heavily crocketted, rising to a turned and carved **finial**. Between the ribs are pierced tracery panels with little crocketted **pediments**, and below them, a deeply moulded and crested base. To the r. of the vestry entrance, there are remains of a **stoup**, so that the C14 doorway on that side may well have been the one in common use before the advent of the new s. porch. Most of the seating in the nave is good C19 work, but there are medieval bench ends at the w. end, and the four just e. of the font have figures which face inwards, an unusual variation. Second from the w. on the s. side is the figure of gluttony which has lost half its head but still holds a ladle over the stock pot between its knees, while clutching a rosary in the

other hand. The irony was probably intentional. The **hammerbeams**, **wall plates**, and **collar beams** beneath the ridge of the nave roof are all embattled, and it looks as though there were angels tenoned into the ends of the hammers. The white ceiling panels between the main timbers set them off very well. The wide chancel arch has no **screen** now and a large modern crucifix hangs very effectively within it. During extensive restorations in the 1880s, the **chancel** was partially rebuilt and given a new roof, but some medieval bench ends were re-used in the new choir stalls. On the n. side there is a grotesque and a castle, and on the s., a seated figure, and a tower with a portcullis which has a head poking out of the top, entirely out of scale. The rear stall on the n. side has the front of a **Jacobean** chest used as part of the back. In the **sanctuary** there is a C14 **piscina** under a wide **trefoil** arch, and in the top **lights** of the e. window, some of the C15 glass remains in the form of rather jumbled figures without heads. Two of them, however, are identified by their emblems; the second from the l. is **St Simon** holding a fish, and to his r., **St James the Great** with his scallop shell.

Finningham has some interesting monuments. Look first at Sir John Fenn's on the chancel n. wall by **John Bacon** - a delicately sculpted figure of a woman kneeling over a table tomb; set against grey, veined marble, it has the epitaph below. Sir John was a leading C18 antiquarian and the man who discovered and published the Paston letters in 1787. He lived at East Dereham in Norfolk, but his wife was a Frere and so he was buried here, the home, since 1598, of that important Suffolk family. Lady Fenn died in 1813 and her tablet, within a Gothick arch, is alongside:

> Though not herself a mother, she took an interest in children... hence arose the literary works which rendered her a distin-

guished supporter of the improved system of early education.

That refers to her rather earnest books for children under the pseudonyms of 'Mrs Teachwell' and 'Mrs Lovechild'. She was incidentally, the model for Lady Bountiful in George Borrow's *Lavengro*. A little to the w. is a charming tablet by John Golden of Holborn whose work spans the end of the C18 and the beginning of the C19. He was fond of using coloured marbles combined with details borrowed from the brothers Adam. This tablet is a good example of the technique; pale brown mottled stone sets off the white marble epitaph tablet and the base carries motifs often seen on chimney pieces and ceilings of the period. It commemorates John Williamson who died in 1871, a friend of the Freres and felicitously described as being 'cheerful in his social connections...'. There are, of course, a number of Frere memorials and quite the nicest is for the rector Edward Frere who died in Bath in 1841, aged 36. It is on the nave n. wall and is an oval coat of arms in coloured marble, with a swooping and heavily curved scroll beneath - much better than the average design of the period.

Flempton, St Catherine (C4): Standing at the village crossroads, this is a neat and trim church. Most of the tower collapsed in the mid-C18 and it was rebuilt in 1839. This was followed by an almost total reconstruction of the rest of the building later in the century, with a ponderous **vestry** added outside of the old n. door. A C15 timber and plaster **porch** was replaced by the present one at that time, but the heads of the C15 entrance doors have interesting **tracery** cut in the solid. The interior is light and fresh, with plain white walls, and over the tower arch is a pretty little set of George III **Royal Arms**, dated 1763 and having the distinction of being signed by the artist, a Mr Boynton of Bury. A plain octagonal early C14 **font** stands within the tower. Despite **Cautley's** slighting comment, the Victorian bench ends are attractive, their small **finials** carved with leaves and the shoulders decorated with **paterae**. A window on the s. side of the nave contains glass by G.E.R. Smith in which the figures of **St Francis**, **St John the Evangelist** and **St Christopher** stand out effectively against clear glass, with shields of arms in the tracery. It commemorates Sir John Wood, last of the Hengrave squires, who died in 1951. Opposite is the 1927 memorial window for Lady Wood, with figures of **St Catherine of Alexandria**, with her palm and sword (rather than the more usual wheel) and **St Gertrude**, bearing a crozier and the Sacred Heart. The pulpit is a good late C16 or early C17 design with two tiers of blank arches in the tall panels. Although there is now no **screen**, one can see where the chancel arch was notched on the e. side to accommodate the **rood loft**. In the window just beyond on the s. side, one of the **lights** is **transomed** to form a **low side window** below. The **priest's door** is just beyond, and above it is a tablet for John Harcourt Powell who died in 1840. It is by Matthew Wharton Johnson whose rather dull work is scattered all over England. There are plain C17 **communion rails**, but within the **sanctuary** is a very handsome double **piscina**. The arch encloses pierced tracery, with a single **reticulation** above the **cusped** arches, and there is a small opening in the side through to the window sill. The late C17 **altar** table stands on a slab which, although it was later engraved as a grave slab, was probably the church's original **mensa**. The **Decorated** e. window has flowing tracery and is filled with 1890s glass - the Crucifixion spread across three lights, with a row of small shields painted with **Passion emblems** above. There are one or two riveting Christian names to be found here - Fitz Nun Lambe (1733) lies by the priest's door, a brass platre on the s. wall is for Arthur, wife of Zilpha Frost (1918), and you may take my word for it that behind the organ there is a memorial to an C18 rector called Blastus Godley.

Fornham, All Saints, All Saints (C4): The broad grass verges of the village street form a pleasant approach to the church which stands on a bend in the road. The base of the plain, unbuttressed tower is early C13 but the bell stage is about 100 years later, and the pinnacles which mark it from a distance were added in the C19. The **nave** was refashioned about 1300 and the **chancel**, with **reticulated** tracery in the e. window, dates from the first quarter of the C14. The **aisles** and **porch** were added in the late C15 or early C16, with a slightly unusual layout - the aisles abutting the e. wall of the porch. There are attractive parapets on this side, with **flushwork** initials and shields and 'I.H.C. have mercy' carved on a panel at the e. end. There was a full-scale restoration in the 1860s under **Sir Arthur Blomfield**, when the roofs of chancel and s. aisle were replaced and the majority of the windows renewed to the original designs. The porch was extensively restored at that time and the parapet has a niche at the centre. Part of the roof is original and there is a good centre **boss** carved as a human face. The inner door, although restored, is a visible survivor from the C12 church. The restored roof of the nave is C15, as are the **arcades**, and the one on the s. side has one arch opening into the chancel. The very large and plain octagonal **font** is probably the same age. On the tower wall is an elegant C18 set of the **decalogue**, Creed and Lord's Prayer in black and gold, hung originally on the e. wall of the chancel. There are a dozen medieval benches in the nave, and three more in the n. aisle, all with **poppyheads** and square, **castellated** elbows. The front row of benches has carved

animals but at least one is a modern replacement and others are suspect. There is an image bracket with **fleurons** at the e. end of the n. arcade which carries a small modern figure of **St Edmund**. There is another bracket on the wall of the s. aisle, where the chapel has a C17 **altar** table. Beyond it, on the e. wall, are matching image stools and the one to the r. has a fine square canopy set in the corner, pierced by **quatrefoils** and flanked by **crocketted** pinnacles with a plain **piscina** nearby. A **Tudor** arch at the e. end of the n. aisle leads to a **transept**, and in the s.e. corner is a **squint** (although the organ now blocks the line of sight to the **high altar**). The church's collection of **brasses** has been mounted on the w. wall of the transept. The most interesting is the remaining top half of a little figure commemorating Thomas Barwick, a professor of medicine at Bury who died in 1599. He is dressed in a gown and bears a staff; the brass includes his arms, an inscription and a Latin verse. The rest of the brasses are inscriptions for Ann Adams (1607), Thomas Manock (1608), John Manock (1656 but died in 1611), Mary Manock (1656 but died in 1615) and Thomas Manock (1656), with some fulsome phrases worth reading. The remaining shield is probably for a member of the Carewe family. over the entrance arch is a tablet for Lieut John Cowsell, who died in 1811 while 'gallantly leading on his company to charge the enemy' in a minor action of the Peninsula war. Opposite, the church's only **hatchment** is a large one for Sarah Elizabeth Halliday who died in 1834. The chancel arch was rebuilt by Blomfield and his new roof, although of pine, is attractively painted and has oak bosses. The arch through to the s. aisle has a modern screen which incorporates sections of medieval tracery, probably from the old altar and on the s. side is a most unusual arrangement. Normally the piscina is to the s. of the altar, with **sedilia** to the w. of it, but here the order is reversed and the C14 piscina, with its **cusped** and crocketted **ogee** arch, is set in the wall between the stepped sedilia and the priest's door. The e. window glass is by **Hardman**, appropriately illustrating Christ reigning with all his saints.

Fornham, St Martin, St Martin (D4): The s. **aisle**, with its small rose window to the w., repeated an earlier Victorian model in 1870 but, apart from that, the church is **Perpendicular** and the tower is particularly handsome for its size. Chequerwork battlements match the **base course** and the **transomed** bell openings are unusually tall. There is a heavy stair turret on the s. side and the **string courses** are well defined, with the lowest dipping under the w. window, which has distinctly cheerful **headstops**. There are headstops in fact to all the window arches, including the belfry **lancets**. Although they are not all in use, a whole family of **gargoyles** studs the parapet and stone **put-log holes** show on the faces of the tower. The **Tudor** brick n. **porch** has a crow-stepped gable and there is a **stoup** recessed in the r. hand buttress.

The organ was placed sensibly at the w. end of the s. aisle and thus the view through to the e. end is not obscured for a change. The squat C14 **font** has shields within circles on four sides of the bowl and varied **tracery** on the others. Overhead, the tower arch has large, coloured king and bishop headstops and the **roofs** of nave and chancel are plastered. A very dark set of George II **Royal Arms** hangs over the n. door, and in a **nave** n. window is glass designed by R.F. Ashmead for the Lancaster firm of Abbot & Co on the theme of the Benedicite: 'All ye works of the Lord, bless ye the Lord'. Two angels with outflung arms rise from a fiery star below the dove of the Holy Spirit in one **light**, and the sun, moon, earth, ske and sea are pictured in the other. The church's treasure lies in two **miser-icord** seats with very interesting subjects which have been adapted for re-use. The first forms the front of the C19 lectern and shows **St Thomas of Canterbury** kneeling at an altar while a knight cleaves his skull with a large sword; a second knight hovers menacingly and the archbishop's chaplain holds his crozier. Unlike continental examples, English misericords nearly all have flanking scrolls, called supporters, but they have not survived on this one. The second misericord, inset in the front of the **chancel** prayer desk does, however, have supporters carved with angels bearing crozier and mitre, and the central figure is the church's patron saint, **St Martin**. He is shown on horseback in front of a doorway with pierced tracery and the figure behind holds a portion of the cloak which the saint is cutting with his sword. What may well have been a section of the old **rood screen** is made up into a stall in the chancel and the C17 **communion rails** have shapely, turned **balusters**. The two fat and gilded cherubs that sit on the posts at the back of the **altar** are likely to have come from an C18 German or Austrian altar-piece. On the n. wall of the chancel is a tablet, by Hanchet of Bury, for Sir William Gilstrap of Fornham Park who died in 1896. His **hatchment** hangs above it and there is another, more interesting example further along. It bears the arms of Bernard, 12th Duke of Norfolk, who died in 1842. The **achievement** includes the batons of the hereditary Earl Marshal, but because he divorced Lady Elizabeth Belasyse in 1794, her arms do not appear in any form. To the s. of the chancel arch on the nave side is a tablet in memory of Sir Harry St George Ord, who was the first Colonial Governor of the Straits Settlements. On the nave n. wall is a tablet for Henry Claughton, 38 years an inspector of schools in the county. The tablet is unremarkable, except that it was put there in 1924 by his wife and his hunting and cricketing friends. An

HMI who rode to hounds must have brought an invigorating whiff of fresh air and the stable into dull old County Hall.

Freckenham, St Andrew (A3): Open to the fields on the w. but virtually hidden from the village street, the church stands on rising ground at the end of a little lane. **George Edmund Street** carried out a major restoration and rebuilding here in 1867-89, adding a new **vestry**. Because the work was carefully done it is difficult to distinguish old from new. The tower collapsed in 1882 and was rebuilt in the original style two years later, with the exception of the e. and w. windows, all the windows have been handsomely reglazed in clear glass so that the attractive interior is full of light. Street added two dormer windows of different sizes at the e. end of the **nave**, and a taller one which rests on the lintel of an ugly **priest's door** in the **chancel** - eccentric and uncharacteristic alterations. The restored early C14 **arcade** has **quatrefoil piers** and the **capitals** have a frieze of shallow blank arches. The arches into what is now the organ chamber are largely original, but whether there was ever a chancel arch is hard to say (although there is certainly a break in the wall line). The restored waggon **roof** of the nave is panelled, with beautifully **cusped** openwork **bosses**. The chancel roof panelling is simpler, with central bosses of leaves and one **woodwose**; the colouring is C19. The n. aisle has an **arch-braced** roof, animal and human head **corbels** below the **wall posts**, with angels and leaf bosses at the main intersections. The tower arch escaped in the 1882 collapse, as can be seen from the graffiti going back to the C17. Many of the pews are modern but there are some good medieval bench ends, expertly repaired; nave s. side from the w., priest at desk (new head), kneeling woman with rosary at desk (new head), kneeling woman (new head),

kneeling angel (new head and arms), kneeling woman at desk (new head), spotted devil thrusting a priest into hell's mouth. Opposite is a double-headed pair of birds. At the w. end there is a pair of beasts with renewed heads and on the n. side fourth from the back, a damaged **pelican** in her piety. The conventional **poppyheads** are a mixture of old and new work. The plain octagonal **font** rests on a matching shaft with nooked corners and is likely to be early C14. By the n. door is a most interesting alabaster panel which is thought to have been part of a **reredos**. It was discovered by workmen in 1776 and, although damaged, it is the tale of **St Eligius**, with the horse's owner looking distinctly doubtful. The C17 **altar** table in the n. aisle has simple decoration on the top rails. The C19 stone pulpit is typically indigestible. The chancel e. window dates from around 1300, with three stepped **lancets** (**tracery** renewed). The deeply moulded arch has slim **jamb shafts** and the **hood mould** rests on clustered flowers. There is a moulded ledge at various levels round most of the **snactuary**, terminating in foliage balls. Look for the tiny creatures among the leaves. The double **piscina** has **trefoil** arches set flush with the wall, but the niche has been deepened and the **sedilia** remade so there may have been outer mouldings to the arches originally. Over the sedilia is an 1899 **Annunciation** window in attractive **Arts and Crafts** style by **Horatio W. Lonsdale** and the e. window glass of 1869 is by **Hardman and Co**. (Street's chosen firm of the period). The composition of Nativity, Last Supper and the three Maries is characteristic, and uses strong, clear colours very effectively.

Gazeley, All Saints (B4): Standing within a spacious, open graveyard, the church is end on to the village street and slightly above it so that one has a clear view of the highly individual e. window in the C14 **chancel**. Dating from about 1330, its three tall and narrow **lights** have **trefoil** heads, the centre one a little lower than the the others. On them rests a **cusped** triangle with curved sides and the outline dips in to follow the **tracery** instead of being contained within a conventional arch. The tower was largely rebuilt in 1884, repeating the original C14 design and retaining the w. doorway. The C16 **nave** roof is lower and flatter than its predecessor so that the old **sanctus-bell window** can be seen outside on the e. face of the tower. **Aisles** and **clerestory** have early C16 **Perpendicular** windows and beneath all the parapets there are **string courses** studded with little **fleurons**. The Perpendicular s., **porch** now has a pitched roof but the line of the old one can be seen and although they now serve no purpose, the **gargoyles** remain. The **jambs** of the unglazed windows have lots of C17 and C18 graffiti and the first slopes gently down to the inner C14 doorway.

The **arcades** within show that the nave was built in the late C13; they have **quatrefoil piers** and heavily moulded **capitals** and bases matching the chancel arch, C19 angels bearing shields were added to the tower arch, and above it there is a dim set of George III **Royal Arms** painted on canvas and in poor condition. The early C14 **font** has a deep bowl and the panels are carved with a representative selection of the simple window tracery patterns that were in vogue at the time. The centre shaft of the plain **Stuart** cover has an acorn **finial** and is supported by four brackets. The low medieval benches at the w. end of the s. aisle have **poppyheads** and one of them has a back that offers a little puzzle to the curious. Its pierced carving is in the form of attractive capitals but some pieces have broken away and one has to guess the meaning: 'Salaman Sayet' is a possibility, but if so, the 'S's are reversed. There are more pierced backs of varying design n. of the font and the two blocks of pews at the w. end of the nave appear to have been made up, using tracery panels that may have formed part of the **rood loft**. Other benches at the w. end of the n. aisle have rudimentary poppyheads and are probably C17. By the n. door is a vast oil painting of Christ's Presentation in the Temple. By Jacques Stella, it once hung in the chapel of Trinity Hall, Cambridge. The C16 nave roof has **tie-beams**, with **archbraces** above and below and traceried **spandrels**. It was repaired in the 1880s and angels were added below the **wall posts**. It is well worth while using binoculars to study the early C16 glass in the clerestory windows on the n. side. Working from the w. there are: two angels and a shield of **Passion emblems**; two demi-angels; the three crowns of East Anglia or Ely; the figures of **St Faith** and **St Apollonia**; a shield representing the **Trinity**; a mitred bishop and three more angels. Set in the wall by the altar in the s. aisle is a tomb chest in **purbeck marble** - now very worn and irregular. The square canopy is carved with quatrefoils and there is a band of tracery below the recess. There were once **brasses** within but they are gone and it is quite anonymous. In the floor of the aisle there are two **ledgerstones** bearing brass shields - the westernmost dates from about 1500 and bears the arms of the Heigham family, while the other is about 60 years later and has the arms of the Blennerhassets impelling those of Heigham and Francis. The glass in both aisle e. windows is by **Lavers & Barraud**, all in deep colour. The n. aisle design is by H.S. Marks and the medieval treatment of the figures is much more marked there. Standing on a new base, the early C16 pulpit has simply traceried panels and the chancel **screen** is C19, although old tracery has been applied to three of the bottom panels. Just to the w. is a brass inscription in the floor for Robert Tailour who died in 1586. With the organ at the w. end of the church the wide chancel is made more spacious and it has a beautiful early C16 waggon roof; a pale brown colour, its boards are covered with a grid of moulded ribs forming **cusped** panels, with small **bosses** at the intersections. There are little angels bearing scrolls, carvings and wheat ears, vine sprays and leaves, and traces of paint show that it was once coloured. The chancel windows on both sides have low **transoms** forming **low side windows** below, with wide embrasures and deep sills. The frame on the s. side is rebated and the hooks for the wooden shutters are still there. It is strange that what appears to be a pair of **scratch dials** are incised in the sill. They cannot have been very effective and are perhaps doodles (or possibly that particular stone was removed from outside). There is a **priest's door** in the s. wall and a medieval door opposite leads to the **vestry**. To the w. is a **consecration cross** and to the r., a deep recess with a solid stone slab as its base. It has a **crocketted** arch with attached columns each side and the stumps of pinnacles. There is no trace of it having had a door and its position suggests that it was a small **Easter sepulchre**. In the **sanctuary** the early C14 **piscina**, with its **cinquefoiled** arch and stone **credence shelf**, stands next to stepped **sedilia** separated by an arm rest. With a little imagination the beast on top of it could be a lion. The design of the e. window surprises again because the splays have elongated arched panels. It is filled with glass by **Burlison & Grylls** of 1886; there is Christ in Majesty at the top and six panels in the main lights; a Crucifixion with the **Blessed Virgin** and **St John**, three scenes from the life of Christ and, at the bottom, the Garden of Eden. Moses with the serpent, and an **Annunciation**. High on the s. wall of the chancel is a monument to Edmund Heigham and his family. He died in 1599 and his little figure kneels in armour with sword laid by his side. His wife, in Elizabethan bon-

net, kneels behind him and his shield of arms is placed within strapwork on the top. In the chancel floor on the n. side is a small **chalice brass** for a priest dating from the 1530s and in front of the **altar rails**, a brass inscription for Mary Heigham who died in 1618. Before leaving the chancel look for Thomas Nuce's ledger-stone on the s. side. He was a vicar who died in 1617 and his rhyming epitaph is a good one. Next to it is one for Alice Peer:

Unfortunate she was, yet here she lies
At rest (secure) from all her enemies

And I wonder what lies behind those words!

Gedding, St Mary (E5): A long path leads through the large churchyard to the s. door of the church and an old boundary ditch runs parallel with it to the w. This little church had become very dilapidated by the 1880s and the upper stage of the tower was rebuilt in thin red bricks, with **lancet** bell openings. It was given a low, tiled cap as a prelude to something more ambitious. Nothing more was done, however, and weathering has made it very attractive, with the bulge of a tower stair on the s. side. A feature of the w. buttresses are the arms of the Chamberlin family in **flushwork**, with crowned 'M's for the dedication above them. There is no porch and one steps straight into a homely little interior of some considerable charm. Evidence of its **Norman** origin was uncovered at the restoration in the form of two lancets (only 2 in high and 6 in wide) set in deep splays in the **nave** walls, and the one on the s. side has **chevron mouldings** outside. Either side of the wide tower arch there are stubs of buttresses which come down to arches in the corners, and roughly carved heads lie within them. The C15 **font** has shields in the panels of the deep heavy bowl, carved with the cross of **St George** and the arms of the Shelton family while the others are filled with **Perpendicular tracery**. There was once a pillar **stoup** by the door and its bowl now lies on the font step. It is in good condition with a **quatrefoil** on one face and angel heads at the lower corners. The nave **roof** was re-framed as part of the restoration and a three-decker pulpit and box pews were removed, but a couple of medieval benches were suffered to remain at the w. end with their low, traceried backs and time-worn **poppyheads**. The narrow **chancel** arch has plain, continuous mouldings with no **capitals** and it is flanked by two unusual openings. They are tall, only 20 in wide and have **cusped** arches. Beneath the one on the l. is a deep recess divided in two by a **mullion** and it is some 20 in by 6 in overall. Judging by its position it is likely to have been a **reliquary chamber** associated with a nave **altar** and this explains the presence of the two openings: they turned the dividing wall into a form of **screen** and gave a view of the **high altar**. On the chancel side they are splayed and in the C19, **crocketted ogee** arches with **finials** and leaf **stops** were added. There is a **low side window** within an angled recess on the s. side of the chancel and a **priest's door** further along. Two more worn medieval benches are to be found here and note that the floor levels were raised to such an extent in the 1880s that the simple **piscina** in the **sanctuary** is almost at floor level. With the exception of the Norman lancets, all the windows are early C14 and the e. window has attractive flowing tracery.

Glemsford, St Mary (C6): The church stands on the edge of the village and commands a broad view across the valley to Stanstead. The C14 tower has an **ashlar base course**, renewed w. window, and fine three-**light** bell openings with **reticulated tracery**, The rest of the exterior is **Perpendic-**

ular. The w. end of the early C16 **aisle** is decorated overall with **flushwork**, while a base course of **quatrefoils** and shields continues round the s. **porch**. The windows of the **chancel** s. aisle are taller than those in the aisle and have **ogee** shapes in the tracery - a re-emergence of an earlier fashion. Above them is an inscription which records that John and Joan Goldyng were the founders of the chapel. There is more flushwork on the s. frontage, the battlements are pinnacled, and there is a **priest's door** on that side. Beyond the very broad, five-light e. window of the chapel the chancel walls are faced with flint pebbles - probable evidence of the 1870s restoration. On the n. side there is a matching side chapel, again with an inscription in the parapet which refers to a John and Margaret Mundys, and their son John and his wives. Both n. aisle and porch are plain and the **clerestory** windows of 1475 illustrate a late use of **cusped** heads in the tracery. The s. porch has flushwork matching the aisle and over the entrance arch there are three tall, stooled and canopied niches. Its **roof** is lovely; all the timbers are carved with a curling leaf and there is a vine trail on the **spandrels** and **wall plate** over the inner doorway. This has king and queen **headstops** and there are tiny **fleurons** in one moulding and equally tiny niches in another. The worn, but still handsome tracery of the medieval door is cut in the solid and has a folded leaf borders.

The interior is spacious with broad aisles, and the C14 **arcades** with their octagonal **piers** do not quite match - one side is higher than the other and the **capitals** differ. The **nave** roof is steep, in C19 pine, and the line of the original shows above the renewed tower arch. Within the tower there are two charity boards (painted on canvas as it happens), and the frames have the names of the rector and wardens for 1833. The traceried stem of the C15 **font** is very worn, with the remains of four figures. There are

Evangelistic symbols in the e. and n. bowl panels, a bishop's head on the s. side, an angel with shield on the s.e., a king's head on the n.w., and on the n.e. what was probably the **Blessed Virgin** of the **Annunciation**. In the n. aisle stands a huge C14 poplar chest, its curved top eaten away with age between the iron bands. The s. aisle roof is modern but in the n. aisle there is an excellent early C16 cambered **tie-beam** roof. All the timbers are moulded and the tie-beams are carved with leaf and scroll. There are **wall posts** at the corners and in the n.e. chapel the effect is slightly richer, with pierced **spandrels** and figures carved on the wall posts. On the aisle wall is a monument to Elizabeth Morgan who died in 1776. We are told that 'To enumerate her amiable qualifications and distinguished virtues needs no participation' and I am left wondering what that means. There are painted **decalogue boards** above the n. aisle **altar** and the C17 pulpit has interesting variations on the stereotyped decoration of the period: the upper panels are conventional blind arches with compartmented panels below, but the scroll brackets of the bookledge are carved with birds whose tongues extend as flowering plants and they have perky bird-head terminals. The s. chapel **Holy table** is roughly the same period but quite plain. The **high altar** has bulbous C16 legs but most of the rest is replacement and the **reredos** behind is an oak bas relief of the Annunciation dating from the 1880s.

Great Ashfield, All Saints (E4): On the western edge of a scattered village, the church stands by the entrance to Hall farm, and one crosses a water splash to reach the gate. The tower has a panelled **base course** to the w. where the doorway has slim attached shafts. Above it is a nice little **Decorated** window, with the remains of similar **tracery** in the bell openings. Brick **put-log holes** show in

the closely set flints of the walls and there is a spirelet above the plain parapet. The door in the n. aisle is blocked and there are square-headed **Perpendicular** windows on that side. Apart from a C13 **lancet** in the n. wall, the **chancel** seems to have been largely rebuilt in the 1870s. The attractive C16 s. **porch** is a pleasing mixture of brick and flint, with dressed flint panels and tracery in moulded brick. At the bottom of the niche, over to the door, there are small heads which match those on the brick pinnacles of the porch at Ixworth Thorpe a few miles away. There are remains of a sundial below the crow-stepped gable, and the **spandrels** of the arch contain the arms of the de Pakenham and Cricketot families, at one time Lords of the Manor. The porch's **arch-braced roof** has carving in the spandrels and the pillar which supported the **stoup** stands to the r. of the C13 doorway. The ancient door retains its original lock plate.

When the **nave** was rebuilt and the **aisle** added in the C15, the **arcade** pillars were placed on sections of the old n. wall and it also formed a base for the plain octagonal **font** that stands against the westernmost **pier** (like the one at Worlington). The nave has a simple C15 arch-braced roof, and at the w. end there are contemporary benches with **poppyheads** and grotesques, including the remains of two mermaids on the one nearest the tower. Nearby are two chests: one is large and iron bound and is remarkable for being of walnut than the usual oak; the other is a small C16 example with very interesting naive carvings in the front panels. The centre is a grotesque, symmetrical ram's head, to the l., a female head, and to the r., a fine portrait of a bearded shepherd. There is now no **screen** but the **rood loft** stairs can be seen to the n. of the chancel arch, with square-headed doorways facing w. On the s. side is a magnificent, square **Jacobean** pulpit - quite the best thing here. The base is supported on fat cushion legs and there are two ranges of panelling in the body, the lower with plain lozenges and the upper with the familiar arch and **pilaster** design. The reading desk is supported by winged beasts and the backboard has another pair of arched panels, togther with the intials of the probable donor, William Fyrmage. The carved **tester** is dated 1619 and the back continues up to the flat scrolls and a crown. The whole piece is distinguished, not only by carving of high quality, but also by individual touches like the masks beneath the side ledges. In front of the pulpit stands a prayer desk which has been reconstructed. It has a fine bench end carved with the tools of a blacksmith or farrier, and the groove of the original bookledge can be seen on the inside. A unit of the U.S.A.A.F. was stationed locally during the war and they have their own memorial in the n. **aisle**. It is an **altar**, backed by a **reredos** which is flanked by tall canopied panels - a design by **Cautley** which reflects his love and understanding of C15 woodwork. Above it is the original e. window, now lighting a C19 **vestry** beyond. A continental chalice veil in Bruges lace is framed on the wall. Just to the w. stands an interesting framed example of an early C19 church terrier - an inventory of church property and parish responsibilities that is well worth reading. On the s. wall of the **nave** there are two **hatchments**: one with a greyhound crest for Edward, 2nd Baron Thurlow, who died in 1829, and other for Sarah, wife of the 3rd Baron, who died in 1840. Her husband's hatchment hangs on the n. wall of the **chancel**, alongside another for the 4th Baron, who died in 1874. Below them is a well restored charity board in the unusual form of a long painted scroll. It records the 1620 Fyrmage charity (a link with the pulpit) and until the early C19 it was fixed to the top of the now vanished **rood screen**. On the s. wall is another hatchment which has not been dated but was probably for James Richard Bolton. In *The Suffolk*

Gypsy, Richard Cobbold, the C19 rector of Wortham, told the story of John Steggles' flight from the rigours of a Walsham le Willows boarding school, his rescue by gypsies and his many subsequent adventures. He came at length to serve as curate of this parish for over 50 years, and his memorial is on the s. wall above the **priest's door**. The early C18 **communion rails**, with their spiral **balusters**, came to the church from elsewhere in 1945 and, at the same time, the early C17 altar table was returned to its proper place. The plinth that it stands on matches the pulpit and so does the panelling of the reredos, so that it has been suggested that they formed part of a **three-decker**. If that were so, the complete unit would have been enormous and the pulpit construction makes it unlikely. In the e. wall of the **sanctuary** there is a C14 niche with an **ogee** which appears to have been canopied originally. The glass of 1926 in the e. window is by A.K. Nicholson - the risen Christ and two praying angels with pale yellow wings. The flesh tints are steely against deep blue backgrounds, and below there are vignettes of the sower and the angel reaper.

Great Barton, Holy Innocents (D4): This handsome church lies s. of the main road and most of the village and its dedication is a rare one; there are only four other medieval examples in the whole country. The mid-C15 tower is well proportioned and has a chequered **base course** and prominent **string courses**. The three-**light** bell openings have stepped **transoms**, and above the fine **flushwork** of the stepped battlements is an elegant C18 weather vane. **Nave** and **aisles** are C15 work but the **chancel** and was built in the late C13. The side windows have **plate tracery** and above the three **lancets** of the e. window are deeply recessed **quatrefoils** within circles. On the s. side, the archway of the **priest's door** stands on slim shafts. To the r. is a large, gabled tomb recess with a C13 coffin lid in the base. On the other side of the doorway you will see that a former **low side window** has been blocked up. There are handsome hexagonal buttresses at the corners of the chancel, reminiscent of Brandon and Raydon, rising to gabled pinnacles, and on the n. side the octagonal **rood stair** turret rises above the roof line. The s. **porch** boasts a fine sundial with the unusual text: 'Periunt et imputantor' (They perish and are reckoned), and while we know that porches assumed a significant role in medieval church life, it is interesting to learn that in the early C19 this one served not only as sleeping accommodation for homeless labourers but was also used for threshing corn. Over the inner door there is a pretty little niche with **crocketted** canopy and flanking pinnacles.

The feeling of spaciousness within is accentuated by the width of the chancel arch, and the whiteness of the chancel with its plastered ceiling draws the eye eastward. The early C14 s. **arcade** has alternating octagonal and circular **piers** with **fleurons** in the **capitals**, but the n. arcade is late **Perpendicular**, with half capitals within the arches studded with fleurons. Overhead, a C15 **hammerbeam roof** has recumbent figures that have nearly all lost their heads. To the l. of the entrance, a **vestry** enclosure incorporates parts of the old **rood screen**, and beyond is a simple C13 **font** resting on four plain shafts and a centre column. The tabernacle cover is modern. To the r. of the tower arch is a benefactions board dated 1858. It mentions the late C15 vicar, William Howerdly, and it is fitting that the parish's first known benefactor should be commemorated in the C19 glass of the w. window. The greater part of the benches are good quality reproductions dating from 1856, but there are six original bench ends beneath the arcades with **poppy-heads** and **tracery**. The e. window of

the s. aisle is early C14 (like the arcade on that side), and there is a roughly shaped **piscina** nearby. The most interesting thing in the s. aisle is the glass. The centre window commemorates Queen Victoria's Golden Jubilee and is by **Heaton, Butler & Bayne**. Beneath the old queen's full face portrait roundel is a bible held by angels, and below that, the **Royal Arms**, the tracery lights contain the stars of six orders of chivalry, but the extraordinary thing is that the two supporting full length figures are those of the Queen of Sheba and Queen Esther - a very peculiar conjunction. The window to the w. is a memorial put in by members of the Suffolk Hunt for their MFH, F.R. Smith, in 1913. It is a fine composition from **Morris & Co**, and although the artist had been dead for nearly 20 years, the designs are by **Sir Edward Burne-Jones**, with figures of the Centurion as Faith, the Good Samaritan as Charity, and Joshua as Hope. There are blue backgrounds with dense foliage, and in the tracery, seraph heads and angels with dulcimer and double pipe. Across in the n. aisle windows there are remains of C15 canopy work. The capitals of the C13 chancel arch are carved with leaves and the door to the **rood loft** stair is on the n. side. The Bunbury family were Lords of the Manor here from the C17 to the early C20 and just within the chancel on the n. side, within a Victorian Gothic arch, is the memorial to Lieut General Sir Henry Edward Bunbury, soldier, scholar, and Under Secretary of State, his was the delicate task of informing Napoleon, captive on the 'Bellerophon', that he could not hope to live in England but was to be exiled to St Helena. The soldier's father, Henry William, died in 1811 and was well known as a political caricaturist. His tablet is an excellent and deceptively simple design by Magnus of London - a well-lettered light tan scroll draped over a grey slab. The scroll motif is taken up again further along, where one hangs from the branches of a willow on the 1828 tablet for Lousia Emily Bunbury. It is by Thomas Milnes (the sculptor of the Nelson statue in Norwich Cathedral Close). In the **sanctuary** the C13 piscina has a crocketted gable flanked by pinnacles and within it, a pierced **trefoil** above an **ogee** arch. The heads at the base of the pinnacles are new. The level of both the piscina and the **sedilia** alongside show that the floor levels were raised in the C19.

Great Bradley, St Mary (A6): Set in an attractively extended open churchyard, much of the church's exterior is cement rendered including the whole tower. This is C14 and has a slim octagonal stair turret rising above the parapet as at Withersfield. The **base course** is chequered in flint and the unusual feature is that the slopes of the w. and s. buttresses are carved with heraldic devices, as they are at Hundon. Also uncommon is the large fireplace within, from which a flue emerges some way up the n. wall-,protected by a heavy stone baffle slab. The early C14 **chancel**, with its **priest's door** to the s., was shortened in the C18 and the e. end has been repaired in brick. The **nave** was originally **Norman** - see the tall n. door with its plain roll moulding and worn scallop **capitals**. The early **Tudor** s. **porch** is built of lovely, glowing red brick, with a steep crow-stepped gable and ranks of simple niches surrounding the entrance. There are **quatrefoils** pierced in the **spandrels** and the small side windows are formed from moulded bricks. The porch shelters a grand, late Norman doorway which is tall, with a deep **chevron moulded** arch edged with a band of crosses. The capitals are carved with scrolly birds and the twist decoration on the shafts changes direction section by section. Under the lintel there are two projecting heads that turn their faces slightly outwards.

Notches show that the tower arch had a screen at one time, and in the s.w. corner of the nave there is a deep recess that is likely to have been an **aumbry** for baptismal oils, salt, and similar items. The late C14 **font** has a shallow bowl, carved with quatrefoils and centre **paterae**, a panelled shaft, and paterae round the base. There are traces of colour and sizeable chunks have been broken from the rim. The nave has a single-braced **roof** which has been renewed in part, and there are rustic **tie-beams** with **king posts** to the ridge. The 1952 stained glass in the s. window is by **Powell & Sons** - a Nativity group, with the shepherd offering a posy and an English country background complete with castle, thatched cottages and a carpet of flowers. There are roughly shaped recesses cut in the walls at the s. end of the nave and it seems that the **rood stair** was on the s. side. To the w. is a stone **corbel** which, by its position, suggests that the loft was a deep one, underneath which there would have been nave **altars** on each side. (See the remains of a **piscina** on the s. side and another in the large behind the pulpit). The small square window on that side was probably an afterthought to give more light. The chancel arch is early C13 and the footings have been exposed on the s. to show the original floor level. The early C18 pulpit has a **tester** decorated with a marquetry sunburst and until recently it was a two-decker but the **clerk's** pew has been removed. There is a moulded **string course** in the chancel below the window sills and in the corner of the **sanctuary** is a tantalising remnant of early C14 **sedilia**, with a heavy shaft and a deeply moulded **ogee** arch. They must have been beautiful in their entirety before the chancel was truncated.

Great Finborough, St Andrew (F5): This is a fine specimen of confident Victorian rebuilding by **R.H. Phipson** in the 1870s, using traditional materials and not having to spare expense. The style is **Decorated** (with variations) and the church's memorable feature is the tower. it rises conventionally to an average height, and then flying buttresses support a tall octagonal belfry stage which carries a stone spire boldly banded in colour and pierced by two ranges of windows. A local tradition asserts that the squire's wife had difficulty in finding her way home after hunting and persuaded her husband to provide a marker. The spire is certainly visible from as far away as Woolpit where, incidentally, the same architect designed a quite different tower and spire in the 1850s. The s. **porch** is the only part of the building that remains of the original church and although it was largely reconstructed, it has a chequer **flushwork base course** and large octagonal corner pinnacles. These are elaborately **crocketted**, and despite the decaying stone the tiny animal heads at the base of the crockets survive. Inside the porch there are corner roof **corbels** in the form of large **Evangelistic symbols** bearing scrolls. The interior is spacious and within the tall tower arch there is a C19 **font** displaying some of the wilfulness of Victorian design - the octagonal bowl stands on a reeded classical shaft surrounded by a ring of veined marble columns in Decorated style. Beyond two C13 grave slabs are clamped to the w. wall, one with a fine floriated cross. The **nave roof** is **arch- braced** and the main timbers are surprisingly badly placed in relation to two window arches on the s. side. There are large angel corbels now painted in a variety of sickly colours. Many monuments were transferred from the old church and the first to be seen is an anonymous fragment of a large design which now rests on a window sill at the w. end of the nave; a trio of well nourished **putti** drape a garland round an urn carved with the profile of a lady. At the e. end, on the same side, is a monument to Jane, the artist wife of Sir William Hotham, who died in 1855; large **acanthus** scrolls

flank the tilted **capital** of a column surrounded by mallet, chisels, a palette and brushes. The n. **transept** is now a side chancel but was built to house the memorials of the Lords of the Manor - the Pettiwards and the Wollastons. On the n. wall is a 6 ft by 4 ft bas relief of the Good Samaritan under a **pediment** carved with the Chi Rho **sacred monogram**. Sculpted by **Sir Robert Westmacott**, it commemorates Roger Pettiward who died in 1833, a Fellow of the Linnean Society and, in a local capacity, commandant of the militia. To the r. is a handsome marble tablet in the form of a large open book resting on a cherub's head within outstretched wings. The Latin inscription has lost most of its colour and is consequently hard to read but it is for William Woolaston and his wife. He died in 1724 and was a moral philospher whose doctrines anticipated many C20 beliefs. His major work was *The Religion of nature Delineated*, first published in 1724 and noteable for its literary elegance. He was an ordained priest but having inherited a comfortable fortune he lived secluded, for the most part, in London. The tablet with a draped urn against a black triangle is by John de carle of Norwich for another William Woolaston who died in 1797. On the transept w. wall are bas relief portrait medallions of William and Elizabeth Wollaston (1769) and opposite, a large putto lets fall a scroll from his waist bearing the epitaph of Charles Wollaston who died in 1729. The **chancel screen** has angular lattice tracery and on it stands a small cross bearing an ivory figure of Christ, with attendant statues of the **Blessed Virgin** and **St John**. The **piscina** and **sedilia** are in the Decorated style and there is a satisfying range of **Clayton & Bell** glass in the chancel, s. nave and w. windows.

Great Livermere, St Peter (D4): The church stands just within the park and the view to the w. takes in the lake and the ivy-covered ruins of Little Livermere church, with its tall tower a little distance away. The plain early C14 tower now has a weatherboarded belfry with a pyramid top and the **Decorated tracery** in the w. window contains the popular four-petalled motif above a pair of **ogee** arches. The plain, blocked n. doorway dates from about 1200 and all the **nave** windows have Decorated tracery. In the **chancel** is **low side windows** on each side, also with Decorated tracery, the lower sections having been filled in. On the n. side is a heavy C19 flint and white brick **vestry**. The e. window has renewed tracery under a four-centred arch with a deep **label**, and there is a small **quatrefoil** opening over it. The blocked **lancets** in the s. wall of the chancel shows that it was built originally in the C13, although the three-**light** window is late Decorated, there is a simple **priest's door**. The whole of the outside has recently been rendered with plaster, including the battlemented s. **porch** which is quite without ornament. To the e. it stands a very interesting headstone, with a curly **cartouche** edge, over the grave of William Sakings. He was 'forkner [falconer] to King Charles ye 1st, King Charles ye 2nd, King James ye 2nd' and died in 1689. Alongside is a smaller and more rudimentary stone for his son Edmund, who died in 1682 aged 17. The porch has an **arch-braced roof**, stone seats and tall **Perpendicular** side windows. The nave roof is plastered over and there are modern benches below. On the wall by the organ there are two large C14 painted figures which were probably part of a **Three Living and Three Dead**. There are three **consecration crosses** on the s. wall and one on the n. There is a section of wall painting at the e. end of the nave on the s. side which **Cautley** described as a post-**Reformation** Christ, but now only a foot and a hand can be seen. Just inside the door, a portion of the deep **stoup** bowl remains under its worn

trefoil arch, and there is a coarsely cut wooden set of **Royal Arms** over the blocked n. door. The panels of the large C14 octagonal **font** contain one shield in a quatrefoil and a variety of tracery shapes, including a complete Decorated window design; the cover is modern. The plain niche halfway down the nave on the n. side may be the remains of a C13 lancet. Beyond it is the top half of an elaborate image niche which has an oddly shaped canopy with a **crocketted** ogee arch beneath Perpendicular tracery and small side pinnacles; there are remains of blue background colour. The **three-decker pulpit** is a solidly handsome late C17 example in oak, with a minisule **clerk's** enclosure facing w., and a broad band of carved **acanthus** below the canted ledge of the reading desk. The stocky pulpit has the same motif in a deep moulding round the top. On the opposite side of the nave is a Decorated **piscina** with a tiny recess to the r. It is rebated to take a door and might, therefore, be an **aumbry**, but there is a hole drilled in the bottom and another in the arch which is puzzling. The early C15 **screen** has buttresses crocketted at rail level, those by the entrance being coloured red and gold and the bottom crockets carved as grotesque heads. The two panels on the n. side have original diaper decoration but the woorwork as a whole is fairly coarse and there has been a good deal of replacement. This, however, has not extended to the extensive worm damage on the s. side of the base. You will see where the chancel arch was drilled to hold the **tympanum**. On either side there are moulded **corbels** which supported the **rood beam**. There is another consecration cross on the s. wall of the chancel and opposite, a medieval bench with blind tracery on the ends and half **poppyheads**. In front of it, the stall has roughly carved ends and bears the initials of either the maker, the donor or the churchwarden of 1601. Like nearby Ixworth Thorpe, the **commu-**

nion rails are three-sided, but here they are a very nice Georgian set, with turned and carved delicate spiral **balusters**, and **Corinthian capitals** to the corner shafts from which the top rails drop away in a gentle curve. What is most unusual is that both the **altar** and the **reredos** match the rails, employing spiral turning and Corinthian capitals in their designs. The chancel roof is arch-braced with **king posts**, and the very deep **wall plates** are finely pierced with tracery. Over the priest's door, on the s. side, is a length of C14 wall decoration - thin scrollwork in red and there is a faint painted shelf high on the e. wall. Below is a plain lancet piscina and to the r., a brick recess that was probably an aumbry. The e. window is flanked by large niches that were extensively renewed in the C19. The vestry door on the n. side lies within a much larger Perpendicular arch that has leaf carving in the small **spandrels**. Its position suggests that it may originally have framed an **Easter sepulchre**.

Great Saxham, St Andrews (C5): The route to the church is a delightful lane which skirts the park and winds through wooded country. The churchyard with tall red brick walls to the s. and w. is blissfully peaceful and when I was there barnyard fowls with broods of chicks were foraging among the headstones. The early C15 unbuttressed tower has a **trefoil lancet** to the w., a narrow lancet above it, and a stair turret to the belfry on the s. side. The church was largely rebuilt by its patron Thomas Mills in 1798. In the 1820s, new windows were inserted in the **nave**. then a **vestry** on the n. side of the **chancel** and a new **Perpendicular** e. window followed. The medieval s. **porch** was not altered and the side windows have deep sills awith seats below. The roof is original and there are the remains of a cross on the gable. The oldest survivals here are the **Norman** doorways - attached shafts with elementary leaf **corbels** on

the n. and a perfectly plain arch on the s. The C15 **font** has a plain shaft and **cusped** lozenges with centre rosettes in the bowl panels. Over the s. door is a very dark **Royal Arms** of Queen Anne dated 1702 and painted on boards, while a Mills family **hatchment** hangs over the n. door. One of the features of Great Saxham is the continental glass collected by William Mills and installed by his father Thomas in 1815, the year of Waterloo. It originally filled the e. window and one of the s. chancel windows, but some was transferred to the tower lancet - bright little Swiss panels depicting the Virgin and Child, Christ's baptism, the three Maries at the tomb, and a scourging. One of the many fragments is dated 1630 and there are bands of brillantly coloured miniature shields. Medieval bench ends with leaf **finials** are to be found at the back of the church and the manorial pew opposite the pulpit has large **poppyheads**. The centres of the C17 front panels are carved with cherub heads and the Mills' coat of arms, while the rear seat has two **renaissance** panels. Above it is a simple scroll tablet by Gaffin for William Mills who collected the glass and who died in 1859. The small **Stuart** pulpit has two ranges of typical blind arch panels and stands on a later base. Close by is an elegant and deeply carved stone **cartouche** in late C17 style set against black marble for Sir Christopher Magnay who died in 1960. The chancel e. window is filled with the rest of the French and Swiss glass and there are many figures, coats of arms and fragmnts. Look in particular for the Swiss **Pietà** in the top of the centre **light**. In his *Principall Navigations, Voiages and Discoveries of the English Nation* Richard Hakluyt described the travels of that fascinating Elizabethan, John Eldred, who died aged 80 in 1632. As Lord of the Manor, he lied buried here. Originally his tomb was on the s. side of the **sanctuary** but now his **brass** is in the centre of the chancel.

The 20 in effigy is in perfect condition and almost certainly a portrait; he wears cap and ruff, doublet, trunk hose and fur-lined gown. There are Latin and English inscriptions and the eight shields of arms link his family with his status as a merchant. Along the top from l. to r. are the arms of Eldred, Eldred impaling Rivett, and Rivett (his wife's family who used trivets as a pun). On the l. of the slab are the arms of the City of London, on the r., his guild, the Clothworkers. At the bottom on the l. is the East India Company (with all the ship's pennants streaming against the wind!), Levant Merchants in the centre, and the Russia Merchants Company on the r. On the s. wall of the sanctuary is a portrait bust of Eldred in a circular niche, re-coloured and gilded, with arms in an oval above and an epitaph on a separate **touchstone** tablet below. The sculptor of the bust is not known but on the basis that the border is characteristic of Maximillan Colt's work it has been attributed to him by a leading authority. Eldred was in Arabia for five years and came back in the year of the Armada bearing the first nutmegs in 'the richest ship that ever was known to this realm'.

> ...the Holy Land so called I have seene,
> And in the land of Babilon have bene.

But the inscription on the brass by his son ends:

> But Riches can noe ransome buy
> Nor Travells passe ye destiny.

He may, I suppose, have had his fill of travellers' tales from his father!

Great Thurlow, All Saints (B6): The church stands on a rise above the infant River Stour in this attractive village. There is an outstanding collection of C18 and early C19 headstones in the churchyard. In particular, seek out Mary Traylen's n.w. of the tower; the oval at the top is

Great Thurlow, All Saints: tombstone

a naive carving of a corpse, with a figure drawing the curtain against the skeletal figure of Death armed with a spear. To the s. of the tower Elizabeth Snazell's stone has the symbol of reversed torches against a sauceboat funerary urn, and there are others nearby with reversed trumpets. The work of this rustic sculptor can be found in a number of local churchyards. The church has been very heavily restored, with all windows renewed, and the w. belfry window of the late C14 tower is pure C19 invention. Nevertheless, it is a handsome building, with lots of **septaria** in the walls. The tower sports a lead-sheathed open bell turret topped by a pretty wrought-iron weathervane. The clue to an early foundation can be seen at the corners of the **chancel** - little **Norman** shafts carved in the **quoins**. The squared-off restored n. **porch** is very small and the C14 entrance has a medieval door with a C13 oval closing ring on which are riveted two lizards like those at Withersfield, ancient emblems of good fortune.

There is a **sanctus-bell window** above the tower arch, and a modern ringers' gallery in **Jacobean** style has been inserted. The Norman **font** is a massive square with slightly canted sides, carved with a varying arrangement of blank arches and there are nook shafts at the corners. The C15 **arcade** is very plain; there are no **capitals** to the lozenge-shaped **piers**, and above is a **clerestory** with four widely spaced windows on each side. The roofs are modern and three magnificent chandliers hang in the **nave**. Are they C19 Austrian or Russian? The s. **aisle** has an early 1900s window by J. Cameron - the **Blessed Virgin** and **St Elizabeth** with a young **St John the Baptist**. Beyond the very attractive modern **parclose screen** there is a C14 **piscina** in the aisel chapel, and above it the window contains four medieval glass shields with modern name labels. James Vernon's arms are in a fine baroque shield at the top of the e. window and the inscription tells us that he was Lord of the Manor and 'repaired and beautified this church in 1741'.A similar message and arms below relate to Ronald Arthur Vestey's work in 1956. To the l. there is a long **squint** through the wall giving a view of the **high altar**. To the r. is a large oval alabaster tablet for Florence Vestey, with arms at the top in coloured metal and a fighting dove below cast in polished aluminium. The octagonal pulpit is early C17 with typical blind arches in the top panels, and modern base and steps. All the chancel fittings are modern and include a large classical **reredos** in blue and gold, with kneeling, gilded **putti** holding candlesticks on top. Beyond, the e. window has modern glass - Christ the King, **St Michael** with his sword and scales on one side. **St Catherine** with other saints on the other side, and purple- winged cherubim aloft. All are bright and light but strangely wooden. There are restored medieval angels in the s.

chancel window, as well as **Evangelistic symbols**. In the n. aisle is an early 1900s **Kempe & Co** window portraying **St Cecilia** and two musical angels. In the s.e. corner of the **sanctuary** is an interesting **brass** which probably commemorates John and Margery Gedding of about 1470. He was the Lord of the Manor and his armour is a good example of the Yorkist period. The effigy is unusual in that he wears his helmet and carries his sword slung behind him. His wife's mantle and veil **head-dress** shows that she was left a widow; her dog crouches underfoot wearing a bell collar. On a nearby slab is the brass of Thomas Underhill who died in 1508 and who probably built the tower. Only his torso survives, dressed in **Tudor** armour with a helm behind his head, but the 18 in figure of his wife Anne is complete. (She was a Drury. Two shields of arms remain, as well as a plate of nine sons (the daughters' plate has vanished). Another **ledger- stone** on the n. side of the chancel has a single shield left of four, and may mark the frave of John Blodwell (1534) and his wife Ann.

Great Whelnetham, St Thomas à Becket (D5): The building is finished in depressing grey pebble dash (apart from the n. **aisle** which is cement rendered). There are two **Norman lancets** under the eaves of the **nave** on the s. side and another in the n. wall at the w. end. One of the **quoins** of the s.e. corner is carved with a serpent that might well be **Saxon**. At the w. of the nave are more high-level windows, but of the C14, and there is a circular window in the w. wall enclosing a **quatrefoil**. The n. aisle, with its Gothick window **tracery**, was built in 1839, replacing an earlier chapel, and the C13 **chancel** has three of its original lancets on that side, C14 windows and **priest's door** to the s., and a C19 e. window. There was money left in 1453 for the building of a tower but the church has only a white weather-board bell turret of 1749, topped with a decorative weather-vane. The outer doors of the **porch** are ugly plywood but the roof timbers (with prominent joint pegs) are late medieval and pieces of C14 tracery have been used to build the side window. The inner door is medieval too and the doorway has one **headstop** remaining. A C19 **sanctuary** lamp has been converted and hung overhead to light the porch. A **Stuart Holy table** stands just inside and the blocked n. doorway frames a very decorative collage of the church's patron saint. The C14 two-bay **arcade** opens into the C19 n. aisle and the **font** is sited there - octagonal, with quatrefoils, centre **paterae** and two blank shields in the bowl panels. The pulpit is modern but it makes use of panels which date from about 1520. They are similar to those in the Hawstead pulpit not far away. On the other side of the nave is a very small late C13 double **piscina** under a single **trefoil** arch. Further w. are three rather dull C19 tablets for members of the Phillips family - two by Farrow and one by de Carle of Bury. The nave **roof** has simple **arch-braces** and it would seem that the chancel arch was rebuilt as part of of the C19 restoration of the chancel. The n. **vestry** is medieval and has a curiously angled entrance. The early C18 monument for Charles Batteley on the n. wall is a peculiar design, with a mottled marble sarcophagus standing on a bulky oblong block, with draped marble behind and above it. Much nicer is the **touchstone** and alabaster memorial in the sanctuary for Richard Gipps who died in 1660; there is a **cartouche** within the broken **pediment** and a large bas relief skull and crossbones below. On the s. side, a late C13 double piscina under a plain arch stands next to low **sedilia** with finely moulded arches and well formed shafts. The e. window is a World War I memorial with glass by **Burlison & Grylls**. The standing figures are a slightly unusual selection - King David, **St George, St Nicholas**

and Joan of Arc, and there are scenes from each of their stories below. The sanctuary s. window contains some interesting medieval fragments - two female heads, **quarries** painted with little birds having texts in their beaks saying 'Jhu Magi' (Lord Jesus) and 'Jhu Help', and large shields bearing the arms of Raynsford impaling Brokesborne.

Great Wratting, St Mary (B6): The church has a very attractive setting among mature trees, with a path from the handsome **lynch-gate** rising over the sloping churchyard to the s. door. There is a memorable exercise in topiary along the road frontage, where bushes of the box hedge have been shaped into a chair, a chruch, a cross, and a diverting whirligig by the other gate. The church was subjectewd to rigorous restoration in the C19 and the majority of the windows, the s. door, and the **priets's door** have been renewed. The buttresses and lower walls of the **chancel** are original C13 work and there are a lot of **septaria** with thin (possibly Roman tiles on the s. side. The tower has restored **Decorated** bell openings and it was repaired at some time at the top in red brick. There is a belfry stair to the s., and a line on the e. face shows where the original **nave** roof stretched. Sheltered by a **porch**, the handsome **Tudor** n. doorway has **quatrefoils** in the **spandrels** and the door itself is medieval. Within, the tower arch is very tall and thin with no **imposts**, and the organ is tucked in below. The massive C14 **font** is a plain octagon with slightly canted sides. The nave bench are good-looking modern work with **linen-fold** panelling in the ends. Overhead, a modern waggon roof is separated from the **scissors-braced** chancel roof by a curious **cusped** division which has a **tie-beam** above the spandrels. The **screen** below is again good quality modern work in oak, with a coved cornice. The wide, **crocketted** arch has little heads and roses at the ends of the cusps and there are more in the **tracery** of the **lights**. A handsome wooden lectern keeps up the standard, and behind the pulpit is a **piscina** under a shaped and pierced **trefoil**. Above it and on the opposite wall there are stone **corbels** which will have supported the front of the **rood loft**. The recess beyond the pulpit is probably all that remains of the stair to the loft. In the **sanctuary** there are two large **aumbries** behind the altar and an attractive C13 suite of piscina and stepped **sedilia**, with triple-shafted columns and deeply moulded arches, the piscina has an unusually heavy stone **credence shelf** and a deep drain. Across on the n. side stands a good and solid late C17 chest the colour of brown ale, decorated with marquetry vases and foliage in the front three panels. The three stepped **lancets** of the e. window are filled with 1870s glass by Constable of Cambridge - the crucified Christ in the centre, a Nativity **Blessed Virgin** and Child to the l., and the risen Lord to the r. The figures are formalised and the paint is deteriorating in places. I think the side lancets have Constable glass too, but wartime bomb damage called for extensive replacement.

Hargrave, St Edmund (C5): Half a mile n. of Hargrave Green a long cul-de-sac of a lane leads to the Old Rectory and a farm, with the church hidden behind them. It is a quiet and peaceful place, with rabbits popping in and out of the hedges. Until relatively recently there was a s. **porch** but now the simple late C12 doorway, with small nooks at the spring of the arch, is open to the weather. There is a **Tudor** brick window to the l. and by the **priest's door** in the **chancel**, one with **Perpendicular tracery**. The **lancets** are C19 and the n. **aisle**, with its long and low-pitched roof, was added in 1869. The tower is in Tudor red brick with a stair turret on the s. side. A Perpendicular w. window was re-used, its stonework now being decayed. Within is a **stoup** to the r. of the door with half its bowl gone, and to the l. there is a niche with no obvious purpose. There are two simple **box pews** at the w. end and the C15 **font** has blank shields within the **quatrefoils** of the bowl panels and long, slightly curved chamfers down to the plain shaft. With the exception of the **tie-beam** at the w. end, the roof and benches are unremarkable C19 work but the C15 **rood screen** is of some interest, despite its mutilation. All the **cusps** of the wide **ogee** arches are broken off and the front **crocketting** has been stripped away. There are still **paterae** on the top rail but the canopy has gone. The **spandrels** over the entrance are carved with a king's head and an eagle but the unusual feature is the carving on the e. side where there is normally little decoration. There you will see bold and interesting designs, uncommonly large - a fox with a goose in its mouth, a **wyvern**, two fish, two dragons, a **unicorn**, and the head of a man wearing a cap. Above the **screen** the **rood beam** remains, decorated with a line of chevron and **billet** moulding. At the e. end of the nave, on the s. side, there is a plain image niche in the window splay. In the **sanctuary**, the arches of the C13 angle **piscina** have been renewed and there are plain, stepped **sedilia** alongside. On the walls, the C18 **decalogue**, Belief and Lord's Prayer boards are attractively painted in gold and two shades of grey.

Harleston, St Augustine (F5): This is not a common dedication, being one of two in the county. Prettily placed outside the village by the lane that leads to Haughley, a track leads up across a meadow to the churchyard surrounded by a scattering of Scots pine. The little church has no break between **nave** and **chancel** and its thatched roof runs in an unbroken line from end to end. The small **Norman** s. doorway has a plain arch on square **imposts** although the n. doorway is blocked, a section of its arch remains embedded in the masonry. There is a pair of renewed **lancets** and one tall, deep-set lancet in the s. wall of the nave; the C13 chancel has a **trefoil**-headed lancet on that side. The e. window is C19 and there is a single lancet on the n. side. The w. end was rebuilt in the C19 and given a pair of lancets below a foiled circular window, with a wooden bellcote perched on the gable. Within, there is a plain octagonal C14 **font** and a plastered ceiling, with two exposed **tie-beams**, runs the length of the building. The pews and openwork pulpit are Victorian, but the **screen** is C14 and a good one. The uprights between the main **lights** are turned shafts echoing the prevailing style in stone and the centre arch is a broad **ogee**. The deep **spandrels** are filled with **tracery mouchettes** within roundels and the original plain panels remain below the centre rail. The C13 **piscina** in the **sanctuary** has a simple trefoil arch, and although everything else is C19 it was well done. The stall ends carry four lovely kneeling angels with their hands masking bowed faces and their wings raised. A band of tiles decorated with alternating **sacred monograms** and chalices runs under the e. window and the sanctuary floor of Minton tiles displays the **Evangelistic symbols** in blue roundels within large lozenges. In all, this would be a lovely place to celebrate a Harvest Festival.

Hartest, All Saints (C6): The church nestles attractively with the village in a little valley which is quite steep sided for this part of the world. The tower is C14 with a renewed w. window, but the red brick and flint mixture at the top is a reminder that it collapsed onto the **nave** and **aisles** one October Sunday in 1650, 'by which fall a great part of said church is beaten down and the rest much shaken'. Repairs were soon put in hand and the C14

arcades of the nave were rebuilt, the walls lowered, and a new **roof** provided. The n. aisle, with its **transomed Perpendicular** windows, is C15 and although the lean-to **vestry** has been restored, it has a small C13 **lancet**. To the l. of it is a small stone set in the wall which is carved with a tun (i.e. a barrel) and is probably a **rebus** for a name like Shelton - no doubt moved from elsewhere. In the churchyard not far away is a stone which is either the base of a **preaching cross** or a leftover from the C17 rebuilding. The short **chancel** and much of the s.e. Lady chapel was reconstructed in the late 1870s and the **priest's door** has recently been converted into a picture window. The C19 s. porch shelters an **Early English** doorway, and in the corner an angled **stoup** has the remains of a head **corbel** below. This was the main entrance originally but a new n. **porch** was added in the C16, probably at the behest of John Phillipson who asked to be buried there with his wife Anna in 1546 (the two small shields in the **spandrels** carry their initials). Like the s. porch, it is virtually all in squared **knapped** flints and was over-restored by the Victorians. Its cambered **tie-beam** roof is heavily carved, and note the chalice and wafer shield on the spandrel to the l. of the medieval door.

There is a C19 **font** just inside and the short nave, with its three-bay arcade, has a roof which is a Victorian replica of the C17 predecessor. The benches are pitch-pine but those in the n. aisle have oak **linen-fold** panels that may have been saved from an earlier set. The bench at the front of the s. range has well-carved C15 **tracery** which probably came from the old **rood screen**, but note that it is backed by C17 panelling decorated with various shallow roundels and the initials 'R.P.' (another Phillipson?). There is a tall **Stuart** pulpit with four ranges of panels which was cleaned as part of the restoration and given a new base. The simple **piscina** at the e. end of the s. aisle is Early English but the one on the n. side is C14, retaining half of its **crocketted** canopy and placed unusually on the last **pier** of the nave arcade. Before leaving the nave, note the square of C18 roofing lead on the s. wall cast with churchwardens' names and a handsome **hatchment** above the tower door. This is for Thomas Hallifax of Chadacre Hall who died in 1850 and whose monument is in the s. aisle at Shimpling. The only memorial here of consequence is by Henry Westmacott in the n. aisle - a sail carved as a drape to carry the epitaph of Lieut James Harrington RN, who was 'entombed in a distant land' in 1812. (Not how most would describe Miñorca nowadays!) There are **Tudor** arches at the e. end of the aisles and the chancel arch was rebuilt in the 1870s, along with the arch to the organ chamber on the n. side, where the rich leaf-trail carving in the roof recalls that it was once a chapel. The **sanctuary** has a Victorian blind arcade **reredos** and the piscina, in its shapeless recess, was originally sited in a window sill. After all the chancel's vicissitudes there is still a medieval door leading to the vestry. The glass in the priest's door has made the s. chapel very light and two of the brackets from the medieval nave roof have been fixed to the wall - one supporting a **credence** table. The **altar** is starkly modern in stained black, with the top resting on a pair of box frames.

Haughley, The Assumption of the Virgin (F5): The official dedication of the church is to **St Mary**, without qualification, but until 1871 there was a yearly Toy Fair in the village on 15 August, the Feast of the Assumption, and that supports the belief that the specific dedication is valid. The late C13 tower is on the s. side and has massive **gargoyles** in the plain parapet; its ground floor frames the entrance **porch** and there is 'Y' **tracery** both in the bell openings and in the porch, with thick diagonal but-

tresses to the s. The s. **aisle** windows have attractive **Decorated** tracery and the aisle e. window offers an interesting variation - each **reticulation** shape is quartered, with a small lozenge in the centre. The **chancel** is early C14 (witness the **priest's door**) but all the windows are **Perpendicular**, as are those on the n. side of the **nave** (with the exception of one with Decorated tracery at the e. end). A small **sanctus-bell turret** crowns the nave gable. Over the outer entrance arch of the porch is a wooden lintel on which is carved 'C.H. 1699 T.W.' - no doubt churchwardens' initials with the date of repairs or alterations to the tower. The handsome late C13 inner doorway is deeply moulded and has pairs of attached columns with ring **capitals**.

The carving on the octagonal C15 **font** is exceptionally deeply cut and it is intriguing that the bowl panels are not aligned as usual to the cardinal **points** but placed diagonally. They contain the **Evangelistic symbols**, together with angels holding shields carved with the **Trinity** emblem, **St Edmund's** arms, three chalices and wafers, and the cross of **St George**. There are angel heads below the bowl, and against the shaft are lions and **woodwose**, with no two alike. The early C16 s. aisle **roof** is splendid and has angels with delicately spread wings on the **wall posts**; most of them hold books or scrolls but two, towards the e. end, are playing theorbos. The main timbers are all crested, the **spandrels** carved, there are centre **bosses**, and the **wall plates** at the e. end are carved with more angels. In the late C14, there was a chapel of the Holy Cross in the church which attracted pilgrims and the present aisle chapel has taken that dedication on the assumption that the original was there. There is a large **piscina** with a **cinquefoiled** head, and **dropped-sill sedilia** alongside. The 1860s glass in the e. window is by J. & J. King of Norwich, and the artist was the young Thomas Scott who went on to become the firm's chief designer. It is a consciously medieval design across all four panels, illustrating the raising of Jairus' daughter - pale colour with most figures in profile. The octagonal **piers** of the **arcade** rest on square bases that may have been part of the original s. wall before the aisle was built. There is a Perpendicular **clerestory** on both sides and money was left to build a n. aisle, but the will was successfully contested and the work was never done. The nave roof has alternate cambered **tie-beams** and **arch- braces**, and there are huge flower- er bosses reminiscent of snow crystals. In the large Perpendicular w. window there are two interesting medieval glass shields - the three crowns of East Anglia and the arms of Thomas Beaufort, earl of Dorset, who was John of Gaunt's son and grandson of Edward I. All the fittings are C19 and the chancel was largely reconstructed in the 1870s; it now has a barrel roof which follows the curve of the e. window arch. In the **sanctuary** is a nice square-headed piscina, the **cusped ogee** arch having blind **trefoils** in the spandrels. For those interested in heraldry there are five **hatchments**: w. wall, s. side, the Rev Richard Ray, vicar here for 55 years, and dying at a great age in 1758; w. wall, n. side, Elizabeth Tyrell, his daughter (1826); n. wall, w. end, William Crawford of Haughley Park (1835); n. wall, e. of **vestry** door, Richard Ray (1811); over the pulpit, Sir George Wombwell (1780). Before you go, have a look at the leather fire buckets hanging on the wall at the e. end. They are dated 1725 and 1728 and at one time 30 of them hung in the porch, readily available for use in the village.

Haverhill, St Mary (A7): On the High Street and cheek by jowl with the busy market place, the church suffered with the rest of the town in the disastrous fire of 1665 when it was reduced to a shell. Then in 1866 the Decorated **nave arcades** were rebuilt, the C14 **chancel** arches through to the Lady chapel re-opened, and other work was carried out in an attempt to restore the church to its original form. The tower, with its tall and narrow bell openings, has a prominent s.e. stair turret characteristic of the area, with **Evangelistic symbols** at the corners of the battlements. There is a blocked C13 **lancet** in the n. wall of the chancel and, as a change from the usual grotesques, the nave **gargoyles** are good carvings of demi-figures, best seen on the s. side. There is a line of **paterae** below the s. **aisle** parapet and on the **porch** which is the main entrance. Within, the w. end has been adapted by inserting a low ceiling and a folding, glazed screen to form a community area. The base of the tower is now a fitted kitchen. A glazed section of the ceiling peaks up to the tower arch and the church's two **hatchments** are just visible above, but not clearly enough to describe - a pity because one of them is out of the ordinary. Entry to the church proper is from a vestibule and through a **screen** which is, like much of the modern work here, a product of local craftsmen. Below the flat **roof** of the nave there is a **Perpendicular clerestory** with four large windows each side and, over the tower arch, a **sanctus-bell window**. In the s. aisle, two of the windows have glass by Percy Bacon, a glazier active at the turn of the century - large figures of **Saints John, Paul, Peter, James the Great, James the Less, Bartholomew, Simon** and **Jude**. The designs are conventional and surrounded by dense canopy work. There is a C16 chest with **linen-fold panelling** and three locks in the Lady chapel. The Mothers' Union banner is a lovely piece of work designed by Leslie Moore and made by the Wareham Guild - appliqué outlined with thread and the flesh painted. The restored late Perpendicular **font** now stands at the e. end of the n. aisle and its cover was designed in 1967 by Sir Frederick Gibberd, architect of Liverpool's Roman Catholic cathedral and planner of Haverhill's post-war expansion. Counter-weighted, its close-set fins radiate from the centre and rise to a brass **finial**. There is another Percy Bacon window nearby, a conventional but pleasing composition of Christ with a child on his knee and other figures grouped around. Below stands a fine late C18 headstone brought in from outside, and further to the w. is a tablet for the aged spinster Johanna Atkinson of London and bears a long and mellifluous epitaph in C18 mode. There is now no chancel **screen** but to the l. of the entrance is a small doorway with a Decorated arch which led to the original **rood loft stair**. The panelled roof of the chancel was decorated by **Heaton, Butler & Bayne** and in the sanctuary there is a restored **piscina** and a totally iron-clad chest. By the door to the **vestry** is an interesting and eccentrically designed memorial for John Ward, a C16 vicar here. There is coarse strapwork round the small panel, and within the steep gable there is a Latin epitaph which Thomas Fuller in his *Worthies of England* translated:

> Grant some of knowledge greater store,
> More learned some in preaching;
> Yet few in life did lighten more,
> None thundered more in preaching.

The little portrait in oils, dated 1622, to the l. is of his eldest son Samuel who became the Puritan lecturer here, and then for many years at St Mary le Tower, Ipswich. Fuller described him as an excellent artist, divine, linguist and preacher, and the portrait, like his father's memorial, is labelled 'Watch and Warde'.

Hawkedon, St Mary (C6): The church is not large but stands quite proudly in the centre of a broad, sloping green, fringed with scattered houses and barns. in common with a number of others locally, the C14 tower, with its tall bell openings, is angular rather than graceful (an effect caused by the spread of the e. face across the buttresses and an abrupt stair turret on the n. side). There are no **aisles** and the **nave** has a C14 n. door, **Perpendicular** windows, and a C15 brick **rood stair** to the n., covered by a little continuation of the main roof - much nicer than the gaunt C19 furnace chimney alongside. The C14 **chancel** has a later e. window and quite a lot of early graffiti can be found in the mouldings of the **priest's door**. Completing the circuit, there is a **scratch dial** on the buttress nearest the attractive s. **porch**. The entrance is very weather-worn but a **stoup** nestles under a canopy in the angle of the corner buttress (as at Denston) and a triplet of small niches fills the gable. it would seem that it was re-roofed in the C15 and given a battlemented parapet of brick, with a pretty frieze of moulded brick blind arches along the sides below. The cambered roof has a heavy carved **wall plate** over the **Early English** inner door and there is a roughly-shaped recess in the corner that housed an earlier stoup.

The 1912 **gallery** at the w. end was designed by Detmar Blow (an architect better known for his houses). From it, a fragmentary wall painting on the n. wall may be examined at close quarters; it probably formed part of a **St Christopher** over the n. door, but nothing can be identified now. In its place hangs the **hatchment** of Philip Hamond of Hawkedon Hall who died in 1779, which has careless heraldry. By the stairs is another for John Oliver. The third hatchment of 1708, over the entrance, is Edmund Plume's; it is in a frame roughly painted with crossed bones and skulls. The square **Norman font** had two corners of the bowl removed later and the shallow carving is much more developed on the n. and w. sides. The nave **roof** has two **arch-braced tie-beams** and **castellated wall plates**, while below there is a fine range of C15 benches with heavy sills raised on brick ledges. The **poppyheads** are carved with a diversity of forms: to the n. of the font is a lovely little figure of a lady, and towards the front on the same side, three heavily moustached faces under conical hats combine effectively. There has been some careful restoration and the three benches at the e. end on both sides are modern. On the s. wall hangs a handsome set of **Royal Arms** painted on boards - close enough for you to see how the 'C' for Charles II was painted out and George II's 'G' substituted in 1750. In between, Queen Anne's motto had been added and removed but the parish baulked at the complications of the heraldry and the quarterings are still **Stuart**. The blocked door to the rood stair shows on the n. side and opposite is a simple **Jacobean** pulpit, with small strapwork panels under the rim. Beneath the nave carpet at the e. end is a very worn **brass** - 16 in figures of an early C16 man and wife, he in furred gown with a large rosary, she in **kennel head-dress**, with her girdle drooping to the weight of book and rosary. There are small plates of five daughters and three sons but the inscription has gone. The mutilated base of the **rood screen** is still in place and the outer panels seem never to have been painted, so nave **altars** doubtless stood against them. The **tracery** in the other panels was of high quality and there are shadowy figures of saints. Enough remains to identify **St Dorothy** on the far r., with another female saint beside her, and the pair on the n. side were identified as **St James** and **St John** at the turn of the century. It is likely that the chunky tracery fronting the s. choir stalls in the chancel came from the vanished **rood loft** and there is an unusual chained bear carved on top of the sloping and (the complementary beaver opposite is modern). The late C17 **altar rails** are excellent, with diminishing twist **balusters** closely set, and the small early Stuart **Holy table** is now used as a cre-

Hawkedon, St Mary: poppyhead

dence. The church's ancient glass has recently been collected and re-set in the s. window. There are C17 continental panels at the top: from l. to r. **Saints Matthew, Andrew, Paul** and **James the Great**; a fine Royal Arms of Richard III within the Garter is in the centre and there are three panels of fragments. it is a shame that the C15 wall painting over the window has faded into obscurity because it was a rare representation of the Transfiguration and was injudiciously restored in 1938. A C16 priest left his mark in the embrasure to the l. of the chancel door: 'John Lah-dnge curate of Hawkedon anno 1583'. Turning w., one is confronted by the completely pagan Everard monumewnt of 1678 in the angle by the chancel arch - a **touchstone** tablet flanked by **Corin-**

thian columns, urns with a **cartouche** and heavy swags on top, together with flamboyant **putti** on either side. the choirmen's hat pegs jutting out below seem to redress the balance somehow.

Hawstead. All Saints (D5): The village is small but the church is impressive, standing proudly in a large churchyard with a massive early C16 tower whose stair turret reaches above the battlements on the s. side. Over the w. door a line of shields includes five that are charged with arms of the Drury family and alliances by marriage. The Tau cross (like a 'T') was added to the shield by a C14 Drury after a visit to the Holy Land, and the family's history is interwoven with this building. The **base course** of the tower is panelled in **flushwork**, with stars and interlace patterns to the w. and more flushwork in the stepped battlements, with a **pelican** and two crocks on the e. face. W. of the tower, a sundial has been mounted on a medieval stone shaft and on the n. side stands the remains of a **preaching cross**; the base has the remains of Drury shields and at one time it served as a step for the n. door. The **chancel** dates from about 1300 and has a variety of windows - a **lancet** and a two-**light** window with **Decorated tracery** on the n., a late C15 e. window, and a lancet as well as a late C13 window on the s., both of which are blocked. On that side there is also a **priest's door** and a C14 window with a **transom** that formed a **low side window** below. Like the **nave**, the s. **porch** dates from the late C15 and the **Norman** doorways, with their single shafts and **chevron mouldings**, were retained. The porch windows display an attractive selection of C19 shields of arms of local families - Drurys, Cullums and Metcalfes, and the early Drury obsession with badges even extended to the ring of the door handle.

There are no **aisles** but the nave is spacious, with a span of 30 ft. The large **Perpendicular** windows give plenty of light and their sills are lowered to form seats along the walls. The tower arch is tremendously tall and narrow, and within the tower hang five **hatchments** of the Metcalfe and Hammond families - C18 and C19. Below stands a C13 **font**, a plain, deep square on a C19 base, and the coved wooden cover carries a figure of **St John the Baptist**. The set of C17 **communion rails**, complete with gate, has been moved here and its dog-defying **balusters** and intervening uprights would have pleased Archbishop **Laud**. A pale, heavily banded C14 chest is nearby and over the n. door is a fine window (who is it by?). On each side of a Calvary it shows the kneeling figures of Joseph Hall, the persecuted bishop of Norwich, whose first cure of souls was the rectory here in 1601, and the Rev Sir John Cullum, a respected local antiquary and late C18 rector. Below, replica **brasses** are handily mounted for brass rubbers. The nave is spanned by a C16 **roof** which has been described as 'over-restored in 1858' but which is undeniably impressive. Angels, with their new raised wings, are carved on the **hammerbeams**, the **spandrels** are pierced with tracery, and the **collars** of the **arch-braces** support **king posts** to the ridge. There are double-depth **wall plates**, dragons carved on the braces and all the principal timbers carry a twisted roll decoration. At the w. end of the s. wall is a tablet for Claire Colville (1829) by Edward Hodges Baily, a successful sculptor whose vast output included the statues on the facade of the National Gallery. Here he is content with cleverly reproducing a crumpled sheet of paper in marble to carry a long and affecting epitaph. The nave is a good place to compare the merits of sculptor **John Bacon** with those of his son **John the Younger**. The father has a late work at the e. end of the n. side - a fine bas relief of Benevolence for Lucy Metcalfe (1793) - and the son sculpted the memorial for Mary Buckley, Viscountess Carleston (1810) on the s. side of the chancel arch - a female holding a pendent scroll while reclining on a sarcophagus. It's interesting that the son takes the father's favourite cliché of the **pelican** to fill a space in the corner. In his later years the younger Bacon went into partnership with Samuel Manning and the firm turned out masses of rather hackneyed pieces but those for members of the Metcalfe family here are rather better than average. The **Jacobean** family pew in the s.w. corner has some marquetry inlay and used to stand in the chancel arch. Also at the w. end are a few early C17 benches. In the corner beyond the organ is a faint C14 painting of a tall figure - probably a saint-bishop - which was discovered in the chancel and (such is the ingenuity of modern restorers) moved to its new site. The centre window on the n. side contains interesting fragments of medieval glass. There are five shields of arms (variants of Drury), the **Evangelistic symbols** in roundels, and two panels of continental glass (one of the Crucifixion is enamelled, dated 1530, and signed). The plum, however, is the roundel in the centre which shows the wolf finding **St Edmund's** head which cries 'Heer, heer, heer!'

In the wall n. of the chancel arch there is a C13 **piscina** and in the s.e. corner of the nave stands the tomb of Sir William Drury. The base is decorated with a line of **quatrefoils** with tracery panels of lozenges above. The worn **purbeck marble** top carries a fine brass, with 2 ft figures of the nobleman and his two wives Joanne and Elizabeth, each with a bible on a long cord. Elizabeth survived him and is shown with her eyes open. There are shields, a large inscription and a group of daughters, but the complementary clutch of sons has gone. Sir William was knighted by Edward VI and went on to serve Bloody Queen Mary as a Privy Counsellor before dying in 1557. We are lucky to see the brass because it was given to a collector in the 1860s and only returned to the church in 1909. Other brasses have been transferred to the wall behind - early C16 figures of a boy and girl and four shields from Roger Drury's grave of 1495. On this side the s.e. and s.w. windows have **Powells** glass designed by **Henry Holiday** in his own particular **pre-Raphaelite** style. The pulpit dates from about 1520 but has been over-enthusiastically restored and covered with glistening varnish. There are varying designs in the centre panels, **linen-fold** at the bottom and, at the top, the **Tudor** emblems of pomegranate, rose, and portcullis. There, too, are the ubiquitous arms of Drury, linked this time with Calthorpe. Sir Robert married Anne Calthorpe who died in 1513 and the couple lie buried in St Mary's Bury. Close by stands a rare example of a late C15 wooden lectern. It has been restored but retains the simple carving on the ends below the double slope and there are rudimentary buttresses formed where the square shaft becomes an octagon. The nave benches are C19 but the front range incorporates C16 **finials** which, like the pulpit, have been unkindly varnished. There is a collared beast with long jagged horns (**ibex?**), a grotesque, and two differing versions of the pelican. The heavily restored late C15 **screen** had a rood group added in 1906 but is remarkable for the very rare **sacring bell** that hangs on top of the s. side. It is conveniently close for the acolyte stationed by the low side window below; you will see that the latter still retains the hooks for the wooden shutter. The stained glass is a 1908 **Annunciation** in delicately pale and creamy colours by (possibly) Powells. In the quatrefoil at the top there is a small C15 Virgin and Child in yellow stain. The window opposite has glass by the A.K. Nicholson studios, with full length figures of **St George** and **St Géry**. There are low C16 stalls with a couple of **poppyheads**, and overhead

the roof is coved and painted with **sacred monograms**, the **Angus Dei** and chalice emblems. The e. window glass is worth noting as the earliest surviving example of the work of **Heaton, Butler & Bayne** dating from 1856. It is a fully pictorial Ascension scene across the whole arch, well drawn and using bright (one might say virulent) colours and grainy flesh tones.

Large monuments loom everywhere in the chancel and the earliest is the effigy of a knight (reputedly Sir Eustace Fitz-Eustace who died in 1271). Very little damaged, it lies cross legged with feet on a dumpy lion. The level of the early C14 tomb chest below shows how the floor has been raised over the years. The rounded C14 arch is decorated with encrusted foliage in a deep band. Within the arch is a disc of stone pierced at the centre and this may well be a turban finial from a Moslem grave, brought home from the Crusades as a trophy. On the n. side of the

sanctuary is the impressive monument to Sir Robert Drury, the earliest known example of **Nicholas Stone's** work in Suffolk. It has a severe sarcophagus in polished black marble with a death's head clasp, separated from the base by lion-masked pedestals. Polished columns with alabaster **capitals** flank double alabaster arches within which are **touchstone** tablets lettered in gold. Sir Robert was knighted by the Earl of Essex at Rouen in 1591, sailed in the Cadiz expedition of 1596, and died in 1615. The Richmond and Chester heralds saw him to his grave with ceremony and John Donne composed his epitaph. The bust in the oval at the top is of his father, Sir William (another soldier, who died after a duel in 1590). On the s. side of the sanctuary is the tomb of Sir Robert's daughter Elizabeth who died when only 14 in 1609. Donne sent her grieving parents the verses that were later called *A Funerall Elegie* and he almost certainly composed the Latin epitaph. The monument is

Hawstead, All Saints: Elizabeth Drury monument

by Gerard Christmas, carver to the Royal Navy and a sculptor of high reputation in James I's time. This is arguably the best of the effigies attributed to him. The alabaster figure of the young girl lies resting on one elbow with faintly smiling face, two collared hounds fawn at the sides of the tomb and her shield is carved within a wreath held by prancing **putti**. Had she not died young, Elizabeth would have been the bride of Henry, Prince of Wales. On the n. wall is Dudley Cullum's memorial (1720), a sensitive piece with excellent detailing by a local mason of quality, Robert Singleton of Bury and Norwich. The largest monument takes up most of the s. wall and is an extravangaza in painted plaster, mainly black. There is overblown heraldry at the top, freestanding pilasters and twin ovals with shields at each side and, at the centre a sarcophagus - all on a stone base. It was made by Jacinthe de Courcy, shipped by Sir Thomas Cullum from Italy to grace Hawstead Hall, and then used as his tomb in 1675 (strange that de Courcy should claim this work by scratching a little note on the n. pier of the chancel arch). It is almost a relief to return to quieter things and study the brass of Ursula Allington, a Drury daughter who died in about 1530. It is in the centre of the chancel and shows her wearing a **kennel head-dress**, with a long rosary and reticule at her belt.

Hengrave, Church of Reconciliation (C4): The calm serenity of this little church in an idyllic setting is memorable. It nestles unobtrusively in a bower of tall hedges and fine trees beside the great house built by Sir Thomas Kytson in the 1530s, and wisteria climbs the **chancel** wall. Its original patron saint is uncertain. In 1589, Hengrave was amalagated with the parish of Flempton and the church

became a family mausoleum until it was re-opened as a private chapel in 1901. So it continued until 1952 when the Sisters of the Assumption took over the Hall as a boarding school, and then in 1974 a community embracing different Christian denominations established it as an ecumenical retreat and conference centre, and the challenging dedication of Reconciliation was adopted for the church. The round tower is not tall, but it is over 12 ft across inside and its tapering shape, coupled with the layered masonry, mean that it is much more likely to be **Saxon** than **Norman**. There are small round windows in the base and an engaging single-handed clock set in a lozenge. The stair is C19. The 'Y' **tracery** of the chancel windows suggests a date of 1300 but part of the fabric there may be a century earlier. By the n. wall is the base of a **preaching cross**. A Gothic- lettered inscription over the s. door tells us that Sir Thomas Hemegrave and his mother Joan rebuilt the church (he died in 1419). Sir Thomas altered the **nave** in the early C16, and his widow added the n. chapel in 1540. The s. nave battlements have **quatrefoils** and the arms of the abbey of Bury. Just below, there is a frieze of lozenge tracery which continues along the chancel parapet. Beyond the pair of very tall **Perpendicular** windows, the **rood stair** bulges out in red brick. The **porch** has minor **flushwork** and the doorway displays the shields of Hemegrave and Harling a **unicorn**). Inside is a small, delicately canopied **stoup** and the inner door has a lovely arch whose mouldings are carved with crowns and **fleurons**, again with Hemegrave and Harling shields in the **spandrels** and angel **corbels** bearing **Passion emblem** shields (the r. hand one is renewed).

The interior is charmingly compact and the little nave has been cleared except for a semicircle of benches in front of the plain modern **altar**. The tomb chest beyond is vested as an altar and before it, a driftwood cross stands in a barrel, with curtains masking the looming bulk of the Kytson tomb in the old chancel. Within the tower, the **cusped** panels of the **font** contain blank shields and the panelled shaft stands on a base decorated with fleurons (which **Cautley** believed was the inverted bowl of another C15 font). The w. **gallery** houses the organ, with its lovely little coloured and gilded case. The nave **roof** was rebuilt in an 1890s restoration, retaining fragments bearing the arms of Kytson and Passion emblems as **bosses**. There is a **clerestory** on the n. side and the **piers** of the graceful **arcade** between nave and n. **aisle** have varied carving in the **capitals** - oak leaves, angels, and a vine trail. Demi-angels perch at the apex of the arches and there are tiny **paterae** in the mouldings of the windows above. Marks in the chancel arch show where the old **tympanum** was fitted and the rood stairs rise on the s. side. There are fragments of medieval canopy work in the windows of the n. aisle and the Wood memorial windows of 1927 in the nave have glass by F.C. Eden more of his work can be seen at Clare and Whepstead. A tablet in the n. aisle remembers Lieut Thomas Gage Crauford of the Guards, who 'fell cheering on his men in the orchard of Hougomont during the battle of Waterloo'. The n.e. chancel is crammed with monuments and is dominated by the huge six-poster tomb of Margaret, Countess of Bath, who died in 1561. She lies beneath the ponderous canopy in red, ermine-cloaked robe and wearing a coronet, with a greyhound at her feet. beside her, the armoured figure of her third husband John Bourchier, Earl of Bath, wears a long beard over a deep ruff. Her first husband, Sir Thomas Kytson, lies on the shelf below. A wealthy merchant adventurer and builder of the hall, he was one of Henry VIII's supporters in the Boleyn marriage and was knighted in consequence. The second husband, Sir Richard Longe, does not appear but

there is a recessed tomb chest in lieu beyond Sir Thomas which carries five large shields. **Putti** hold shields above the canopy on either side of a square superstructure adorned with yet more heraldry. To the r. is the wall monument for Sir Thomas Gage who died in 1742. It is by Benjamin Palmer, and has a vacuous portrait bust on top against a pyramid. Palmer's father was the better sculptor and one of his works can be seen at Little Saxham. Below is the tomb chest under a plain black marble slab of Sir Edmund Gage, the 1st baronet, who died in 1707. Set in the s.w. angle of the chapel is the lovely alabaster monument, with much of the original colour preserved, of the young Thomas, Lord D'Arcy who died in 1614. The superb figure kneels with shield on shoulder and helm in front, with **Corinthian** columns reaching to an open **pediment** bearing seated allegorical figures. Below, a tiny skeleton delicately draws back the shroud with its fingertips to reveal a minutely detailed anatomy. Moving through to the chancel, the tomb of John Bourchier, Lord Fitzwarren (1556), is on the l., with seven roundels of arms in the panels. The s.e. corner of the chancel is filled with another massive six-poster, this time for Sir Thomas Kytson who died in 1608. He lies between his two wives, and all three are stiffly modelled, with small heads. The nearer wife wears the fashionable calash hood and a big ruff with her furred gown; the stag at her feet lies by her husband's unicorn crest. There is a large strapwork frame on top enclosing the arms, two shields flank a heavy **Tudor rose** on the tomb chest, and two daughters kneel against the w. face - with much original colour everywhere. There are a number of **hatchments** to be seen: above the chancel arch to the r. Sir Thomas Gage (1741): to the l., Sir Thomas Rookwood Gage (1796): s. wall w. end, Charlotte, first wife of the 6th Baronet, Sir Thomas Gage (1790); n. wall, her husband (1798);

chancel s. wall (and difficult to see), Sir Thomas Rookwood Gage (1866); chancel s. wall, Sir Edward Rookwood Gage (1872). The church's only **brass** is an inscription in the n. chapel for Ann Cornwaleys who died in 1599.

Hepworth, St Peter (E3): The church is easily seen from the Bury-Diss road. To the n. there are wide vistas of big, open fields. It was once a thatched building, but on the Easter Monday of 1898, there was a calamitous fire that destroyed not only the roofs but almost everything else, leaving only the tower, the walls, and the s. **porch**. The architect for the rebuilding was J.S. Corder of Ipswich. The C13 tower had already suffered in 1677 when the upper stage was taken down, the stair dismantled, and the date writ large on the w. face. Some of the iron reinforcements were applied then and more, lower down, in 1828. The diagonal buttresses are very deep on the e. side and there are small, early C14 **quatrefoil sound holes**. The C14 w. doorway has a C19 **lancet** over it, but the belfry windows were part of the C17 reconstruction, as was the little pyramid tiled roof with its perky bellcote on the side. The porch that survived the fire was two-storied (see the marks in the **nave** wall where the stair went up to it) but it had to be replaced and much of the old fabric was incorporated. The nave was given new windows in **Perpendicular** style, although the renewed **tracery** in the **chancel** windows is **Decorated** and probably repeated the old patterns. There is a separate **low side window** which is unusually small and has the distinction of being traceried. A C14 **priest's door** is also nearby, and on the n. side of the nave is another doorway of the same age, with animal **headstops** to the **dripstone**. In the porch there is the fragment of a **Norman** scallop **capital** and a section of shaft (evidence of an earlier church than the one that was

Hepworth, St Peter: font cover detail

burned down) and above is an image niche. The door still has its medieval closing rings and lockplate. Just inside to the l. is the blocked doorway that led to the upper room of the porch. The tower arch is low and completely plain, pointing to an early C13 date, and to the r. of it is the church's real treasure. One would not dare to hope that a medieval **font** cover of this size and weight would be saved from a major fire, but happily it was, and it now stands on top of an 1870s font. Originally telescopic, it is over 12 ft high, and two bottom sections are hinged for access. It is tabernacled and buttressed, but its individuality lies in the lower section. There, the image stools are pierced and carved in the form of miniature **castellated** towers, complete with window tracery and doorways wherein tiny men at arms come and go in lively fashion. It is perhaps unfortunate that it was not very well restored and repaired by a Mr Brooke of Hopton in the 1850s; his work can be fairly easily identified and should not distract one from the delights of the Lilliputian fortress. The nave roof of 1898 is a double **hammerbeam**, with heavy pendants on the upper hammers. Corder installed a waggon roof in the chancel and put down black and white marble paving. On the s. side of the chancel arch is a C14 **piscina** with a worn **trefoil** head, and in the n. wall is a blocked doorway that led to the **rood loft** stair. The openwork oak pulpit of 1923 is a handsome piece of work by Sir Henry Methold, a skilled amateur craftsman who also made the litany desk. The choir stalls date from the fire but they incorporate medieval bench ends with castellated elbows and fine, bulbous **poppyheads**. The **altar** is a little out of the ordinary because it is mahogany, with spiral legs and stretchers, but unfortunately it has been badly attacked by woodworm. On the s. wall of the **sanctuary** is a modern oak tabernacle for the reserved sacrament of unusual, if rather heavy, design. The tiny low side window, with its **ogee** tracery within a square frame, is deeply recessd and was only rediscovered after the fire. The stained glass coat of arms it contains occurs again in the window on the n. side of the chancel - a memorial for Mary Ellen Methold who died in 1903. The glass is by **Powell & Sons**, and shows the angel of the Resurrection appearing to the two Maries - all in cool colour. The face of the **Blessed Virgin** is apparently a portrait of Mrs Methold, and her cloak is decorated with the family arms.

Herringswell, St Ethelbert (B4): This is one of four churches dedicated to **St Ethelbert** in the county, and in the Middle Ages there was a **guild** here dedicated to him, with a priest to celebrate a weekly mass. Walking round the outside, columns and **quoins** of the original **Norman** church can be found at the n.e. and s.e. corners of the **nave**, and this was succeeded by a C14 building. In 1869, however, a disastrous fire destroyed nearly everything and there was a rebuilding to the designs of **Sir Arthur Blomfield**. The tower had not been damaged significantly and presents a highly individual profile from almost every angle. There is a stepped buttress up the centre of the w. face as far as the belfry stage and on either side of it there are stubby blocked **lancets** that were once **traceried**. There are substantial stepped projections n. and s., the latter containing the tower stair, and the two-**light** bell openings are renewed below panelled battlements. The e. wall of the tower and the stair turret both show an earlier and higher roof line, indicating that the unusual design is original. Most of the exterior is new work but there is a niche above the s. **transept** window, as well as a little **trefoil** over it. Similarly, in the **porch**, there is a niche over the door, and that has very fine double mouldings, although the top has been partially obscured by the roof. A **stoup** has been re-set beside the door. Inside, the tower continues to surprise. The arch is carried on octagonal **piers** supported by flying buttresses angled from the side walls, and behind it, tall and narrow arches open on either side. Apparantly, this arrangement is original and not part of the rebuilding. The nave roof has plain **arch-braces** and there is a waggon roof in the **chancel**, panelled with **bosses** at the intersections. There is a trefoil-headed **piscina** in the s. transept and a blocked window in the e. wall. To the l. of the entrance to the transept is a blocked doorway which will have led to the old **rood loft**.

Close by is a small marble statue of a lush young maiden on a pedestal. She reclines in an attitude of langorous abandon against a crescent moon, one hand flung back behind her back, with a star on her forehead and another on the diaphanous drapes that just fail to reveal all. It is an extraordinarily voluptuous piece to come across unawares. The s.w. chancel window retains its **Decorated** tracery and one of the lights is divided by a **transom**, showing that the lower section was used as a **low side window**. Beyond the stepped sill **sedilia** in the **sanctuary** is a C14 double drain piscina, but the canopy and pinnacles are C19 replacements. On either side of the e. window are tall C14 niches with trefoil **ogee** arches and **crocketted finials**. The original **vestry** door on the n. side of the chancel is deeply recessed and has devil **headstops**

Herringswell is memorable for the outstanding series of stained glass windows designed by artists of the **Arts and Crafts movement**. The e. window of 1902, on the theme of The Good Shepherd, is by **Christopher Whall**. The figure of Christ, in a rich red robe lined with fur, was adapted from a design first used by him in the chapel of Fettes College, Edinburgh, in 1899. The Suffolk black-faced sheep were drawn by his sister-in-law, Alice Chaplin, better known as a distinguished sculptress patronised by Queen Victoria. The bottonm of the l. hand light portrays the biblical ram caught in a thicket, and the r. hand light includes a distant vignette of a shepherd tending his flock. The 1904 s.w. chancel window is a memorial to the uncle of Whall's friend, Selwyn Image, and is a good example of the artist's ability to combine contemporary detail with traditional religious themes. Texts on the virtue of charity are interwoven and Christ stands as a robed king in the l. hand light, with angel heads above and below. The other light is divided by a transom and the figures praying in the upper scene have portrait heads,

while a sickbed group is shown below. Also by Whall is the Resurrection window in the s. wall of the nave and it repeats a design he used at the church of the Holy Cross at Avening, Gloucester, in 1908. As the sun rises, Christ stands within a pointed oval oriole, his hand raised to show the wound, while an angel with multicoloured wings raises the stone; below a soldier in armour sleeps prone across the two lights. The glass in the n. chancel window of 1902 was designed by Paul Woodroffe, another member of the Arts and Crafts Movement. Mothers and children gather on the l. and Christ draws more children to Himself on the r. - one with a doll flung over her shoulder. Both lights are framed in a deep band of Celtic foliage scrolls, and the general treatment is softer and more indefinite than Whall's. The windcw on the s. side of the sanctuary is by Jasper Brett, a pupil of Christopher Whall. On the theme: 'Come unto me all that are weary and heavy laden...'. Two of the loviest windows here were designed by James Clarke and made by A.J. Dix of Gower Street, London - memorials to Leopold Frederick Davies. The first, in the centre of the nave n. wall, takes the text: 'All thy works praise thee O Lord', and the design spreads over both lights; there is a centre clump of Scots pine, and silver birches rise up on either side; a brilliant cock pheasant struts in the heather and swallows wheel across the sky. It is an enchanting piece. The s. transept window illustrates 'O Lord how manifold are thy works' and a brilliant landscape fills the whole of the three lights. Slender boles of laburnums and a Scots pine strike upward and in the upper branches there are pigeons and squirrels, one seeming to pause on a ledge of tracery. Rabbits sit by their burrow at the bottom and in the centre, vivid flowering cherry and lilac overhang a river where stands a heron. This is an intensely romantic concept that skilfully avoids sentimentality. Next to

Hessett, St Ethelbert

the pulpit in the nave is a 1950s window for Llewellyn Sidney Davies, whose enthusiasm for field sports prompted a **St Hubert** theme, designed by H.W. Luxford. The saint stands in the r. hand light with spear, hunting horn and Gospel book, while a springer spaniel, in the likeness of one of Davies' dogs, sits at his feet. The other light has a stag at bay with a crucifix within its antlers; there are woods and hills in the middle distance and the foreground is richly carpeted with spring flowers. Lastly, a window at the w. end of the nave (whose designer has not been identified) shows **St Francis** scattering seed while holding a hare in the crook of his arm; a dog sits before him and flocks of birds swoop down to feed. Thin tree trunks rise through the composition to foliage at the top, and in the background is a rocky hermit's cell.

Hessett, St Ethelbert (E5): This lovely church fronts the village street against a dense background of yews and avenue of small limes leads up to the s. **porch**. There are only 18 dedications to Ethelbert in England, four of which are understandably in Suffolk. By the gate is the shaft of a C15 **preaching cross** and the mortices cut in its sides indicate that it once had substantial arms and possibly attendant figures. The well proportioned tower has been restored and there are new pinnacles at the corners of the pierced battlements which are moulded and set with shields bearing the initials of John Bacon who financed the late C15 enrichment. There is a deep band of ornament under the battlements and the arches of the **Decorated** bell openings are picked out with red brick and flint and there are pairs of shields below. The w. window is **Perpendicular** and there is a chequerwork **base course** in flint **flushwork**. As a final touch, the tower now boasts an elegant weathervane in the form of a gilded, crowned

'E' for St Ethelbert. The parapets of the C15 **aisles** and **nave clerestory** are as richly decorated as the tower, with pinnacles at frequent intervals and openwork battlements carved with shields and roses. All the windows are Perpendicular and there is an interesting late C15 inscription carved on the parapet of the **sacristy** n. of the **chancel**. Its medieval English translates:

> Pray for the souls of John Hoo and Katherine his wife, the which made the chapel, heightened the vestry and battlemented the aisle.

Most of the word 'souls' was hacked away by one of the Commonwealth despoilers of 'superstitious inscriptions'. The original roof line of the **vestry** is marked by the **gargoyles** still embedded in the wall. The chancel is C14 and there is attractive flowing **tracery** in the e. window which has a niche above. There is a renewed **priest's door** in the s. wall and from there one can see the strangely awkward way in which the parapet is carried over the angle of the nave roof, with the battlements at right angles to the slope. As was often the case, the C15 s. porch in stone and flint was given special attention and it has standing angels bearing scrolls at the corners of the openwork battlements. The three canopied niches over the entrance with their miniature vaults are very like those at Woolpit, while the buttresses have carved and flushwork panels where initials of the Bacon family occur again - and again in the panelled base course. The carving of **St George** and the dragon in the **spandrels** of the outer arch is now very worn. The timbers of the porch roof are bleached almost white and to the r. of the small C14 inner doorway is the base of a **stoup**, whose bowl (or that of another) lies by the entrance.

The church interior is light and spacious, the slender columns of the Perpendicular **arcades** having typically wide and shallow mouldings. There is an extra bay on the n. side forming a chapel which was no doubt part of John Hoo's legacy. At the w. end stands the **font** made in Norwich in the 1450s and given by Richard and Agnes Hoo in 1500. A very worn inscription on the step asks us to pray for their souls and the sides of the wide octagonal base are traceried. The panels of the stem are carved with **paterae**, with more beneath the bowl, the panels of which are decorated with a variety of **cusped** patterns and centre ornaments. In the tower wall overhead is a **sanctus-bell window** and the C15 **arch-braced** nave **roof** is flattish, with remnants of angels below the **wall posts**. Unlike most in the area, the C15 benches are low with plain, square ends, but some of them have a simple leaf twist carved on the top molulding and along the back rail; one bench end in the s. aisle has the remains of a crouching hound. There is a **piscina** in the s. aisle chapel under a finely moulded and pierced **trefoil** arch. In the n. aisle chapel the plain recess to the r. was probably a piscina originally. Nearby is a long iron bound chest. Cromwell's commissioners were given the keys but the canny churchwardens kept back the rod that is also required to open it and so it remained inviolate. Just as well, because the unique C15 **pyx** cloth and **burse** (both now in the British Museum) were inside. Illustrations and details of them can be seen at the back of the church. A fine set of Charles II **Royal Arms** has been well restored and placed above the chest. Medieval church walls were the picture books of the people and we are fortunate that some fine examples survive here. Over the s. door there was a **St Christopher** but what remains is not likely to be recognised as such, although a second version over the n. door is better. Plain to see are the saint's legs, tunic and staff as well as two small figures and some fish in the river. Over the s. aisle piscina is a very good painting of **St Barbara** with her tower, but the most interesting subjects

are on the n. aisle wall. There we see the **Seven Deadly Sins** as figures on the branches of a tree which springs from the dragon jaws of hell, with demons either side. The painting dates from the 1370s and the figures represent Pride at the top with (in descending order) on the l., Gluttony, Vanity, Avarice, and on the r., Anger, Envy and Lust. Perhaps it is just an accident of time but Lust is almost worn away. Immediately below is one of the best representations of the rare **Christ of the Trades** dating from about 1430. Our Lord is contrasted with, and perhaps neglected as a result, the common cencerns of life. His faint seated figure is surrounded by pincers, hammer, scissors, chisel and gridiron, and in the top l. hand corner is the six of diamonds - one of the earliest illustrations of 'the devil's picture books'. Below to the r. is a C15 **consecration cross**.

The **rood loft** stairs go up on the s. side of the chancel arch and the C15 **screen** remains in place. The unusually broad bottom panels have stencilled decoration and there is a shield-shaped **elevation squint** to the l. of the entrance. The **lights** have cusped and **crocketted ogee** arches with panel tracery above them. There are the remains of **gesso** work on the uprights which are impressed with a highly individual bird pattern. The wrought-iron gates are modern. The medieval stalls, with **poppyheads** and carved elbows, are arranged in collegiate fashion so that some of them back against the screen. Their fronts are traceried; look for a **pelican** in her piety in one of the spandrels. One bench on the n. side was almost certainly made for a private house; it is particularly fine and its back is carved with a repeat design of birds and leaves above a line of **quatrefoils** enclosing shields. Nearby is the Decorated doorway to the sacristy complete with original door. If it is open (as is sometimes is) you will find a piscina with a **cinquefoiled** arch and medieval wooden **credence shelf**.

Within it is a **squint** is cut through to the **sanctuary** and the low chamber must therefore have been used as a chapel or **chantry**. The upper room is reached by a ladder with triangular baulks of timber used as rungs, and it has been suggested that the whole thing was an **anchorite's** cell, with chapel below and living room above. Remember, however, that the inscription outside calls it a vestry. The squint is framed in a quatrefoil in the sanctuary wall and below it is a ledge with substantial decoration whose position suggests that it was used as a Gospel lectern. The 1860s **reredos** is a small stone version of da Vinci's 'Last Supper' and is flanked by the **decalogue**, Creed and Lord's Prayer painted on stone panels. Piscina and **sedilia** are also C19. The church has a good deal of C15 glass (mostly re-set by **Warrington** about 1850), and in the s. aisle e. window there is a fine mitred figure of **St Nicholas**, holding a long cord threaded with gold coins and accompanied by four children. One holds what some people have described as a golf club but medieval artists sometimes showed saints as children holding their adult attributes and is likely to be a young **St James the Less** with his fuller's club. The figure behind may likewise be intended for a **St Stephen**. In the s. aisle centre window on the l., there is an unusual panel showing the **Blessed Virgin** in front of the emperor with her parents behind and **St Joseph** to the r. in the r. hand light is the favourite medieval way of showing Christ's Ascension - a pair of nail-pierced feet below two angels. The window to the w. has an excellent figure of **St Paul**. In the centre window of the n. aisle you will find a scourging of Christ and in the easternmost window, Christ rising from the tomb, with fragments of the sleeping soldiers. The chancel e. window tracery contains C14 glass but the main lights are by Warrington. There are three rows of good figures: top, **St John**, Christ, the Blessed Virgin; centre, **St**

Peter, **Edward the Confessor** (or St Ethelbert), St Paul; bottom, **St Edmund**, **St Etheldreda** and **St George**. The s. sanctuary window of 1867 is by **O'Connor**, with two Nativity scenes. The monument in the s. aisle to Lionel and Anna Bacon (1653) is credited to **Nicholas Stone**. Draped fabric carries the inscription below a **cartouche** of arms flanked by skulls; there is an urn on top, two miniature shields below and the design terminates in a sizable pinnacle as a pendant.

Higham, St Stephen (B4): The village, with its lower, middle and upper greens was part of the parish of Gazeley but in 1861 it became a separate benefice and a new church was built, designed by **Sir George Gilbert Scott**. He had a hand in a number of C19 restorations but this is his only complete church in Suffolk and it is a stolid little building, with **nave**, **chancel** and n. **aisle** in **Early English** style. The flint walls are banded with **ashlar** and the **dripstones** have finely cut **headstops**. The round tower with its conical cap lifts the design above the ordinary and Scott let himself go on the belfry stage where tall, blind **arcading** (with bold shafts and stiff leaf **capitals**) links the bell openings. Entry is via a s. **porch** into a dark interior under a pine **roof** with **tie-beams** and tall **king posts**. There is a four-bay n. arcade with **hood moulds** coming down to headstops above octagonal **piers**. As with the outside, the tower provides the interest. Designed as a baptistry, it has a rib vault resting on shafts with stiff leaf capitals. Below them are heavy leaf **corbels**, one with a bird and another with a hound clutching at the base. The tub **font** with its cable rim rests on short, closely set marble columns and has a flat iron-scrolled cover. The C18 or early C19 benefactions board in the n. aisle is headed 'Parish of Gazeley, Hamlet of Higham' and was transferred here in 1944. All the woodwork is plain unadorned work by Rattee and the pews still have their numbers. It was one of the conditions of a grant by the Incorporated Church Building Society that 31 of them should be reserved for the poor of the village - part of their campaign to get rid of the iniquitous pew rent system. C19 stone pulpits are nearly always indigestible and this one is no exception; standing on polished green marble columns, it was two roundels carved with busts of **St Peter** and **St Paul** and a shaft of liverish marble supports the built-in book rest. Opposite is a wooden tablet with a coloured coat of arms at the top for members of the Barclay family spanning more than a century. The arch of the organ chamber on the n. side of the chancel has a pair of very well cut head corbels which are typical of the fine detailing in this church. The e. wall is boldly banded with ties on either side of a narrow **reredos** panel in patterned marble. All the 1870s glass is by **Clayton & Bell** and the e. window depicts the Crucifixion, with two Maries on one side and two saints on the other. The **sanctuary** d. window shows the martyrdom and burial of **St Stephen** - the latter an interesting composition, with the draped coffin being borne away on the shoulders of vested bearers preceded by cross and banner, with a young taperer by the side. Scott designed a set of altar frontals to go with his new church and it is pleasant to find them still in use more than a century later.

Hinderclay, St Mary (F3): The church is nicely situated except for the fact that on the s. side of the churchyard one is confronted with a line of black corrugated iron silos that are quite awful in their ugliness. There is a small **Decorated** w. window in the tower but it is otherwise **Perpendicular**, with bell openings that have deep **labels** over the fine **tracery**. The window shape is continued downwards below the sills in the form of panels with **cusped ogee** heads and filled with flint chequer. The tower has a plain flint **base course** and the **flushwork** in the battlements contain the letters SSRM for the dedication. On the n. side of the **nave** is a blocked late C12 door of simple design and in the n. wall of the **chancel** is an early Decorated window with elongated **trefoils** in the two **lights**. The chancel is early C14; the e. window has **reticulated** tracery. and there is a **priest's door** with worn **headstops** on the s. side. A **quoin** at the s.e. corner (about 4 ft 6 in from the ground) has a **scratch dial** but only the hole for the centre peg can now be seen. One of the Decorated windows on this side has **transoms** which formed **low side windows** at the bottom. The tracery matches that in the e. window of the s. aisle. The aisle s. windows are square-headed with three lights and, like nearby Thelnetham and Rickinghall Inferior, the **aisle** is gabled. The w. end has been repaired in red brick but note that a C14 **gargoyle** is placed in the angle between the aisle and the nave to take water from the gulley between the roofs. Entry is by way of the s. **porch**, one of the few wooden examples in this part of Suffolk. It stands on a brick base and, although the sides have been renewed, the outer arch is C14, with the **jambs** and half of the curve cut from a single piece of timber. Through a simple and quite small doorway one passes into a pleasant little interior. There is a plain C14 **font** at the w. end and the tower arch is filled with an C18 **screen** at the bottom and the **Royal Arms** of George III on canvas above. The **vestry** enclosure matches the tower screen and there is a Perpendicular w. window within. The early C13 **arcade** between nave and aisle is carried on low round **piers** and the benches are a late and interesting C17 set. The **poppyheads** are small and diamond-shaped, bearing mainly carved fleur de lys and rosettes. Those on the rear bench are lettered: JSK SK and RL 1617 TC - no doubt the churchwardens' initials at that time. Not all the seating is benches, for there are C18 low **box pews** of pine in the s. aisle and more in the eastern half of the nave, with panelled ends. The **capitals** of the chancel arch were cut into to accommodate the **rood**, and the end of the beam that supported the front of the loft may be seen in the n. wall. There is a shadow of a niche in the window embrasure by the pulpit and this could have been the site of an altar for the **guild** of **St Peter** that was here in 1474. The square-headed chancel screen is a late example, with open tracery and moulded **mullions**, and looks as though it may have been re-set subsequently in another frame. To the r. you will see that the hinges of the original shutters are still set in the jambs of the low side windows. On the n. wall of the chancel is a monument for George Thompson, a rector who died in 1711. The execution is fairly coarse, with a **cartouche** of arms supported by garlands at the top, standing **putti** at each side, and **acanthus** leaves below. The only other memorial of note is a well lettered oval tablet on the s. wall for Charlotte Doe who died in 1917. Behind the organ there is a very narrow plain arch connecting the aisle chapel **sanctaury** with the nave, and I can only think that it was to give a view across to another **altar** on the n. side - in other words, a very large **squint**. Hinderclay has some interesting modern glass designed by Rosemary Rutherford in 1973. There are three windows in the s. aisle, with simplistic figure shapes against streaky leaf-like faces to the figures, and one of them is treated quite differently from the rest and looks like a portrait from life. With contemporary glass, the iconography can be elusive but Moses in the bullrushes seems to figure in one of the side-windows. In the chancel e. window, the tracery along has stained glass and there are bird, fish and flame abstracts. If you are fortunate enough to visit on a sunny day, the body of the church is filled with warm, enticing colours.

Honington, All Saints (D3): Robert Bloomfield, whose pastoral poem *The Farmer's Boy* sold 26,000 copies between 1800 and 1803 and which still holds its reputation as a work of rustic genius, was born in 1766 in the cottage just across from the church. His parents' double gravestone is the one nearest to the s.w. corner of the early C14 tower. This has a modern w. window but there is a **quatrefoil** window above, bell openings with **Decorated tracery** and a red brick stair turret to the second story, probably added in the C16. The **chancel** and the s. side of the **nave** date from the C14 while the n. side has late **Perpendicular** windows. Because of their important role in church and village life, **porches** were favourite subjects for lavish treatment and valuable bequests, and this one is a good early C15 example. It has a quatrefoil **flushwork base course**, step-**transomed** side windows and a battlemented parapet with stone panels carved with symbols which include a crowned 'M' for the **Blessed Virgin** and two 'J.S.' monograms which may be the initials of the donor. The s. front has panelled flushwork, with three canopied niches, and the **dripstone** of the arch rests on weathered angels. The arch itself is enriched with leaves and shields and there are shields in the **spandrels** - one of them for **St Edmund**. Save for two ugly and obtrusive brick chimneys in the nave roof, the view from the street is most attractive. Note the line of the old roof showing above the new on the e. face of the tower. Once inside the porch, the fine **Norman** doorway betrays the real age of the building. There are three bands of decoration in the arch, with a battered head over it, as well as a carved **hood mould** coming down to beast masks on weither side. Below, pairs of shafts decorated with chev-

Honington, All Saints: font panel

ron and spiral on the l. and chevron with three carved blocks on the r. (4th shaft is a replacement). Passing through, note the shallow slot on the r. and the deep one on the l., made to house a drawbar to secure the door.

C14 carvers sometimes produced the equivalent of a mason's pattern book of window tracery on **font** panels and here we have the best example in the area. In addition, the e. panel has a Crucifixion that is remarkably good. Christ is portrayed with long hair, and the Blessed Virgin and **St John** weep convincingly on either side, and both sun and moon are represented overhead. The condition of the whole piece is such that I suspect it was plastered over to shield it from the itinerent C17 image breakers. There were faint but extensive wall paintings of **St Nicholas** and **St Thomas** of Canterbury on the s. wall when **Cautley** visited before the war but not a trace can be seen now - all plastered over 40 years ago at the incumbent's behest. Shame! The second clue to the original Norman

church is the chancel arch, entirely plain now, with small corner shafts on the nave side and fragments of carved **imposts** above them. Although the **screen** has gone you can see how a stair to the **rood loft** was cut into the n. wall. There is a large recess on that side of the chancel arch, with a plain image niche close by, the site of a nave **altar**. The handsome wooden eagle lectern of 1872 was transferred from nearby Sapiston, now in the care of the **Redundant Churches Fund**. Here, a restoration before World War I replaced the roofs and unfortunately exchanged a fine set of C15 benches for dull pitchpine pews. Some bench ends were suffered to remain and they are now part of the choir stalls. Carved on their gabled armrests are: (s. side, **unicorn**, **wyvern**, dog with a goose in its mouth and a hare; (n. side), monkey, two birds, and a rare example of a bagpiper that could have stepped straight out of a painting by Brueghel. On the s. wall by the **priest's door** is a 2 ft **brass** for George Duke (1594), in ruff, cloak and sword, typical dress for gentry of that period. The inscription that goes with it can be found on the e. wall behind the curtain, and another for Anne Curteis (1585) is to the l. of the altar. On the s. side of the **sanctuary** is a C14 **piscina** with a square drain under a flattened **ogee**arch, with **dropped-sill sedilia** alomngside. The **Stuart communion rails** have shapely twisted **balusters** and on the n. wall is a large white marble tablet for Robert Ruskbrooke (1753). His arms are in a roundel at the top and the long inscription is cut in as fine an italic as you will see anywhere, with every stroke doubled.

Hopton, All Saints (E3): The main fabric of the building is C14 but there have been a number of subsequent alterations. The tower has a pair of small **lancets** in the ground floor, an **ogee**-headed niche above, and a lancet belfry window. The upper stage, with its round-headed bell openings was attractively rebuilt in the C18 and is decorated with flint and stone chequework. The line of the original **nave** roof shows clearly on the e. face, above the handsome battlemented **clerestory** in warm, **Tudor** red brick. Its window arches and **tracery** are formed from shaped bricks and there are rcessed panels at intervals. The w.end of the s. **aisle** betrays evidence of a late C13 predecessor, not only by a lower roof line but by the **plate tracery** in the two- **light** window. There are renewed **Perpendicular** windows in the s. aisle, but the e. window there has **Decorated** tracery within a widened Tudor arch. One sometimes finds **low side windows** on both sides of a **chancel** but here, most unusually, there are tow on the s. side, both divided by centre **mullions**. The e. window has three **trefoil** lancets and there is a **priest's door** on the n. side of the chancel. The late C13 n. door survives, but the rest of the n. aisle is Perpendicular and its four-light e. window contains pretty curvilinear tracery under a Tudor arch. The buttress at the n.w. corner has an interesting variation - the lower stage as v-shaped before returning to a conventional angle under a gable at the top. The simple C14 s. **porch** has had angled brick buttresses added and the side windows are C19 replacements. The **dripstone** of the inner door has **headstops** and there is a niche over it. Within, the tower arch is plain and very steep, and there is a **trefoil**-headed **sanctus-bell window** in the wall above. At the w. end of the s. aisle you will see that the door to the tower stairs is heavily banded with iron - a reminder that, apart from church property, parish valuables were often kept for safety in the tower. The **font** is C19, but there is a huge and impressive C14 chest at the w. end of the n. aisle. The ends and base have suffered badly from worm, but the inset lid retains its original seven hinges and three great locks. The C14 **arcades** have octagonal **piers** and,

above them, the brickwork of the clerestory has been carefully repointed and is very attractive. The low-pitched **roof** has alternating **hammer-beams** and **arch-braces**, and the hammers are coarsely carved figures holding books, organs, patens and chalices. The robed, seated figures on the **wall posts** have lost their heads and, above them, the double depth of **wall plate** is decorated with crudely carved flowers, painted angels, and two lines of cresting. The whole roof is painted, with red as the predominant colour, and the figures have ermine collars. They were apparently repainted by the vicar's five daughters a few generations back. The aisle roofs display delicate foliated and painted **bosses** and the bay at the e. end of the n. aisle has a carved cresting on the wall plate, possibly the remains of more extensive distinction. There is a C14 **piscina** and **dropped-sill sedilia** in the s. aisle chapel. The inside of the e. window shows more clearly than the outside that it was reconstructed in the C16. The **Stuart altar** has a carved top rail but two of its stretchers are missing. Tall niches are let into the walls at the e. end of the nave arcades and the **rood loft** stair goes up behind the pulpit; there is no lower door now but the hinges are still there. When the order came to take the rood and its loft down, the workmen sawed through the main beams but left the stumps in the wall; both ends of the **rood beam** itself can be seen and one end of the joist that supported the front of the loft. The frames of the low side windows are rebated on the inside as well as the outside for shutters. In the **sanctuary** the piscina, under its trefoil arch, its original wooden **credence shelf**. On the n. side of the chancel there is a large tablet in memory of Thomas Raymond; he died in 1680 and was 'first sole keeper of the papers of state and council to King Charles II'. It has a **cartouche** within a broken **pediment** at the top, and a skull with crossed fronds carved in shallow relief at the bottom. The 1890s glass in the e. window is by **Ward & Hughes** (designed by **T.F. Curtis**) and displays good colour, with a nice attention to detail. Christ in glory with his disciples, and the Crucifixion panel below is flanked by figures of the **Blessed Virgin** and **St John**. Other panels have a variety of figures, including Noah, **St Cecilia** and **St John the Baptist**. The **Annunciation** window in the s. aisle is a typical **Kempe & Co** design.

Horringer, St Leonard (C5): By the main entrance to Ickworth Park, in a very attractive setting on the village green, lies the church. The top of the tower was rebuilt in 1703, and in 1818 the scale of rebuilding was such that the *Bury and Norwich Post* reported that 'nothing remains of the former edifice but the plain masonry of the walls.' A n. **aisle** with organ chamber and **vestry** was added in 1845, the **chancel** was virtually rebuilt in 1867 and most of the fittings replaced in 1883. The tower and battlements were rebuilt again very handsomely in the early years of this century and so was the **porch**. All of this adds up to a C14 building in which almost everything has been replaced, largely in the style of the original. What looks at first sight to be a s. aisle is in fact the C15 Horsecroft chapel; built on to the e. side of the porch, it was never a **chantry** apparently but was always associated with the hamlet of Horsecroft and particularly with the Lucas family. The outside of the church is attractive, with weathervanes on the tower pinnacles and extensive **flushwork** on porch and battlements. The w. window is unrestored **Perpendicular** and the chancel e. window with its good **Decorated tracery**, was carefully repaired rather than replaced. There is a **stoup** to the r. of the entrance door and just inside hangs a respectable late C19 copy of the **Pietà** by Francesco Francia. The **capitals** of the tower

arch are **castellated** and carved with **fleurons**, and the heavy octagonal C13 **font** has repainted shields on the bowl: the abbey of Bury and the families of Brooke, Gipps, Jermyn and Lucas. The retractable cover in C17 style is hung on a counterbalance. Not far away on the w. wall of the n. aisle the C18 epitaph for Valentine Munbee says that 'he was a person of great good sense' - a comforting thought. The tablet is by Thomas Singleton who, incidentally, carved the reliefs on the outside of Bury Town Hall. Before the aisle was built Dame Elizabeth Gipps' memorial was on the n. wall and her husband lay below her. He was knighted by Charles II and died in 1681, she in 1715, and their stones were transferred first to the chancel and then to the aisle w. wall. His crest was nearly worn away by passing feet (as you will see) but her arms are still sharply cut and displayed in the manner of a **hatchment**. The entry to the s. chapel is through funny little swing gates and the low **screen** incorporates some medieval tracery that may have come from the old **rood screen** or loft. Within the chapel there is a tablet for John Crooke who died in 1653 - wilful lettering and amateurish cherub heads, with a skull below. The e. window glass of 1872 by **Clayton & Bell** is a Deposition scene and the three Maries at the tomb, all in fairly virulent colour. As part of the 1880s work, the **nave roof** was stripped to reveal the original single-braced roof. The capital on the s. side of the wide chancel arch is notched where the rood screen once fitted and there are marks to show that a **tympanum** filled the space above. A hook remains in the apex of the arch and this may have been used to secure the rood itself or a **Lenten veil** over it. Beyond is a C19 waggon roof and, on the n. side, the eccentric 1860s two-bay **arcade**. The C14 entrance to the vestry has a nicely Gothick early C19 door. The glass in the e. window is by J.E. Nuttgens of High Wycombe, installed in 1946 -

elongated figures of **Saints Etheldreda, Leonard, Edmund** and the **Blessed Virgin** taking up the lower two-thirds, with dull blue borders for the rest of the lights and the tracery, relieved only by deep red symbols at the top. (Another of Nuttgens' windows can be seen at Kedlington.) There is very little **Art Nouveau** church furniture about and the prayer desk that stands in the chancel is a rare item. The beaten metal side panels, with their characteristic shape and decoration, are lettered 'Christ Church Chester 1900' and 'Laborare et orare'; there are metal caps to the uprights and a folding kneeler - in all, a thoughtful snippet of design evocative of the period.

Hundon, All Saints (B6): Approached by a little lane from the village street, the church stands in a spacious churchyard where there are many excellent C18 headstones, some carved by members of the Soane family. It was a mainly **Perpendicular** building but one Sunday evening in February 1914 it was gutted by fire, leaving little more than a charred skeleton. It was rebuilt over the next two years to the designs of Detmar Blow and Ferdinand Billeray in a conservative style that produced no surprises and largely followed the original. There is a little wooden bellcote complete with weathercock on top of the stair turret and the slopes of the buttresses to s. and w. have fine, bold carvings of grotesques which are simliar to those at Great Bardley. The **nave** parapet on the s. side is a very decorative frieze of pierced **quatrefoils** with feathered **cusps** on top, reminiscent of Woolpit **porch**. There are three- **light** windows in the **aisles** dating from about 1300 and the w. windows have **Decorated tracery**. The large s. **porch** is very weathered and the late C14 inner doorway has shields in the mouldings and **headstops** that do not match. There are tall niches with **crockelled** canopies each side and a band of qua-

trefoils along the top. It has an upper room reached by a stair whose doorway is just inside to the r. n the window sill to the l. of the entrance stands the old gable cross - a rare opportunity to examine one at close quarters. The **font** nearby is a modern drum octagon and beyond it on the w. window sill there are remnants of what must have been a fine C13 tomb. The interior is wide and open, with chairs used judiciously, but all the walls and **arcades** are a sad shade of grey. Two of the old **roof corbels** remain on the s. side below the **clerestory** and there are four more in the n. aisle. The **Royal Arms** of George III painted on board hang here and on the window sill at the w. end stands a large wheatsheaf **finial** which is all that remains of a 'noble pyramid of marble' that used to be outside by the porch. It was a monument to Mrs Arethusa Vernon who died in 1728 but it became unsafe and was demolished in 1983. At the e. end of the n. aisle is the doorway to the old **rood loft** stair which emerged on the **chancel** side, and there is a **squint** through the outer wall. Close by, a small C14 **piscina** is tucked in behind the end of the rebuilt arcade, indicating that there was a medieval **altar** here. The new chancel arch is wide and there are no furnishings or stalls. The **high altar** is a solid block that matches the width of the five-**light** e. window. The Decorated piscina has survived in very battered state, having had a new drain inserted (which does not happen very often). The s. chapel is at a lower level and approached through an arch from the chancel. The dark, traceried panels in the dado were in the vicerage at the time of the fire and thus were saved. A tablet on the n. wall of the chancel commemorates vicar John Norfolk who died in 1749. Below, a Latin epitaph, there are the letters: 'A.O.L.M.F.F.P.M.R.S.' which must surely be the longest acronym on record. It has been suggested that it stands for 'Adami olim lapsu mortales facti fuimus, post mortem resurrecti sumus' (By Adam's fall we became mortal, by the resurrection we live).

Hunston, St Michael (E4): This little church hides itself away, with a pond and some farm buildings for company at the end of a rough track. Its origins are **Norman**, and it is strange that, like nearby Pakenham, and despite its smallness, it has a full blown s. **transept**. There was a restoration in the 1880s and the three-stepped **lancets** in the transept s. wall were renewed then and match the main e. window. The **chancel** was given six new windows in all. Walking round, a relic of the Norman building can be seen at ground level by the n.e. corner buttress of the chancel - a very small segment of an arch, with pellet and cable ornament, that was re-used to fill a space. There is a **priest's door** on that side, in company with two C13 lancets, and there is a door on the n. side of the **nave**. The unbuttressed tower has **Decorated** bell openings to the n. and s. and a matching w. window, although money was left as late as 1472 for its building. Although entry is through a C19 openwork wooden **porch**, the C13 transept has its own w. door, with single shafts and renewed arch mouldings. Within, there is a small C13 **font**, a plain drum standing on C19 columns. Beyond it, the **tester** belonging to a small **Jacobean** pulpit leans against the wall next to an attractive little chest that has both carved and panelled strapwork. On the wall above are three **hatchments**: to the r., for Maria Catherine Heigham who died in 1837; in the centre, for the Rev Henry Heigham; to the l., for his wife Elizabeth. You will find a memorial for this couple on the s. wall of the **sanctuary**. The nave **roof** is a rustic form of **hammerbeam** and **arch-braced** construction and the chancel has a C19 copy of it. The blocked lancet in the s. wall was used to house a marble slab setting out the terms of an C18 village educational

charity which, among other things, was to pay for 'a mistress for teaching three poor little girls to read, knit, spin and sew'. Coade stone was a popular late C18 and early C19 artificial substitute for marble and there is a good, late example of its use on the n. wall - a monument for Capt George Heigham of the Royal Irish Dragoons (1854), and his son, Major George Heigham of the Royal Welsh Fusiliers, who served at Lucknow. The wide and rather shapeless arch into the transept rests on peculiar **corbels** that disappear into the walls, but between the lancets in the e. wall there is a niche with extraordinarily flamboyant decoration. The wide moulding contains large petals which rise to a centre point, like an oversize form of **dogtooth**. They vary in design and some are backed by tendrils, while the **hood moulds** has little roses and two stiff-leaf forms to the r., as though the mason changes his mind or got bored. Corner **piscinas** normally jut out of an angle but the one here reverses the convention and sits in the s.e. corner, with one drain in each wall. The **trefoil** heads of the arcades have been re-cut and the r. hand **capital** renewed. Below the lancet in the e. wall is a large **aumbrey**, and on the w. wall, a memorial for James Ellis who died in 1832. It has a small urn within the broken **pediment**, and the bold lettering marks it out as one of the better efforts of George Tovell, the Ipswich mason. The chancel arch has slim attached shafts on the outer corners and thicker, ringed shafts against the **jambs**. The capitals sprout very odd little leaves (rather like seedlings seeking the light), and the arch above has a thin centre groove that once held the **tympanum** behind the **rood**. The tall recess by the pulpit will have been the entry to the **rood loft** stairs. In the chancel there is a blocked priest's door on the s. side with a plain round arch, and it is very curious that it lies within the embrasure of another, later, arch which has a semi-circular window within the head. This has trefoil tracery with floriated **cusps**, and one wonders whether it was a tympanum originally, rather than a window. The stalls carry some attractive bench ends in good condition; on the n., two dogs (one, a collared greyhound), on the s., a monkey and a creature with long, curved horns. This is likely to be a very rare representation of the **ibex**. The two lancets on the n. side are filled with glass by **Heaton, Butler & Bayne** - one as a war memorial, with an angel bearing the palm of victory, and the other the **Blessed Virgin** and Child. Pause as you leave by the s.e. corner of the transept to read the 1846 epitaph of John Juggins which begins:

> It was so suddenly I fell,
> My neighbours started at my knell,
> Amazed that I should be no more,
> The man they'd seen the day
> before ...

Icklingham, All Saints (C3): Standing on a little hillock above the village street, this thatched church escaped restoration until the late C19. It is simply beautiful, a place of quiet homeliness and infinite charm. Now in the care of the **Redundant Churches Fund**, its future is secure. The only remains of the original early C12 **Norman** building are the w. and n. walls of the **nave**, where there are two blocked slit windows, and one can see a variation in the pebble work above the C14 windows where the walls were heightened at the time of the rebuilding. This took place about 1360, when a tower and s. **aisle** were added, followed by the **chancel**, which is probably a little longer and higher than its predecessor. The C15 s. **porch** was then built and lastly, a few decades later, a window was set in the w. wall of the nave. The C14 windows have **Decorated** motifs and the head of the s. aisle e. window is filled with a splendid web of **reticulated tracery**. A line of **ball flower** ornament runs along the top of the s.

nave wall and in the chancel wall is a **low side window**.

Entry is now by the n. door and close to it is a fine C13 stone coffin and lid that were found under the floor nearby. There are only a few simple C15 benches on the **pamment** floor of the nave and this accentuates the sense of spaciousness. At the w. end is an early C14 **font** with a series of tracery designs in the bowl panels as though from a mason's pattern book; it stands on five shafts which were at one time encased in rubble and plaster. The w. door is blocked and a typical late C19 **bier** stands in front of it. The lovely C14 chest that belongs here has been taken down the road to St James', leaving its plain C16 poor relation behind. **Roofs** of both nave and aisle are replacements in oak, following the original designs; the plaiting of the underside of the thatch was copied exactly. By the s. door is a square **Jacobean box pew** with a canted ledge and a simple poor box fixed to the corner. The s. aisle must have been splendid in its youth; there are carved stone cornices tucked under the roof and the e. window is flanked by two large and very ornate niches: most of the r. hand canopy survives, the uprights are encrusted with coloured **paterae** and the carved beasts that supported the statue pedestal still crouch in the stone. The design of the opposite niche is quite different with its panelled side shafts and the outline of a big reversed **ogee** below. There is a contemporary **piscina** in the corner. The stairs to the **rood loft** were cut into the wall on the l. after the building was finished and the base of the late C15 **screen** remains beyond. It has a huge sill and a centre door was added in the C17 which has bobbin shafts in the top half. Only the outer shafts of the top of the screen survive but note the four **elevation squints** bored in the tracery panels on the s. side. The arch above still has the notches for the **rood beam** and for the **tympanum** that backed it. The octagonal C17 pulpit, on a modern base, has very crude and shallow country carving in its panels which attempts to reproduce a popular Jacobean design. Behind it are a **dropped-sill sedilia**, an **aumbry**, and the vestige of an image bracket, showing that there was an **altar** here, probably for a **guild**. The chancel e. window had become decayed and was bricked up until the late C19 or early C20; the present one is modern. On the n. side of the sanctuary is a double aumbry, rebated for doors and slotted for shelves, and to the s., a piscina with a large **trefoil** arch and its original wooden **credence shelf**; alongside are dropped-sill sedilia. The C17 **communion rails** have flat serpentine uprights. One of the most interesting features of the church is the medieval floor tiles covering the **sanctuary** and the centre of the chancel. Probably laid early in the C14, the type was once common in eastern England but few examples of this magnitude remain; they compare with those in Prior Craudon's chapel in Ely cathedral. Set as mosaic, they have a variety of designs and colours; many are decorated with pairs of tiny birds in roundels reminiscent of Picasso, and there are human faces too. The remnants of C14 glass re-set in the s. chancel and s. aisle windows were recovered by a C19 sexton from the churchyard. The arms of John of Gaunt, father of Henry IV, are to be seen in the window nearest the altar and there is a full- length figure next to it. Two more are in the next window but the heads are not original. Similarly, the heads of the demi-figures in the window in the s. aisle look like amateur replacements.

Icklingham, St James (C3): A village with two churches, and this is the one currently in use. The tower collapsed in the C18 and was rebuilt some time before 1820, using much of the old material. There was a heavy-handed restoration in the 1860s and the out-side of the building reflects this. There are large expanses of **flush-work** made up of very small squared flints, and two of them on the n. side are marked 'Joseph Needham 1865' and 'H.A. 1865', possibly the churchwardens. The panelled parapets are plain and the tower has battlements in yellow brick. The **chancel** was built in the late C13 or early C14 but the **nave** is **Perpendicular**, retaining the old windows with **Decorated** tracery. The old chancel roof line is still visible and marks on the n. wall suggest that there was once a door and perhaps a chapel here. Enter via the original medieval n. door to find a treasure just inside, but one which does not really belong here. It is the magnificent early C14 chest which has sadly been taken from its true home in Icklingham, All Saints, where it could be seen to much better advantage. Beautiful scrollwork, with **trefoil** terminations, covers the sides and top; there are six wrought handles and security is ensured by three long hasps. This is probably the best example of its period anywhere in England. The old hassocks of sedge, which also belong to All Saints, have been brought here and are like those at Lakenheath and Eriswell. Nowadays, kneelers are often bright examples of embroidery (you can see some in the chancel), but these are their rustic ancestors; clumps of the sedge *Carex paniculata* were known as hassocks and were cut and brought into church, either to kneel or sit on - very comforting, no doubt, in their verdant youth but harsh and prickly now. The Perpendicular nave **arcade** matches the chancel arch and is tall for its length, with **clerestory** windows above having Decorated tracery. There was another window over the chancel arch but this was blocked up by the C19 barrel roof beyond. The tower arch was entirely re-done at the restoration and the simple octagonal **font** below has **quatrefoils** in the bowl panels with varied tracery on the shaft. The n. aisle e. window is C19

Icklingham, St James: chest

but there is a niche with a **cinquefoiled** head beside it and, in the n. wall, an **aumbry** still with its original door (evidence that there was an **altar** here, as there was in the s. aisle where the **piscina** remains with square drain and cinquefoiled arch). The steps up to the old **rood loft** are in the wall between the chancel arch and the s. nave arcade and there is an image bracket to the l. The pulpit is C19 and so are the chancel stalls in the main, but note that the s. range incorporates tracery panels from the missing **rood screen**. The s. chancel wall has a pair of tablets, 1844 and 1879 memorials to the rector's family, one of them signed by Jackaman of Bury - plain ovals with matching urns on top. The e. window of about 1300 has slim internal shafts and the **hood mould** comes down to tiny **headstops**. The glass is very uninspired C19 and the window to the s. has **St John** and **St James the Great** in yellow and deep red that is not much better. There is a pallid C19 stone and marble **reredos** behind the plain mid-C17 altar table which has a new top. The C13 piscina

has **cusped** openings on either side of a central pillar. One of the internal walls is sharply angled and was possibly altered at the time of the restoration.

Ickworth, St Mary (C5): This church has been declared redundant and its future is now uncertain; hopefully, however, it will continue to be accessible and used occasionally for services. The reward for a National Trust entrance fee is a pleasant drive through the park, skirting the house and discovering the church some distance to the s.w. in a splendidly pastoral setting. A mellow brick wall and tall yews surround the churchyard and the cement rendered tower abuts the track - triple coupled **lancets** as bell openings and beasts jutting from the corners below **crocketted** pinnacles. It was built by Augustus John, Earl of Bristol, in 1778 and was partially rebuilt by the same marquis who added the s. **aisle** in 1833. The **nave** and **chancel** have been extensively repaired and restructured but the lancets in the chancel are C13, as is the e. window with its three stepped lancets and the roundel above. A slanting **squint** cut through the n. wall shows that there was once a n.e. chapel. Part of a C13 grave slab with a **Lombardic** inscription lies in the n. **porch** and one passes into a very dim interior. There is a w. **gallery** and beyond it by the w. door lies the curved head of a **Norman** lancet carved with a series of diagonal crosses. The plain C13 octagonal **font** has a late C17 pyramid cover topped by a gilded dove, and by the window in the n. wall is the church's showpiece, an exceptionally fine double **piscina** dating from the early years of the C14. The position is unusual because it is at the w. rather than the e. end of the **dropped-window sill** and it spans the corner of the embrasure. Its steep encrusted gables rise to crocketted pinnacles, and within them are attenuated **trefoil** arches, with ledges for a **credence shelf** behind. The arch of the contemporary window has **headstops**, above slim shafts with ring **capitals** and bases. The chancel arch was removed in the C18 but there would have been an **altar** here, possibly dedicated to the **Blessed Virgin**. There are some fairly startling C17 Flemish roundels set in the window, including a male martyr being boiled alive, **St Nicholas** with his three boys being saved from the pickling tub and, top r., Judith triumphantly brandishing the head of Holofernes who sits up in bed bereft and spurting blood (Judith 13:15). The late C17 **three-decker pulpit** made use of an earlier pulpit and the stair has finely turned **balusters** which match the **communion rails**. In the chancel there are more C17 Flemish roundels, including one in a s. window of horrifying creatures straight out of the paintings of Hieronymous Bosch. The roundels are likely to have come from the same source as the much more extensive collection at Nowton and sacred mingles with secular (another roundel in the chancel illustrates the Trojan Horse). To the r. of the e. window is a tall, late C14 or early C15 figure of the archangel **Gabriel**, plainly outlined in reddish brown. It was uncovered in a 1911 restoration and the incomplete canopy was carefully copied and repeated. Strangely, there was no trace of an **Annunciation** scroll nor of the figure of the Virgin on the other side of the window as one would have expected. Below, the early C14 piscina lies within a **cinquefoiled** arch with just the hint of an **ogee** shape. The good 1907 glass in the e. window is a memorial to the 3rd marquis from his Suffolk friends and takes the form of a **Jesse tree** spread across the three **lights**, with the Virgin and Child in the roundel above. The Hervey family has been at Ickworth since the C16 and, naturally, the evidence in **ledger-stones** and tablets is all around although, and this is a surprise, there are no monuments of distinction. The s. aisle turns out to be a family pew at high level, approached by flights of stairs at each end and boasting a separate cloakroom. There are cushioned high-backed settles with 1830s Gothick panelling at their backs and on the rear wall a marble tablet lists the burials in the vault from 1779 to 1960, including George III's unfavourite prelate, the mitred earl (whose body was shipped home from Italy in a packing case labelled as an antique statue to fool the sailors who would not have kept company with a corpse). A dull grey slab on the n. wall is all that is here to remind you of the beautiful Mary, Lady Hervey, once the toast of Pope, Gay and Voltaire. She died in 1768 and her epitaph is credited to Horace Walpole:

Awhile, O linger, Sacred Shade
Till every Solemn due be paid...

And so it goes on for nine whole verses!

Ingham, St Bartholomew (D4): There was a full-scale restoration and partial rebuilding here in 1861 and the **chancel** is nearly all new work. However, the tower, built about 1455 is much as it always was - tall and handsome, with diagonal buttresses to the w. and two prominent **drip courses**. The **base course** is panelled, the w. door has king and queen **headstops**, there is a **Perpendicular** w. window and the bell openings have **Decorated** tracery. **Put-log holes** framed in red brick show up clearly, and there is a stair turret on the n. side up to the second stage. The arches of the large Perpendicular-style **nave** windows feature thin red bricks and there is a blocked C14 n. doorway. On that side, the churchyard has been entirely cleared of headstones. Entry is via the w. door and the tall and narrow inner arch of the tower has head **corbels** that appear to be C19 work. The roof of the nave has been panelled in, and there are now chairs below instead of pews. The s. **porch** has been converted into a utility room but is worth exploring because it contains medieval glass in the side windows: on the e. side, a female figure with another head added, a roundel with an 'MR' monogram for the **Blessed Virgin**, and another with the eagle, symbol of **St John**; opposite, an angel and a roundel containing an eagle clutching a harp. The C19 pulpit has sections of medieval tracery let into the panels, and behind it are the stairs to the **rood loft**. There is a substantial ledge just below the upper doorway which formed part of the rood loft floor. The chancel roof was rebuilt in 1861, using the old **arch-braces** and the **spandrels** that are laid lengthwise between them. These are finely carved with **Renaissance** motifs, including two fine grotesque birds at the e. end on the s. side, and a pomegranate in the centre section on the n. side. The main braces now come down to angels holding books, crowns, and scrolls. Robert Lowe was rector here for 57 years and was 91 when he died in 1727. His memorial is on the n. wall of the chancel - a veined marble tablet set between fluted **pilasters**, with a **cartouche** of arms at the top and all set against a dark background. To the e. is a memorial for Edward Leedes and his wife Anna - pilasters either side of the tablet, with rather coarsely carved cherubs flanking a broken **pediment**, Leedes' arms at the top, and two skulls and crossbones at the bottom. Leedes was the master of the grammar school at Bury and died in 1707. There are C19 **decalogue** panels either side of the e. window and the **reredos** is probably C19 too - a low relief in gold of the Virgin and Child, with **St Elizabeth** and the baby **St John the Baptist**, and side panels containing the **Evangelistic symbols**. As you retrace your steps, note the medieval **poppyheads** applied to the chancel stalls, and a tablet on the nave n. wall by William Steggles of Bury for Lieut Col Martin Cocksedge of the West Suffolk Local Militia who died in 1824.

Ixworth, St Mary (E4): The church is tucked away in a quiet churchyard behind the village street at the lower end, and its entrance is easily missed when driving past. For the most part, the building is late C15 and early C16 and the tower can be dated accurately by a stone panel on the s.e. buttress. This panel is the third above the **nave** roof, and with binoculars one can read the inscription: 'Mast Robert Schot Abot', together with the crown and arrows badge of the abbey at Bury. Schot was abbot from 1470 to 1473. The tower has emblems set in the **base course**, on the buttresses, and below the deep, stepped battlements, very like the decoration at Walsham-le-Willows. The early C14 **chancel** was virtually rebuilt during the 1855 restoration and the n. **aisle** was extended to form an organ chamber and **vestry** at that time. The **rood staircase** protrudes from the angle between the s. aisle and the chancel (as at Walsham-le-Willows only on the other side), and there is a **priest's door** in the s. wall of the chancel with a **stoup** in the wall beside it. There is also a blocked **low side window** to the

l. In the e. wall is a wide niche with a **cusped ogee** arch that is the right shape to have contained a rood group; on the other side of the window is an image stool.

Entry is by way of the handsome late C14 **porch**, with its **flushwork** front and diagonal buttresses that have grotesques lying on the slopes. Below the battlements there is a line of small heads in the moulding and there are heavy **gargoyles** at the sides. There are low stone seats within the porch and the inner early C14 doorway has a canopied niche over it.

The ground floor of the tower was converted into a small meeting and activities room in 1980, with a glazed screen separating it from the body of the church. Three tiles that were originally set in the outer walls of the tower are now displayed here and they give further evidence of its date. One is inscribed: 'Thome Vyal gaf to the stepil iiii£', and Thomas Vyal's will was proved in 1472. He was a carpenter and is likely to have done work in this and other churches in the neighbourhood. The C15 octagonal **font** has a plain bowl, but there are shields set in the **tracery** of the shaft and two of them bear emblems that appear to be woodworkers' tools - a draw knife and two bills. The nave **arcade**, with its **quatrefoil** piers, and the **clerestory** are C15. The low pitched **roof** has tracery in the **spandrels** of the **archbraces** and there are angels at the base of each brace, with more on the **wall plate**. Money was left for the leading of the roof in 1533, indicating that it was finished just before the **Reformation**. The nave benches came in at the 1855 restoration and they are now complemented by a bright array of embroidered hassocks. Prior to the Reformation there were **guilds** of **St Thomas** and **St John**, but apparently the n. aisle chapel (now a Lady chapel) was dedicated to **St James**. There you will find an **aumbry** in the n. wall and a small, plain **piscina** to the r. of the **altar**. The stairs to the **rood loft** can be seen at the end of the s. aisle

and a modern bottom door has been fitted. The nicely traceried base of the **screen** remains, and the arch overhead shows the groove that was made to secure the **tympanum** behind the rood. The a text painted on tin is Victorian. When the C19 vestry and organ chamber were added, a three-bay arcade was built on the n. side of the chancel. The tall priest's door and the blocked low side window can be seen on the s. side, and in the **sanctuary** is a large early C13 piscina with a double drain below twin cusped arches. In the n.e. corner is a most interesting tomb, that of Richard and Elizabeth Codington. The chest has strapwork on the shallow **pilasters**, with three shields of arms between. At the back there is a **brass** of the couple kneeling at desks; he has medium length hair and wears a moustache and beard (note that the sleeves of his fur-trimmed gown become pockets lower down): she wears a French hood, and two children of a former marriage kneel behind her. The couple's shield of arms, together with those of his family and her first marriage were originally inlaid with colour. Codington died in 1567, and the inscription is fascinating because it tells how he was granted the manor of Ixworth by Henry VIII in 1538 in exchange for his manor of Cuddington in Surrey. It was at the time when the king was gathering in the spoils from the suppressed religious houses like Ixworth priory that he started to build the fabulous palace of Nonesuch. To do so, he swept away the village and church of Cuddington, having acquired the site by this exchange. The irony is that he never lived to see it finished and the palace was pulled down in 1670. There are C19 painted metal **decalogue** plates either side of the altar and on the sanctuary s. wall, a **touchstone** panel in an alabaster frame with a roundel of arms for John Norton who died in 1597. The 1944 memorial window on that side, with its figures of the sower and the Good Shepherd, was designed by **James Powell & Sons** in 1966. As you leave, have a look at the fine C17 bible box at the w. end; it has 'H.B.' on the top and the front is richly carved.

Ixworth Thorpe, All Saints (D3): A small church, it stands on a slight rise away from the tiny village, within a churchyard ringed with trees and affording views over gently rolling countryside. The upper part of the tower fell at some time and has been replaced by a weatherboarded bell-turret, while the lower section incorporates stones from an earlier structure, particularly noticeable on the s. side. **Nave** and **chancel** are thatched, and on the n. side is a very simple blocked **Norman** doorway, square-headed **Decorated** windows and the bulge of the **rood loft** stair. There are two small C13 **lancets** on the n. side of the chancel and the e. window has wooden C18 or C19 **tracery** under a **Tudor** arch with long **labels**. On the s. side are Decorated windows, a **priest's door**, and an extraordinary collection of glaziers' graffiti scratched on the diamond **quarries** of the windows; apart from some crude modern additions, there are signatures of Edward Thibbald of Starston (1830), G. Hurrell of Ixworth (1852), Ambrose Cobb of Diss (1852), and an earlier one of 1703. This seems to have been a local habit and there is another example not far away at Stanton. The attractive Tudor **porch** in red brick has a crow- stepped gable and at each corner there are stumps of brick pinnacles with **crockets**, one of which is carved as a human head reminiscent of an Easter Island statue. The sides of the porch are decorated with diamond patterns in darker brick and below the battlements there is a frieze of dressed flints set in brickwork, with similar panels on the buttresses. There is a nice little **arch-braced roof** within, although the **bosses** along the ridge have disappeared. Entry is via a plain and low

Ixworth Thorpe, All Saints: bench end harvester

Norman doorway less than 3 ft wide and a C13 grave slab has been used as a step just inside, with two more beyond it. The floors are pleasant pale yellow brick and the ceilings are plastered throughout. The plain octagonal C14 **font** has a flat board cover, decorated only by gouge cuts on the rim, and a neat set of George III **Royal Arms** painted on board hangs over the simple tower arch. The range of C15 benches has large **poppyheads** and there are grotesques and figures carved on the gabled elbows. Some of these are very good - look for a bird with a human head (w. end, s. side), the harvester (second from the door on the s. side), the mermaid with her mirror (next but one along), a **unicorn** (next along), and the lady taking her little dog for a walk (middle of the n. side). On the n. side of the nave, a small door leads to the rood loft stair and a vestige of the chancel arch juts out of the wall beyond it. On the s. side stands a tiny **Jacobean** pulpit, only 3 ft 6 in high and 2 ft 9 in across, with shallow carvings in the top panels, and there is a typical arch and **pilaster** arrangement below. In the C18, those who 'intend hereafter to enter into the State of Matrimony, Godly and agreeably to the Laws' were deflected from unholy alliances by a printed set of degrees of marriage, published in 1771 and hung in all churches; most have disappeared but there is a framed copy in good condition here on the n. wall of the chancel. Further along is a memorial to Charles Crofts who died in 1617 - a round-headed **touchstone** tablet in an alabaster frame which carries two shields of arms and two crests, still with some of their colour. Three tiny cherub heads decorate the cornice, and above is an **achievement of arms** surmounted by the small figure of a naked man minus his head, with his foot on a skull. The spelling of the epitaph is delightfully wilful. Opposite is a small marble tablet flanked by **pilasters**, with an attractively lettered epitaph for Sir John Crofts who died in 1640. The lancets on the n. side of the chancel have deeply splayed embrasures and there is a plain lancet **piscina** in the **sanctuary**. The Lord's Prayer, Creed, and **commandments** are painted on boards with marbled frames hung on either side of the **altar** Three-sided **communion rails** are not common, but here is a late C17 set with turned **balusters** and gates staggered to n. and s.; the front top rail is badly wormed in one section. The prayer desk in the chancel is an interesting example of a piece of furniture that has been adapted for church use. It is, I think, part of a console table - a finely carved and angry wooden eagle bearing a **Corinthian capital** on its head, now mounted on a new base and fitted with a bookledge on top.

Kedington, St Peter and St Paul (B7): This is one of the most fascinating of the county's churches but it does not wear its heart on its sleeve, presenting as it does a strange and gawky aspect to the road. The **chancel** roof is not visible above the walls, the **nave** roof has had its top sliced off, and the porch gable juts above the plain **aisle** parapet. There was a church here in very early times and the **Saxon** cross that you will see inside was found under the floor in the C19. The C14 tower was probably built by the Lord of the Manor, John de Novo Mercato and there is a little gable at the foot of the s.w. buttress that shelters a lump of stone which was apparently his effigy. Above the next stage, a **trefoil** niche has a faint inscription over it which is said to read 'Dame Amicia' for John's wife. A heavy stair turret with an outside door rises to belfry level on the s. and a band of flint chequer work reaches up to the sill of the **Perpendicular** w. window. An original **Decorated** bell opening remains to the e., with a replacement to the n.; the others are decayed. There are early flint-filled window shapes by the side of the bell openings and on the e. face of the tower, like a strawberry birthmark, is a very strange **cinquefoil** in brick that seems to bear no relation to anything else. The line of an earlier nave roof can be seen and the clock, with its weathered octagonal face, was made in Braintree in 1729. The body of the church is late C13 - early C14, with two doors on the n. side, one for the convenience of the family from the Manor house which was pulled down in 1780. The chancel has tall windows with **cusped** 'Y' **tracery** (the soft stone is very decayed on the s. side) and a C15 e. window. To the r. of the **priest's door** there are two **scratch dials**, one of which has almost flaked away. Before moving on, have a look at William Phillips' 1690s tomb nearby, with its range of the symbols of mortality. The s. porch, over a charming cobbled floor, has been repaired and altered through

Kedington, St Paul & St Peter: Saxon cross and three-sided rails

the years and there are lots of C18 graffiti in the window embrasures and on the deeply moulded inner door.

The low C15 **arcades** and lack of **clerestory** must have made for a fairly dark interior until someone in 1857 was inspired to insert three skylights in the roof. Vandalism is one view and common sense another, but there is no doubt that they make a big difference and they show off the early C16 false **hammerbeam roof** very effectively (the only parallel that comes to mind is the parish church at Whitby). Kedington is one of the churches that the Victorians left alone and the furnishings are a wonderful conglomeration of styles and periods, a time capsule that gives a very good idea of how things were managed and how they changed between the **Reformation** and the 1840s. To the r. of the entrance is a pillar **stoup**, its large bowl chopped away, and nearby, the remains of a **Norman piscina** are used

for the same purpose today. The long and low iron-banded parish chest with divided top dates from the late C14, and there is a contemporary but unidentified area of painting on the s. aisle wall. By a n. arcade pillar stands the worn C15 **font**, with shields and **quatrefoils** in the bowl panels; there are traces of colour and the steps have two gridiron marks which, like others elsewhere, defy reasonable explanation. In the C17 there was an attempt to follow current fashion and the sides of the **piers** were painted in imitation of fluted classical columns. The mid-C18 w. **gallery** is bow-fronted and on either side, at the w. end of the aisles, are tiers of C18 children's benches: s. side (with hat pegs) for boys, n. side for girls. At the end of the nave benches there are two special seats that face w. so that the Master and Dame could keep an eye on their charges. A rare C17 **bier** (extensively restored) stands on the boys' benches and is similar in style to those at Dalham and Little Saxham but much simpler, and its C19 successor stands near the door. There is a charming irregularity about the seating in the nave and aisles. The backs of the benches at the w. end are warped and gnarled with age and have a delectable patina, while the main range is a plain, late C15 set with **linen-fold panelling** in the ends. **Box pews** with shaped divisions face inwards all along the n. aisle, there is a high, square range at the e. end of the s. aisle, and at the front of the nave on the n. side another group evolved its own pattern of heights and widths - they date from the C17 to the C19. Beyond is the fine manorial pew built about 1610, with turned openwork above the sides and slim, turned columns supporting a flat panelled ceiling. It is divided into two compartments, each with its book box and hat pegs, and the front was formed from a 1430s **parclose screen** that stood at the e. end of the n. aisle. It has lovely Perpendicular tracery, cusped and **crocketted**, with much of the original colour revealed by a 1930s restoration.

The **three-decker pulpit** is arguably the country's best and is an early example dating from 1610, with an unusual layout - the reading pew, with **clerk's** desk in front, stands beside the pulpit. The clerk's desk, facing w., is built into the range of pews and has its own hat pegs beneath the book slope. The reading desk is long and narrow, with steps rising awkwardly right through it. There is a hinged kneeler and rough seat, and the full length book slope is carved on the underside and on the brackets, matching the upper panels on all three sides. The pulpit on its turned pedestal is tall, but a mere 26 in across, and two sides of the octagon form the door. It has a canted bookledge and above the backboard there is a square **tester**. All the carving is of

high quality and there are two extras that emphasise its individualy - a turned post on the front pew on which the minister could place his wig and an **hour-glass stand** whose wrought-iron cage rests on a separate turned pole. This was the pulpit used by the Puritan, Samuel Fairclough, whose eloquence drew congregations from far and near for over 30 years. His successor was the John Tillotson who went on to become Archbishop of Canterbury in 1691. Across the aisle is a curious C14 or early C15 almsbox formed from the trunk of a tree, bound with iron and only 15 in high. By the side door at the e. end of the n. aisle is a stairway in the wall that led to the parclose screen loft, and the **altar** there is a beautiful little early C17 communion table; it is honey-coloured and the melon legs are delicately carved with **acanthus** leaves. Beyond it, the wall is recessed and probably housed a **reredos** for the medieval altar. The Decorated window has glass by J.E. Nuttgens of High Wycombe (see his e. window at Horringer) and portrays the risen Christ flanked by the two Maries. To the l. is a portion of medieval wall painting and to the r., a narrow archway leads through to the front of the late C13 chancel arch whose **responds** are earlier, possibly mid C12. The **screen** is a severe **Jacobean** design and is dated 1619 in the scrolled tracery that has turned pendants in each **light**. It is one of the oldest post-Reformation screens in the country and its unusual feature is that there are two folding sections to the n. and one to the s. The fine hanging Calvary above was made in 1926 by George Jack, the well-known woodcarver, and is just the right size for the arch. The stair to the old **rood loft** was rediscovered in 1920 and can be seen within a cavity in the n. **jamb** of the arch (an uncommon, if not unique, position) and the upper exit is in the n.e. angle of the nave. A stone **corbel** and the remains of another flank the chancel arch and will have supported the original **rood**

beam. The chancel now has modern chairs and benches, sensibly converting it into a convenient chapel, but the old practice of using it only to assemble the congregation for occasional communion lingered on, and in the C18 a special set of communicants' pews was made. Such things were normally swept away by the Victorians to whom they were anathema but, by good fortune, some of Kedington's survive and one section stands just to the w. of the screen on the n. side. They are of deal which has been grained to look like oak and have blank Gothick arches before and behind. Two more ranges with high, settle backs, stand by the s. door and e. of the pulpit (See also Glossary entry: **Housel bench**). The late C13 chancel side windows have slim shafts and a **string course** below them lifts over the priest's door. The **sanctuary** is paved in the black and white chequer that was so fashionable in the C17, and the walls are deeply panelled in oak. On the s. side, a section hinges open to reveal a **piscina** which was probably shorn of its front moulding when the panelling went in. The **reredos** was painted by Professor Tristram in 1935 and above it is the church's oldest treasure, the Saxon cross. This probably formed the head of a **preaching cross** and is said to date from the early C10. The lovely set of three-sided **communion rails** fits the space to perfection and their shapely **balusters** match the legs of the **Holy table**. As his memorial on the wall in the s.e. corner tells us, they were given by Samuel Barnardiston who died in 1707. The tablet is strangely old-fashioned, in the style of 100 years earlier. Sir Samuel made his fortune as a Levant merchant; as a young man he demonstrated with the London apprentices in 1641 and his cropped hair prompted the queen's remark: 'See what a handsome round head is there' and gave the Roundheads their name. The Barnardistons were once one of the most important families in the county and flourished here over 27 generations. In their prime they crowded some massive tombs into the e. end of the s. aisle, but before moving there, note the slab with four shields set in the n. wall of the sanctuary. It probably formed part of Sir Thomas Barnardiston's 1540s tomb which also served as an **Easter sepulchre** before it was dismantled.

The largest monument in the s. aisle is for another Sir Thomas who died in 1610 with his two wives. Standing behind tall iron railings, it rises to the roof, with polished marble **Corinthian** columns each side and twin arches at the rear, in which kneel the figures of the two wives, Mary and Katherine, the latter as a widow with veil and heavy ruff. A little tree bearing shields decorates the **pilaster** between them and a full **achievement of arms** is carved on top, flanked by a funeral helm and gauntlets on brackets; a gruesome pile of skulls with bones in their mouths rests on each corner. Sir Thomas' effigy is finely carved on the tomb chest and much of the original colour survives overall. The most extraordinary feature is the pseudo-coffin that protrudes at right-angles from the front of the tomb chest, as though the undertakers got it wrong and just gave up trying! At the e. end of the aisle is the tomb of the Sir Thomas who died in 1503 and his wife Elizabeth (some families seem to have a fixation about favourite names). Their worn effigies have been shamefully treated by generations of idle hands and the helm behind his head is broken away. An inscribed tablet set beyond their feet in the wall tells us that he was the founder of the **chantry** in the n. aisle and that after his death Elizabeth provided the new roof for the nave. To the s. of the chancel arch stands the tomb of yet another Sir Thomas, who died in 1619, and Elizabeth, his wife. Worn figures of children kneel in the side panels and the family arms are framed in stone and placed over an image niche in the wall beyond. His armour and her clothes are excellent examples of the fashions of the period. Thomas married again and had a daughter called Grissell, whose kneeling effigy, in the s.e. corner of the aisle, is perhaps the most memorable of all. She died in 1609 and her monument is of high quality, raised on the wall so that it can be seen from the nave. The figure is remarkable for the way in which the hair is mounted over a frame, with the back curls looped and knotted, and for the way the epaulettes of the sleeves extend as spikes almost to the ground. Across in the n. aisle is the monument to Sir Nathaniel and Lady Jane (1653 and 1669) - an attractive pair of alabaster demi-figures whose hands gently overlay a skull between them; he wears armour and she a very fashionable gown with slashed sleeves and a profusion of lace. A Puritan MP, he suffered imprisonment with John Hampden over the matter of ship money. Finally, the family left an excellent array of **hatchments** which are hung above the nave arcades. On the n. side, from w. to e., they are for Sir Thomas (1669), Sir Thomas (1700), Sir Thomas (1698), Lady Anne (1671), Sir Robert (1728); on the s. side, from w. to e., Lady Anne (1701), Sir Samuel (1735), Sophia, Viscountess Wimbaldon (1691), Thomas (1704) and Nathaniel (1837).

Kentford, St Mary (B4): The church stands well above the village street which once formed part of the main Bury to Newmarket road. It is a C14 building and the **nave** windows have flowing **Decorated tracery**. The three **lights** of the e. window have **ogee** heads, with **reticulations** above, but the single **lancet** on the n. side of the **chancel** shows that there was an earlier and simpler predecessor. The s. chancel windows are modern and much of the exterior stonework has been renewed. The memorable feature of the tower is a small and pleasing rose window just above ground floor level, with **cinquefoiled** tracery.

The bell openings are small lancets on the w. and n. faces, but on the s. side there is a round-headed (possibly C18) window which appears to have been part of a reconstruction, mainly in thin red bricks, following a collapse of the upper tower on that side. The parapet is plain brick and a former roof line shows on the e. face. The C14 **porch** is badly decayed and one of the angle buttresses has been rebuilt in brick. It has a crow-stepped gable and the side windows have been blocked up, although the Decorated tracery survives in the one on the e. side. There is an C18 sundial above the entrance arch. The s. door is C18 panelled pine and there is a **trefoiled** niche above it. Until relatively recently there were remains of extensive wall paintings here, on both nave walls and at the w. end. Now, all is plain plaster except for an area on the n. wall opposite the entrance. Figures of the three young kings from the legend of the **Three Living and Three Dead** can be recognised and the figure of **St Christopher** was probably to their r. The background colour is mainly pale red with hints of green. The roofs are modern, and in the nave there is a plastered ceiling. Below is a lovely pale brick floor and a suite of C18 **box pews**, of unvarnished pine and in fine condition. The two-light window in the centre of the nave n. wall has 1902 glass - Christ as the Good Shepherd on one side, with an **Agnus Dei** within a wreath below, and the Virgin and Child alongside, a pot of lilies within a matching wreath underneath. The chancel was restored in 1877 when the arch was renewed and, possibly, the floor raised. The lancet in the n. wall contains a nice little roundel of stained glass, a 'G.G.' monogram with a bee on a tussock of grass as a crest. The window opposite contains shields of the Ely diocese and Trinity Hall, Cambridge, the patrons of the living. The glass in the e. window is a memorial to three members of the Lord family. The bottom centre panel shows

Christ crucified, with a young knight kneeling before Him (obviously a portrait); there is a church in the background against a red and gold sky. On either side are scenes of Christ's presentation in the temple and the visit of the Magi, with the Resurrection and Ascension above them. A fine window.

Kettlebaston, St Mary (E6): Winding lanes rise up to the little hamlet where the church and churchyard are blissfully peaceful, with a lovely whiff of pigs drifting across from the farm over the road. Passing through a little tunnel of yew, the first thing to catch the eye is a late C14 niche with **dripstone** and **finial** set in the s.e. **chancel** buttress. It was originally shuttered to hide the image during Lent and was restored in 1946 when a wrought- iron grill in the form of 'M.R.' for the church's patron saint was fitted. The bas relief within of the Coronation of the Virgin is a reproduction of one of the Kettlebaston alabasters; it was carved by Mr Green (Saunders of Ipswich) and coloured by Edith Chadwick. The chancel is C14 and there are interesting variations in the **Decorated tracery** of the windows; the **reticulations** in the e. window were renewed in 1902 but probably repeat the original. On the n. side there is an C18 brick **vestry** and the **rood stair** shows in the wall beyond. The **priest's door** on the s. side has **headstops** to the dripstone and there is a faint **scratch dial** still discernible on the s.e. buttress of the **nave**. The buttresses further w. are brick and so is the C18 **porch** with its rough wooden seats. The sturdy C14 tower has a belfry stair turret on the s. side, Decorated bell openings, and a later w. window. The early C13 doorway is an excellent example of transition in architectural styles. The shafts and **capitals** are **Norman** but the arch is pointed; however, it is still decorated in the old way with a band of triangles. This motif crops up again on

the s. side of the square **font** and could mean that the same mason was involved. The rest of the bowl is carved with simple shallow patterns and there are rudimentary attached shafts at the corners. (It is odd that one of the supporting columns has been reversed at some time.) Despite the **Perpendicular** windows, the nave was originally Norman and one of the small **lancets** has been uncovered in the n. wall, its wide splays decorated with early C14 scrolling. A plain C16 chest stands in front of the chunky tower arch and its early C17 successor by the n. wall has bands of shallow carving and roundels in the four panels. In 1864 an important series of mid- C14 alabaster panels illustrating the **Annunciation**, Ascension, **Trinity** and Coronation of the Virgin was discovered in the chancel wall and is now in the British Museum. However, casts were made and they are displayed in a case at the w. end. There is a section of small medieval tiles in front of the n. door but the rest of the floors are in homely brick, and it must be one of the last churches in regular use to depend on paraffin lamps and candles for evening light. Betjeman would have loved it. The nave **roof** has **tie-beams** and **king posts** and on the n. side the rood stair has been fitted with a wrought-iron grill designed by **Sir Ninian Comper**. In the window sill there is the simplest form of **piscina** marking the site of a medieval **altar** and now the old **Jacobean high altar** table stands there, with ponderous turned legs and prettily carved top rail and brackets.

Notches in the chancel arch show where the **tympanum** was fitted and the present screen was installed in the 1890s. Designed by the Rev Ernest Geldart, an architectural cleric active in the Anglo-Catholic movement, it does not stretch across to the old access stairs. It has attractive tracery although the panels are too squat in relation to the overall height. The colourful decoration in medieval manner was applied by Edith Chadwick in 1950 and the figures from l. to r. are **St Felix**, Sir Thomas More, **St Thomas of Canterbury**, Cardinal John Fisher, **St Alban** and **St Fursey** - an enterprising choice to include two victims of Henry VIII's malice. Although the chancel roof is largely C19, the **wall plates** are carved with a running C17 motif, and in the n. wall below there is a C14 tomb recess under a shallow **ogee** arch topped by a replacement finial, with a repainted **consecration cross** nearby. On the s. side, the wall leans outwards and so does the handsome early C14 suite of piscina and **sedilia**, its **trefoil** arches deeply moulded and the spaces divided by **quatrefoil** shafts. The **reredos** behind the free-standing high altar is another Geldart 1890s design painted by Edith Chadwick - a centre Annunciation and flanking figures of **St Peter**, **St Edmund**, the **Blessed Virgin** and **St Paul**. On the n. wall of the **sanctuary** is an alabaster and **touchstone** tablet for Joan, Lady Jermy 'whose arke after a passage of 87 yeres long through this deluge of teares on ye 6 Day of May Ano 1649 rested upon ye mount of joy'. Her epitaph is equally enchanting; do read it! On the floor of the chancel on that side is a **brass** inscription for a lady who was probably constrained to live as she died, within her husband's shadow, without the courtesy of a Christian name:

> The corpse of John Pricks wife lyes heere,
> The pastor of this place.
> Fower moneths and one and thirty yeerr
> With him she ran her race.
> And when some eightye yeres were past,
> Her soule she did resigne
> To her good God in August last,
> Yeeres thrise five hundreth ninety nine.

Lackford, St Laurence (C4): The church has a delectable setting in an acre of churchyard away from the village, surrounded by mature beeches

and approached by a longish track. Davy's 1829 journal says: 'I have not seen a place of religious worship so utterly neglected as this is; it is a great discredit both to the rector and to his parishioners'. Not surprising, therefore, that the 1868 restoration was on a large scale, both inside and out. The n. **aisle** had been pulled down in the C16, the **arcade** blocked up and windows inserted, so a narrow new one was substituted, lit by a line of sharp little **lancets**. On that side, the new **roof** slopes in one sweep over **nave** and aisle. The mid-C14 tower has a bulging stairway up to the belfry stage on the s. side and two prominent **drip courses**. The upper level was altered in the C15, stepped brick battlements applied in the C16, and the bell openings renewed in the C19. The mid-C14 **porch** has stone seats along each side and inside the church is a fine **font** of the same period. Standing on a Victorian base, with stub shaft and deep bowl, the panels are carved with different foliage patterns, including ivy and roses, with more on the chamfer below. It was plastered over to protect it in the C17 and is in better condition than most. The simple **arch-braced** roofs in nave and **chancel** are C19 but the n. arcade is early C14 and there is a matching arch further e. which has leaf decoration on the outer sections of the **capitals**. This arch leads into an extension of the n. aisle which was originally a chapel. There is a **squint** from here through to the chancel, and both ends of it have sharply gabled **trefoil** arches on **Early English** capitals and shafts, and a **piscina** drain is set within it at the chapel end. You will notice that there is a break in the line of the nave walls at the e. end and that they turn inwards. One possible explanation for this is that there was a central tower early in the church's history. The chancel arch was remade at the restoration and gives no help, but it might be significant that the squint from the chapel aligns with a point well to the w. of the **high altar** and might be evidence of an original short chancel beyond a centre tower. The C19 bench lining the aisle wall incorporates some medieval bench ends; one at the w. end has the remains of a carved animal and another is decorated with quite fine **tracery**. The C17 pulpit is in plain panelled oak, raised on a short centre stem. A window on the s. side of the nave has a dropped and stepped sill and there is a piscina on the r. hand side, marking the site of a **guild** altar. The large C13 grave slab clamped to the s. side of the chancel arch has three discoid crosses spaced down the centre spine (there is another like it outside by the porch) and in the **sanctuary** there are C13 stepped **sedilia** under unequal restored arches separated by a pillar. Beyond is a simple piscina with a trefoil arch. There is a tomb recess in the n. wall of the sanctuary and in the e. wall nearby is a very tall niche under a **cinquefoiled** arch. The 1871 glass in the e. window was designed by **Henry Holiday** for **James Powell & Sons** of Whitefriars and is poor stuff. Christ stands in the centre blessing a mother and child on the l. and a father and babe on the r. The flesh work has lost nearly all its colour and curious tendrils of wispy foliage rise up from behind the figures, with the rest of the window taken up by close patterning. On the n. face of the chancel arch is the only list of incumbents that I have ever seen engraved on a large brass plate. Returning to the s. door, you will see a memorial in the nave to the Rev William Greaves, a rector who died in 1806. It is one of the chaste little tablets with good lettering produced by de Carle of Norwich, a simple shallow sarcophagus standing on a pair of lion feet, set against a grey background.

Lakenheath, St Mary (B2): Standing a little above the village street, this is a church not to be missed, with lots of interest and beauty. The first thing one notices is the two- storey extension built on the w. face of the tower, in mottled brick and flint with a **Perpendicular** window above an C18 door and brick arch. This was a post-**Reformation** schoolroom built of material filched from the old church of Eriswell, St Peter. Manor business was at one time transacted there and it was still doing duty as the village school in the C19. The lower stages of the C13 tower have blocked **lancets**; above them are two-**light** bell openings with attractive **tracery**, and worn symbols of the **Four Evangelists** stand on the corner battlements around the centre spirelet. Traces of **Norman** work can be seen on the outside of the **chancel** walls - a fragment of a window or blind **arcade** on the n. side and a clear mark on the s. side where the building terminated before a C13 rebuild extended it eastwards. The evidence for this is a lancet on the n. side and the outlines of a C13 chapel which became a **vestry** before being demolished in the C18. Within is a substantial Norman chancel arch with roll mouldings, on scalloped **capitals** and triple columns. Beyond it on the n. side of the chancel is a short column and fragment of an arch which may have been part of blank arcading round the e. end of the original building. The doorway to the old n. chapel has been re- set within the blanked-off arch that linked it with the chancel. There is a small **piscina** tucked into the s.e. corner of the chancel, with **dropped-sill sedilia** alongside. There is no **screen** now but the stairs to the old **rood loft** are within the wall on the s. side of the chancel arch. Next to them is a wall painting of the risen Christ, in monochrome. The head shows that this was fine work but much is now lost under two large obliterating patches.

The **nave** arcades have interesting variations; on the s. side cylindrical Norman sections support C13 bases which in turn carry C15 octagonal **piers** whose concave faces have **trefoil** tops. These are seen again at the w. end of the n. arcade, and e. of them is a section of wall which probably marks the w. end of the Norman church. This is directly opposite the s. door and on it is some C14 wall painting that needs to be studied with some care before the fragments make sense because part of it has been over-laid with a diaper pattern in black. At the bottom on the r., **St Edmund**, with crown and nimbus, holds three arrows in his right hand; above this, one arm and the shadowy figure of **St John** is all that is left of a Calvary. From the cross, a tree branches out with scenes from the life of Christ - the flagellation on the l. and Christ carrying his cross on the r. Above to the l., the jaws of hell have largely to be imagined, but some of the naked souls can be seen and there is a Judge-ment scene to the r. Further e., the arcade **spandrels** contain faint paint-ings of the **Annunciation** and the Res-urrection, and on the pillar below are life-size figures in dusky red that are too indistinct to identify. Across the nave above the arcade, an Elizabethan text in gothic lettering from St John's Gospel reads: 'Labour not for ye meate which perisheth'. The fine C15 octagonal pulpit, with good and var-ied tracery at head and foot of the pan-els, stands on a shapely coved stem. Across from it, on the s. side of the nave, is a **brass** with 18 in figures of a civilian of the early C16 and his wife; he in a gown with high lapels, she with a turban head-dress. The inscription has been lost, but the cou-ple are likely to have been a local farmer and his wife, John and Cecily Lacey. The C14 n. **aisle** has **reticu-lated** tracery in the side windows and a beautiful little roundel window over the **altar** contains glass of 1905 - a fine Virgin and **St Michael** flanking Christ in majesty. On the n. wall is a memorial to Lord Kitchener who went down with the cruiser *Hamp-shire* in 1916. One of his forebears came, oddly enough, from Hampshire in 1666 as bailiff to the Styward fam-ily, Lords of the Manor. The C13 octa-gonal **font** to the w. is the finest of its period in the county and is thought to

have come from the old church of St Peter of Eriswell after the **Reforma-tion**. The centre shaft is ringed with alternating thick and thin shafts, and each face has a sharply defined gable from which exuberant **crockets** sprout. Above are deeply recessed arches enriched with **dogtooth** orna-ment. The elegant cover provided in 1961 has a dove on the **finial**. At the e. end of the C15 s. aisle is a **Jacobean box pew** with panels of scroll carving, probably used by the Styward family. In the corner next to it is the tomb of Simeon Styward who died in 1568, its grey **purbeck marble** very worn, with a battered heraldic **achievement** at the back. Everything about it is old fashioned for the period except the inscription in Roman capitals on the cornice and the bevel of the tomb slab. Before the space was thus taken up, there was an altar to the Holy Trinity here and the piscina and dropped-sill sedilia remain. To the w. of the large tomb, an oblong panel in the wall is the memorial to Simeon's wife, Joanna, with a shield of arms hung on a tree with crossed swords below, all in shallow relief. Further w. can be seen a large **Royal Arms** of Charles II on boards, dated 1678 and rescued from neglect and decay 300 years later.

So far, very little has been said about the church's woodwork, but the lovely range of C15 benches is per-haps the one thing that draws enthu-siasts to Lakenheath. Their pierced and traceried backs gleam like newly fallen chestnuts, and though many have been cruelly defaced, the range of animals and grotesques on the but-tressed armrests is one of the best to be found anywhere and echoes the medieval **bestiaries** excellently. On the s. side of the nave, look for the tigress with the mirror; legend had it that to catch a tiger cub one must ride off with it and elude the parents. If the tigress followed too closely, the trick was to throw down a mirror so that she would mistake the reflection for her cub and lick it while the hunter

Lakenheath, St Mary: bench end tigress with mirror

escaped. Call the tigress 'humanity', the cub 'the soul', the hunter 'the Devil', the mirror 'sinful wordly pleasures' and there you have a sermon in a carving no bigger than your hand. On the n. side of the s. aisle is a dog licking itself because the bestiary taught that thus dogs heal their wounds. In the n. aisle at the e. end is an elongated beaver bent over itself; it was believed that it was hunted to extract certain drugs from its genitals and that, when cornered, it would bite them off to show that the whole thing was not worth it. (There is another carving very like this at nearby Wilton in Norfolk.) Further w. in the n. aisle, a whale swallows a fish (the fate of sinners at the hands of the Devil), and elsewhere you will easily identify the elephant and castle, the contortionist and the **unicorn** similarly inclined. This century has added its quota of good work in oak - the benches at the w. end have crisp **poppyheads** and a variety of subjects on the elbows, including St Edmund, a **griffin**, a chalice and paten, and a bell and wheel. Above all this is a lovely early C15 **roof**, surely designed by the master who worked at Mildenhall, Hockwold and Meth-

wold. **Arch-braced tie-beams** have tracery in the spandrels and either side of the **queen posts**, and they alternate with **hammerbeams** bearing angels with outstretched wings. These were defaced more successfully than those at Mildenhall during the Commonwealth and the wings were not restored until often marvels of meticulous embroidery, but by the n. nave pillar opposite the door you will find two of their rustic ancestors. A clump or tussock of the sedge *Carex paniculata* was known as a hassock and they were brought into church to kneel or sit on. Now harsh and prickly as a week-old beard, they must in their youth have been balm to the knees. Others like them survive at Eriswell and Icklingham.

Langham, St Mary (E4): The church is quite hidden from the road and a visit entails a quarter of a mile walk across meadow land, so a careful look at the map and an enquiry about the key are advised. The setting is a lovely one, with the Hall to the n.w. and mature trees grouped attractively round the church. The **nave** was entirely rebuilt to the design of **E.C. Hakewill** in 1877 in **Early English** style, using a great deal of material from the old building. A western double bellcote and a s. **porch** were added, and ten years later the **chancel** was rebuilt to match, together with a **vestry**-cum-organ chamber on the s. side. Although all the windows are C19 their **tracery** may well have been copied from the originals. For some obscure reason, the head of a small **lancet** was used to form a niche in the e. face of the n.w. nave buttress next to the blocked n. door. As one would expect, the interior is largely C19 in feeling but there are some interesting things to see. The late C14 **font** with its **castellated** rim, stands on a high step and the bowl panels contain **cusped** and **crocketted ogee** arches; an heraldic shield is repeated within four of them and there are squared-off grotesque heads in the rest; the carving is curiously crude. At the angles below the bowl there are worn human heads, but the odd thing is that one to the e. is a lamb's head. I wonder why? On the n. wall there is a **brass** recording a benefaction by John Jollye who died in 1630, leaving £100 to buy land to be let for the benefit of the poor, stipulating distributions at Christmas and on Midsummer day. The C19 benches have lozenge-shaped **poppyheads**, except for the pair at the w. end which have kneeling angels. After 100 years they have lost their arms, showing that ordinary wear and tear as well as deliberate mutilation can figure in the life cycle of an average bench end. The **rood loft** stair rises on the n. side and the C15 **screen** is a very interesting example. It is sadly mutilated but note that the openwork tracery front of the old rood loft has survived, having been moved back and placed on top of the screen itself. The base panels have been cut down so that the traceried plinth now obscures their lower sections, and although those on the l. retain their original colour and stencilled patterns, those on the r. are rough replacements. The tracery in the panels must have been fine but all the applied crocketting has been

stripped away. The main **lights** have cusped ogee arches, with dense tracery above them. The clue to the unusual feature of this screen lies in the mortices cut at sill level on either side of the entrance, and the long grooves above them. They show that originally there would have been projecting wings forming bays each side of the entrance for **altars**. The same arrangement may be seen on the more elaborate screen at Ranworth in Norfolk and, like Ranworth, there would have been a coved canopy beneath the loft, probably across the entire width. In the chancel there are niches with tall crocketted **finials** each side of the altar and it is strange that, although they are of the same period, they do not match (the heights differ and the one on the n. has blank shields each side of the finial). Both have traces of colour within. The **piscina** has a reconstructed arch on which is cut 'H.K. 1875'. It is unusual to find graffiti in the **sanctuary** and it may have been taken from elsewhere in the old building. The wooden **credence shelf**, however, looks original.

Lavenham, St Peter and St Paul (D6): Suffolk is rich in splendid churches but for many people Lavenham is the finest, and is remembered with affection and respect by the thousands who visit year by year. It is solidly magnificent and the exterior has a unity and strength that bears comparison with any parish church in England. Apart from the early C14 **chancel**, with flowing **tracery** in the e. window and the unusual **trefoil** shapes in the single s. window, the building is a coherent essay in the mature **Perpendicular** style. It was raised on the wealth of the Earls of Oxford and the Lavenham clothiers (particularly the Springs); the great rebuilding and extension began about 1470 when Thomas Spring II built the **vestry** at the e. end. Just before he died he saw the base of the tower laid in 1486 and it rose to just above the

level of the belfry windows in the first phase. John de Vere, 13th Earl of Oxford, that powerful champion of the first **Tudor** king, Henry VII, counted the manor of Lavenham among his many possessions and he joined with the Springs in the new project. The **nave** was rebuilt from e. to w. and at the time of Lord Oxford's death in 1513 it was finished, together with the **aisles** and **porch**. Meanwhile, the chapel of the Holy Trinity, n. of the chancel, had been built by Simon and Elizabeth Branche about 1500. The tower was finally completed in the 1520s, using the bequests of wealthy clothiers, particularly that of Thomas Spring III. He and his wife Alice began the building of the Lady chapel s. of the chancel in about 1523.

Having generalised, let us look at the outside in detail. The splendidly proportioned tower is a landmark for miles and has substantial square projections at each corner which are themselves buttressed. **String courses** break the profile up to the top of the first building stage (where the star of the de Vere family is set in the walls), and then it sweeps up past large three-**light** bell openings to a decorated but severe parapet. It has been suggested that pinnacles and perhaps a spire were envisaged but there is little evidence for this and I do not think it likely. The design may have been the work of Simon Clerk who was the king's master mason at Eton and Cambridge. The deep **base course** is decorated with shields (many of them worn) which carry the de Vere arms and three versions of Thomas Spring's merchant's mark. By the time the tower was completed, Thomas Spring III had been knighted and the parapet repeats his arms no less than 32 times. The w. door with its worn tracery is original, and note that besides the de Vere arms there is a chalice and wafer carved at the top.

An indent in the lowest niche on the s.w. buttress shows that there was once a **brass** placed there. The battlements of nave, porch, and aisles are pierced with carvings of pointed trefoil leaves and the tall, closely spaced **clerestory** windows act as a foil to the heavier aisle windows below. The aisle buttresses are decorated with **cusped** and **crocketted ogee** arches within which leaf shapes echo the theme of the battlements. All the surfaces are **ashlar** and, as the style is reminiscent of Saffron Walden and Cambridge, Great St Mary's, it may follow that John Wastell (who followed Clerk at King's College) was the architect. The distinctive octagonal **rood stair** turret at the s.e. corner of the nave was part of the earlier church and is capped by a tall crocketted pinnacle embellished with a delicate openwork **finial**. The matching chapels that flank the chancel are slightly higher and broader than the aisles and their e. walls carry the best **flushwork** on the building. There is an inscription below the parapet of each recording their foundation, and the words asking us to pray for the souls of the donors were chiselled away during the Commonwealth. The C16 door in the s. wall has **linen-fold panelling** with the Spring arms in the **spandrels** and there are headless figures on the parapet. There is flushwork on the e. wall of the vestry and a stone panel bears the faint marks of a brass, another instance of the unusual placing of a brass outside. Just round the corner is a gargantuan **gargoyle**, and the replica **churchyard cross** nearby is a memorial to John Croker and his wife; he was the rector largely responsible for the restorations and alterations of the second half of the C19. It is unique in my experience because not only does it carry verses of well-loved hymns but their tunes are set out as well. The s. porch was the particular gift of John, 13th Earl of Oxford, and is correspondingly lavish. The s. front has recently been cleaned and restored. Below the

stepped and pierced battlements the centre canopied niche contains modern figures of the church's patron saints. On either side shallow niches contain arches with tall crocketted finials, within which are the shields of the 9th to 13th earls; they are each enclosed within the Garter which is embellished with little animals on the r. hand side. Full details of the heraldry are displayed just within the church. The spandrels of the outer arch are carved with a weathered boar, a punning badge of the de Vere family from the Latin 'verres'. The **fan vaulting** within is likely to have been a John Wastell design and it was comprehensively restored in 1865. The fine inner doors with their linen-fold panelling are original and in the upper corners boars are carved hanging from fire jacks, another de Vere punning badge which presumes that Sir John was familiarly known as 'Sir Jack'. A few steps down lead to an interior of great spaciousness and dignity. The openback C19 benches do not obtrude and the w. end has been largely cleared. The **piers** of the **arcades** have attached shafts on all four sides whose **capitals** vary in detail and the entire space between arches and clerestory is filled with blind tracery - blank shields in **quatrefoils** and lozenges predominating, under a line of cresting below the windows. Half-round shafts rise to carved **corbels**, on which stand the **wall post** figures. The nave **roof** is a restrained cambered design and the two bays at the e. end are panelled to form a **celure** for the **rood**. There you will see **bosses** freshly painted and gilded displaying the **Evangelistic symbols** in the centre, flanked by the Oxford and Neville arms and two of Thomas Spring II's merchant's marks. There are a few fragments of medieval glass in the clerestory windows and by using binoculars a medieval beacon can be identified in the sixth window from the w. end on the n. side, with another further along.

The lean-to aisle roofs have richly

carved main timbers and **wall plates**, and there are seated figures on the wall posts of the s. aisle, with standing figures in the n. aisle, including **Saints Simon**, **Jude** and **James the Less**. The recurring themes in the decoration are the de Vere stars and boars, but over the **font** the carver relented and gave us children scrambling along a vine. A vine trail can also be seen carved in stone beneath the s. aisle windows; there are corresponding **paterae** in the n. aisle. Within the tower there are seats below blind panelling at the base of the walls and the w. window has glass designed by J. Milner Allen for **Lavers & Barraud**. It won a prize at the 1862 Exhibition but unfortunately the whole window was blown in by a landmine during World War II. However, the eight main panels were salvaged and re-set and they have a **St Peter** theme: top r., he strikes off Malchus' ear and denies Christ, and bottom r., he is crucified upside down. The **purbeck marble** C14 font now stands by the s. door and will have belonged to the earlier church. It is very worn but the design is interesting because, apart from one which has shields of the patron saints, each panel of the shallow bowl was carved with two figures. They are scarcely recognisable now but the one to the s.w. appears to be a mother and child with a satanic angel turning away. There are now only vestiges of the four figures and the four beasts around the stem. Three sets of **Royal Arms** are grouped around the s. door: e. side, a **Hanoverian** set delicately carved in relief, coloured and gilded; w. side, a set for George II painted on canvas; overhead, a brash Queen Elizabeth II achievement. The w. end of the n. aisle has a solid oak **screen** installed in 1917 and by it on the wall is a dark brass for Alleyn Dister who died in 1534:

A clothier vertuous while he was
In Lavenham many a year,
Ffor as in lyefe he loved best,

The poore to clothe and feede,
So with the riche and all the rest,
He neighbourlie agreed...

He and his wife kneel, their children behind them, his arms are in a **cartouche** at the top and the gothic lettered inscription is framed with strapwork below. Over the n. door there are traces of the painted surrounds of Elizabethan texts and in the tracery of the adjoining window two lovely little C15 angels have bandeaux adorned with large crosses. A **sacred monogram** can be seen in the tracery of the next window, together with sections of medieval canopy work. At the e. end of the n. aisle is the **chantry chapel** of one of the church's principal benefactors, Thomas Spring III. He died in 1523 and directed that he should be buried here before the altar of **St Catherine** and arranged for a chantry priest and bedesmen to pray daily for him, his wife, Henry VIII and Queen Catherine, and Thomas Wolsey, Archbishop of York. His tombstone, reaved of its brasses, lies within and the **parclose screen** is the finest example of woodwork in the church. Dark and lustrous, the luxuriant carving is full of lively **Renaissance** detail, with foliage tracery in the lower panels, pierced main uprights, and rope-like carving with twisted chains of beads. There is openwork cresting over **groined** canopies and the tracery of the main lights is enlivened by grotesques while some of the Spring shields are supported by small figures. A small St Catherine stands within a niche at the s.w. corner and **St Blaise** can be found at the s.e. corner. The work has affinities with the screen in Henry VII's chapel in Westminster Abbey and is likely to have been the work of Flemish craftsmen. An extremely skilful restoration was carried out in 1908.

Beyond is the screen to the n.e. chapel, tall and square-headed, with dense Perpendicular tracery above ogee arches. The little angel over the entrance is, I suspect, from the hand

of **Henry Ringham**. On the e. side can be seen a door which led originally to a loft above the screen. The chapel is divided from the chancel by two varying sections of Perpendicular screenwork in which are cut three **elevation squints**. The n. wall has low arcading above stone benches and the e. window glass (almost certainly by Lavers & Barraud) dates from 1864. The top half shows one of Christ's miracles of healing while below there is the first miracle at Cana, with hieratic figures in C13 dress. The **altar** here is an excellent melon-legged early C17 table. In the s. aisle is another fine early C16 parclose screen. It is by no means as luxuriant as the Spring chantry but the design has perhaps more clarity and grace. Pairs of main lights with dolphins in the tracery are contained within large ogee arches decorated with spaced crockets; the lower panels have Renaissance tracery and there are elevation squints to the w. The shield bearing dolphins belongs to the Spourne fam-

Lavenham, St Peter & Paul: Spring chantry

ily and as that emblem recurs in the tracery it was probably their chantry. It now contains the tomb of clothier John Ponder (who died in 1520), which was moved in from outside in 1908. There is a **piscina** set in the wall. Across the aisle is the entrance to the rood loft stair and one of the upper doors gave access to a loft above the Lady chapel screen. The base of this is medieval and the beautifully carved top cresting is dated 1958. Within the Spring or Lady chapel the vine trail of the s. aisle is continued below the windows and there is a tiny piscina. The roof is particularly rich and one needs a bright day to appreciate it fully. On the s. side from the e. the wall posts carry figures of an angel, St Peter and St Blaise; on the n. side from the e., **Saints Thomas of Canterbury**, **Paul** and **James the Great**. The wall plates are carved with the Spring arms and their stag's head crest, flowers and animals' heads, while the spandrels of the **arch-braces** carry **Tudor** emblems of rose and pomegranate. To the l. is a standing bronze of the **Blessed Virgin** and Child of 1983 by Neil Godfrey, and in the centre of the **sanctuary** a very good C20 heraldic brass. The chapel has three lovely windows by Lavers & Barraud, with scenes effectively arranged and in rich colours. In the s. wall you will see the stoning of **St Stephen** and the conversion of St Paul in one window and scenes from the life of Christ in the other; both are in deep, fairly sombre colours with little animation. The e. window has Christ blessing children below fruiting trees, and the lower panels contain the scene from St Luke's Gospel where **St Mary Magdalene** washes Christ's feet with her tears and dries them with her hair. The clothes and general feeling of the composition are Renaissance and the church's principal benefactors are included in the group. The altar here is a good, early C17 table with a carved top rail and centre pendant.

The tall and wide C14 chancel arch has very small male and female **headstops** like tragic masks on the **hood mould** and there are two more on the e. side. The hook that supported the rood still remains in the apex of the arch and below is an excellent screen dating from about 1330 and retained at the rebuilding. As with nearly all early screens, the lower section is plain and each panel was drilled with trefoil elevation squints. Each main light contains a heavily crocketted ogee arch divided by a slim **mullion**, with the head filled with **mouchettes** of flowing tracery, the pattern alternating. The main uprights have crocketted gables and at their bases are tiny heads of men and beasts. The screen doors were discarded during the 1861 restoration but luckily they were recovered from a stable and their hinges from a pigsty, and were replaced in 1909. Some of the clergy stalls backing on to the screen have

misericords; the one on the s. side is carved with a man using a pig as a set of bagpipes. The three on the n. are: a **pelican**; a man playing the bellows with a pair of tongs, paired with a lady who holds a vielle (similar to a violin but fitted with a handle that turned a rosined wheel within which produced a continuous bass note, and a rare illustration of a popular instrument which became known as the hurdy-gurdy); the two figures are backed by a dragon. Next there is a jester and, beyond him, a spoonbill and an ibis dip their beaks to the small head of a man. The stall ends have heavy tracery and **poppyheads** and there are remains of **griffins** on the n. side, with a camel and a winged lion on the s. Henry Ringham was at work here during the C19 restoration and much of his meticulous work can be recognised. In front of the sanctuary steps is a small **chrysom** brass with a Latin inscription for Clopton d'Ewes who only lived ten days and died in 1631, son and heir of Sir Symonds d'Ewes. The fine flowing tracery of the e. window is filled with an outstanding example of the stained glass of Lavers & Barraud. Designed in 1861 by James Milner Allen, the main lights contain the crucified Christ flanked by the Virgin and **St John**, with St Peter to the l. and St Paul to the r. There are Evangelistic symbols below the Christ in Majesty at the top, and while the key colour is blue, the overall effect is kaleidoscopic. Below it is an alabaster **reredos** installed in 1890; it is arcaded, with busy gables, pinnacles and standing figures. The contemporary **sedilia** to the r. is far more pleasing an attenuated arcade with polished marble columns supporting pierced gables. High on the n. wall of the sanctuary is the large monument to Henry Copinger, rector here for over 40 years, one of whose early duties was to receive Queen Elizabeth when she visited the church. He died in 1622 and the memorial was erected by his widow. In **touchstone** and alabaster, much of the original colour survives and the couple face each other across a faldstool between **Corinthian** columns. Rather ungainly angels stand each side and the children are neatly graded in the panel below.

Lawshall, All Saints (D6): The church was rebuilt in the middle of the C15 on a fairly large scale, with **nave**, **aisles** and **clerestory**. The earlier tower is well-proportioned, with four strong **string courses**, angled buttresses, and **flushwork** crosses set at intervals in the **base course**, a motif used again on the nave and **porch** buttresses. **William Butterfield** rebuilt the **chancel** in restrained **Early English** style in 1857 and the random flint finish is relieved by lines of thin red tiles. These occur in the parapets too and suggest that they also were restored, along with the porch. That displays little beast **paterae** below the parapet and there are two stunted **gargoyles**. The entrance doorway is **Perpendicular**, with blank shields in the **spandrels**. Within, there are elegant **arcades** with **piers** that are shafted on four faces and rise to **castellated capitals**. A string course runs below the clerestory and lifts over the chancel arch. It is punctuated by **fleurons** and demi-angels, from which slim shafts rise to support the **wall posts** of the closely timbered cambered **roof**. The **arch-braced** aisle roofs rest on castellated **corbels** that match those in the nave. The string course angels and spandrels over the chancel arch were brightly coloured some years ago, and the C15 **font** received the same treatment. It has varied **tracery** in the deep bowl panels, with defaced heads at the angles, and the underside is unusually moulded. Above the tower arch is a squat and wide **sanctus-bell window**, and to the l., an interesting memorial for Pilot Officer Johannes van Mesdag who was killed in 1945. It is a panel of cream, 3 in, glazed tiles bearing a noble inscription impressed in dull gold, with a blue and gold

enamelled shield at the bottom. Made at Gouda, it was designed by the eminent typographer Jan van Krimpen. The aisles are lit by large Perpendicular windows and at the e. end on the s. side is a massive mahogany chest with filigree brass decoration and a large lockplate engraved with a double eagle, possibly C18 work from the East Indies. In the n. aisle the e. window was partially blocked when the 1850s organ chamber was added, and in front of it stands a second chest of the C17 with marquetry panels and strings, shallow bands of carving and split turnings on the front. The mid-C19 wooden lectern is a very good, high quality example of the period; the turned shaft of the desk top rises from a miniature octagonal gallery which has a sloping roof over the colonnade. The chancel is all Butterfield and a **cusped** division separates the painted waggon roof above the **sanctuary** from the rest. There are **Ecclesiological Society** candelabra, tiled fronts to the steps, and the **communion rails** are cast metal in dull red, gold and black. The tiled **reredos** has a centre cross with attractive blue enamel lobes bearing the **Evangelistic symbols** in beige. There is a mock **piscina** without a drain to match the Early English-style **lancets**. The stained glass by Alexander Gibbs is not memorable.

Lidgate, St Mary (B5): A lane leads past the large village pond up to the church which stands on what was once a fortified hill; there are still deep ditches to w. and n., and the remains of a castle to the e. The churchyard is beautifully kept and the C13 or early C14 tower has a plain parapet. The stair lies within the s.w. buttresses so that its slit windows peep out on two sides. The **aisles** are C14 while the **lancets** and **priest's door** in the **chancel** date it as C13, with two C14 windows on the s. side and an e. window with flowing **tracery** of the same period. The brick s. **porch** is likely to be C17 and the lower roof line of its predecessor shows on the aisle wall. The inner door, with its square lintel and blank **tympanum** is probably early **Norman** but the **jambs** have C15 mouldings. A possible **consecration cross** is incised within a circle on the r. hand side, and Thomas Willyamson cut his name above it some time in the C17.

Inside, there are tall C14 **arcades** and the church is rather dark, mainly because there is no **clerestory**. All the floors are in pale brick and, at the w. end, the low tower arch is deeply moulded and fitted with a medieval door complete with three strap hinges and centre closing ring. There are many examples of medieval graffiti to be found in the church and they include three late C14 fragments of music (very rare), a beautifully drawn head of the **Blessed Virgin** on a s. arcade pillar, together with inscriptions, windmills and birds. The plain C15 **font** also has its share of scribbles, and there is a curious three-pronged recess like a gridiron cut into one of the steps which has no obvious purpose. (Similar examples can be found on other fonts in the county.) The roofs are C19 but the benches below are medieval and, in their way, interesting. Unlike more flamboyant sets, they are plain and low with square ends, and seem to have been made in three blocks; those on the s. side have heavier top mouldings than the rest, and a single bench end on the n. side of the nave has tracery cut in the solid (possibly a pattern that was not accepted). In the n. aisle the ends are decorated with early C16 **linenfold** and one of them is spectacularly warped. A C19 **bier** stands in the n. aisle and at the e. end there is a late C15 **parclose screen** with doors to w. and s. The main **lights** have **cusped ogee** arches with attractive flowing tracery over them, and the top cresting is pierced and battlemented. Balance has been nicely achieved by a modern parclose screen enclosing the chapel in the s. aisle - solid, competent work in the medieval idiom. The chapel has a **piscina** with a **cinquefoiled** arch, and to the l. of the **altar** the **rood stair** is set squarely in the corner with a high level window. The early C17 pulpit is an unusual design; octagonal, with strapwork panels above very plain and shallow blind arches, it stands on a square base with turned **finials** at the corners, and there is a carved top rail with partially carved blind arches in two panels. The C15 **rood screen** has a base of plain boards and the centre arch is a double cusped ogee, with **mouchettes** and panel tracery above it. The gates are modern. The chancel is wide and open and in the **sanctuary** is an early C14 piscina, the arch resting on short shafts with ring **capitals** and bases. There is a small recess to the r. with a hole in the base, and one wonders whether this was an auxiliary piscina installed during the short period when two drains were the rule. In the sanctuary n. wall there is a pair of **aumbries** with C19 doors, and in front of the modern **communion rails** is an interesting late C14 **brass**. It is the 20 in figure of a priest in eucharistic vestments, one of only four in Suffolk thus dressed. The head is a modern replacement and it was once enclosed within an octofoil cross. Although it has often been suggested, the brass has no connection with the poet-monk John Lydgate - he may have hailed from the village but the memorial dates from about 1380, some 20 years before he became a priest. It is more likely to be the brass of Thomas atte Welle who was rector here at the relevant time. John Isaacson was an early C19 rector and his **ledger-stone** nearby has the unusual distinction of being signed by the mason, Parkinson of Newmarket. In the s. lancet is some 1860s glass by **Clayton & Bell** which has good colour and composition - a Crucifixion with the three Maries in a **quatrefoil** above and the Entombment in a quatrefoil below, forming an excellent example of this firm's better work.

Little Bradley, All Saints (B6): This lovely little church is tucked away down a long lane that leads to the Hall Farm through gently undulating countryside. There are humps and hollows in the field beyond the church, marking the site of the deserted village. The **Saxon** round tower was given an octagonal belfry with stepped battlements in the mid C15 and the arms of Underhill are displayed on a shield below the s. window. The **nave** has **Perpendicular** windows on the s. side but the masonry of the nave and w. half of the **chancel** is probably Saxon, judging by the **long and short work** at the e. angles of the nave. There is the bulge of a **rood loft** stair in the angle between nave and chancel on the s. side, and the low wall top of the original Saxon chancel and its e. corners can be seen reaching halfway along the present chancel. The extension was evidently early **Norman** because there are faint remains of little **lancets** on either side of the renewed e. window. There are two similar lancets (one blocked) on the n. side where, again, the Saxon wall can be seen. The n. side of the nave has square-headed **Decorated** windows and one of the C19 inserted in the old n. doorway. Before going in, have a look at the fine C18 stones on the s. side, evidently by the Great Thurlow mason.

Entry is via a plain Norman doorway which has circle graffiti just inside to the r. The early Norman tower arch is low, with squared **imposts**, and a medieval door frame with carved **spandrels** was added later. By the door is a large and plain octagonal C14 **font**, and the simple interior was fitted with benches as part of a rigorous 1870s restoration. The pulpit seems to be early C19 but the **tester**, with its marquetry star, may be a little earlier. The plain chancel arch had deep notches cut in the imposts to take the **rood screen** and beyond it on the r. is a blocked **low side window** which now contains a **brass** moved from the floor. It is the headless figure of a man in **Tudor** armour, with kneeling groups of children, and it may be for Thomas Knighton who died in 1532. Further along is the large monument in soft, pale stone for Richard le Hunt who died in 1540. It is raised up on a ledge and reaches to the **roof**, with two **achievements of arms** in frames on top. He, his wife and family kneel in line, and all have lost their heads except father who lacks his hands and lower legs; his helm is neatly stowed in an alcove beside him. In the **sanctuary** the **piscina** is very strangely positioned in a shapeless recess above the **dropped-sill sedilia**. Here is an excellent late brass for Thomas and Elizabeth Soame, 1612. A large plate, it shows them kneeling, he in armour with five sons, she in a variation of the Mary, Queen of Scots, cap and large ruff, with her two daughters. Thomas died in 1606 but his sons are dressed in the new fashion of doublet, hose and short cloak. Like the Soame monument at Little Thurlow, there is a quotation from the psalms, but in Latin in this case and from psalm 88. Another brass is laid in the floor on the n. side - 18 in figures of John and Jane le Hunte (1605) - and note that in the inscription Cavendish has its old spelling of "Candish'. On the n. wall, set within a shallow Tudor arch, is a brass of a man and woman kneeling on either side of a stone shield of arms to which they were once linked by scrolls. He wears a long fur- trimmed gown, she a **kennel head-dress**, and the heraldry identifies them as an early C16 Underhill and his wife but the inscription has gone. Above this memorial is a beautiful and important brass set in a moulded stone frame. It is for John Daye, the renowned Elizabethan printer, who died in 1584. Born at Dunwich in 1522, he produced the first book of church music in English, and printed Queen Elizabeth's prayer book in six languages. Works by Latimer and Archbishop Parker came from his press but he is perhaps best remembered as the printer of John Foxe's *Acts and Monuments of these Latter and Perilous Days*, that great folio of 1563 that caused an immediate sensation and was dubbed *The Book of Martyrs*. He and his second wife Alice face each other across a faldstool on which are engraved images of two **chrysom children**, and six sons kneel behind him, with five daughters ranged behind his wife. At the top, his achievement is in the centre, with the arms of the Stationers' Company (of which he was Master) on the l. He was fond of punning and used the device of a sun and "Arise O man for it is Daye'. His wife evidently caught the habit when she composed his epitaph:

heere lies the Daye that darkness could not blynd
When popish fogges had over cast the sunne...

She by that time had married a Mr Stone and the temptation to have another go was too strong, for the last lines read:

Als [Alice] was the last increase of his stoore,
Who mourning long for being left alone,
Set upp this toombe, her self turned to a Stone.

He probably laughed in heaven.

Little Saxham, St Nicholas (C4): A very attractive setting at the village cross-roads. The round tower is arguably the best in Suffolk and the base may well be **Saxon**, although the belfry stage is **Norman**. There, two-**light** openings are deeply recessed and linked by an **arcade** of blank arches above a course of **billet** moulding. It has been suggested that the detailing was copied from the Norman gateway of the abbey at Bury. There is a small **lancet** lower down on the w. side within sections of **chevron moulding**. Some particularly pretty **Decorated tracery** is to be found in one of the C14 n. **aisle** windows and the C16 Lucas chapel, with its large

Perpendicular n. window, juts out on that side. Large three-light windows were inserted in the s. wall in the C15 and the churchyard has been cleared in front with headstones lined up - some of them C17 and C18. Within the **porch** are a small **stoup** and a Norman doorway with a plain **tympanum**. The thick roll moulding of the arch has a rim of billet decoration and the shafts have volute **capitals**. Just inside on the l. there is a Norman archway in the w. wall, and this has been identified by some as the n. doorway. If so, it must have been cut down and there seems to be no good reason for it being where it is. The C11 tower arch is tremendously tall and narrow and there is a doorway or large window opening above it. At the back of the aisle two base sections of the old **rood screen** rest against the wall and the buttresses have **crocketted** pinnacles at the top, while in the tracery **spandrels** you will find tiny carvings of squirrels, birds, lions, a rabbit and a pig. Nearby stands a C17 **bier** - a rarity of interesting design; it has a slatted top, rudimentary carving on the ends and, instead of the usual hinged arrangement, the handles retract into the frame. (Another example is to be found at Dalham.) Two of the church's pre-**Reformation** bells now stand at the w. end, and both were cast by the Brasyer family of Norwich in the C15. It is a good opportunity to study the shield mark of the foundry, with its three bells and ducal coronet, and to admire the characteristically splendid lettering on the crown. The treble has 'Ave Maria gratia plena Dominus tecum' (Hail Mary full of grace, the Lord is with thee) and will have been used to sound the angelus. The second is inscribed 'Missus de celis haber nomen Gabrielis' (I have the name Gabriel sent from heaven). On the n. side of the nave there are medieval benches which have birds and beasts instead of **poppyheads** and one of them is a dragon biting its tail. Near the front, one bench has traceried ends with **paterae** on the chamfers, the remains of angels on the elbows and dumpy poppyheads. Across on the s. side, one **finial** is carved as a lady in a cloak kneeling at a prayer desk on which is a large open book. The **Jacobean** pulpit has two ranges of panels with the usual blank arches; it was extensively restored in 1891 when a new **tester** was added. The stairs to the old **rood loft** are at the e. end of the n. aisle and the position of the bottom door is most unusual. With the hinge hooks still in place, it is a good 6 ft from the floor and one wonders whether part of the loft served as a secure place for valuables. In the wall below is a **piscina**, indicating that there was a medieval **altar** here. Sir Thomas Fitz Lucas was Henry VII's Solicitor General and it was he who built the n. chapel. He died in 1531 and was buried in London but he had already prepared a tomb here and it stood within an archway in the n. wall of the chancel,opening into his chapel. However, when the chapel was appropriated by the Lucas family in the C17, the panels of the tomb were piled one on another to block the arch; so they remain, with eight coloured shields bearing the arms of Lucas, Morrieux, Kent and Kemys, all set within tracery. Little Livermere church is now an abandoned ruin but its lovely set of **communion rails**, with their turned and reeded **balusters**, were salvaged and have found a home here, with the **sanctuary** floor amended to follow their elegant double curve. The **Heaton, Butler & Bayne** glass of 1902 in the s. chancel window contains large figures of **St Luke** on the l., the **Blessed Virgin**, and **St James the Great** on the r. There are three angels above them, and both the predominance of pale yellow and the texture of the painting are in strong contrast with the E.R. Suffling glass in the e. window.

The n. chapel is normally locked but it is worth making local enquiries for a key because of the important monument within. It commemorates

William Lucas, 1st (and only) Baron Crofts (1677) and his wife, and is the work of Abraham Storey, one of Wren's master masons whose monuments are of great importance. This is his finest work and takes up the full height of the chapel on the s. side. The life-size figure, in flowing robes and baron's coronet, reclines with head thrown back, his fleshy face framed by an abundant wig. In his uplifted hand he holds a folded parchment and its seal is carved with the artist's monogram. Lady Crofts lies in front and just below him, head strained back as though to catch a glimpse of her husband. The features of both are finely modelled and note the quality of his left hand. The front panel of the massive base carries the Croft shield, **corinthian** columns flank a large epitaph panel framed in coloured marble, and there is a coloured **achievement** set between scrolls and draped urns above the cornice. Apart from chipped noses and two missing fingers, the dazzling marble is in lovely condition. Baron Croft was a Gentleman of the Bed Chamber to Charles II and guardian to his natural son the Duke of Monmouth so that the king frequently stayed at the Hall, particularly if there was racing at Newmarket. Samuel Pepys was with the king when he stayed at Saxham in October 1668; Charles got so drunk that he could not give audience to Lord Arlington who had come over from Euston. That means they probably did not come to church! Elizabeth Crofts died in 1642 and her memorial on the e. wall is particularly interesting because few were commissioned during the Civil war, and the design is defiantly at odds with the Puritan spirit. It is possibly by Henry Boughton and the alabaster frame is carved with cherub heads in profile, while fat **putti** support a **cartouche** of arms resting on a skull in the curve of the top. Above that, a small bust of the lady displays a generous and undraped busom. By way of confirmation, her husband tells us in the epitaph that 'she had a large proportion of personal beauty and handsomeness', but hastens to add: 'ye endowments of hir minde beinge much more eminent ... in sum a woman of extraordinary perfections'. The C18 memorial to Mrs Ann Crofts is by William Palmer, and on the w. wall there is a tablet in a simple architectural frame for William Crofts who died in 1694, his achievement within the scrolled cornice and another coloured shield at the base.

Little Thurlow, St Peter (A6): This is a late C13 to early C14 church. The tower has a large w. window with **cusped**, intersected **tracery**; the tall bell openings are later, with **headstops** to the **dripstones** and the battlements are flint chequer overall. As with other churches in this corner of the county, a lot of **septaria** show in the walls of the s. **aisle** and **chancel**. The Soame family chapel was added in the early C17 and it is as large and tall as the chancel next to it; there are blind circular windows and another on the n. side has curious tracery. The large **trefoil clerestory** windows were replaced on the n. side with plain circles in the C17. The low and simple C18 brick **porch** shelters a C14 n. door which retains one shapeless headstop. The C14 tower arch is tall and thin and the position of C17 and later graffiti in the w. window embrasure shows that there was once a ringers' gallery half way up. The square C12 **font** is large and deep; there are scrolly and very varied carvings on three sides of the bowl with a cross roundel on the s. face, and thick shafts with **chevron capitals** mark the corners. The **Jacobean** pews are very interesting, with curiously shaped tops to the ends - inverted scrolls coming to a point at the top, the outer surfaces carved with a range of flower and leaf motifs. They are so like those at Clare that they may have been carved by the same man. The roofs are modern and a lovely twelve-branched chandelier

hangs in the **nave**, topped by a dove. London made, it is similar to others at Burton-on-Trent and Steyning in Sussex and dates from about 1725. The church's only **brass** is in the centre of the nave - 18 in figures of a C14 man and wife. It may be for Thomas and Anne Gedding, but he died in 1465 and the wife's early form of **kennel head-dress** was not fashionable until the 1480s so there is some doubt. The late C13 **piscina** in the s. aisle still has its wooden **credence shelf** and the e. window nearby contains 1937 glass by Geoffrey Webb - the post-resurrection scene of Christ and his disciples (John 22: 15). In the corner to the l. is a fragment of large C13 **dogtooth** moulding. The very narrow doorway that led to the **rood loft** is in the n.e. angle of the nave wall and round the corner in the n. aisle is a piscina rather oddly placed within what was the stairway. There were **altars**, therefore, in both aisles. Traces of wall painting show on either side of the wide chancel arch and the base of a C15 **screen** remains which has jumbled sections of stencilled colour on the s. side. A pedestal to the l. carries a 16 in bronze figure of **St Edmund** sculpted by Elizabeth Frink in 1974 in memory of her father. The late C17 **communion rails** enclose the **sanctuary** on two sides and have a very shapely range of **balusters** below a heavy, smoothed-over top rail. There is a C13 double piscina here, with heavily moulded arches and centre shaft, while on the e. wall there are unusual **decalogue** panels of slate, the lettering incised and gilded. **Jacobean** arches lead to the Soame chapel and two of them have strapwork decoration. The chapel was built by Sir Stephen Soame, Lord Mayor of London and local squire who died in 1619, having founded a village school and provided some almshouses. It was designed to accommodate his superb, enormous tomb whose sculptor is unknown. The magnate's bulky alabaster figure lies above and behind his wife Anne, with the armour picked out in gilt. She wears a French cap, a gilt chain is draped over her bodice, and both their heads rest on bulky, tasselled pillows. There are flanking pavilions of **Corinthian** columns and within them four sons kneel in varying attitudes, while two young daughters stand in niches behind; three daughters in long veils kneel along the front behind the iron railings and there are two more children at the sides, a bountiful quiverful. It is notable that all the family are scaled down to child size even though the sons are bearded. Small coloured shields of arms surround the large **touchstone** panel with its extended epitaph, a quotation from psalm 144 runs along the edge of the tomb chest, and overhead lurks the figure of Old Father Time with his scythe. The large contemporary family pew, with delicately pierced panels around the top, is set in the arch behind the choir stalls and a funeral helm is placed on a bracket high in the s.w. corner of the chapel. Near to it, the circular window has C17 glass painted with the 'in coelo quies' so often found on **hatchments**; five of these hang on the walls. Those for Sir Stephen and his wife (at the w. and e. ends of the n. wall) are not contemporary but may be later copies. The hatchment in the centre of the n. wall is for Anne Soame who died in 1781, that on the chancel side at the e. end is for Stephen's grandson John (1709) and the last, over the arches to the chancel, is for Margaret Hare, the heiress wife of an C18 bishop of Chichester. Another Soame monument worth studying is floridly signed by John Walsh, a talented C18 sculptor. To the l. of the large monument, it is a large tablet for the Stephen Soame who died in 1771, with a portrait medallion of Mrs Soame and her child. There are two poignant epitaphs, one for the husband and one for the child. In the first she writes: 'Thy Frances only waits the child to rear...' and then she had to add the verse for her son less than a year later.

Hitching rings for horses are sometimes found on church walls (Sapiston has two) but this church has a very rare C18 or C19 dog chain attached to the n.w. buttress of the tower. Have a look as you leave.

Little Whelnetham, St Mary Magdalene (D5): The church is attractively sited, with fields falling away to the w., and e. of the **chancel** there is an enigmatic circle of low flint ruins. It has been variously described as an **anchorite's** cell or the **apse** of a **Saxon** or **Norman** church, but the more likely solution is that it was a C10 watchtower that may have had a small church added to it. The unbuttressed tower of the present church has a C14 w. window but is likely to be older and there are bands of Roman tiles embedded in the fabric. The **nave** windows are **Perpendicular** but the corner **quoins** look C12 or C13 and there is a **scratch dial** at the s.e. corner. It has recently been provided with a metal gnomen or pointer. There is a C14 **priest's door** on the s. side of the chancel and by it, a **low side window** still fitted with its original grill. The C16 red brick **porch** has a crow-stepped gable and there is a niche above the handsome outer arch. The inner doorway is of the same period and has the unusual addition of a scroll-bearing angel at the apex of the arch. Although the door itself is modern, a medieval floriated cross has been retained in the centre. The C15 **font** has **quatrefoils** with centre **paterae** in the bowl panels, one blank shield and a shield bearing the cross of **St George** to the e. Its interesting feature, however, is the shields below the bowl, two with **Passion emblems** and one with the **Trinity** device. The C15 nave **roof** is both handsome and unusual. It has **hammerbeams** and **arch-braces** but instead of the usual layout wherein the forms alternate, here we have hammerbeams separated by two sets of arch-braces. The other individual feature is that, unlike their fellows in the body of the nave, the large individual figures carved on the hammerbeams against the e. and w. walls lie on their sides and face each other. All were badly mutilated during the C17 and restored as part of a major restoration in 1842. At least two of the crowned heads are new, but if there were once wings these were not replaced. The grotesques at the base of the **wall posts** are an excellent sample and include two devils and a lion with foliage sprouting from his jaws like a **green man**. The tower **screen** is modern and incorporates two ranges of **traceried** panels that may well have formed part of the **rood loft**. The C15 benches have large **poppyheads** and a pleasing variety of tracery on the ends. You will find a coarsely carved bull and the initials 'I.B.' on a bench near the front on the s. side which means that the donor was likely to have been a John or James Bull. Four of the benches on the n. side are good C19 copies. Below the easternmost window on the s. side is a Norman **pillar piscina** - another indication of the church's early origin. To the e. of it there are two Perpendicular image brackets decorated with paterae under **castellated** rims and the larger may have had a demi-angel below. Over the **Decorated** chancel arch is a sexfoiled circular window of the same period. The base of the C15 screen has good tracery in the panels, with a band of carving along the bottom. The lectern is intriguing. Given by a C19 rector, it is a great eagle excellently carved in wood and standing on a ball (the base is modern). It has had a bookledge added but the stance is so upright that one wonders whether it was not originally a purely decorative piece of the C17 or early C18 from Europe. There is a deep embrasure to the low side window and the piscina in the **sanctuary** has a plain C12 arch, with a small image bracket to the l. In the n. wall is a tiny C13 **aumbry** and if you care to look under the **altar** you will find the church's original **mensa**

which was recovered from the churchyard during one of the C19 restorations. There is a pleasant variety of late C17 and early C18 **ledger-stones** in the chancel and it is worth recording that the church depends entirely on candlelight for evening services, surely one of the very few that remain. The rowel-style candelabra in the nave were designed and made by Sydney Peters, craftsman and churchwarden.

Little Wratting, St Mary (B7): This diminutive church is ringed by trees and there are two distinct levels separated by a curving bank which means that it may stand in a rare example of a circular churchyard. Large pebbles, stones laid with wide joints, and rough **herringbone** work in the **nave** walls and part of the **chancel** point to an early C11 date. The plain rectangular doorways bear this out, and the lintel of the s. entrance is carved with an inscription whose faint but unmistakable letters shapes mark it as **Saxon**. It has been suggested that the few words that can be deciphered form part of a dedication but the whole has defied an acceptable translation. There are two large floriated 'C's and three straps of late C12 wrought-iron on the door which may well be as old. As you enter, note the draw-bar hole to the r., it is over 5 ft deep. There is no tower and the C19 bellcote with its shingled spire is supported within the church by C15 **arch-braced wall posts** resting on huge floor plates - a unique arrangement in Suffolk but common in Essex. The plain octagonal C14 **font** has a Victorian cover and the C15 low benches have unusual **tracery** in the end panels which is more akin to screenwork. The three front rows on the s. side are modern copies, but part of the wall panelling with its **castellated** top is original. A **box pew** at the w. end has been craftily converted to house a modern organ console. A deep **rood loft** staircase is built on to the n. wall and there are matching stone **corbels** each side of the nave which carried the front of the loft, with a ledge showing in the n.e. corner. They are only about 6 ft up but the floor level was probably raised during the C19 restoration. There were nave **altars** beneath the loft and larger windows were inserted to give more light (fragments of original glass remain in the one to the n.). The C15 **screen** was removed when the wider brick and stone chancel arch was inserted in 1895, and the chancel was partially rebuilt and re-roofed at that time. The shallow stone sink built into the n. **jamb** of the arch was found in the churchyard near the porch and it may once have been a **reliquary** associated with an altar. A chapel for the Turnour family was built on to the n. side of the chancel in the early C16 but it decayed and was demolished in 1710. All that is left is a section of the connecting **arcade** embedded in the wall just beyond the chancel arch, and a fragment from one of the tombs. This is an early C17 kneeling woman in ruff and voluminous gown which now stands on the ledge of one of the early C16 s. windows. Another possible survivor from the chapel is an armorial plaque inserted alongside a roof corbel on the n. side of the chancel. The C14 **piscina** was rebuilt into the **sanctuary** wall and has a deeply moulded **ogee** arch, with vestiges of **headstops**, **crockets** and a **finial**.

Long Melford, Holy Trinity (D7): Apart from Lavenham, Suffolk has nothing that can compare with the grandeur of Long Melford, standing in solid magnificence above the broad sweep of village green. At the turn of the century the unsatisfactory C18 tower was at last encased to a design by **George F. Bodley** which, with its west country bell openings and Norfolk sound holes, is not locally inspired but which nevertheless matches the scale and character of the building. The quality is impeccable;

note particularly the tall **flushwork** panels at the base. The whole of the rest of the building is an epitome of the **Perpendicular** style and the s. front is one continuous series of verticals thrusting up through **transomed aisle** windows, buttresses and deeply recessed **clerestory**. All that is lacking are the pinnacles on parapet and battlements. The rest of the wall surfaces are meshed with flushwork and a continuous **base course** of shields in **quatrefoils** runs the length of the building. One of the remarkable features is that an unbroken band of inscriptions is cut in the parapet of **porch** and aisle and below the clerestory battlements, identifying those who paid for the building and dating the work between the 1460s and the 1490s. There is no linear break or change in height but the chapel at the e. end of the s. aisle, built in 1484, has two windows with the four-petalled flower motif in the **tracery**, a style of 30 years earlier. They may well have been re-used to allow the original glass to remain in place. This is the chapel of the Martyn family and the merchants' marks of Roger and Lawrence Martyn can be seen on shields below the **string course** of the **chancel** parapet at the e. end. The chancel extends one bay beyond the aisles with deeper windows, with a bridging **vestry** at lower level below. Originally there was a Lady Chapel outside the main building but in 1496 a new one was added to the e. end under three long, steeply gabled roofs, which, for all its splendour, does not combine happily with the rest. The windows are shorter and the entire wall surface is filled with flushwork; again, there is a continuous parapet inscription. Although the n. clerestory has flushwork and inscription, the aisle is wholly without decoration and there is an unadorned n. door; a brick **rood stair** turret rises on that side. The outer arch of the lofty s. porch is decayed, with a niche on either side, and overhead there are three stooled and canopied niches

Long Melford, Holy Trinity: alabaster panel

linked by blind-arched panels.

Within this great church the **arcades** march in a splendid unbroken line from end to end, although the **piers** of the five w. bays are the C14 originals and the rest adaptations of the same style. The wall space between arches and clerestory is filled with blind panelling that matches the windows, and the **arch-braces** of the almost flat roof meet in a continuous curve beneath the **tie-beams**. All the roof timbers are moulded, the **spandrels** pierced with tracery, and dumpy figures in heavy robes stand beneath canopies on the **wall posts**. Looking eastward, the silhouetted gables of the off-centre Lady chapel appear awkwardly beyond the e. window, making one regret that it no longer has stained glass. By the door stands a C15 **purbeck marble font**, with shields in the traceried panels and a deep mould beneath the bowl. The counter-weighted cover dates from 1935. Turning back, you will see over the door one of the finest sets of **Royal Arms** in the county; they are probably for George I, and are beautifully delicate, and carved three-

dimensionally in limewood. To the w. of the door hangs the oldest diamond-shaped **hatchment** in the county and one of the earliest in England; it is for Thomas, Viscount Savage, who died in London in 1635 of 'the running gout' and was buried at Macclesfield. The rest of the church's hatchments are grouped conveniently within the tower and all carry names and dates on the frames.

Long Melford is justly famous for its C15 glass. In the C19 it was collected in the e. window and in the aisles, but in the 1960s Christopher Woodforde directed a complete rearrangement by Kings of Norwich and it is now excellently displayed in the n. aisle. There you will find a unique series of medieval portraits, together with saints and martyrs. Name labels have been helpfully inserted under the major figures. John Clopton was the church's principal benefactor and he included portraits not only of himself and his family but political colleagues and powerful national

Long Melford, Holy Trinity: medieval glass [St Edmund and donor]

figures. You will find Chief Justice Sir William Howard (third window from w.), Sir Ralph Joscelin, the Lord Mayor who defended London Bridge against the rebels in 1471 (fifth window from w.), and Elizabeth Howard, Countess of Oxford, wife of the 12th Earl beheaded in 1461 (third window from w.). **St Apollonia** with her pincers is in the first window and over the n. door is a lovely **Pietà**, with **St Peter Martyr** alongside. Below the Pietà is the tiny roundel of the three

rabbits who share three ears. The only other known version of this symbol is on a roof **boss** at South Tawton in Devon, and while it is familiarly known as 'the **Trinity** rabbits', there is some doubt about its religious significance. In the eighth window from the w. is a fine **St Edmund** with an abbot of Bury kneeling before him. Further along there is another St Edmund, with **St George** and **St Martin**, in the **Kempe** window of 1903. The portrait of Elizabeth Talbot, Duchess of Norfolk (second window from the w.) is said to have inspired Sir John Tenniel's illustration of the Duchess in *Alice in Wonderland*. At the e. end of the n. aisle is a beautiful mid-C14 alabaster panel of the Nativity. In almost perfect condition, it was recovered from beneath the chancel floor in the C18 and is an early example of a **reredos** panel. The **Blessed Virgin** lies on a couch with the Child, the Magi are ranged with their gifts, and an attendant woman stands on one side while **St Joseph** dozes in a chair; the heads of two oxen peep out improbably from under the bed. The angular stone pulpit of 1884 is interesting in that its panels contain the figures of saints to whom altars were dedicated in the medieval church: the Virgin and Child (for the Jesus chapel and the Lady chapel), Saints **Anne**, **James**, **Edmund** and **John**. Through the **screen** from the n. aisle is the n. chancel aisle or Kentwell aisle, as it is called, where there are a number of **brasses**, some relaid. The first one is for William Clopton (1420), and beyond it is one for a lady of his family of the same period. Beyond the organ, there are three more: nearest the outer wall, for Alice Harleston (1440), half-sister of John Clopton; she wears an heraldic mantle with her husband's arms, her kirtle bears the arms of Clopton, and a fragment of the elaborate canopy remains. In the centre is the effigy of Francis Clopton (1578) wearing Elizabethan armour with a vestigial codpiece. Beyond him is the brass of Margery Clopton

(1424), mother of the church's great benefactor. Like Alice Harleston she wears a **butterfly head-dress** with transparent veil over the plucked forehead, and an heraldic mantle. Again there is a portion of the canopy work and both brasses must, on the evidence of costume, have been commissioned by John in the 1480s; both were inlaid with colour. The door in the n. wall was the private entrance from Kentwell Hall and alongside is a **consecration cross**. Beyond it is the tomb of John's father, Sir William Clopton (1446). It has been extensively restored and, apart from the freshly coloured shields, is a uniform and shiny beige. The effigy lies in armour under a low arch on the tomb chest which has a **stoup** built into it by the door. Within the recess is a lengthy Latin inscription on brass, and a helpful, beautifully lettered translation is provided. On the floor in front there is another inscription for Thomas Clopton who died in 1597. There is a **piscina** in this chapel and a most unusual **squint**. By cutting through two walls it gives a view across the corner of the Clopton **chantry** next door to the **high altar** beyond. The chantry chapel is entered through a vestibule which is only 5 ft across but which contains a fireplace and has an intricate little **fan vault** which is almost flat. The chapel is a beautiful room lit by a seven- **light** e. window in which is set the late C14 or early C15 'lily crucifix'. Less than a dozen examples survive of this most interesting form - the resurrection implied by Christ crucified on the lily of the **Annunciation**. The rear of the chapel has a low ceiling, like a **gallery**, but which glazed above, and there are remnants of verses on the w. wall. The **wall plate** is decorated with as a folded scroll through which is threaded a vine, and a hand is carved in the s.e. corner as though opening it out. It is painted with two poems attributed to John Lydgate, the monk of Bury, and the ceiling rafters carry little painted scrolls of 'I.H.U. mercy' and 'Gramercy'. There are the

remains of a piscina and two **sedilia** to the r. of the **altar**, a line of Clopton shields in quatrefoils above them, and below the ceiling, twelve niches with exquisitely pinnacled canopies designed no doubt for statues of the apostles. A low arch connects the chapel with the **sanctuary** and within it stands the tomb of John Clopton, the church's principal benefactor, who died in 1497. A large figure of Christ holding a cross and displaying his wounds is painted on the underside of the arch, and on the top of the tomb was placed the painted timber frame of the **Easter sepulchre**. In the sanctuary, the high altar is backed by a large 1870s reredos of the Crucifixion under heavy canopy work by Farmer and Brindley in dun coloured Caen stone. It is a pity that Bodley, having done so well with the tower, could not have provided a reredos on the lines of his work at St Margaret's, King Lynn, or Sudbury, St Peter's. On the s. side is the massive tomb of Sir William Cordell who died in 1581, having been Speaker of the House of Commons under Queen Mary and Elizabeth's Master of the Rolls. Fuller in his *Worthies of England* says of him: 'great offices he had and good offices he did to posterity'; he founded the Trinity Hospital almshouses close by the church. It is highly likely that the monument is by Cornelius Cure, master mason to the Crown in the closing years of the C16, and it is in beautiful condition. He lies in armour on a rolled straw mat below two deeply coffered arches supported by polished marble **Corinthian** columns. Against his feet is his **cockatrice** crest and the four figures of Prudence, Justice, Fortitude and Temperence stand in shallow niches at the back. Such was the influence of the **renaissance** that the head of Bacchus enlivens the scrollwork at the top. Returning to the s. aisle, there is 1880s glass by **Ward & Hughes** in one window, (six Resurrection scenes), and at the e. end, a small **trefoil**-arched piscina and **dropped-sill sedilia**. Beyond the modern screen is the Martyn chapel or chapel of the Jesus **guild**; parts of the screen dividing it from the chancel are original. There is an iron-bound chest in one corner and against the e. wall, a fine C15 settle which came from Granada cathedral; it has Gothic tracery on the back and bottom, and bears the arms of Ferdinand V of Castile and Isabella. There is a **purbeck marble** tomb chest reaved of its brasses, with shields in lozenges along the sides and beyond it there is a piscina in the corner. There are two fine brasses here: Roger Martyn and his wives Ursula and Margaret (1615); the ladies have French hoods and ruffs and there are two groups of children. The second is for Richard Martyn and his three wives (1624); he is in doublet, hose and gown, his wives are in Paris caps, and there is a group of two sons (one bearing a skull to show that he died before his parents); in addition, there are two **chrysom children** and there was originally another group of children and another baby. The Lady chapel is entered by a door in the s. wall and is a charming building in its own right. It centres on a three-bay sanctuary which has a stone screen at the w. end and a solid wall behind the altar; around it on all four sides is an ambulatory or processional way. The centre chapel has canopied niches above the piers together with blind arcading under a cambered tie-beam roof. The lovely ambulatory roofs also have cambered tie-beams with canopied niches in the corners. There are stubby figures bearing emblems on the wall posts and the wall plates are similar to those in the Clopton chantry chapel. The floors are pale brick and in the n.e. corner a multiplication table is painted on the wall - a reminder that the chapel served as a schoolroom from 1670 until the early C19. As you leave, have a look at the fine **Act of Parliament clock** at the back of the chapel, with its painted chinoiserie case marked 'Thomas Moore, Ipswich'.

Market Weston, St Mary (E3): Some way beyond the village street to the n., the church lies with open fields about it. The early C14 tower has a panelled **base course**, diagonal buttresses to the w. with four **set-offs**, and two **drip courses**. Both w. window and bell openings have **Decorated tracery** and there is a plain C19 parapet. The line of a much steeper original roof shows on the e. face. There was a major restoration by L.N. Cottingham in 1846 and the **chancel** was entirely rebuilt. The s. **porch**, however. is **Perpendicular**, although the outer arch has been re-cut, with crowns and **fleurons** in the mouldings. There are niches either side in the **flushwork** front, with another under a canopy above, and it is lit by tall, two-**light** windows. Stone seats line the walls below them and the deeply moulded inner C14 doorway has worn **headstops**. Above it is a delightful niche, with **crocketted** canopy and nodding **ogees** that terminate in tiny heads, containing a fine statue of the Virgin and Child. As you enter, note that the door is medieval, complete with closing ring and key escutcheon. Within, the hand of the C19 lies heavy, but there are interesting things to see. The small tower arch is fitted with a medieval door, and on the n. wall hangs a large, pale set of **Hanoverian Royal Arms** painted on canvas. In the tracery of the westernmost window on the n. side there are two small roundels; the smaller of the two contains a kneeling figure robed in red with his name 'Thomas Asbi' inscribed underneath, and the other has the eagle symbol of **St John** in yellow stain. Above them is a small coat of arms. On the wall by the C19 **font** is a length of oak carved with pierced roundels that was found in the local post office after wartime bomb damage. In the 1840s the parish clerk was also the postmaster, and it may be that he found it when the building work was going on and took it home. If so, it could well have formed part of the **rood screen** or the loft. The **nave** has dark pine benches with rounded and pierced tops to the ends, and the **roof** overhead is a crude version of the double **hammerbeam**. On past the massive pine pulpit and reading desk to the chancel, where there is a small marble tablet on the s. wall to John and Margaret Thruston (1849) by de Carle of Bury. By the **priest's door** there is a much more elegant memorial signed by **John Bacon the Younger** classical white, with shapely urn on a pale grey background. It is for Framingham Thruston who died in 1789. This makes it a very early work of Bacon's, for it was only in that year that he entered the Royal Academy Schools, and a decade before he took over his father's business. Further e. is an 1858 memorial to another Framingham Thruston, by Bower of Highgate, which shows just how much the trade's design sense had faltered in those 70 years. On the opposite wall is a shapely unsigned tablet for Dr John Thruston who, when he died in 1776, was honoured by his friend Samuel Peck as one who was 'many years Lord of this Manor and a blessing to this neighbourhood'. On the subject of memorials, there are four good **ledger-stones** before the **altar** rails, spanning the years 1692 to 1743, with deeply cut armorial roundels for members of the Bokenham family. The e. window tracery is filled with mid-C19 glass painted with patterns of vine leaves and scrolls, and in the **sanctuary** s. wall is an intriguing **pillar piscina** of the same vintage. It has a cluster of slim shafts under a semicircular bowl, and on the wall behind is a small, framed bas relief of Christ and the woman of Samaria (John 4:7). I do not recall having seen another like it.

Mildenhall, St Mary (B3): In every way this is one of the great Suffolk churches. Not only is it 168 ft by 65 ft, but it abounds in richness, variety and interest. Mildenhall has sprawl-

led since the war but the nucleus of the old town laps the spacious churchyard on three sides and the mighty tower is a landmark for miles. It is 120 ft high and must have been even more commanding before the C15 spirelet with its lantern was removed in 1831. The tower was completed by 1464 and has a plain stone **base course** with virtually no decoration on the main surfaces. Alternate stages of the gabled buttresses carry tall **crocketted** pinnacles set diagonally, but essentially it is an austere design, massive and well proportioned. By the mid-C19 there was a deep fissure in the s.e. angle and in 1864 it was refaced and the stair turret extended above the battlements. The w. door, with its ample side niches, and the great w. window were both renewed. At that time, masses of fine **dogtooth** mouldings were found reversed in the tower buttresses, remnants of the C13 predecessor. The large and plain s. **porch** was virtually rebuilt in 1876. The s. aisle is restrained, with only crocketted pinnacles to the buttresses, but the e. end is another matter altogether. The great window fronting the High Street is a magnificent composition dating from about 1300 which can stand comparison with any in England. The seven **lights** are graduated in width and the outer pair are continued up and over the head as a band of **quatrefoils**. In the centre is a large **cusped** oval, itself set within a rim of tiny quatrefoils, and on either side are **tracery** shapes reminiscent of the pleated paper bells used for Christmas decorations, or so it seemed to me as a child. The **chancel** corner buttresses are very inventive; they begin as standard right-angled pairs, rise to **cinquefoil**-headed niches in the angles and then reduce to slim octagonal pinnacles extend rise above the roof line. Four of the image stools rest on carved head **corbels**. On the s. side, the chancel windows alternate attractively between stepped **lancets** within a single arch and intersected 'Y' tracery, and on the

Mildenhall, St Mary

n., matching stepped lancets. Churchyards were systematically re-used in the Middle Ages and displaced bones were often placed in a charnel chapel. There was one here and its ivy covered ruins can be seen s.e. of the chancel. It was founded in 1387 by Ralph de Walsham (who had a hand in the murder of the Prior of Bury Abbey during the Peasants' Revolt of 1381). With a crypt below for the bones, it was endowed with a priest to say masses for the dead, and the sunken depression towards the street shows its size. Although there has been a church here since the Conquest, the earliest dateable work is the early C13 chapel built of limestone (now the **vestry**) n. of the chancel, with an e. window of three stepped lancets. Part of the chancel is the same age and you will see the break in the wall line on both sides where it was extended a few decades later. A parish often chose one side of its church on which to lavish attention and here it is the n. **aisle** and porch. The C14 buttresses have pleasing niches under **groined ogee** canopies, and in the early C15 rebuilding much more was done - new windows, a parapet panelled in two tiers with small blank shields and a line of small grotesques within the moulding below. The whole of the aisle is faced with chequered **flushwork**. Built about 1420, the n. porch of two storeys is the largest in Suffolk and, as the main entrance, its decoration matches the aisle. The ground floor is stone faced and there is a line of shields over the outer arch with a window above them. Within is a ribbed stone vault with **bosses** at the intersections and the inner doorway is set within a larger arch of blind tracery, with ogees each side, which probably backed **stoups** that have been hacked away. Over the door is a stooled and canopied niche and the shields in the **spandrels** are those of **Edward the Confessor** and **St Edmund**. The doors

themselves are original, with three ranges of fine **Perpendicular** tracery in the heads.

Once inside, the sense of size coupled with richness is intensified. The **piers** of the C15 **nave arcades** are tall and slim, with minimal enrichment, and light floods in from large aisle windows and **clerestory**. To the r. of the door is a stairway leading to the porch upper room; the spandrels of the arch have carvings of the **Annunciation**, underlining the fact that the chamber was a Lady chapel in an unusual location. There is a smaller, earlier, doorway below which led to the original stairs. The early C15 **purbeck marble font** is very eroded and, although they are well nigh illegible now, the shields in the bowl quatrefoils bear the arms of the City of London and the donor, Sir Henry Barton, who may have been involved in the great rebuilding of the 1420s. Lord Mayor in the year after Agincourt and again in 1428, he had introduced the first street lighting in London as Sheriff in 1405. He was buried in old St Paul's but a memorial tomb was placed here at the base of the tower and is now at the w. end of the s. aisle. Sir Henry's arms are on a brass shield on one end of the tomb and those of the City were on the other. The scale of the stone w. **gallery** matches the church; set within the tall, deeply moulded tower arch, it has a line of blank shields over the arch and the parapet is pierced with closely set quatrefoils. Underneath is a beautiful **fan vault**, one of the very few to be found in Suffolk or Norfolk. It is likely to have been inserted between 1530 and 1555, and there is some evidence that it was the work of Thomas Larke, the surveyor of the final phase of King's College Chapel, Cambridge. It may well have been designed and used as a **galilee porch**.

Glass in the two small windows here commemorates church workers often overlooked: that on the n. side is by J. Dudley Forsyth of a woman in medieval dress cleaning, as did Anne

Mildenhall, St Mary: angel roof

Jolly here for 18 years, and on the s., **St Cecilia** and a robed lady bellringer for Mary Fordham - rare, if not unique, subjects. Above the gallery is a wall to wall w. window and to the l. what must be the largest set of **Royal Arms** in any parish church. At least 12 ft by 9 ft, they are for George II, dated 1758 and used to hang over the chancel arch. Over Sir Henry Barton's tomb at the w. end of the s. aisle is a modern tablet commemorating William Gregory, the second Mildenhall man to be both Sheriff and Lord Mayor of London, in 1436 and 1451. Here also is the long iron-bound C14 parish chest and a stone coffin found under the n. aisle in 1851. One of the features of the church is the magnificent suite of benches designed by **Cautley** and bequeathed by his wife in 1959. The intricately traceried bench ends and **poppyheads** are all different and the standing figures in the niches at the w. end are reminiscent of Wiggenhall St Mary in Norfolk. They portray: nave, the **Blessed Virgin** and **St Etheldreda** holding a model of Ely cathedral; n. aisle, the Virgin and Child; s. aisle, **St Anne** teaching the Virgin. The aisles now have open boarded floors and the outer walls are lined with benches.

Overhead is the glory of this church, C15 roofs which in their magnificence are unsurpassed and where everything points to a designer and craftsmen of more than local standing. The nave has moulded and richly carved **tie-beams**, whose **arch-braces** rise from deep **wall posts** to meet at the centre, the spandrels filled with tracery. Above them, **queen posts** are braced up to the ridge, flanked by tracery with demi-angels adorning the sides. Alternating with the tie-beams are **hammerbeams** carved as ten mighty angels and their wings, spread wide and raised, are held in grooves behind the figures and have no other support; each holds a **Passion emblem**, a book, or a lute. Yet more demi-angels line the deep cornice on each side. The height of the roof saved it from the worst excesses of the C17 image breakers but in their frustration they riddled it with buckshot and blunderbuss bolts. Some of the wings had to be replaced, but in the main it is as the makers left it except that close examination has revealed traces of colour. The wide aisle roofs are fitting companions and they too have arch-braced hammerbeams, carved in the n. aisle with an astonishing array of beasts and men. Here, binoculars are invaluable in revealing the richness and vitality of the imagery. Starting from the e. end, the hammerbeams are carved as: a hideous woman in a horned head-dress, a king wielding a sword followed by a lion, a lion with another behind it, a **wyvern** (the badge of Lord Bardolph), a rich merchant with his dog, and another lion. The spandrels below teem with life and, from the w., the scenes are: a pardoner blessing a lady, demons playing an organ, **St George** and the dragon (the queen's 1430s head-dress dates this closely), baptism of Christ, a collared swan (Henry V's badge), the Bethlehem shepherds, a chained antelope (Henry V again), Abraham and Isaac, a huntsman with dogs, deer, hare and squirrel, the Annunciation, a **griffin**, **St Michael**, and a **green man**. Even then, there is a carving next to the wall that cannot easily be seen. Between the hammerbeams, large, very mutilated figures jut out that have lost their arms. Slots for wings remain and they must have been angels that matched those in the nave. The damage doubtless dates from 1651 when the parish paid a man a shilling a day to smash popish images, and the figures carved on the wall posts lost their faces too. They have angels poised protectively above them in lieu of canopies - a brilliant conception. The s. aisle is not so evocative but the work is still rich. The design of the hammerbeams, with their deep cresting, is slightly angular and blind tracery rather than carved scenes fills the spandrels. Tall figures nestle in the corners and miniature carvings abound, including at the e. end, a man attacked by a wyvern thrusting a stick between its jaws. As in the n. aisle, mutilated angels reach out over the windows. Among the mass of carved detail, Henry V's badges appear time and time again.

At the e. end of the s. aisle is the church's only large monument, the elaborate tomb of Sir Henry North (d. 1620), Lord of the Manor. He was knighted in 1586 at Zutphen (a skirmish with the Spaniards in the Neth-

erlands where Sir Philip Sidney fell). He lies in full armour next to his wife who wears the fashionable large hood of the period. Their heads rest on tasselled cushions and there are traces of colour. Purbeck **Corinthian** columns rise either side to obelisks on the cornice, with a coloured **achievement** above, and an inscription on two **touchstone** panels at the back under cherubs within a pair of enriched arches. The tomb was restored in 1885 and the figures of the children were replaced, although Sir Henry still lacks his feet. His funeral helm hangs above. To the r. is a handsome memorial to his son Roger North (d. 1651) - oval touchstone tablet set in alabaster swags and scrolls heightened with gilt; cherub, crest and two shields over, with a skull crowned with laurel on top, a macabre conceit. Nearby is a window commemorating Sir Charles Bunbury (d. 1886), one of the family that were Lords of the Manor from the C18 to the C20. The glass is by C. Elliott, with centre panels on a theme from the book of Ruth and parable panels on either side. The s. aisle chapel is dedicated to **St Margaret** and the **altar** bears a **mensa** dated 1420 which was in use as a floor slab until 1936. To the r. an **aumbry** and to the l. a clutch of Bunbury memorials. It is interesting that Thomas North's 1661 tablet was copied almost exactly for Henry Bunbury 60 years later. The 1870s brass lectern is a good solid design and came from nearby Worlington (where the loss has not been forgotten). The remains of the church's C17 pulpit can be found at Beck Row, while here we have a robust 1870s piece in oak by **J.D. Wyatt** on a stone base and with green Irish marble **colonnettes**. For some inscrutable reason the whole thing is now mounted on runners. The n. aisle chapel is dedicated to **St John the Baptist**, patron saint of one of the six **guilds** associated with the church. There is a **pillar piscina** here with a very shallow drain. Behind it was a **squint** to the **high altar** which is now blocked. The fine **Early English** chancel arch has triple shafts with dogtooth moulding between them, and more is set in the **hood mould**. The stiff-leaf foliage of the **capitals** continues as a band into the corners of the wall and there are renewed **headstops**. The present **screen**, with its rather fussy tracery, was installed in 1903 but the original **rood screen** must have been very grand and in keeping with the scale of the church. The stair turret for it lies to the n. and rises to roof level. It housed the **sanctus-bell** and you will see that there are three blocked doorways. This prompts the conclusion that there was a double screen or two separate lofts. The upper would have been used for maintaining the rood itself and its lights, while the lower one may well have carried an altar. If the lower loft was a deep one, the space beneath would have borrowed light through the **mullioned** opening from the s. aisle chapel. There is an interesting 1670 memorial in painted marble above this opening for Sarah North, with clasped hands above a shield of arms. Her husband, Sir Henry, was the melancholic and finally suicidal author of *Eroclea, or the Mayd of Honour*. Part of the epitaph translates: 'Dead while living, oh how hard; you are happy because your life has ended, I am desolate for I cannot die'. The C13 chancel was extended and given new windows in the C14. Note that although the choir stalls are modern, there are sections of medieval tracery in the second range on the s. side, with a **woodwose**, dragon, wyvern and mask in the spandrels. The e. window has purbeck shafts which rise to angels at the spring of the arch. To the r. is a C13 double piscina with purbeck shafts and stiff-leaf capitals (the whole of the upper section is new work), and stepped **sedilia** with simply shaped armrests. Look for the grave slab in the floor on the n. side, e. of the vestry door. The inscription around the edge is in **Lombardic** capitals and translates:

'Here lies Richard de Wichforde, some time vicar of the church of Mildenhall who made this new work'. He was vicar from 1309 to 1344 and so we know who to thank for the beautiful e. window. One regrets the large unsightly radiator that stands on part of the slab. There are two aumbries in the s. wall, one with a **trefoil** arch, and a brass shield and inscription for Mary Warner who died in 1601. Her husband, Sir Henry, has a **brass** on the n. wall and wears Elizabethan armour in the simplified style favoured by the **Stuarts**. He was High Sheriff in 1599, MP for Thetford in 1601 and knighted in 1603. The inscription is for father and son but the latter's effigy has gone.

Mildenhall, Beck Row, St John (B3): In 1876 this was a late entrant at a fairly low level in the great Victorian church building boom. Designed by **J.D. Wyatt** in flint, it has a faint echo of the previous decade's taste for structural colour in the form of bands of red and white bricks, with matching window arches. The windows are vaguely **Early English** but hardly consistent, with simple **plate tracery** on the s. and **trefoil**-headed **lancets** on the n. A stubby s. **transept** separates the buttressed **nave** from the **chancel** and a bellcote with shingled spire caps the w. gable. With little but the village street to shield it from the stupefying noise of aircraft using the Americans' 'Gateway to Europe', one would not expect much calm and serenity in this little church, but it manages well enough. The interior originally had patterning in brick but now all is white, with only the stone dressings of the lancets picked out in ochre, apart, that is, from the chancel and transept arches on **colonnettes** stopping well short of the floor. They contrive to look rather splendid in the original red and white bricks. The 1863 glass in the e. window is not particularly memorable except for the fact that one **light** portrays Jesus, John and Judas at the Last Supper, an unusual combination. The glass in the roundel above the lancets at the w. end has an angel blowing a trumpet that would have liked a larger window to stretch in. The C17 octagonal pulpit has shallow carved floral panels and a canted ledge supported by coarsely carved heavy scroll brackets. Now set on a modern base, it was discarded by Mildenhall, St Mary's, in 1875 when the architect of this church designed a new one there. There is a lumpish **font** at the w. end and, in the n.w. corner, the propeller blade from a Stirling of 90 Squadron which crashed on a training flight in 1943. It has been mounted as a memorial for those on board who all, save one, lie buried outside. There, on the n. side of the church, are the ranks of graves that remind one that Mildenhall was a wartime bomber aerodrome. Only a tithe of those who were lost lie here but they came from all over the world; R.H. Middleton VC, of the Royal Australian Air Force, was killed in 1942 aged 26 and lies closest to the n.w. corner of the church.

Mildenhall, West Row, St Peter (B3): In the mid-C19 church architects often designed schools as well and liked to use the same **Early English** style. When, therefore, this National School of 1850 came to be used as a church in 1874, all that it needed was a matching **chancel** and now one cannot tell the difference. By the green at the s. end of the village lies a simple building in flint and white brick, faintly enlivened by hexagonal slates on the **roof**. Inside is a **queen post** roof over the nave and a **scissors- braced** construction for the one beyond the **trefoiled** chancel arch. The stepped **lancets** at the e. end repeat those at the w. end and the n. chancel lancets have 1883 glass of Christ on the waters and with **Saints Peter** and **Andrew**. The glass at the w. end is by J. Dudley Forsyth, one of **Henry Holiday's** apprentices, and is a fine composition in

deep, rich colour. The group of Christ with attendant figures spreads over the three **lights** but is contained within Gothick **tabernacle work**. It has almost monochrome flesh tints, and the face of Christ is reminiscent of the young Prince Consort (There is more of his work at Culford, Mildenhall and Warlington). Below it is a heavy, square **font** with multiple chamfers. Equally solid is the chocolate brown organ case, with a pair of Early English- style turned shafts each side and **quatrefoils** along the front. The pulpit is not, as some guides have said, the C17 piece discarded from Mildenhall, but plain C19 pine.

Monks Eleigh, St Peter (E6): This handsome church stands above the village street to the n., approached by a steepish lane, and in many ways reminds me of Cavendish. What we see is largely C15 and the solid stair turret on the s. face of the tower is set back where it rises above the parapet and is crowned by a bell in an openwork metal frame. There are two tiers of **flushwork** in the battlements and large three- **light** bell openings. An unusual feature is the way in which the corner buttresses are stopped short of the top and capped by carved masks. From them, small octagonal buttresses continue up to **crocketted** pinnacles. There is a flushwork **base course** in two ranks and the w. doorway is particularly rich although very worn. Constructed of clunch, the chalk building stone, there are lion masks and crouched lions and bears in the mouldings, while the square **label** terminates in large and jovial **headstops**. Stooled niches flank the doorway and the **tracery** of the tall window above was renewed in 1845. It was at that time that the long **chancel** was entirely rebuilt, with a **vestry** on the n. side. The **Perpendicular** n. **aisle** has a simple C14 doorway that was probably part of the older building. In walking round you will find a number of good C18 headstones, for example, Elizabeth Green's of 1734 by the e. end of the s. aisle; it has a cherub's head and skull above a skilful combination of Gothic and Roman lettering. Further to the s. is an example of quality modern stone cutting by John Green - the headstone for June-Mary Dalton who died in 1981. The C15 s. **porch**, approached by a miniature avenue of pollarded limes, has large flushwork **consecration crosses** outlined in thin red tiles on either side of the entrance, with a **scratch dial** to the l. The inner doorway is deeply moulded and there is worn tracery at head and foot of the medieval doors.

You will notice that the **nave arcades** do not match and the C14 s. side probably formed part of the earlier church; the **piers** and **capitals** have concave faces as opposed to the plain octagons on the n. and the arch mouldings differ. The single-framed rafter **roof** of the nave had a **canopy of honour** for the **rood** at the e. end which is now a plain band of plaster. Below it hangs a large and handsome set of Queen Anne's **Royal Arms**, excellently restored recently by Anna Hulbert. The organ stands in front of a tall tower arch and near the s. door is a plain pillar poor box dated 1636. The C13 **font**, with its C15 cover, by the n. door, has a centre shaft and four columns supporting the square bowl; there are octagonal shafts inset at the corners and a strange strapwork design on the s. side, with the remains (or the beginning) of an incised pattern on the n. A simple C16 chest stands at the w. end of the s. aisle and another at the e. end has pierced corner brackets and wrought handles. Nearby, a rectangular projection houses the stairs to the old **rood loft** and the entrance is over 6 ft from the floor. The level of the upper doorway shows that the **screen** was lofty and on the n. side another opening connects with a high level doorway in the n. aisle; a **squint** aligned with the **high altar** is sited in the intervening passage. The arrangement suggests that

there were **parclose screens** round both aisle chapels and that they were connected by a walkway to the main rood loft (as at Rattlesdon). The notches cut in the e. **respond** of the s. arcade are further evidence of a **screen** being fitted there. There is a tall and elegant image niche with a **cusped ogee** arch set crosswise in the n.e. corner of the n. aisle, and to the r. of the altar you will find a **pillar piscina**. The pre-**Reformation** pulpit rises from a coved pedestal and there is squared tracery in the bottom of the panels, with applied tracery in the tops (some of which is replacement). A chancel n. window has glass by T.F. Curtis of **Ward & Hughes**; dark and sombre colours, with the figure of Dorcas and her handiwork in one light. Opposite, a window illustrating the text 'But when the morning was come Jesus stood on the shore' has a Victorian gentleman's portrait head peeping out behind the disciples. The e. window glass of 1880 is by **Henry Hughes** of Ward & Hughes, an Ascension flanked by a Nativity and the three Maries at the tomb, with three vignettes beneath; the figures are stilted and the colour sharp. The **sanctuary** has C17 panelling and there is a C19 blind arch stone **reredos**. The high altar is a fine and solid **Stuart Holy table** which is higher than average and does not appear to have been altered as so many have.

Moulton, St Peter (B4): Secluded at the s. end of the village, the church stands very attractively on rising ground, with a footpath leading through the churchyard to a beech hanger beyond. The tower nestles among yews, with a few Scots pines at the w. end. Originally it was a wide and tall **Norman** building and the C12 columns marking the corners can be found in the angles where the **nave** meets the **chancel** and at the w. end. There was probably an **anchorite's** cell between the w. end of the n. **aisle** and the tower - a blocked doorway led

TO SUFFOLK CHURCHES

into the aisle and there is a fragment stub of wall to the l. The late C13 tower has a truncated w. window immediately above the door, a **corbel table** just below the battlements and heavy **gargoyles**. There are **transomed lancet** windows on either side of the bell openings on the n. and s. sides, a very unusual formation but likely to be original. The weathervane is in the form of a most distinctive and well nourished fish. The body of the building dates from the early C16, with large **Perpendicular** windows; those in the **clerestory** have stepped transoms and a continuous **hood mould**. The whole building was heavily restored in 1850 and the s. **porch** is completely C19. Inside, the nave, aisles and **transept** chapels are linked by arches that have a common design but which differ in detail, with the arch between the s. aisle and transept lower and heavier. All the **capitals** are battlemented and decorated with **fleurons**. The tower arch is now filled-in above a low oak screen. Above the nave **arcades** is a most attractive stone frieze, battlemented and carved with fleurons; it incorporates demi-angels from which attached columns rise to support the nave **roof**. All the roofs are good replacements; **hammerbeams** in nave and chancel with demi-angels carved on the **wall plates**, and the **arch-braced** aisle roofs come down to **wall posts** linked by transverse arches. The **font** is probably C19, but if not, it has been comprehensively re-cut; four of its **cusped** panels contain shields with **Passion emblems** and the others are carved with closely set fleurons, with more under the bowl and on the stem. The C16 cover is crudely carved and has been badly attacked by worm. In the curtained **vestry** at the w. end of the s. aisle there is an ancient stone panel carved with two figures; a man with his arms raised in prayer and a woman with her hands folded over her belly. It appears to have been part of a larger design and could conceivably represent Adam and Eve. The nave

and aisles have C19 oak pews with rather good **poppyheads** and in the n. transept chapel there is the pillar of a **piscina** with just a fragment of the bowl. To the r., a very narrow doorway to the **rood stairs**. Nearby is a massive, heavily carved C19 wooden eagle lectern. Unless they were moved in the C19 restoration, the two stone brackets near the rood stair opening on the n. side of the chancel arch are likely to have been supports for the loft rather than image brackets. On the s. side there is a tall and slim **trefoil**-headed niche for a statue. The s. transept contains a piscina with a **cinquefoiled** arch under a square **label**, with blank **quatrefoils** in the **spandrels**. There are medieval bench ends worked into the modern choir stalls, with carvings on the elbows - a **unicorn** and a rabbit on the n. side, a deer with large antlers and a dog on the s. The chancel was raised well above the level of the nave in the 1850s and a crypt was discovered beneath the **sanctuary**. The C16 piscina to the r. of the **high altar** has a **crocketted** arch with **finial** and, although the cusping has been broken, there are large fleurons in the side mouldings. The n. wall of the chancel carries a **touchstone** tablet framed in marble, with an alabaster **cartouche** of arms within a broken **pediment** above. It is for Francis Seyliard who was rector here and died in 1676. To the l. is a very plain marble tablet on a grey surround by R. Brown of London for another rector, George Greenall, who died in 1845. There are examples of Victorian **brasses** on two **ledger-stones** in the sanctuary for Edmund Mortlock, the rector who carried out the big restoration, and his sister Mary Ann.

Newmarket, All Saints (A4): Built as a memorial to Lord George Manners in 1875, it replaced an earlier church and part of the original tower was incorporated. A heavy and uninspired building in random flint with slate roofs, designed by the Lowestoft architect, W.O. Chambers, it has a conventional layout, except that the tower is offset to the s.w. There is a **clerestory** of paired **lancets** alternating with **quatrefoils** and a main **porch** entrance at the w. end. Within, the smooth cylindrical columns of the **nave arcades** have **capitals** heavily carved with stiff flower forms, vaguely **Norman** in style. The **chancel** arch comes down to triple **colonnettes** whose capitals are carved with wheat and grapes, and there is a boarded waggon roof beyond. The chancel was enlarged in 1887 and a new e. window installed - three large stepped lancets, deeply splayed, with polished marble shafts. Below, the **sanctuary** is panelled in oak, with a carved and gilded surround to the **reredos**. The **sedilia** and **piscina** match the e. window. The tapestry panels of angels standing under canopies on the n. wall of the chancel were worked by Sir George Mellers in 1940. The oak pulpit has painted panels of **Saints Mark**, **Paul** and **Luke**. The window arrangement at the w. end is unconventional, with a row of five short lancets below the w. window proper. They have glass by C.A. Gibbs - the **Four Evangelists** with the Good Shepherd in the centre. The w. window itself has glass of 1880 - figures of **Saints Peter**, **James the Great**, **Paul**, **Philip** and **Stephen** in the tall main **lights**, and conventional angels in the **tracery**. The westernmost window in the n. aisle has glass in somewhat virulent colours by W.C. Constable and the heads of the figures are in Victorian portrait style, now rather faded. The window in the n. side of the sanctuary is probably by the same artist. The two other windows in the n. aisle are by **Powell & Sons** - Christ with his disciples in one and the **Annunciation** in the other. The w. end of the church has been rearranged to provide a meeting room in place of the old baptistery and a general purpose area, cleared of pews, at the w. end of the nave. The church's only treasure, a **Burne-Jones** cartoon, was sold to help meet the cost of the new venture.

Newmarket, St Agnes (A4): The Bury road into Newmarket, lined with spacious houses and racing stables, is the setting and this small church lives up to it. It began as the Crawford memorial church, a private chapel built by the Duchess of Montrose as a burying place for her second husband, and it was consecrated as a parish church in 1887. Designed by R.H. Carpenter and built in 1885 with a lavish disregard for cost, it has happily been left alone and encapsulates late Victorian taste. Contrasted with Elveden, it is richness with restraint, devoid of eccentricity, using traditional forms to create a genuine style. In red brick with stone dressings, it has a slim octagonal tower on the n. side, the belfry stage carrying a small spire ringed with **crocketted** gables. The w. window is cut short by a lean-to baptistery below, the **chancel** rises slightly above the **nave** and its e. end has **Early English**-style blind **arcading** continuing over recesses which reach to the ground. The interior is very dark and does not come to life until the lights are switched on, but then the impression is exciting. Simple **scissors-braced** nave **roof** with **cusped** braces and a waggon roof in the chancel keep the attention down, and the eye is drawn to the e. end where, instead of a window, there is a large white marble **reredos** set in a round-headed recess. Sculpted by Sir Edward Boehm, this bas relief has **St Agnes** carrying her lamb being borne up by angels from the Colosseum, while cherubs peep from the clouds. The subject was the cause of some agitation at the time, but the Duchess (Caroline Agnes) had her way. Above is an arcade within which are mosaic figures of saints against a gold background, and this treatment is sumptuously continued up to the roof.

There is another mosaic of the **Blessed Virgin**, **St Patrick** and **St George** on the n. wall of the **sanctuary**. A two-bay arcade on the s. side of the chancel opens on to a family pew area which has its own entrance. The nave and part of the sanctuary walls are lined with majolica tiles patterned in blue, cream and buff - again, a rich effect, but the woodwork is rather dull (oak for the chancel, pulpit and altar, pitchpine for the nave). A large painting of the Last Supper by an unknown Italian artist hangs on the n. wall but is not well enough lit to be appreciated. All the windows have stained glass, most of it by **Clayton & Bell**; there are saints (mainly women) in the nave, all with their emblems, and the w. window contains attractive figures of the angels **Gabriel**, **Michael**, **Raphael** and **Uriel**. By way of a little period postcript, the organ was designed by Sir Arthur Sullivan - what better setting for 'The Lost Chord'!

Newmarket, St Mary (A4): The church lies n.w. of the High Street in an area transformed since the war by new housing and a shopping precinct. Newmarket was part of the parish of Exning until the C16, but there was a chapel of the Blessed Mary here in the C13. It was rebuilt and extended on the s. side in the C15 but most of what we see now is the result of major rebuilding in 1857, 1867 and 1887, during which a n. **transept** was converted into an **aisle**, the **chancel** was completely rebuilt and a new **vestry** added alongside. The tower is C15, with a slim shingled spire set well back from the parapet, and has a separate bellcote on one corner. Within the restored s. **porch**, the doorway is C15 (now badly damaged) and has an angel with a shield set in the moulding at the top. Inside, the chancel is rather dark, but the **nave** is tall, bright and spacious. The C15 s. **arcade**, with **quatrefoil piers** and battlemented **capitals** was matched on the n. side in

the rebuilding. The w. window **tracery** is original and the glass of 1930 is by Christopher Webb an **Annunciation** set in clear glass, with a backing of **Renaissance** architectural detail. This is most attractive and there is more of his work in the n. aisle a series of different compositions in three windows on the childhood of Christ. Again, Renaissance **cartouches** and architectural frames, set in clear glass. How fine it would have been if the set could have been completed with a Flight into Egypt in the fourth window. The wrought-iron tower screen has an interesting mixture of Gothic and **Art Nouveau** motifs, and on either side there are large benefaction boards. These are worth studying for the practical details of C17 charity - cades of herrings, stones of beef, twopenny bread, and warps of salt fish. On the w. wall of the n. aisle is a large painting of the Virgin and Child with **St Elizabeth** and **St John the Baptist**. It is by Giovanni Battista Caracciolo, an early C17 follower of Caravaggio. Clamped to the wall in that corner is a section of lead from the old roof, embossed with the names of C18 churchwardens and the plumber. A small glass case on the wall at the e. end of the n. aisle contains a linen purse that was found when the **high altar piscina** was uncovered in 1857. It contained three early C16 Nuremberg trade tokens but these are no longer on display. The screen to the n. aisle Lady chapel is a war memorial and the shafts on either side of the doorway carry small, well carved figures of **St George** and St Joan of Arc. There is a large painting on the **sanctuary** n. wall here by James Wood of Jesus entering Jerusalem, but having been placed over an unshielded radiator it is deteriorating. There is a section of wood placed behind the **altar** which carries a medieval inscription asking us to pray for the soul of Thomas Wydon who had benches made in 1494, possibly in conjunction with the first rebuilding. To the r. is a **Deco-**

rated piscina with foliage in the **spandrels**. The high altar is backed by an oak-panelled **reredos**, and to the r. is the C13 angle piscina rediscovered in the C19. It is **groined** within and one of the **corbel** heads is original. The C19 stone pulpit is more pleasing than most and has openwork tracery panels. The s. aisle has a number of well lettered C18 tablets which illustrate the move from Renaissance to classical detailing. There is a C19 coarsely cut epitaph in Latin to the unfortunate (or he might have said fortunate) Robert Cook, a C17 rector who died while preaching in the pulpit. Further e., the **cinquefoiled** recess in the wall was probably a piscina, although there is now no sign of a drain. Nearby, a 1907 window by **Kempe & Tower** shows a very traditional rendering of 'Suffer little children...' across three **lights**, with musical angels above. The s. aisle chapel of the Blessed Sacrament has two oil paintings, both unattributed; one is a 'Descent from the Cross' and the other 'The Blessed Virgin and St Elizabeth' in C17 Italian style. Nearby is an interesting sidelight on the social attitudes of 1886 - a masonic memorial window, with figures of Solomon and **St Etheldreda** (the name of the lodge) and innumerable and no doubt significant symbolic objects. A very minor footnote to history: Cardinal Wolsey's father was an Ipswich butcher, but he was born and buried here, although nothing marks his grave.

Norton, St Andrew (E4): The church is very isolated at the end of a lane off the road to Great Ashfield. It is however a sweet situation, with a line of tall limes leading up to the s. door, and the old rectory standing foursquare beyond. Flint and stone chequerwork was a popular decoration locally in the C15 and here it can be seen on the s. **porch** parapet and in the **base course** which continues along the s. **aisle** with its large **gar-**

goyles. The **chancel** dates from the end of the C13 but there were restorations in the 1880s and the s. wall was rebuilt with new windows, although a **lancet** remains above the **priest's door**. On the nearby buttress, the centre hole of a **scratch dial** will be found some 3 ft from the ground. The e. window **tracery** illustrates how **Decorated** and **Perpendicular** forms may sometimes be found in charming conjunction. Round the corner, the little C15 **vestry** has been fitted with diminutive sash windows, only the second time I have found them in an East Anglian church. There is a Decorated window in the n. wall of the chancel with **headstops** on the **dripstone**. Outside the early C14 n. door is a compact **stoup** under a **Tudor** arch. The early C14 tower has Decorated tracery in the w. window, but it was a long time in the building because money was left for its completion in 1442. By the n.w. corner of the n. aisle, a monument topped with a draped urn for the Williams family is strong on epitaphs. For Charles (1877) we have:

> Forbear dear children to mourn and weep,
> While sweetly in the dust I sleep.
> This toilsome world I've left behind,
> A glorious crown I hope to find.

Amen to that! Like the s. aisle, the porch was added in the C15 and there is a modern **St Andrew** in the niche over the entrance.

Just inside the C15 doors is a lovely little chest, hewn out of a solid trunk whose natural curve forms rough feet at each end. Although churchwardens' initials and the date '1604' have been carved on the front, it must date from the C13. To the l. of the tower arch is a curious and interesting monument. It is a large stone block painted grey and dull pink, with an **ogee** arch forming a recess on top. There are three obelisks, painted with scroll patterns, and within the arch is the faint figure of a skeleton with hour glass and scythe and the inscription:

Norton, St Andrew: medieval glass [St Christopher]

Norton, St Andrew: medieval glass [St Ethelreda]

'As the glasse runneth, so life wasteth'. There was a brass plate fixed to the front which recorded the charity of Daniel Bales who, when he died in 1625, established a bread charity for the village; loaves for distribution to the poor were still being placed in the arched recess within living memory. Photographs of C19 rectors hang within the tower and the **quoins** of the former **nave** walls show up on either side of the tower arch. Idle hands have long been at work on the stonework; Robert Fuller cut his name quite elegantly in 1754 on the n. **jamb** of the arch. The early C15 **font** is in superb condition and is highly individual; the square shaft panels contain two tiers of tracery and there are standing figures at the corners, including those two old adversaries the **woodwose** and the lion. The bowl panels are deeply carved with **Evangelistic symbols**, together with a **grif-**

fin, a double-headed eagle, and a **pelican** in her piety. The last panel contains a **unicorn**, and although it often occurs on bench ends, it is rare on a font. It was one of the symbols of the **Blessed Virgin**, and underneath the bowl there is another, the winged hearts sprouting flowers. The octagonal **piers** of the nave **arcades** have concave faces topped with blank **trefoiled** ogee arches. The nave and aisle **roofs** were rebuilt in 1897 and the nave benches installed in 1907, but those in the aisles are C15. They have **poppyheads** and grotesques on the gabled elbows like the ones at Stowlangtoft (including a priest with his rosary on the n. side). The ends, however, are not traceried and there are no poppyheads by the walls. There is a plain niche **piscina** in the s. aisle and in the n. aisle, the vestige of another - just a rough mark in the stonework with a drilled hole. There will have been **altars** by both of them and the sill of the window in the n. aisle is lowered so that it probably housed a **retable**. The stairs to the **rood loft** went up on this side (see the fragmentary steps behind the C19 pulpit and the small window above the piscina). The **hood mould** of the chancel arch comes down to small **corbel** heads and the arch itself is grooved to house the **tympanum**. To the r. is a stone block which may have served to support the rood loft, and it is pierced by a hole so that a rope may have passed through it to control the **Lenten veil** over the rood itself. Two **brass** inscriptions have been moved to the wall beneath, both for rectors - Edmund Coket (see also the Ampton entry), and John Rokewood, a member of the family who not only entertained Queen Elizabeth at Euston but provided one of the conspirators in the Gunpowder Plot (see also Stanningfield). The chancel roof is medieval, with **arch-braces** and embattled **collars** under the ridge. The bay over the **sanctuary** was painted as a **celure** and the decoration can still be seen on the deep **wall plates** and on the braces. Although they will almost certainly have come from elsewhere (perhaps even the abbey at Bury), three fine ranges of stalls with **misericords** can be found in the chancel. On the n. side, the raised seats reveal carvings of the martyrdom of St Andrew, the pelican in her piety, and a lovely vignette of a woman carding wool. On the s. side is a monk at his books and a martyrdom of **St Edmund** which is much more spirited than the **boss** in the Norwich cathedral cloister. In the sanctuary, the misericords are carved with three animal groups - a lion savaging a woodwose, a pretty pair of greyhounds, and the fragment of another. The elbows are carved as well, and one in the last group has a young lad being soundly birched. Overhead, the tracery of the window contains some C14 and C15 figures: from l. to r., **St Margaret**, a beautiful **St Christopher**, a saint with a palm

frond, an unidentified figure, **St Etheldreda** and St Andrew. In the lancet above the priest's door is a very good panel of an angel with a **thurible** that was once in the e. window, and in the top r. of the s. aisle e. window is the figure of **St Appollonia**, complete with a tooth held in massive pincers. Four C15 shields of Ashfield family arms are set in a n. aisle window. William Clarke, who was rector for the first 30 years of the C19, has a plain tablet by de Carle of Bury on the n. side of the chancel. More pleasing are the memorials for two other rectors on the e. wall - the one for Andrew Pern (1772) has a very perky shield and crest. In all this is a sweet little church.

Nowton, St Peter (D5): This little church is well away from the hamlet and stands on a rise among open fields, backed to the w. by pine trees. The building was enlarged and altered in 1843 and the **chancel** restored in 1876, all so thoroughly that the result was practically a new building, with a neo- **Norman** n. **aisle** and heavy **arcade**, windows to match on the s. side, and quaintly domestic ventilation dormers in the roof. However, the original Norman n. doorway was re-set beneath a steep little gable - it has leaf **capitals** to the columns, and there is a plain Norman s. doorway; a tiny Norman **lancet** was placed in the e. wall of the new aisle. The chancel retains its late C13 or early C14 windows with intersected **tracery** in the e. window, and the arches of the side windows betray a hint of the **ogee** shape. The C14 unbuttressed tower has two strong **string courses, Decorated** tracery in the windows, and renewed battlements with corner pinnacles. The interior is rather dark and a ponderous C19 polished marble **font** stands beyond the tall tower arch. On the w. wall of the **nave** on the s. side is a small memorial by the fashionable sculptor **John Bacon the Younger**. It is for Elizabeth Oakes

Nowton, St Peter: Flemish C16 glass [Christ carrying the cross with St Veronica]

Nowton, St Peter: Flemish C17 glass [Christ taken captive]

who died in 1811, and a mourning woman drapes herself over an angled sarcophagus. There is no chancel arch and the **arch- braced** roof is continuous, with plastered and boarded ceilings. The C19 benches are replicas of those at Little Whelnetham and there is a C19 eagle lectern, but the northern half of the **screen** is medieval. The tall C14 niches on each side of the e. window were drastically restored, probably when the panelling below was installed in the 1870s; the original **piscina** is set within it. It is most unusual to find C19 **misericords** but there are six here, and the undersides are well carved in traditional fashion with the arms and names of rectors from 1750 to 1875; all is the work of the Bury carver Henry Wormald.

What makes Nowton so special and puts it high on the list of churches not to be missed is the fabulous series of 84 continental C16 and C17 glass roundels, one of the finest in England. They were collected by Col Rushbrooke in the early years of the C19 and then sold to Orbell Ray Oakes, the Lord of the Manor, who had installed them here by 1820. They are set within richly enamelled painted rosettes, borders and other decorations and these were probably the work of Samuel Yarington of Norwich. Most of the colour in fact, in the e. window particularly, derives from the setting rather than the roundels. The C19 rebuilding entailed rearrangement of the glass but the collection is virtually complete and the bottom panels of the e. window came from a collection formerly at Dagnam Park, Essex, being added in 1970. The roundels display both religious and secular scenes and are mainly from the Netherlands. Binoculars are useful when studying the e. window but one of the pleasures of the collection is that the majority of the roundels can be seen at close quarters, and they are fascinating. I found the following particularly interesting: n. aisle w. end, the nailing of Christ to the cross in chilling detail; chancel n. window, top l., a professor and students of (probably) the university of Leuven, with a little academic dog in the middle; chancel n. window, top r., Anger (one of a series on the human passions), in which a man holds another by the throat as he stabs him; chancel n. window, Job kneeling with his back to us while assorted chunks of classical architecture rain down on his unfortunate family; e. window, l. **light** towards the bottom, Adam naming the animals; e. window, centre light, centre, **St Christopher** being tortured by having a red- hot helmet lowered on his head; e. window, centre light, bottom, Christ taken captive - a very vigorous scene full of movement, with Peter striking off Malchus' ear; s. chancel, bottom l., Christ carrying the Cross assisted by Simon, while **St Veronica** holds the cloth with the imprint of Jesus' face upon it one of the outstanding pictures here; nave, easternmost window, Christ and the woman of Samaria at the well, and the Judgement of Solomon, with the soldier about to cleave the tiny child in swaddling bands. The space at the bottom of some of the windows has been filled (rather strangely) with C19 figures of knights in the style of monumental brasses - all lying on their sides. At the w. end is a much smaller German roundel, dated 1643, of the Baptism of Christ, which is a good example of enamelled work as opposed to painted glass, and below are the C19 arms of squire Oakes, the benefactor who 'embellished and decorated' this church in such splendid fashion. For those who would like to know more, there is a full description of the glass in the Suffolk Records Office in Bury, and a shortened version by William Cole was published in *Crown in Glory* edited by Peter Moore.

Onehouse, St John the Baptist (F5): The church is set apart from the village down a lane but is easily seen from the road. Round towers are peculiar to East Anglia and this one is likely to be **Saxon** rather than **Norman**; it has **lancet** bell openings and the later battlements are mainly brick. The **nave** windows on the s. side are C19 and so is the **chancel**, with an e. window in a Victorian version of **Perpendicular**. There are rather brutal little yellow brick pedestals corbelled out below the gable ends, and on the n. side of the nave, two late C18 or early C19 wide lancets; however a small Norman lancet survives high in the wall beyond the small n. door. The s. **porch** is built of pleasant pale pink **Tudor** brick, with heavy angle buttresses each side of the low C16 archway. It has a simple **arch-braced roof** and there are remains of a **stoup** to the r. of the inner door. The interior is plain and uncomplicated under a **scissors-braced** roof with **tie-beams**, and at the w. end is a C12 **font**. Its heavy bowl has become mis-shapen over the years and at the top corners there are shadowy outlines of heads and outstretched arms; the square plinth is later. In the tower w. window there are three small panels of continental glass painted with the figures of **Saints John the Baptist**, **Paul** and **Matthew**. There is a fragment of stone embedded in the nave n. wall that may possibly have been an image stool, and the roughly shaped beam above the entrance to the chancel is likely to have been the original **rood beam**, with faint traces of a C19 text on the chamfer. The pews are C19 and so is the pulpit, but that is an excellent piece carved by Herbert Green in 1893. Everything is sharply cut and the tiny **crocketted** pinnacles show

how much care was taken in the detail. Beyond it is the one remaining medieval bench end, with a strange web-footed creature turning its head over its shoulder.

Ousden, St Peter (B5): The church stands on rising ground at the w. end of the village and it has a central **Norman** tower which has remained virtually unaltered apart from the parapet. It is extremely simple, with attached shafts at the corners above the shallow set-off. The arches of the bell openings have plain roll mouldings and there is a small **lancet** at ground floor level. There may have been an **apse** at the e. end but a new **chancel** was built about 1300 and its roof line shows on the e. wall. This in its turn was replaced in the late C18 and new windows were inserted a century later. A chapel which served as a manorial pew was added on the n. side of the **nave** in the C18 and the nave was extended westward some 20 ft in 1850, with windows typical of the period. The main entrance used to be on the s. side and more evidence of Norman work is to be seen there. The blocked door (with a modern window inserted) has three bands of chip carving in the lintel, and within the arch of thin Roman tiles the **tympanum** is deeply carved with a large chequer pattern. On the l. **jamb** is the faint outline of a very early **scratch dial** which has holes as markers instead of radial lines. The lancet in the nave is Norman but the larger window with 'Y' **tracery** is C13 as is the tower lancet; to the r. of it a window was inserted in the early C14, probably to give more light to the **rood**. The n. **porch** is modern and the entrance has been fitted with a well designed wrought-iron grill. The doorway itself is an intriguing mixture. The shaft on the l. is Norman but the other has an **Early English capital** and the arch is pointed - all signs of a reconstruction using whatever came to hand. The design of the late C14 **font** is uncommon; the

Ousden, St Peter: Laeititia Mosley memorial detail

attached columns of the tall and graceful stem curve out to meet the bowl, the panels of which are carved with various tracery shapes and a single blank shield. Behind the font stands a simple **Jacobean** chest. There are **paterae** on the **wall plates** below a waggon panelled ceiling and two **hatchments** hang on the walls; on the s., for Thomas James Ireland of Ousden Hall who died in 1863, and on the n., for the Rev Thomas Frampton, rector, who died in 1803. Above the tower arch hangs a large set of **Royal Arms** painted on board, with three turned **finials** on the frame. They are **Hanoverian**, although **Cautley** suspected that they were an early **Stuart** set originally and the frame design supports this. The n. chapel is entered through a creditable imitation of a Norman arch and on the wall within is a tripartite Victorian Gothick memorial for members of the Ireland family by I.E. Thomas. To the l. of the tower arch is an excellent memorial for Laeticia Mosley of 1619. Two female virtues recline on the

pediment which encloses an hourglass, and the **touchstone** tablet is flanked by matching **Corinthian** columns; below, in a marble oval, a shrouded skeleton is exquisitely carved. The inscription is gilt and although the epitaph is too long to quote, it should not go unread. The plainness of the C18 pulpit is subtly relieved by marquetry banding on the panels and beyond it there is a C13 recess which will have backed a nave **altar**. The Norman tower arches are typically massive, with roll mouldings, and there are two beasts carved on the capitals of the easternmost arch. A close look at the s. jamb of the w. arch will reveal a roundel in low relief carved with an interlace design. It seems to be quite isolated and there is no clue as to its significance. There are **decalogue**, Belief and Lord's Prayer boards in the **sanctuary** and the **communion rails** have clusters of four turned **balusters**, with all the signs of having been three-sided originally.

Pakenham, St Mary (E4): Standing on high ground above the village street, this was originally a **Norman** church with **nave**, central tower and **chancel**. In the late C13 the chancel was rebuilt and a s. **transept** added, while in the C14 the tower was given an octagonal top with **Decorated** bell openings (the parapets are now of brick). At some time the transept was destroyed by fire and in 1849 **Samuel Saunders Teulon** carried out an extensive restoration and rebuilding. He opened up the old arch and built a new s. transept, adding another on the n. side, together with a new tower stair turret and a n. **porch**. Walking round the outside you will see the original Norman w. and s. doorways with their simple roll mouldings and scalloped **capitals**. There is a stone coffin built into the wall under a window on the s. side of the nave (unlikely to have been there originally), and there are four C13 coffin lids fixed upright on

the s. wall of the chancel. Within, below the large **Perpendicular** w. window, is an excellent C15 **font**. Four of the bowl panels have **Evangelistic symbols** but on the e. there is a **pelican** in her piety, on the s., a lion with a staff topped by an encircled cross, and to the w., a **unicorn**. This is one of the symbols of the **Blessed Virgin** and is not commonly seen on fonts, although there is another example at nearby Norton. There are angels below the bowl and the **traceried** shaft has unusually good figures of seated monks at the corners: one meditating, one holding what is possibly a treasurer's satchel (n.w.), one reading his breviary and the last holding what could be a **reliquary** (s.e.). The nicely detailed tabernacle cover was given in 1931. Thomas Discipline died in 1752 and his **hatchment** is on the n. wall. His wife rejoiced in the name of Merelinda and her hatchment hangs opposite. The **roofs** were replaced in the Teulon restoration and the new nave benches, with their shapely and well carved fleur de lys, were modelled on those at Stanton Harcourt, Oxfordshire. Teulon presumably wished to open up the vista to the e. end and to do so, he replaced the Norman w. arch of the tower with one which is altogether larger and pointed. A modern **altar** now stands below the centre crossing, and to the r. is a small C15 chest. The original Noman e. arch of the tower is undisturbed and has simple cross decoration on the **abacus**. The plain C15 **screen** has been extensively restored and the stalls in the chancel have compact **finials** encrusted with carved foliage. The two bench ends that back on to the screen terminate in grotesque masks with tongues lolling out. There is a **priest's door** on the s. side and the **vestry** door opposite is medieval. The e. window and two of the side windows are Perpendicular but there are C13 **lancets** over the two doors and in the **sanctuary**. A window on the n. side has **Ward & Hughes** glass of 1913 designed by T.F. Curtis. It is an interesting composition in steely tints, with figures of the Sower, the Reaper, and Christ as the Lord of the Harvest. The late C17 **communion rails** have twisted **balusters** and there is a **trefoil**-headed **piscina** in the sanctuary. The C19 **reredos** was designed by Thomas Earp - a series of low arches and roundels backed with gold mosaic.

Palgrave, St Peter (F3): The church sits nicely in the centre of the village, and in walking round the outside, look to the s. of the **chancel** for the gravestone of John Catchpole. a waggoner who died in 1787. The top of the stone has a nice illustration of his team of six horses and the epitaph reads:

My horses have done running, my waggon is decay'd,
And now in the Dust my Body is lay'd;
My whip is worn out and my work It is done,
And now I'm brought here to my last home.

The unbuttressed tower dates from the early C14 but the **nave** was rebuilt about a century later. The chancel has rather odd round-headed windows with 'Y' **tracery** and is work of the early C18, while the n. **aisle** was rebuilt in the C19. A good deal of attention was given to the s. **porch** in the C15 rebuilding and it has an ornate front to the street, with **flushwork** panelling and battlements. **Crocketted ogee**-arched niches flank the doorway and there is another canopied niche at the gable. The doorway **spandrels** contain carvings of **St George** and the dragon, there are **fleurons** and crowns set in the mouldings, and fine lion terminals. The porch is two-storied but the upper room has now gone. To the l. of the entrance door is a fine tablet commemorating 'honest' Tom Martin, 'that able and indefatigable antiquary' who died in 1770 - placed

there by Sir John Fenn, the man who first published the Paston letters in 1787. On entering, you will see immediately above your head, one of the suits of parish armour that used to be kept in the room above the porch, and the door to that room lies to the l. The mouldings of the tower arch fade into the **imposts** and above is a very dark set of **Royal Arms** dated 1850. The large and square late **Norman font** is not typical of East Anglia in its decoration. It stands on a central octagonal shaft, and columns at each corner have scalloped **capitals**. There are heads at the corners and the sides are decorated with large crosses. When the n. aisle was rebuilt in the 1860s, the whole **arcade** was replaced on the original bases and the **quatrefoil piers** match the triple shafts of the early C14 chancel arch, with its wide concave mouldings.

The joy of this church is the splendid **hammerbeam roof**. The **archbraces** rest directly on the hammerbeams and they sweep over in a continuous curve below the ridge. The roof retains its original decoration and there are dark tracery patterns on all the main timbers, with lighter stencilling in between. Even the spandrels and arch-braces are painted rather than carved. There are remains of delicate cresting on the hammerbeams and the **wall posts** come down to rest on head **corbels**. Below, a legacy of the C19, are the pitchpine pews, each with its little gate. There is no **screen** to the short chancel and the e. window has 1850s glass - patterned **quarries** and borders, with inset quatrefoils and roundels. Below is a late C17 oak **altar** table with shapely **baluster** legs. On the n. aisle wall is a set of painted boards bearing the Lord's Prayer, Creed and **commandments**. They were carefully restored in the 1960s and look very well indeed. Over the n. door is the church's single **hatchment**, for the rector Charles Martin, who died in 1864.

Poslingford, St Mary (C6): The church stands a little above the street and its solid, well proportioned tower has **Decorated tracery** in the small w. window. Above the belfry **lancets** there are large bell openings, and on the n. side there is a long flight of steps up to an access door, probably a C19 arrangement. The church was heavily restored by the Victorians but on the n. side you will find typical coursed flints, a small lancet and the **jambs** of a door, all of which are **Norman**. The windows range over a number of periods and styles: a tall late C13 lancet (chancel n. side), a Decorated lancet and a two-**light** early C14 window with **cusped** 'Y' tracery (s. chancel), Decorated windows, one with **reticulated** tracery (s. **nave**), and a **Perpendicular** design (n. nave); the e. window lancets are C19 but may echo what was there before. The line of an older roof shows on the e. face of the tower and it is strange to see that the restorers clad the gable wall of the nave with Kentish-style tiles. The early C16 **porch** is very attractive in red brick and has a **stoup** inset by the outer arch. Below the crow-stepped gable there are three large and shallow niches and the side windows have **mullions** of brick. Much of the roof is original. The inner doorway is fine Norman work, with sturdy shafts, and **capitals** carved with a variety of scroll patterns; the **abaci** are decorated with **chevrons** on one side and **dogtooth** on the other. Within the **tympanum**, a deep band is chip-carved with rosettes, interlace and dogtooth. Within, the church is beautifully kept. The roofs are modern and the Decorated tower arch has been fitted with pine doors pierced by leaded **lights**. By the door stands what is probably a C12 **font** which at some time has had the corners of the bowl clipped off and then been restored to a square. On the w. wall is a mid-C17 monument for Thomas and Frances Golding which has its own endearing variety of lettering and spelling on the **touchstone** tablet; there are flanking

trophies of death's sickle and spade, and at the top a coloured **achievement** is set within a broken **pediment** on which voluptuous little angels toy with skull and hour-glass. The upper **hatchment** above the arch is for Samuel Severne of Poslingford Park who died in 1865, and the lower pair for Col Thomas Weston and his wife Mary. It is interesting that their memorial tablets lower down are also lozenge-shaped to match the hatchments. There is a heavy C14 chest in the n.w. corner which is unusually decorated with two bands of coarse carving on the lid, which also bears centuries of graffiti. The **Royal Arms** of James I painted on board hang conveniently in front of the old n. door. The motto in rustic capitals within a strapwork surround is 'Exurgat deus dissipentur inimica' ('Let God arise and let his enemies be scattered', psalm 68); the lion and **unicorn** are surprisingly explicit physically. An enterprising innovation is the use of two light- weight cartwheels converted to candleabra in the nave. There are remains of C14 painting in a s. nave window arch and the sill of the Prpendicular window on the n. side drops to the floor; The blocked door within it was probably the entrance to a **rood loft** stair. To the r. are the remains of what must have been a beautiful niche with a **groined** canopy. The tall C15 **screen** has **crocketted** and **cusped ogee** arches spanning two lights, with panel tracery above them. The lancet in the s. wall of the chancel retains some C13 decoration in the embrasure and the window above the stepped **sedilia** has 1880s glass by **Ward & Hughes** in sentimental mode. The early C14 plain **piscina** has been restored and there is an **aumbry** in an uncommon position. It is round-headed, rebated for a door, and recessed in the splay above the sedilia.

Preston, St Mary (E6): By the mid-C19 the church had become very dilapidated, and when in 1868 the tower was struck for a second time by lightning and collapsed, a wholesale restoration was put in hand under **Sir Arthur Blomfield**.It as then that the tower and most of the **chancel** were rebuilt. The tall C16 **porch** is quite an eye catcher - panelled overall in **flushwork**, with three-**light Perpendicular** side windows; there are three matching niches - two in the buttresses and one over the doorway and the latter has an angel holding a shield below the stool. There are shields in the **spandrels** displaying the **Trinity** badge and **Passion emblems** and **fleurons** stud the arch. In walking round note the **priest's door** on the s. side of the chancel and also the small angel below a stub buttress at the apex of the **nave** roof - an indication that there was probably a **sanctus-bell turret** there. Although the tower was rebuilt, the doors, niches and windows were re-used and the weathervane (in the shape of a feather) is dated 1892. It is interesting that the porch is not centred on the small C14 n. doorway but was offset to leave space for a table tomb. The **purbeck marble** top once carried a **brass** and it is likely that it commemorated the donor of the porch.

The fine C12 **font** stands just inside and the square bowl is carved with simple designs - an intersected arcade to the e., plaits and a rosette to the s., a square cabled border round a stylised Tree of Life to the w., and a floriated cross to the n.; the supporting shafts are modern. Over the n. door is one of the earliest and most interesting **decalogue boards** to be found anywhere. Dating possibly from the time of Edward IV, it is in the form of a triptych, with the commandments painted on the centre section and the wings inscribed with biblical texts on Sabbath keeping and commandment obedience. When closed, the boards display texts on the theme of charity and the spelling is cheerfully haphazard. To match the decalogue, Robert Ryece (of whom more later) set up one

of the most splendid sets of Elizabethan **Royal Arms** in the country, again in triptych form. The wings are painted with Tudor supporters, lion and dragon, against a blue ground, with the sun and moon. Backed by strapwork, the arms are enclosed within the Garter and Ryece concocted an extraordinary collection of quarterings to display the queen's real and imaginary genealogy. Apart from the arms of England and France (reversed), he made a place for Brutus, Uffa, king of the East Angles, Edward, king of the West Saxons, Swanus, king of Norway, Edward the Confessor, and even the SPQR badge of ancient Rome! 'Elizabetha Magna Regina Angliae' is lettered below, and at the top one can trace the faint outline of an 'ER' which has been overpainted. this suggests that the board may have carried Edward VI's arms originally. The back of the wings are painted with Puritan texts on an anti-imagery theme, and in 1987 the set was beautifully restored by Miss Julie Crick. The church hopes to refurbish the decalogue board as well and mount the pair either side of the tower arch where they may be seen to better advantage.

In the n. **aisle** wall there is a low tomb recess and the stair to the old **rood loft** rises to the l. of the chancel arch behind the pulpit, with a little window giving on to the n. aisle. There is a plain **piscina** in the s. aisle chapel and nearby, a **Ward & Hughes** 1880s window - an uninspired Nativity in muddy colours. Roofs and fittings throughout are C19, but although the **rood screen** was destroyed long before, its base was recovered and replaced with new panels inserted. The C14 piscina in the **sanctuary** has a wide **trefoiled ogee** arch, and there is a narrow opening to the **dropped-sill sedilia** alongside. **James Powell & Sons** are best known for their stained glass but they undertook other work; the **reredos** here is by them - mosaic panels of the **Evangelistic symbols** and a centre inscription which informs us that the rector and his curate 'by whose exertions the church was restored in 1868' had it installed in 1883. The flanking walls are tiled and above are two large mosaic panels with the **Agnus Dei** and the **pelican** in her piety within centre lozenges. The Rev James Dunn's tablet on the n. wall has the often-used epitaph which begins 'Adieu vain world I have seen enough of thee, and now I am careless what thou say'st of me'. The chancel glass is uniformly awful but there are two brasses in the sanctuary floor which should not be overlooked: on the s. side for Mary Ryece (1629) with four shields, an inscription and Latin verse, and on the n. for Robert Ryece. This has a lavish display of heraldry - Ryece's shield with mantling, crest and motto and eight other shields. They range widely enough in his family to include the arms of his great-great-grandfather's wife (the centre inscription is modern). Ryece, who died in 1638, was one of Suffolk's earliest antiquarians and was besotted with heraldry. He collected over 150 stained glass shields of arms dating from the C14 to the C16 and 46 of them survive in the aisle e. windows and in the **clerestory**. They figure in his *Breviary of Suffolk* written in 1618 but not published until 1902.

Rattlesden, St Nicholas (E5): This most attractive village lying in a valley has a church which stands proudly on rising ground in the centre. The C14 tower has most unusual five-sided buttresses to the w. which rise to the parapet and are gabled at the top. It has a **Decorated** w. window but the bell openings are C19 and at that time the lead on the broach spire was replaced by oak shingles. This was part of a major restoration in the 1880s under **Sir Arthur Blomfield** when the n. **clerestory** wall was replaced, the **porch** and s. aisle re-faced and many of the windows renewed. The aisles have C19 **crock-**

etted pinnacles at the corners, there is an early C16 two-storied **sacristy** n. of the **chancel**, and an obtrusive chimney rises on the n.e. corner of the nave. The s. wall of the **Perpendicular** clerestory has a most interesting series of **flushwork** emblems. From the w. they represent: Saints **Edmund, Matthew, James the Less, Philip, Thaddeus, Bartholomew, Peter**, the **Blessed Virgin**, the **sacred monogram**, a dragon (possibly for **St John**), and the Saints **Paul, James the Great, Andrew, Simon, Thomas** and **Etheldreda** (an 'A' for her popular name, St Audrey). Round the corner at the w. end are the arms of the Chamberlain and Bourchier families and on the e. face are a mitre and crossed croziers (the arms of Hervey, Bishop of Ely in the early C12). A **rood stair** turret is set in the wall of the s. aisle and the s. porch is tall and handsome. Rebuilt in the 1470s, the **ashlar** of its s. face is panelled overall, it has stepped battlements, and in the canopied niche above the doorway an 1890s figure of **St Nicholas**, vested as a bishop, sits with a child at his knee. The line of an old roof shows over the lovely inner doorway dating from about 1300 which has a deeply moulded arch resting on pairs of attached shafts; above it is a contemporary circular window inset with a **quatrefoil**.

Within are C14 **arcades** on octagonal **piers** whose concave faces are topped by blank **cusped** arches, and capping all is a superb double **hammerbeam** roof alive with the carved angels that were added when it was restored and renewed in the 1880s. There is **tracery** above the hammerbeams and on either side of the **king posts**, which rise from the **collars** to the ridge. All the angels in the aisle roofs are C19 too, with the exception of one in the n.e. corner of the s. aisle. There is a **sanctus-bell window** in the tower wall and access to the belfry is by way of an unusual Victorian cast iron spiral staircase. The set of George I **Royal Arms** is dated 1714. In front of the tower arch stands a section of the C15 **rood screen**, with four-**light** tracery in its panels. The late C14 **font** stands on a wide octagonal step and is satisfyingly solid, with a traceried shaft and a deep bowl whose panels are carved with cusped **ogee** arches flanked by flowers and leaves. Under the bowl are six varied human heads and two lion masks to the w. To the e. is a range of C17 **altar rails** which came from Kettlebaston in 1903. They are finely turned, with groups of four **balusters** at each end; other sections of the same set are placed at the e. end of the n. aisle and at the front of the nave on the s. side. Like Methwold in Norfolk, Rattlesden has a complete replica rood screen, loft, and rood, and it is a lovely reconstruction, lacking only the vivid colours that its predecessor would have had. Designed by G.F. Prynne, it was built in 1909 and in 1916 he designed the matching **parclose screen** in the s. aisle. This completes the original arrangement and its loft provides the link between the turret in the s. aisle wall and the **rood loft**, via a little curving wooden stair. All the carving is excellent, with intricate tracery roundels, cresting, and bands of ornament. The s. aisle chapel retains its **piscina**, although the canopy is chopped away, and the image niche in the e. window embrasure suffered at the same hand, which left only a portion of the vaulting. To the l., a quatrefoil **squint** once gave a view of the **high altar**. This may have been the chapel of the **guild of St Margaret** with the guild of **St John the Baptist** taking the n. aisle where a matching image niche has been similarly defaced. The **Jacobean** pulpit stands on a new base; the bottom panels are plain but the top range of blind arches has better than average carving.

Through the heavy doors of the **screen** one moves into the chancel where the coved and panelled ceiling conceals a hammerbeam roof. It was extensively restored in the C19 but many of the ribs and ornaments are

C16. The stalls, too, were reconstructed but, again, much is original work, including the fronts and slopes; look particularly for the four-headed **poppyhead** on the n. side and the one with six faces (all with tongues out) on the s. side. Until the 1890s the C17 **communion rails** were three-sided but they were re arranged and a section of the set now stands on the n. side of the nave at the e. end. In the n. wall is the medieval door to the sacristy. Although the upper floor has been removed, the stairs remain in the s.w. corner. The ground floor may have been used as a chapel but both windows are barred. There are traces of heavy shutters, and the door frame is slotted for a bar. On the wall hang the **decalogue**, Creed and Lord's Prayer boards painted in 1690 for the **sanctuary**. In the n. wall of the sanctuary is a particularly fine C14 **aumbry**. It has a crocketted gable on tilted **corbel** heads, with a **trefoil** below it and flanking shafts with ringed **capitals** topped by pinnacles. The interior is grooved for a shelf and it is large enough to have served for an **Easter sepulchre** in season. Fitted with a new door it now contains the Blessed Sacrament reserved for the sick. In 1912 a wooden canopied stall was inserted into the **sedilia** and the back panels came from the original rood loft or screen. They were once painted with figures but only the faint outlines remain. There are two quite flamboyant **Art Nouveau** sanctuary lamps in copper and the e. wall is panelled in stone, with a heavy canopy over the 1890s Last Supper **reredos**. The e. window glass by **Clayton & Bell** is the same period but there are three good windows by William Aikman dating from the 1920s: on the s. side of the sanctuary, three scenes against clear glass, with lovely deep colours in the robes, of Thomas Rattlesden meeting King Henry VII at Bury, St Nicholas, and St Edmund; s. aisle, the war memorial window with **St George** flanked by scenes of the sacrifice of Isaac and David versus

Goliath; s. aisle w. end, Christ gathering the children of all nations, with the church's font and altar illustrated at the bottom. The other s. aisle window has late (1913) **Hardman** glass of Christ in Glory with four **censing** angels and it is made very dull by the tree outside. In 1897, **Heaton, Butler & Bayne** took a host of fragments from the clerestory and set them in the w. window; there is a musical angel at the top and lots of small heads in a kaleidoscope of colour. More fragments were arranged in a n. aisle window in 1901 but they are a mere jumble.

Rede, All Saints (C5): There was an extensive restoration here in 1850, the **chancel** was rebuilt in 1874 and the **porch** restored in 1877, so that much of the fabric has that sharp look of the C19. However, a good deal remains of interest and it is worth circling the outside of the building first. A round-headed **lancet** at the w. end of the **nave** on the n. side indicates that the church was originally **Norman**. The next window along has **Decorated tracery**, and C13 lancets were re-used in the side walls of the chancel when it was rebuilt. The late C13 or early C14 tower has half-height w. buttresses, 'Y' tracery in the bell opening and lancets in the other faces. There are good **gargoyles** n. and s., with long snarling metal spouts below the recently restored battlements (in the 1830s there was no parapet at all). The s. porch is handsome in its quiet way, with a floriated cross on the gable and **crocketted** corner pinnacles. The niche above the door is richly decorated with a nodding **ogee** arch, stiff leaf **capitals** to the little side shafts, and a carved stool on which stands a modern figure of Christ the King. Below the corner pinnacles there are jutting demi-angels and the bases of the buttresses are carved with the arms of Turner and Bullock. The C14 s. doorway is tall and narrow and note when you use the heavy key that its wards are stamped '1850'. There is no tower arch - access is by a medieval door, and above it there is a small **sanctus-bell window** with a **cusped** arch. It is backed by a wooden traceried shutter which, if original, is a rare and unusual feature. There are some low C15 benches at the w. end that have been ravaged by woodworm and the C13 octagonal **font** is entirely plain, standing on a shaft almost as wide as the bowl. The ceilings are plastered, with two exposed **tie-beams** and, with a single exception, all the benches on the s. side are medieval, with **poppyheads**, gabled elbows, and **castellated** backs. The C17 pulpit has plain panels with coarsely carved shells applied below the rim and a canted ledge resting on plain scrolls; the square window nearby is a C19 addition. The Victorian chancel stalls have poppyheads and on the ends there are four intriguing hinged seats facing e. Their purpose is obscure and the undersides are carved rather in the fashion of **misericords** (although they have no lips to rest against and are too low anyway). The carvings are: a **pelican** in her piety, **Agnus Dei**, **sacred monogram** with leaf supporters, and floriated cross, also with supporters. Someone obviously favoured hinged seats at toddler level because there are more fixed to the old benches by the font. The jolly little chamber organ with painted pipes held in a wrought-iron frame was built by Bevington & Sons of Soho, probably in the 1860s. The marble **reredos** set in stone panelling with alpha and omega signs is run-of-the-mill Victoriana but the e. window glass is distinctly interesting. It was the first independent commission of William Francis Dixon who had been a pupil of **Clayton & Bell** and who designed for the firm of Mayer in Munich 20 years later. His style is an individual development of the conventions adopted by Clayton & Bell and foreshadows techniques used by other artists. The choice of subjects happens to be more adventurous than usual too; the l. hand **light** shows Cornelius the centurion kneeling before **St Peter** (Acts 10:26) and on the other side of a central Ascension is the Old Testament scene of the death of the Shunammite woman's child before Elisha restored him (2 Kings 4:20); there is a Christ in Majesty (shown as King) in the tracery and the coats of arms across the bottom are Turner on the l., **Royal Arms** in the centre, and Bullock on the r.

Redgrave, St Mary (F3): This is another example of an isolated church; it stands on gently rising ground nearly a mile to the e. of the village and may have been so placed for the convenience of the Lord of the Manor. A fine building, with lots of interest, it was built in the first half of the C14, with the s. **aisle** and **clerestory** following a little later. The original tower collapsed in the C16 and was rebuilt in red brick, but late in the C18 it was cased in the local 'Woolpit whites' and the windows were remodelled. The s. aisle has a parapet of **flushwork** displaying crowned monograms and sporting large **gargoyles**. There is a two-**light** window with **Decorated tracery**, two **Perpendicular** windows, and the aisle e. window has lovely Decorated tracery, with the **ogees** of the three main lights flowing up to enclose two multi-**cusped** and pointed ovals. This design echoes what had already been used in one of the tall **chancel** windows on the s. side and shows how the Decorated and Perpendicular styles overlapped in time. There are ten windows each side of the clerestory, and a continuous **dripstone**, together with panels of flushwork, unites them in a single composition. Again, the flushwork embodies monograms, and the crowned portcullis of the House of **Tudor** can be seen at the e. end. The chancel has prominent buttresses with niches at the second stage, and there is a shape-

ly Decorated **priest's door** complete with **crocketted finial** and **headstops**. The great e. window tracery is delicately moulded but the pattern of tracery above the seven lights is restless, with interlocking ogees enclosing a circle in the head. Above it, you will notice that the line of the original gable was much flatter. The C16 **vestry** on the n. side was altered to accommodate an C18 tomb beneath, and the outside was cased in red brick, presumably at the same time as a large egg-shaped window was introduced in the n. wall. The windows in the n. aisle have flattened Tudor arches and the door on that side has been blocked. Over the wide outer arch of the C14 **porch** is a sundial and the inner doorway is very handsome; there are pairs of shafts with leaf **capitals**, and one of the arch mouldings is enriched with **fleurons** and lion heads, coming down to large king and queen headstops. Above the arch is an image niche with a demi- angel beneath it, and to either side are head pedestals.

Inside the church one can appreciate its spaciousness. The two ranks of mouldings in the arches of the C14 **arcades** match those in the chancel arch and are very effective, but they slightly overpower the slender **quatrefoil piers** that support them. The **nave roof**, clean and light, is a warm brown colour and has alternating **hammerbeams** and **arch- braces**, with braced **queen posts** above. The **wall posts** rest on carved head **corbels**, one with his tongue sticking out. Below, on nice brick floors, there are C19 pine benches, with those in the aisles still marked 'Free', a reminder of the longstanding C17 and C18 tradition of the best pews being rented out to those who could afford them. Over the s. door is a lovely carved and painted set of **Stuart Royal Arms**; in an oval frame, it is very similar to the uncoloured example at neighbouring Wortham and was probably carved by the same man. The C14 **font** at the w. end of the n. aisle also shares a family likeness with Wortham's; the carving is not as sharp but the heads below the bowl are better and, instead of having stepped buttresses at the angles, this one has little attached columns. Beyond it on the n. wall is a huge early C18 **reredos**, designed to stand behind the **high altar**. In wood and picked out in gilt, it has absurdly massive side scrolls, **Corinthian** columns, cherub heads, and panels of the **commandments** flanked by very faded paintings of Moses and Aaron. By the organ is a C15 parish chest with a divided lid; it is cross-banded with iron and still has its original padlocks. The chapel in the s. aisle contains a C14 **piscina** with a multi-cusped arch, **groined** within, and **dropped-sill sedilia** alongside. There is no **screen** now to the wide chancel and the roof is modern, but the late C14 sedilia are beautiful. Divided by lozenge-shaped pillars, each seat has a vaulted canopy, and above there is an exquisitely detailed little range of Perpendicular window tracery; at each end of the straight top cresting are demi-angels holding shields. To the e. is a piscina within a cusped and crocketted arch resting on angled animal headstops. The e. window glass of 1853 is by Farrow, the local Diss glazier. There are figures of **St Peter**, **St Paul** and the **Evangelists** in a line across the centre, with Christ in the centre holding a chalice; below is a Crucifixion against a vivid blue background, and the rest is patterned roundels. The whole is bright and consciously medieval in feeling.

Redgrave has some uncommonly good monuments and memorials and one of the finest is in the n.e. corner of the **sanctuary**. It is for the Lord Chief Justice Holt and is boldly signed by the sculptor, Thomas Green of Camberwell. Green was one of the outstanding artists of his day and this is one of his finest pieces. Defoe called it 'that most exquisite monument'. Sir John sits in the full panoply of judicial robes, wearing the **collar of SS** and holding the black cap in his lap.

The figure of Justice, bearing the scales but without a blindfold, stands on the l., and Mercy with a coiled serpent is to the r. Corinthian columns flank the main figure and there is a **cartouche** of arms above the draped curtains in the arch behind. Three pairs of cherubs and an urn are at the top, while on the upper corners are cock and crane, the symbols of watchfulness and vigilance. The Latin epitaph gives his date of death as March 1709, but apparently he last sat in court in February 1710. Set in the floor of the sanctuary on the s. side is one of the most perfect post-**Reformation brasses** in England and it may well have been engraved by **Nicholas Stone**. Intended to be the top of a table tomb, it is for Mrs Anne Butts, the mother-in-law of Sir Nicholas Bacon. She died in 1609 and is shown wearing a calash (the voluminous hood that was in vogue) and an embroidered petticoat is displayed by her parted gown. Her shield of arms is on the l. and that of her parents (the Bures) on the r. The epitaph reads:

> The weaker sexes strongest precedent
> Lies here belowe; seaven fayer yeares she spent
> In wedlock sage; and since that merry age
> Sixty one yeares she lived a widdowe sage
> Humble as great as full of Grace as elde,
> A second Anna had she but beheld Christ in His flesh who now she glorious sees
> Below that first in time, not in degrees.

On the wall above is an elegant oval in **touchstone**, garlanded at the sides and surmounted by a cartouche below a **pediment**. It is by Nicholas Stone and commemorates the Lady Gawdye who died in 1621. She was Sir Nicholas Bacon's second daughter and, after a first marriage of convenience, her epitaph suggests that she chose for herself and wisely. At the e.

end of the n. aisle is the magnificent tomb of Sir Nicholas and Lady Anne Bacon. The massive chest, in touchstone, has lovely white marble scrollwork panels on each side, with shields of arms at the ends. It was made by Nicholas Stone's colleague Bernard Janssen, the king's engineer, but the recumbent figures on top were carved by Stone himself, for which he charged £200. The baronet wears plate armour, with the visor of his helmet raised, and his wife is in embroidered gown and bodice with a ruff. The modelling of her face is particularly good and reminiscent of Stone's effigy of Mrs Elizabeth Coke at Bramfield (perhaps his finest anywhere). Sir Nicholas, created premier baronet by James I in 1611 and son of Elizabeth's Lord Keeper of the Great Seal, had the tomb made in 1616 when his wife died; the effigies were added after his death in 1624. The pieces of mock armour resting in the niches beyond the tomb were carried as emblems at his funeral. On the n. wall nearby is a good tablet for Robert Bacon, who died in 1652; it may be by Nicholas Stone's son, John. Nicholas himself was responsible for fitting out the w. end of the n. aisle as a Bacon chapel, including the paving and the alcoves. There you will find a severely plain tablet, finely lettered by Stone, for Lady Philippa Bacon, who died in 1626, and there is a memorial for Sir Edmund Bacon on the w. wall and a matching tablet for his wife Elizabeth to the r. in similar style. The church has an excellent array of **hatchments** for the Bacon, Holt and Wilson families, all at some time Lords of the Manor. Having been stored for many years in the vestry, they were cleaned and now make a brave show. Those in the n. aisle are for Bacon, those above the nave arcades for Holt, and those in the chancel for Wilson (including an exceptionally late one for George Rowland Holt Wilson who died in 1929). A very helpful list giving full details hangs by the font.

Rickinghall Inferior, St Mary (F3): This is a very attractive little church at the lower end of the village street. The C12 **Norman** round tower had its top remodelled into an octagon some 200 years later, and the battlements are decked with **flushwork**, with shields in **quatrefoils** and pinnacles at every angle. The bell openings have **Decorated tracery**. The C14 s. **aisle** has very large buttresses at the corners which rise to **crocketted** pinnacles whose gables terminate in grotesque heads. The windows on this side have good **headstops** and their tracery is excellent, with three quatrefoiled roundels above a pair of **trefoiled lights**. The **spandrels** of the tracery in the easternmost window of the aisle are filled with shallow carving. This most unusual feature is found again in the **Perpendicular** s. aisle e. window, as well as in a window at nearby Thelnetham. The e. window tracery of the C14 **chancel** is all renewed, dating, I suspect, from 1858 when **J.D. Wyatt** was at work here. The early C14 **porch** was originally single storey and inside there is a low two-bay **arcade**, resting on a stubby pillar. It is lit by pairs of little windows with 'Y' tracery, as well as a centre quatrefoil. Above the outer arch is a line of flushwork containing crowned 'M's for the dedication, and the inner doorway has very big, worn headstops.

Within the church itself, one notices that the s. aisle is the same width as the **nave**, separated by a fine arcade on quatrefoil **piers**, with **hood moulds** resting on replacement heads. The **imposts** of the tower arch are plain, and there was originally an entry higher up, giving support to the theory that these early round towers were designed as places of refuge. Between the windows in the s. aisle is a blocked doorway that is rather puzzling. It is in the wrong place to give access to a **rood loft** stair or a side chapel and one wonders whether it was originally a **banner-stave locker**. The aisle chapel has **dropped-sill**

sedilia and a C14 **angle piscina** that was restored in a grossly elaborate fashion in the C19 (the same hand was responsible for a similar piece at Thelnetham). The aisle e. window was originally Decorated, and the inner shafts of the earlier design remain, as well as a very decorative band of foliage along the bottom. The nave **roof** is a late C16 **hammerbeam** and, beyond it, the early C14 chancel arch retains the remains of a leaf **capital** on the n. side. Like that in the s. aisle, the **high altar** piscina was unsympathetically restored by Wyatt, who was also responsible for the Minton tiles in the **sanctuary**. The **reredos** is made up of tracery panels that will have been part of the old rood loft, and they have been painted with figures in medieval style. There are roundels and fragments of Flemish glass in the head of the window on the s. side of the sanctuary, and the 1891 glass in the s. chancel window is by **Lavers & Westlake** - scenes from the Via Dolorosa, with canopy work and two angels above. The early C14 octagonal **font** is interesting, not because it has window tracery designs in the panels like many another in the district, but because they are incomplete; only four are totally detailed and one panel has nothing at all. One wonders why the church was content to accept half-finished work, particularly when the design on the e. side is a careful copy of the aisle w. window. Also at the w. end is a C16 chest with carved **Renaissance** panels, and an C18 **bier**. It is a simple design, with drop handles and a series of holes drilled in the bed so that pegs could be inserted to secure the coffin. Another like it can be found up the hill at Rickinghall Superior, so they probably came from the same carpenter. As you leave, note the base of an old **preaching cross** by the porch door.

Rickinghall Superior, St Mary (F3):
The two Rickinghalls now share one parish church on the main road where most of the population lives. This building has been in the care of the **Redundant Churches Fund** since 1980. Still used for occasional services and cared for by local people, it is well worth a visit. Standing attractively on the brow of a hill a short way to the s. of the village, it has a C14 tower with stepped **flushwork** battlements that were added in the C15 and display 'MR' for the dedication and the **sacred monogram**. Do not overlook the **mason's mark** to be found on the s.w. buttress, some 7 ft up; it is a large try- square, with a pair of compasses in the angle, and is one of the finest anywhere. The **chancel** is also early C14 and there is an excellent **priest's door** in the s. wall with an **ogee** arch, complete with **corbel** heads and **crocketted finial**. The e. window **Decorated tracery** is quite inventive, with **ogee** heads to the main **lights** and intersected tracery above, enclosing smaller shapes. The chancel side windows, however, are later **Perpendicular**. There was a major rebuilding in the middle of the C15 and **Cautley** believed that a previous **nave** and **aisle** were absorbed into the present wide nave. This has large Perpendicular windows, with unusually good tracery, whose arches form a pleasing pattern of flint and red brick. Under the windows, a line of blank shields is set in a band of small, finely dressed flints. Judging by the way in which stone, pebbles and dressed flints are carefully arranged in the nave walls, the builders took a good deal of care to make the new work attractive. Two of the nave windows are cut short, one to allow for a n. door underneath, and the other in the s.w. corner over the entrance to a side chapel which is no longer there. It was possibly a **chantry** or a Lady chapel and filled the angle between the **porch** and the corner of the nave. The C15 porch has a room over it and there are flushwork panels above the entrance arch, again with 'MR' and the sacred monogram. The

ceiling is nicely vaulted, and a common human touch is added by the outline of a child's hand scratched in the e. window sill among other venerable graffiti.

Within, the light floods in through great windows across the 30 ft width. Low stone benches line the walls, and from them, delicate shafts rise to form transverse **arcades** over the windows. To the l. of the entrance you will see the **Tudor** arch that led to the side chapel and there also is the door to the porch upper chamber. The C14 **font** stands centrally, its panels intricately carved with tracery patterns and beyond it, high up in the tower wall, is a **quatrefoil sanctus-bell window**. Also at the w. end is a **bier** dated 1763, of the same pattern as that to be found at Rickinghall Inferior, with holes drilled in the bed for pegs to secure the coffin. In 1868 there was a major restoration directed by W.M. Fawcett of Cambridge. The **roof** was replaced to the old pattern but in pitchpine rather than oak, and the nave floor was lowered and tiled. At the same time, the n. door and the tower arch were re- opened and the porch chamber restored. Although the **rood screen** has gone, the stairs to the loft that went with it remain in the n.e. corner of the nave; the upper opening faces w., showing that the loft will have stood forward from the chancel arch. In the C15, there were **guilds** here dedicated to **St John the Baptist**, the **Blessed Virgin**, and **St Peter**; the **piscina** at the e. end of the nave s. wall will have served an **altar** for one of them. The chancel has a C19 waggon roof and in the **sanctuary** there is a very nice C15 piscina which has a **trefoil** ogee arch, complete with flowered **cusps**. The e. window is filled with excellent 1868 glass by the Irishman **Arthur O'Connor** who, with his brother, was active in the formative period of C19 stained glass. In the centre is the Crucifixion and Our Lord as the Good Shepherd. Other panels portray Him teaching and being presented in the temple; a nice touch in the latter is the children holding the thank-offering of two pigeons. The scenes are set in prettily patterned **quarries**, with groups of four lilies repeated. The chancel s.e. window contains two roundels, one a medieval lion, the other an C18 figure. The other window on this side has 1870s glass by **Heaton, Butler & Bayne** on a Samuel theme; it commemorates Samuel Speare, a missionary who died young in Zanzibar, and by some mischance the texts below the panels have been switched over.

Risby, St Giles (C4): The approach from the street is through a **lych-gate** which snuggles delightfully between two huge horse chestnuts. There is a school of thought which maintains that the round tower is **Saxon**, built as a place of refuge, to which the **Norman** church was added later, but others are content to date it late C11 or early C12. Its only original windows are two tiny **lancets** some 20 ft up, capped with arches cut from a single stone. The tiers of slit openings below the parapet are later and a w. window was added in the C14. Typically large blocks of Norman masonry can be seen at the bottom of the **nave** walls but there was rebuilding and the s. nave windows with 'Y' **tracery** date from about 1300. The **chancel** was added in the early C14, with **reticulated** tracery in the e. window, and there is a large **low side window** in the s. wall. On the n. side there is a single late C13 lancet, with a mixture of **Decorated** and **Perpendicular** tracery in the other windows. There was a C14 chapel on the n. side of the chancel and one of its roof **corbels** remains e. of the 1840s **vestry** that replaced it. The last medieval addition was the **porch** of 1435; it is plain but has an uncommonly pleasing floor of pale, narrow bricks.

Within, the tower arch is Norman, with a double roll moulding and simply carved **abaci**. Above it is an opening which lends substance to the theory that the tower was originally a Saxon refuge, for although it may have been used later as a **sanctus-bell window**, it is too large to have been designed as such and is more likely to have been the original entrance - high enough to be secure. The plaster ceiling in the nave was installed in the late C18 and covers the rough-hewn timbers of the original C13 roof. The C15 **font** is particularly interesting; four of the shaft faces are traceried and there are image stools below the rest, although the figures have gone. More damage might well have been done had not the bowl been plastered over; its fine carvings were only revealed when a lady tapped one with her parasol in the 1890s. Four of the panels contain **Evangelistic symbols**, there is a **griffin** to the n.e. and a **pelican** to the s.e. The other two panels make up an **Annunciation** scene, with the archangel on the s.w. and the **Blessed Virgin** on the n.w. face. She kneels at a prayer desk, and behind her the artist added a homely touch in the form of a little dog (contemporary tombs quite often portrayed the pets of great ladies, so why not?). Most of the nave seating dates from 1842 but there are some medieval benches at the w. end, with **poppyheads**, lightly carved back rails and signs that there were originally carvings on the squared elbows. On the s. wall are the **Royal Arms** of George III, still bearing the fleur de lys which dates them before 1800 when the claim to the French throne was finally dropped. The n. wall has an interesting but slightly confusing series of mainly early C13 paintings. Most of them are rather faint but the following can be identified: at the w. end, a life-size outline in red of a mitred priest vested for mass, with yellow hair and beard. He bears no emblem, but the cult of **St Thomas of Canterbury** was at its height and he is a possibility; to the r. is the head of a double axe which might be one of the tools surrounding a **Christ of the Trades**; next is a clear,

late C14 outline of Christ's appearance to **St Mary Magdalene**. The sequence is then broken by the placing of the n. door, a section of Norman window arch and the C13 lancet, and it was further damaged when the walls were heightened in the C14. There was a Nativity sequence of five scenes at the top and, from the l., one can make out the faint outlines of two shepherds, the angel (very dim above the Norman window fragment and followed by a Massacre of the Innocents that has to be guessed at now), and the Flight into Egypt - shadowy figures of Joseph and the Virgin and Child on an easily recognisable donkey. There was another series below, but all that can be seen now is a faint devil which was apparently part of a **St Margaret** painting. Lower down is a **consecration cross** within a decorated roundel, and the scroll work in the lancet splays is late C13. There are puzzling recesses by this window which suggest that the Norman nave ended here and that it was the site of an **altar**. It may well be that the first chancel became an extension of the nave, and it is obvious that when the new chancel was built about 1330, parts of the old arch were re-used to form the new one, as you will see on its e. side. The mid-C17 octagonal pulpit has typical blind arches on the panels, resting on reeded shafts, with shallow carving above, and on the s. side there is a roughly contemporary altar table with a quite individual arrangement of open arches below the top rail. The nearby window has glass by **Kempe & Co** and in the sill is the simplest form of **piscina**, which shows that there was always an altar here. There are stools for images in the window splays on both sides of the nave and they have been associated with the four **guilds** known to have existed in the C15.

The entrance to the chancel is made splendid by a combination of the **rood screen** and pairs of large niches each side which formed **reredoses** for the nave altars. All were beautifully restored in 1966 with the aid of the Pilgrim Trust. Although small, the screen is fascinating in its intricacy. There are only three **lights** each side of the entrance rather than the usual four, and the base panels have stencilled patterns within their tracery; there are **crocketted** gables to the main buttresses at rail level. The main lights rise to **cusped** and crocketted **ogee** arches, and above them the space is filled with a net of cusped tracery contained within a trellis of lozenges. The centre arch has flowered cusps, with eagles and beast masks in the **spandrels**. The pairs of side niches are gorgeously coloured in red, gold and blue, the back walls rich with a lattice of diaper work framing varied flowered centres. The heads are canopied with miniature vaulting and the crocketted ogee arches rise to tall **finials**. One of the r. hand niches has a broad image stool, and on the opposite side another contains a C19 seated figure of **St Giles**, its clumsy plinth the only discordant feature of the whole array. The stairs to the vanished **rood loft** are on the n. side. Passing through to the chancel, note the line of **paterae** at the top of the screen and the sections of Norman stone work in the arch above. The chancel was restored by the rector, Thomas Abrahams, in 1881 and three of the windows commemorate members of his family. His predecessor, Samuel Alderson, was obviously a woodcarver of same skill and individuality, for the profusion of heavy leaf forms on the reredos, altar, **communion rails**, and poppyheads are all his work. On either side of the altar there are large C14 niches with **trefoil** arches under ogee heads to match those in the nave, and the large piscina matches them, with canted head corbels. There are headstops on the arch of the vestry door too, and in the e. window are many fragments of C14 and C15 glass collected there by Samuel Alderson's wife in 1850. The result is rather confused, but there is a good king's head in the l. hand light, a deli-

icately painted pelican in a lozenge above the lion shield in the centre, and among the many other interesting little pieces, an **Agnus Dei**. The window to the s. received the same treatment and there are two larger figures made up of fragments, with new heads, one with an arrow emblem and the other with the wheel of **St Catherine**. Over the low side window is a tablet for John Wastell who died in 1811. He was an intimate friend of the 3rd Duke of Grafton, the famous racehorse owner, and managed his stable for him. Just in front of the communion rails is a **brass** inscription for Edward Kirke, the rector who died in 1580. He was a friend of the poet Edmund Spenser and wrote the introduction to The Shepherd's Calendar. A more recent rector is remembered in a nave window, Canon A.F. Webling, whose books Risby, The Last Abbot and Something Beyond are well worth seeking out.

Rougham, All Saints (D5): A number of Suffolk churches are isolated from their villages and in Rougham's case it was because the **Black Death** visitation of 1349 was so devastating that, as a desperate measure, the parishioners burnt every house to the ground and moved half a mile to the s. Now, the church has only the school, a cottage and the new rectory for company. Isolation only serves to make it more impressive and the C15 tower, with its bold angled buttresses and well defined **string courses** is a landmark. It has a stair turret to the belfry stage on the s. side and, like Hessett, the top is lavishly decorated. The stepped battlements with corner pinnacles are set with **flushwork** and the centre panels are notable for their inscriptions - on the s. side, 'Pray for ye sowle of John Tillot', and on the n., 'Drury', in bold gothic confirms that Robert Drury and John Tillot were chiefly responsible for building the tower. The panel on the e. side carries an 'M' for the **Blessed Virgin** with her lily emblem and there are circled monograms on the w. face. A band of flushwork roundels runs below the battlements and the windows to the w. are firmly anchored in the design by the string courses. William Layer was an important C15 mason who is believed to have been the architect of the nave of St Mary's, Bury. He had property in Rougham and bequeathed 20 marks for this tower and could well have designed it. There had been a large scale rebuilding in the late C13 and early C14 - new **nave**, **chancel** and probably the s. **aisle**. The s. **porch** was part of this work and it is notable. The three-**light** unglazed windows have sturdy columns and pierced **ogee tracery** under square tops, while the entrance arch is finely moulded. The gable shows the original **roof** line and there is a fat **gargoyle**, with its hands over its ears, in the e. parapet. Below the porch w. window you will find a few C13 yellow bricks and there is an angled sundial in the niche over the entrance. Two very large medieval grave slabs lie nearby and a pair of blocked arches show in the wall to the e. of the porch. They are burial recesses, one of their covers is carved with a C13 double omega and lies by the path further along. Nave and aisle parapets have pierced battlements and half way along the aisles you will see a small carved head in a roundel that is taken by some to represent **St John the Baptist's** head on a charger. The chancel was again rebuilt in 1880 and the tall square **vestry**- cum-organ chamber was added in 1900, with a large **low side window** re-sited in the s. wall; the small lean-to vestry on the n. side dates from 1856. The n. aisle has **Perpendicular** windows and can be confidently dated by inscriptions on three of the buttresses. It would be nice to think that the easternmost was put there by the workmen themselves for it reads: 'We pray you to remember us that causyde ye yle to be made thus'; on the next is the date '1514' and the third has the name of the priest John Smith.

Within, the nave has graceful C14 **arcades**, the double chamfered arches resting on **quatrefoil piers** and the chancel arch matches. The early C16 nave **roof** is beautifully solid but the decoration is restrained. **Arch-braces** rise from **hammerbeams** to thick **collars** and the eye is attracted more to the elaborate **wall plates** where two ranks of **paterae** are separated by a band of pierced tracery. The hammerbeams are carved as angels and although they have lost their heads they still hold shields carved with chalices, crowns, books and organs. Below, the **wall posts** carry canopied niches with mutilated figures and rest on stone shafts that rise from a string course that runs below the **clerestory** windows. The aisle roofs too have deep wall plates decorated with large paterae and there are stone head **corbels**. All the roofs were repaired when John Johnson of Bury carried out a restoration in 1856 and although a **Doom** was uncovered over the chancel arch, there is no trace of it now. The panels of the C14 **font** are carved with an unusual mixture of arch patterns and show traces of colour. The early C16 nave benches are unusually good. They are low and chunky and the tracery on the ends is full of invention. There are **poppyheads** and traceried backs but, alas, all the figures have been sawn from the elbows. They are likely to have been angels because the little pads representing clouds on which they stood remain. The matching pews at the front and in the aisles were designed by Johnson in the 1850s. There are matching C14 **piscinas** at the e. end of the aisles showing that there were once **altars** there - that in the n. aisle having been resited. The **Decorated** s. aisle e. window now opens into the organ chamber and its companion on the n. side is largely blocked by a quite nasty Victorian Gothick series of panels commemorating the Bennet family. The tracery above it still has some early C14 glass - a shield with **Passion emblems**, a shield of arms, and a tiny

Virgin and Child fragment in yellow stain. Below the Bennet memorial are wooden **Jacobean** panels that came either from a chest or a pulpit. In the floor nearby is a very good **brass** with 4 ft figures of Sir Roger Drury and his wife Margery. He died in 1418 and his armour is a perfect example of the period, lacking only the helm behind the head. She wears a mantle over her gown and a little dog lies at her feet against the lion which lies under his. Lady Margery's figure is identical with Eleanor Burgate's at Burgate and indicates that such memorials were produced to a standard pattern. The stained glass in the n. aisle window is an 1897 memorial for John Josselyn and his wife. His arms are in the tracery, with angels, an **Angus Dei** and the eagle of **St John**. The main lights have figures of Christ, the Blessed Virgin, St John the Baptist and St John the Evangelist; at the bottom there is a small **Annunciation** panel. Behind the C19 pulpit there is a large image niche with a slight **ogee** top and on the s. side of the chancel arch is the blocked door to the **rood stairs**. **J.D. Wyatt's** reconstructed chancel is depressing rather than uplifting despite its spaciousness and the e. window glass illustrates why the work of the C19 was villified by later artists. However, the late C14 piscina and **sedilia** were undisturbed and form a very satisfying group.

Rushbrooke, St Nicholas (D3): This church has an unbuttressed C14 tower of flint but, like the rest of the building, the walls are plastered. The bell openings have **Decorated tracery**, and a **Perpendicular** w. window, with deep **label** and **headstops**, was inserted later, probably when the **nave** and **chancel** were rebuilt by Thomas Jermyn in 1540. The new work was in red brick and many of the windows have moulded brick **mullions** and tracery. The low nave n. door and the **priest's door** on that side have been blocked up and the gables

of nave, chancel and s. **porch** are boldly crow-stepped in brick. The s. **aisle** extends half way along the chancel, with e. window and small side doorway blocked. The layout within is decidedly eccentric. The s. aisle is divided into three parts - a w. vestibule, a central **vestry** at a higher level that was once a family pew, and an eastern chapel largely given over to monuments. There is a two-bay **arcade** at the w. end, followed by an unmatched arch which is now partially walled off, and then comes a Perpendicular arch which has a separate low entrance to the r., both leading into the chapel. At the w. end of the aisle stands a C19 wooden **font** of vaguely Gothic form and on the floor is the bowl of a large C15 font which appears to have been re-cut; the panelled shaft stands close by. The C16 aisle **roof** has been extensively restored but from the nave one can see that the principal timbers in the centre section are carved. In the 1840s Col Rushbrooke of Rushbrooke Park installed collegiate style seating in the nave facing inwards, and at the w. end it is backed by crudely carved canopy work with steep gables; on a **gallery** there is a showy display of painted organ pipes but no sign of an actual instrument, nor is there room for one. There are medieval bench ends with **poppyheads** incorporated in the stalls and under the gallery a **hatchment** leans against the wall; it was used for Robert Rushbrooke who died in 1829. The nave roof is steep with **arch-braces** and pendants below the ridge, and in the chancel there is a lovely C16 cambered **tie-beam** roof enriched with carving on beams, **spandrels** and **wall plates**. There is no chancel arch or **screen** but the carved **rood beam** is still in place supported on **wall posts** bearing small figures with canopies both above and below them. Above is a **tympanum** against which is displayed a massive set of **Royal Arms**. The crowned shield is supported by carved and silhouetted dragon and greyhound, the **Tudor** badges of portcullis and rose stand alongside, and the motto with the archaic spelling of 'droict' is painted on the beam below. The form of arms was used by Henry VII and Henry VIII and the assumption is that Thomas Jermyn had them put up in 1540 when he received the manor from Henry VIII. That would make them the only example of the period in the country and a uniquely early instance of the practice. The only problem is that apparently they were not in the church in the early C19 and there is a suspicion that the antiquarian zeal of Col Rushbrooke may have had something to do with it. A **piscina** in the s. chapel shows that there was once an **altar** there, although the e. wall is now taken up by a memorial. In 1692 Thomas, the only son of the last Lord Jermyn, died at the age of 15. 'A hopefull Youth', he was killed in a boating accident on the Thames and his monument is against the s. wall - a small marble figure in full wig, profusely buttoned coat and gown, pensively reclining with his hand on a skull, with **touchstone Corinthian** columns on either side. On the w. wall is a monument to Sir Robert Davers who died in 1722 - a dark sarcophagus backed by a tall mottled marble architectural panel with decorative garland. In the chancel, the lumpish tablet to the Countess Dowager Darlington (1763) is made interesting by the cast metal **achievement of arms** at the base. Below it is a **brass** inscription and two shields that were once enamelled for Thomas Badby, 'one of the Quenes Maties receyvers' who died in 1583. Lower down are two C17 Jermyn tombs and across on the s. wall, a tall monument with indifferently carved cherubs for Lord Henry Jermyn, who was exiled with the Royalists in France until the Restoration and who died in 1672. The e. end of the chancel was rebuilt in 1885 and some medieval glass is displayed in the e. window, including two figures and, at the top, the shield of **Edward the**

Confessor with its cross and five martlets. There are other fragments in the nave and you will find rather a nice **unicorn** in a roundel in the centre window.

Santon Downham, St Mary (C1): It is more than likely that you will be able to watch grey squirrels and jays coming and going in this churchyard, set idyllically in a quiet corner of the forest. The church is small but has much of interest. Look first at the panels at the base of the C15 unbuttressed tower: n. side, a crowned 'M' for the dedication. **sacred monogram**, two sets of initials; w. and s. sides, the names of those who gave money for its erection (John Watt, John Reve, John Dow, Margaret Reve, Patsy Styles and William Toller). The **Norman** s. door of the **nave** has simple roll mouldings in the arch, set on spiral shafts, and over it is a contemporary carved panel of an animal that could be a lion, except that it has turned vegetarian and is munching a plant that matches the flourish on its own tail. Further along is a blocked **low side window** that formed part of the **lancet** above, and next to it is the **priest's door** with late C12 **dogtooth** moulding in the arch, and shafts which may be earlier still. The doorway was originally on the n. side where the outline can still be seen. The e. window has been totally renewed and may or may not be faithful to the original. In the C14 there was a chapel on the n. side of the nave dedicated to the **Trinity** and the **piscina** for the **altar** is still embedded in the wall under its **trefoil ogee** arch.

Entering by the n. **porch**, notice that although the Norman shafts of the doorway match the s. door, the arch was replaced in the C14 to allow for a niche to be set above. The door itself is medieval with the original long strap hinges, and behind it is one of the Norman window splays that was converted to a C13 lancet. This has an 1890s stained glass figure of Faith with her shield by **Kempe & Co** and the matching windows in the C13 chancel portray the other two religious virtues - Hope with her anchor and Charity in the form of the **Blessed Virgin** and Child. Below is a C13 arched tomb recess and a short section of Norman dogtooth moulding in the wall nearby, probably associated with the former priest's door. There is an **aumbry** in the n.e. corner of the **sanctuary** and the piscina opposite, under its multi- foiled ogee arch, has the remnants of the original wooden **credence shelf**. The C14 window by the priest's door has 1950s glass by Harcourt M. Doyle - **St Francis** with a colourful selection of birds and butterflies. **Rood screen** builders were very active in the C14 up to the time of the **Black Death** in 1349 and here is a good example from that period. The plain boards of the base have an overall stencil pattern (part of the border has been repainted) and the miniature window cut in a board on the s. side is a contemporary **elevation squint**. Much of the **tracery** and two of the shafts have been replaced, but the shafts on the n. side are original and the whole has been sympathetically treated. The early C17 octagonal pulpit has two ranges of panels carved with simple scrolls above and lozenges below. The base and stairs are replacements and there is an image bracket on the wall beyond. Over the utilitarian stove on the s. side, a fragment of a C13 window arch is decorated with a foliage trail in dark red. On the n. side of the nave is the early C14 arch (now framing a window) which led to the lost chapel. The plain octagonal **font** has a simple pyramid cover with shallow incised carving, matching the pulpit. The lancet in the s. wall nearby contains C19 glass by **Heaton, Butler & Bayne** - a sentimental Good Shepherd with cuddly sheep. On the n. side by the tower arch is a tablet to Lieut Col the Hon Henry Cadogan who fell in the Peninsular campaign at Vittoria in 1813; it is a good portrait medallion on a sarcophagus, with draped flags and a stylish shako. Penetrate the gloom of the tower to take a closer look at the good 1880s glass in the w. window by Kempe & Co. His golden wheatsheaf emblem is right at the top and the two main **lights** contain an **Annunciation** in rich colour. The **hatchment** hanging in the tower is for William John Frederick, 3rd Duke of Cleveland, who died in 1864; another like it is at Raby Castle, Durham. John Rous was minister here from 1623 to 1644 and although it contains no mention of his parish, his diary for the period is well worth seeking out. Published by the Camden Society in 1856, it has fascinating sidelights on the events leading up to the Civil War and the conflict itself. He saw the Parliament men ride out of Bury in 1642 bound for Lincolnshire, and their colours bore the legend 'The warre is just that is necessary'. How often have simple men heard that to their cost!

Sapiston, St Andrew (D3): Down a lane and a good half mile from the village, the church lies in meadow land by an isolated farm. We should be thankful that it is now in the care of the **Redundant Churches Fund** and is used at intervals for services. Apart from the s. doorway, the fabric is early C14, a plain unbuttressed tower with 'Y' **tracery** bell openings, **reticulated** tracery in the e. window and **trefoil**-headed **lancets** on the n. side. There are two C13 grave slabs in the floor of the neat little **porch** but the doorway, a fine piece of Norman work, is what takes the eye. The scale is small, with an opening less than a yard wide between pairs of octagonal shafts under scalloped **capitals**. The arch has two bands of very individual ornament, rather like a series of cloven tongues, with a carved head above. Look for the **scratch dials** on both capitals, obviously in use before the C14 porch was built. Inside is a lovely old brick floor and, above it, a simple **hammerbeam** and **scissors-braced roof**. The **chancel** roof is boarded, with no arch between it and the **nave**. In front of the blocked n. door, a plain octagonal C13 **font**; the bowl has sloping sides and is supported by a centre shaft and four columns. The C17 black cover has large scrolls reaching up to support a turned **finial**. Beyond the tall tower arch is a w. window with **Decorated** tracery, and on the n. wall, a set of **Stuart Royal Arms** with the quarterings altered to suit the **Hanoverian** dynasty. Four **consecration crosses** have been uncovered, one by each door and one each side of the nave e. end. The lancets on the n. side are set in deep embrasures with dropped sills, and over the top of a tomb arch there are tantalising traces of a large wall painting in which one figure with a sheaf of arrows can be distinguished; it is possibly a martyrdom of **St Edmund**. Further along there are stairs in the wall that gave access to the vanished **rood loft** and the later Decorated windows on the s. side may have been inserted to give it more light. There is a **priest's door** on the s. side of the chancel and beyond it, a lovely C14 **piscina**, its large trefoil with blind tracery in the **spandrels** set in an **ogee** arch. What gives it real individuality is the miniature replica cut in the angled side wall. On the n. chancel wall is an alabaster tablet to John Bull (1643). The name is so familiar that it is rather like meeting an old friend. It has a shield of arms in a **cartouche** over the **pediment** diminutive cherubs below, and pendant pomegranates below that. A **ledgerstone** in the chancel for William Crofts (1632) is interesting and, indeed, helpful because it gives family names in the scrolls below the impaled shields of arms. Returning to the porch you will see the remains of a **stoup** inside the door, and on the outside wall below the e. window, two hitching rings remain that once secured the horses of the parson and the squire.

Shelland, King Charles the Martyr (F5): This is a very rare dedication, there being only four others in England. It is also a church that is not marked on the average map and even the village name is elusive. However, it stands by a spacious common on the lane that runs from Harleston to Borley Green and Woolpit and is well worth seeking out. It is small, set within a spacious churchyard overlooking open fields to the s., and it is one of the very few churches in the county that the Victorians hardly touched. It had only been rebuilt in 1767 and its newness, coupled with its isolation, saved it. Outside, it is very plain and the **nave** has **lancets** and 'Y' **tracery** windows. The **chancel** is lit by a C19 e. window and there is a little **vestry** tacked on to the s. side of the nave. The w. gable boasts a substantial bellcote with an attractive **ogee** cap topped by a ball. Within the little brick n. porch there is a marble cherub's head over the inner doorway that is likely to have come from an old tomb. Inside the tiny building there is an air of peaceful calm and orderliness that is so often the hallmark of the C18 village church. The brick floors are laid in herringbone pattern and the symmetry of the high **box pews** is complemented by the matching rails with elegant **balusters** that divide the nave from the chancel and isolate the **sanctuary**. All the joinery is in pine, painted and grained in pale tan, and to the r. of the brick chancel arch is a **three-decker pulpit**. The **clerk's** pew faces w., continuing the line of the pews, and one passes through it to the reading desk at the next level. This is provided with a seat and so is the pulpit just above it. Three hat pegs adorn the wall in front. The chancel ceiling has a little cornice of Gothick arches and pendants and the walls below the dado are covered with patterned uncut moquette fabric which also backs the wooden blind arcading on the e. wall. That must surely be a unique variation in wall finishes. On each side of the chancel there is a low 8 ft long **housel bench** with square tapered legs and carved top rail on which parishioners will have sat to receive communion. There are well cut **ledger- stones** for the Cropley family in the floor and on the n. wall is a memorial for William Cropley who died in 1717. In white marble on pale grey, the tablet is finely lettered within an **acanthus** frame, with a **cartouche** of arms above and three shields below. Turning to the w. the effect is symmetrical once again. Below the circular w. window an attractive little organ case rises from the musician's pew, which has matching wings at a lower level. The organ is very rare - one of the few **barrel organs** still in use for services. It was made by Bryceson of London in 1820 and has three barrels of twelve tunes each. Cleaned and restored in 1956, it had the same 'organist', Robert Armstrong, from 1885 until 1935 whose reported comment was: 'It's not everybody who can do it; you must have an ear'. High on the w. wall is a set of George III **Royal Arms** in scale with the building and below stands the one reminder of an earlier medieval church - the C14 **font** whose panels are carved overall with a variety of leaf forms and three shields to the w. The ogee cover matches the bellcote outside but for a pineapple **finial**, and one of the curved panels is fitted with a neat little door for access. One of the memorable and endearing things about Shelland is the riotous colour scheme; lilac walls in the nave vie arch, bright terracotta **tie-beams** and rafters against a white ceiling, and turquoise cornice to match the chancel arch **capitals**. The walls of the chancel are lime green above the dado and the coved ceiling is deep blue. All is great fun and an excellent foil for the austere fittings. **Prayer book churches** have a fascination of their own and their devotees will not be disappointed here.

Shimpling, St George (D6): An ave-

nue of tall limes close enough to form a tunnel leads to a bridge over the Chad brook and into the churchyard at the e. end. An 1860s restoration has left its mark fairly decisively on what is largely a C14 church, and a three-stage flint and stone chimney rises on the s.e. corner of the **nave**, with another above the **vestry** which is distinctly priapic. The Hallifax mausoleum of 1841 stands by the **chancel**, rather like a superior builder's hut in stone. However, there are windows with nicely varied **Decorated** tracery in the nave, chancel and s. **aisle** and small unequal niches flank the w. window of the tower. The rebuilt s. **porch** shelters a late C13 doorway and leads to an interior made rather dark by the absence of any **clerestory** over the four-bay s. **arcade**. The C14 **font** by the door is a strange design and quite unlike others in the area; it has attached columns round the shaft and a very shallow octagonal bowl carved with **quatrefoils** and tracery panels. **Roofs**, benches and the **parclose screen** in the aisle are all Victorian, and there is a very heavy-handed wooden **altar** of the same vintage in the aisle chapel. Close by is a C14 **piscina** with an exceptionally large drain. Levels were raised in the chancel so that the simple piscina there is now near the floor. Over the shallow arch of the **priest's door** there is a line of **dogtooth decoration** that one would call **Early English** except that it is very sharply cut. Victorian **Decalogue boards** flank the altar and there is a modern **brass** framed behind glass for Augustus Bolton who was rector here. Elizabeth Plampin has a memorial by **Sir Richard Westmacott** on the n. wall - a female in a rather stagey pose stands by an urn with initials and date on the plinth. The epitaph is instructive for, apart from her extensive talents as a wife and mother, 'in epistolary correspondence she displayed a sincerity of friendship and an energy of sentiment expressed in language at once refined and natural'. A rare gift, undoubtedly. The banal 1850s monument to Thomas Hallifax in the s. aisle cannot compete with that. The stained glass at Shimpling is interesting for a number of reasons. Quite a lot of C14 **tabernacle work** remains in the tracery of the chancel side windows, and in the n.e. window of the nave there are unusual **Trinity** emblems, while shields in the centre window include that of St Edmundsbury. In the aisle the centre window has 1864 glass which was **Henry Holiday's** first design in East Anglia and his only early work in Suffolk. In strong **pre-Raphaelite** style and colouring, it shows the Presentation of Christ in the temple, with the priest vested as a medieval bishop. The **Blessed Virgin** holds two purple doves and vivid patterns are deployed in robes and background. The glass was originally planned for the aisle e. window where Holiday angels remain in the tracery; the later figures of Faith, Hope and Charity are by the **Powells**. The chancel e. window glass of 1842 is the earliest example of **Warrington's** glass in the county; **Evangelistic symbols**, central **sacred monogram**, and the arms of Sir Thomas Hallifax are set against opaque **quarries** decorated with oak leaves and all are within pretty borders. The tower window is an instructive contrast in the High Victorian style of the 1860s - a parallel Transfiguration and Ascension by Baillie & Mayer, using dense colour and bright patterning in the tracery. Before leaving, it is worth a detour in the churchyard to view the little building in the s.w. corner. In yellow brick and slate, it has a room with fireplace, bay window and fitted seat, together with a cloakroom and closet. Restored in 1977, it was apparently designed as a 'fainting house' to which swooning C19 ladies could retire if the length or vigour of the sermon proved too much for them - unique in my experience.

Somerton, All Saints (C6): This is a delightfully peaceful situation along the cul-de-sac at Upper Somerton, and there is a pleasant westward prospect over rolling fields and hedgerows to Hawkedon and Stansfield. Coming in from the e. of the churchyard, the s. chapel looks like a second **chancel** and they stand side by side, with matching barge boards on the gables. The C14 tower is small but leggy, with **Decorated** bell openings, chequered **base course** and battlements, and some fearsome devil **gargoyles**. The blocked n. door, with roll moulding in the arch and simple volute **capitals**, shows that the **nave** was **Norman** although it now has C14 windows to the s. and an early **Perpendicular** window to the n. The s. chapel juts well out and has its own w. door; low down in the angle with the nave there is part of a C13 grave slab. Entry is via a nice little s. **porch** in thin red brick and flint, with a simple medieval roof. In front of the tower arch stands a small C16 **font** with shields in **cusped** panels and a defaced carving to the w. There are **paterae** under the bowl and it has all been heavily limewashed in cream. There are the remains of a **stoup** recess by the blocked n. door and at the e. end of the nave on the s. side is a puzzling remnant within a recess in the wall. It is the capital and beginning of an arch that is roughly contemporary with the late C13 or early C14 **arcade** that links the chancel and the chapel. Did the chapel once extend further w. or was there a s. aisle? The roofs are C19 and there being no chancel arch the division is marked by a set of early **Stuart communion rails** which have been moved westward in place of a **screen**; they are tall and gated, with turned **balusters**. The tall **Jacobean** pulpit is like Hartest's although not as decorative, with simple blind arches, lozenges, and grooved panels at the base (the rim and bookrests are modern). The C19 lectern is particularly graceless compared with a contemporary model at Lawshall. The chancel and chapel have Perpendicular e. windows of differing designs but in both cases the late C13 shafts of earlier windows flank the embrasures. There is a blocked medieval door to the n.e. **vestry** and in the s. wall of the **sanctuary** is a most unusual arrangement. There is a **piscina** whose bowl originally projected below a triangular arch and another piscina drain is cut within a **squint** that connects chancel with chapel. As the chapel has its own piscina in the s. wall, the drain in the squint may have been a way of providing a double piscina for the chancel when one was called for at the end of the C13. The squint is roughly shaped and there are remains of side shafts on the chapel side. The chancel e. window has 1890s glass by **Kempe & Co** of Christ in Majesty, and note that there is the bowl of a large stoup in the corner of the spacious chapel, while a pallid set of George III **Royal Arms** hangs on the wall.

Stanningfield, St Nicholas (D5): The church has a 'hunched shoulders' look because when the tower became unstable in the 1880s the upper stage was removed, and it now has a low pyramid cap. There is a square stair turret on the s. side and the **transomed** C15 w. window has been renewed. This was a **Norman** building originally, as shown by two small **lancets** in the **nave** and by the blocked n. door - very worn curly **capitals** and a **chevron moulding** which has little nodules on the inner points. The 'Y' tracery windows date from about 1300 and the very interesting **chancel** built by the Rokewood family followed soon after. The window tracery is exceptionally enterprising, with multi-**cusped quatrefoils** on the n. and pointed **trefoils** grouped within circles on the s. The intersected tracery of the e. window has thin trefoils in the heads of the three **lights** and contains a circled quatrefoil at the top. The s. **priest's door** is blocked and below the window to the l. is a

low side window in the form of a small quatrefoil. A sensitive attention to detail crops up again in the s. doorway where the mouldings are carved with two runs of **fleurons** and **ball flower** decorates the **dripstone**. Just within, a **stoup** is set under a cusped arch. The heavy C15 **font** on its traceried stem has quatrefoils in the bowl panels, with the shield of **St Edmund** to the e. and Rokewood to the w. The sills of the windows at the e. end of the nave are both lowered to form **sedilia** and there will have been **altars** nearby, although only the **piscina** on the s. side remains behind the pulpit. The C15 chancel **screen** is low and simple, with **mouchette** roundels in the **spandrels** of the centre arch, which has just the hint of an **ogee** shape. You may have heard of Stanningfield's fine C15 **Doom** above the chancel arch; if so, you will be very disappointed when you see that it is an expanse of sombre grey colour, with very little detail showing. It was cleaned and treated in the 1930s and was in good condition when **Cautley** saw it. There has been a sad deterioration over the years but if you have binoculars and a little patience much may still be recognised. There were almost 100 hundred figures originally and a life-size Christ is seated in the centre on a rainbow. His wounds still visible; the **Blessed Virgin** intercedes on the r. and the Passion angel, robed in red, is to the l.; each side are angels summoning the dead with long trumpets, and the myriad little figures rise naked from their shrouds and tombs. The faint figures of **St Peter** and an angel can be seen to the l. in a multi-storied heaven and there are fragments of hell opposite. The s. side of the **sanctuary** has a large lancet piscina with plain sedilia alongside, and opposite is the tomb of Thomas Rokewood, who married a Clopton of Long Melford and who died in 1521. It is in fine condition, with cresting and four shields above the long, low recess; the standing angels at the corners were added in 1881. The front of the tomb is carved with four panels of multi- The front of the tomb chest is carved with four panels of multi- cusped quatrefoils, with shields of Roke- wood and Clopton. From its position and type there seems little doubt that it served as an **Easter sepulchre**. The family were staunch Catholics and Ambrose Rokewood was a friend of Robert Catesby. Thus he was drawn into the Gunpowder Plot and met his end on the last day of January, 1606.

Stansfield, All Saints (C6): This is a fairly large church that stands on a hill to the n. of the village. Its C14 tower was encased in scaffolding for a major restoration in 1986. The stair turret lies within the angle of the s.w. buttress, there is a double chequer **base course**, and three niches are grouped round the w. window. There are no **aisles** and the tall **nave** dates from about 1300 with , on the n. side, a handsome octagonal **rood stair** tur- ret. Its battlemented top, rising above the roof line, is decorated with **pat- erae** and tiny grotesques. The early C14 **chancel** side windows have very pretty **tracery** reminiscent of Stan- ningfield, and either side of the **Per- pendicular** e. window are tall **Decorated** niches, with remnants of **headstops** on the **crocketted drip- stones**. The corner buttresses are angled at the second stage, there is an **Early English priest's door** on the s. side, and you will find a **scratch dial** on the centre nave buttress. The tall s. **porch** is battlemented with corner pinnacles, and there are shields with- in **quatrefoils** at the base of the angled buttresses. Its roof is cambered and there is a re-cut **stoup** to the r. of the late C13 inner doorway. The door itself is modern but the medieval closing ring has been fixed in the cen- tre. Just inside, there is an earlier stoup in a **lancet** niche. The **font** bowl is very mutilated and once had corner shafts; it is possibly late C13 and now stands on C19 shafts. In the n.w. cor- ner stands a C14 chest, pale with age;

it is long, low, and heavily banded with iron, and the little turned legs that were added in the C17 have prob- ably helped to keep it dry. The nave is wide and rather bare, with C19 benches. The early C16 roof has braced and cambered **tie- beams**; every other **wall post** is **castellated** and the deep **wall plates** have carved and pierced trails. It has been stained black and is difficult to examine, but by using binoculars some fine carving can be discovered. On the s. side, the last **spandrel** before the chancel arch has a maid peeping from the top of a castle while a sinuous dragon men- aces her, and immediately opposite another dragon wields a huge pair of tongs. On the e. side of the spandrel over the s. door there is a labourer with a variety of tools, and on the n. side opposite is a group of villagers. Under the sill of the s.e. nave window is a little **piscina**, close to a tall image niche which now contains a modern Virgin and Child. This was no doubt where the **altar** of the medieval **guild** of **St Mary** was sited. A late C16 or early C17 **Holy table** with a carved top rail now stands there. The early C17 pulpit has three ranges of panels in standard designs of the period with a modern base and steps. Behind it, an iron door was fitted to the rood stair in the C19 and the upper exit blocked off. The front of the nave pews have tracery which probably came from the **rood loft** and the low **screen** has a modern frame in which is set the excellent tracery saved from the C15 original. The quality was matched by the C19 carver of the pretty trail that runs below the top rail. Similarly, the stalls are good modern work and have standing saints on the bench ends. The chancel roof is single-braced, with two rough tie-beams spanning it at wall level. In the **sanctuary** the pis- cina has a most attractive **ogee**arch with pierced **mouchettes** and a little opening to the side of the **dropped- sill sedilia**. On the e. wall there are three **consecration crosses** and the fragments of medieval glass remaining have been gathered into panels in the s. window. Francis Kedington's memorial of 1715, on the chancel n. wall, is a handsome **touchstone** slab with his arms well displayed in shallow carving; the heavy **acanthus** leaves and head in stone below would seem to be earlier work. William Steggles of Bury cut a gawky little tablet for the Rev Beriah Brook in 1809 and it is interesting for the details it gives of how the upkeep of his tomb was to be financed. The memorial is s. of the chancel arch but there is no evidence outside, alas, that his wishes bore fruit for very long.

Stanstead, St James (C6): This small church was decisively restored by the Victorians. In the 1860s the **chancel** was restored and in the 1870s a new arch was inserted in the tower. The C14 tower has a new w. **lancet** but the very narrow little belfry lancets are original and there are **Perpendicular** bell openings. With the exception of the C19 e. window, the windows are early Perpendicular and there is a blocked C14 n. door. The n.e. **vestry** is a Victorian addition as is the tall chimney that rises at the corner of the **nave** gable. There are impressively fierce dragons at the corners of the s. **porch** parapet and a canopied **stoup** niche remains in an outside buttress. The medieval door still has its original closing ring, and on the floor by the tower arch is a 9 cwt bell cast by Stephen Tonni of Bury St Edmunds, one of only four from that foundry that are known to have survived. Have a look at the inscription and the maker's mark. Above the old n. door hangs a well painted set of Queen Anne's **Royal Arms**, and in the window beyond the medieval fragments include shields of Bernay and Walsham. The **roofs** and fittings are Victorian, the square-topped oak benches having been moulded on the original set, and there are **encaustic tile** floors. The Rev Samuel Sheen's 1867 memorial on the chancel n. wall

is a good example of High Victorian Gothic on a small scale. There is a mosaic cross in the head of the alabaster recess arch below an aggressively **crocketted** gable, with side stub shafts in green marble. The s. **sanctuary** window is a memorial to another Samuel Sheen, also rector and presumably a son. The 1907 glass is by **Heaton, Butler & Bayne** and has full length figures of **St James the Great** and the prophet Samuel as High Priest of the temple; there are drapes behind the figures and the remainder of the lights is filled with patterned squares. The **tracery** contains two angels and at the bottom two more draw out a scroll. The glass in the e. window is earlier - a centre Calvary against a deep blue ground, and roundels of the **Agnus Dei**, **pelican**, alpha and omega and the **sacred monogram**. The rest of the window is filled with opaque **quarries** and there are figures of the **Four Evangelists** in the tracery. On either side of the **altar**, **decalogue boards** are framed in oak panels.

Stanton, All Saints (E3): The village once had two churches, and the **Redundant Churches Fund** now takes care of the empty shell of St John's (where the last service was held in 1876) by the main road. All Saints once had a fine C14 tower but it collapsed in 1906 and the top two-thirds fell - luckily, away from the church. In 1956, the upper portion of what remained was rebuilt and the timber belfry with its pyramid cap was added. The **nave** and **chancel** were built about 1320 and the e. and w. windows, with their **reticulated tracery**, were replaced in 1875 as part of a major restoration. The square-headed s. **aisle** windows have **Decorated** tracery, with a compact reticulated pattern in the e. window. It would seem that the aisle was added to connect the body of the church with what had been a free-standing tower. A line of **ball flower** ornament lines the parapet. There is a **priest's door** on the s. side of the chancel and on the n. side, a heavily restored medieval **vestry**. On that side of the nave, the buttresses carry inscriptions: 'MR' for 'Maria Regina' (the Virgin) and 'Omns S' for 'Omnes Sancti' (All Saints). The n. doorway is blocked and if you look in the angle of the w. wall and the n.w. buttress there is a fragment of **Norman** masonry embedded some 6 ft from the ground. Within the **porch** there are stone seats and it is a nice touch that the builder who repaired the tower was commemorated here when he died in 1982. Within the church, one can see how the heavy corner buttresses of the tower were undisturbed when the s. aisle was built, and a large **stoup** was housed in one of them. The plain octagonal C13 **font** has a centre shaft and slim pillars at each angle. On the wall behind, two shepherd's crooks are displayed which were emblems of a Friendly Society that used to meet in the village (reminding me of those in Norfolk's Walpole St Andrew which are also relics of a similar club). The old door to the tower stair is to the l., and its position high in the wall indicates that valuables were once stored there. The **arcade** between aisle and nave has short octagonal **piers** and the **clerestory** windows are small **quatrefoils**. Floors, **roofs**, benches and most of the fittings date from the C19 restoration. In the wall of the aisle there is a magnificent tomb recess which almost reaches the roof. It has been terribly mutilated but is still beautiful, with a massively **cusped ogee** arch fringed with the remains of **crockets**. Only the stumps of the side pinnacles remain, but the surfaces of the arch cusps are finely carved with leaves, and some of them have tiny faces in the centre so that they resemble **green men**. This was obviously a tomb for a person of importance; that could well have been Hervey de Stanton, King Edward II's Chancellor. The main arch of the C14 **angle piscina** in the s.

aisle chapel is a crocketted ogee with a **finial**, and there are **dropped-sill sedilia** alongside. The **altar** here is a very simple C17 table which came from Great Cornard (how I know not). In the window above are fragments of medieval glass and a nice panel of continental glass portraying **St Margaret** and **St Elizabeth**. The bottom of the **rood stair** was entered from this chapel and the upper opening faces the nave. The George III **Royal Arms** on the n. wall are painted on board and were moved here from Stanton, St John's. The simplest form of medieval piscina was one carved out of a ledge or window sill and an example can be seen here beside the pulpit - once the site of an altar. Nearby is the church's only **brass** - an inscription that was once on a **ledger-stone** to John and Elizabeth Parker who died in 1575 and 1597 respectively. The very tall chancel arch matches the nave arcade and all trace of the **rood screen** has gone except for some marks in the stonework where it was fitted. It is a fine vista through to the chancel, spoiled only by the obtrusive bulk of the C19 organ on the s. side. The **sanctuary** has a large C14 piscina under an ogee arch and the stepped sedilia alongside are separated by stone armrests, a refinement normally found only in larger churches. The centre panel of the e. window is a version of Holman Hunt's picture 'The Light of the World', designed by Luxford of New Barnet in 1955, but it is not a very happy translation. An oddity in the window on the s. side is the diamond cut inscription in one of the bottom **quarries**: 'John Norton glazed me for John Clarke Ixworth - Kenninghall Norf. 1891'. The ledger slabs in the sanctuary provide an interesting contrast of lettering styles; have a look at the pair of tablets flanking the chancel arch. Rector George Bidwell employed the London mason Gaffin to cut the memorial for his wife in 1840, but his own is a carbon copy by the local mason, Sharp of Thetford, and done in 1865 after Bidwell had been rector here for 54 years.

Stoke-by-Clare, St John the Baptist (B7): The church lies in an attractive setting by the entrance to Stoke College. There had been a Benedictine priory previously but the college was founded by Edmund, Earl of March, Lord of Wigmore and Clare in 1419. Matthew Parker, who became Archbishop of Canterbury under Elizabeth, was its last Dean before the Dissolution. He restored the **nave** in 1535 and, being collegiate, portions of the church belonged to the priory. The handsome C14 tower has a stair set in the n.e. corner buttress with an outside door, and two worn C17 headstones rest against a n. buttress - an inscription on one and skull and crossbones on the other. The w. window has 'Y' **tracery**, with a small stooled niche above it, and the bell openings are late **Perpendicular**. To the n. is a one-handed clock with a lozenge dial, and on the s.w. buttress is a wooden sundial. Within the s. **porch**, with its stepped gable, stands a C19 **bier**, and further along a square-cut stub **transept** has yawning **gargoyles**. There is a monument of unusual design s. of the **chancel** for Edward Douglas Loch who died in 1942 - a slim oblong panel with heavy scrolls at the ends, capped with a cornice. The two-storied n.e. **vestry** has barred windows and there is a **priest's door** on that side. The three- **light** windows of **aisles** and **clerestory** are C15 and at the n.e. corner of the nave an octagonal **rood stair** turret rises to the battlements. The n. porch has a gable that matches the s., with a very worn niche over the entrance. The interior is spacious, with pleasing brick floors, and close to the door stands an early C14 chest, with vertical wrought-iron straps on the front which branch out like small trees. The w. wall is blank, but note that there is the outline of an arch which is off-centre. The original church was apparently without aisles, and at the

Stoke-by-Clare, St John the Baptist: pulpit

C15 rebuilding the axis moved to the n., so that what had been the old s. wall became the wall of the new s. aisle. The octagonal C15 **font** has **quatrefoils** in the panels with centre shields and **paterae**, and there are carved heads below the bowl. The nave is lofty, with tall clerestory windows, an almost flat **roof**, and a **castellated**

string course above the **arcades**. The quatrefoil **piers**, with their castellated **capitals**, may have been saved from the C14 church and used again, as at Clare. The short s. transept is also likely to have formed part of the previous building. A plough now stands within, and there is some interesting glass in the window above it. Below the coat of arms at the top is a fine little windmill, a lozenge to the r. is painted with the white hart, and to the l. is a lozenge which has merchant marks, probably for one of the Elwes family. There are two heraldic roundels, and the one on the l. contains the arms of the Clothworkers' Company (note the teazle at the bottom and the two harbicks or tenterhooks, with points at each end). It is a reminder of the dominance of the wool and cloth trade in this part of Suffolk during the Middle Ages. The pulpit is at once one of the best that we have and the smallest, being only just over 20 in across. Money was left for its construction in 1498 and it stands on a coved and panelled stem. It has beautifully dense tracery in the panels, with an overlay of pierced work at the top. Behind it, modern doors have been fitted to the **rood loft** stair. The organ takes up virtually the whole of the n. chapel but by edging round it one can see something of the mid-C16 **Doom** painted on the e. wall. It has a pale green background and the figure of Christ is seated on a rainbow; below Him there is an angel with spread wings and hosts of subsidiary figures. This is an unusual position for a Doom and may reflect the dual use of the church by college and parish. In the wall behind the organ is the small memorial slab for William Dicons, a priest who died in 1567. The archway at high level leading into the chancel is most unusual and I can offer no reasonable explanation for it. The door to the vestry from the chancel is medieval and the benches in chancel and s. chapel have **poppyheads** carved with a fascinating variety of leaf forms, including a pair

of seed pods by the s. wall. Sadly, they have all been cruelly mutilated. There is a plain **Stuart Holy table** in the s. chapel and to the r., a small medieval statue of the Virgin and Child, given to the church some years back. The C19 stone **reredos** is boldly lettered 'This do in remembrance of me', and the **Heaton, Butler & Bayne** glass above it has not worn well. The church has a number of **brasses**: on the s. side of the nave by the lectern is an 18 in figure of a lady in **kennel head-dress** dating from about 1530 (you will notice the stone was re-used for 'F.C.' in 1766); nearby is the 22 in gowned figure of Edward Talkarne who died in 1597, with his coat of arms, and across by the pulpit lies his widow Alice, shown in Paris cap and ruff, who followed him eight years later. In addition, there are brass inscriptions for Ralph Turner (1600) by the pulpit, Elizabeth Sewster (1598) by the pulpit, John Croply (1584) by the lectern, and William Butcher (1611) in the n. aisle.

Stowlangtoft, St George (E4): There are few country parishes that can boast such a church as this, standing tall and handsome by the street, on a hillock that was once a Roman camp. Embedded in the wall by the path that rises to the gate are fragments of **Decorated** window **tracery**, but the present building is well nigh pure **Perpendicular** and was built between about 1370 and 1400 by Robert de Ashfield. Lord of the Manor and servant of the Black Prince, he died in 1401 and was buried in the **chancel**. It had fallen on hard times by the C19 but a new chancel roof was provided in 1832 and a major restoration followed in the 1850s. It is a tall building for its size and the unity of its design is emphasised by the chequerwork that lines the plain parapets of tower, **nave**, and chancel, and is seen again on the buttresses and in the **base course** that circles the whole church.

There is little difference in width between nave and chancel, and a **drip course** lifts as a **label** over the side windows whose arches are shaped like **Tudor** ladies' **kennel head-dresses**. There is a small **priest's door** on the s. side of the chancel and the five-**light** e. window is able to display a wider range of panel tracery than those in the side walls. The tower has the common local feature of an e. wall made broader by the buttresses, and there are square-headed bell openings and belfry windows. A heavy stair turret rises almost to the top on the s. side, and to the w. is a mighty cedar tree. The **porch** has a deep parapet of **flushwork** panels and the whole of the front is covered with chequerwork. There is a lovely little niche above the entrance; it has a **crocketted ogee** arch, stiff leaf in the moulding, and a fine modern statuette of Christ as the Good Shepherd with His sheep and holding a metal crook. A simple arch spans the corner by the inner door where once was a **stoup**.

Stepping inside, one is faced by a huge painting of **St Christopher** on the n. wall, at least, there is a large area of pale brown in which some of the remains can be identified. His legs, body, one arm and a hand are clear, and there are faint traces of the fisherman hermit, wearing a deep hood, standing within the doorway of his hut on the r. Below him, more distinctly, is a smaller figure crouching with a blurred rabbit, but of the heron, otter, and lobster that **Cautley** saw I could discern no trace. In the blocked n. doorway is a gilded and coloured war memorial Calvary designed by F.E. Howard, and in the centre of the nave, a survival from the earlier church - a fine early C14 **font**. It stands on a reeded shaft (as at Thurston), and the bowl panels contain a series of figures under **cusped pediments**. Although mutilated, they are an interesting series; clockwise from the e., the **Blessed Virgin** and Child, **St Catherine** with a small wheel held

in the crook of her arm, **St George** (for the dedication of the church), with a heavy sword at rest and his emblem on his shield, **St Paul**, Christ, with both arms raised in blessing, **St Peter**, a bishop, **St Margaret** and her dragon. Note how the carvings lap over the bottom of the panels. To the w. is a long iron-banded C15 chest with a divided lid. Within the tower the stair door is completely covered with iron straps, with two locks protected by a hinged plate - a sure sign that the tower was used for a village safe deposit. Above hang two **hatchments**: at the top, for Mary Wilson, who died in the early C19; below, for Lady Anne Belasyse, first wife of Sir George Wombwell, who died in 1808. Another on the opposite wall is for Joseph Wilson, who died in 1851. The low pitched nave **roof** has **tie-beams** and, unusually, the space between them and the ridge is boarded in. Note, too, that the **purlins** have little bracketed pendants coming down on either side of the tie-beams. The end bay formed a **celure** over the **rood** and traces of decoration remain on the last tie-beam and on the purlins. The infill panels painted with the **sacred monogram** had been removed for restoration at the time of my visit. There are some very dark fragments of C14 glass in the tops of the westernmost windows, with one good figure on the n. side and a tiny angel in the very top of the tracery. The rest of the nave tracery contains a range of C19 Old Testament figures, with a series of roundels set in patterned glass below them, apparently painted by a daughter of the mid-C19 rector, Samuel Rickards, who master- minded the restoration. The easternmost window on the s. side has a bold St George on a plunging steed, grappling with a psychedelic dragon. This 1934 design, by Hugh Easton, is set in clear glass, with four shields in the top **lights** and a canted **achievement** in the bottom corner. At the e. end of the nave on the s. is a **piscina** under a battered, **cinquefoil** arch and opposite, a gawky

Stowlangtoft, St George: the cock monster

stone pulpit perpetrated by William White in 1855.

The glory of the church is the woodwork, for here we have benches and stalls that vie with Wiggenhall, St Mary, in Norfolk and are, perhaps, the finest to be found in any parish church. In the nave, the blind tracery on the bench ends is varied and inventive. There are large **poppy-heads**, and over 60 grotesques - animals and human figures that perch on the gables of the squarely buttressed elbows. Carved to a high standard, the forms of many can be matched elsewhere but others are uncommon, and one or two unique. Look in particular for the following: n. side, next to tower, a camel and a fox with a goose in its mouth; the first beyond the n. door by the wall, a **cockatrice**; next along, an owl, then a chained monkey; next but one is a wild boar with human feet opposite a dog wearing a saddle; the next one is strangest of all, a cock with a hideous human face. On the s. side:

near the font is a **unicorn**, and on the other end by the wall, a boar playing a harp; next to the e. end by the wall is the rare figure of Scandal, dipping his pen to write upon a scroll; by the door, a mermaid with her mirror, and fourth from the door eastwards, an animal dressed as a friar in a pulpit. The bench backs have varied tracery above the bookledge, and the top moulding is close carved. At the e. end, the front three benches on the n. and the front five on the s. are good C19 work to match the rest, and are likely to have been carved by **Henry Ringham**. The **rood stair** rises from a high step in the n. wall by the pulpit but only the base of the **rood screen** survives. It dates from the time the church was built and the arms of the principal benefactor, Robert de Ashfield, can be seen in the tracery **spandrel** to the l. of the entrance. The other spandrels contain leaves, birds and a cherub head. Between the panels there are deep buttresses which have tall crocketted gables terminating in tiny heads. Although most of the painted decoration is modern, the red leaf pattern showing on the sides of the buttresses next to the entrance is original. The choir stalls are quite outstanding. They form a compact unit, with six clergy seats backing onto the screen, and an L-shaped range of low benches for the choir boys in front. The seats facing e. all have **misericords** and the subjects from n. to s. are: a hawk seizing a hare, the **Evangelistic symbols** in the order of **Saints Luke**, **Mark**, **John** and **Matthew**, finishing with a dragon. The broad ends of the priest's stalls are exquisitely traceried and, instead of poppyheads, the tops are crowned with small figures of priests, one in a pulpit and one at prayer (exceptionally good). The ends of the side stalls also have figures which are paired n. and s.; at the e. end, two taperers holding candlesticks; next, two vested deacons bearing the shields of Ashfield and Pêche; lastly, two acolytes with an incense boat on the s.

and Gospel book on the n. Small feathered angels stand on the front edges of the stall ends and there is chunky tracery backing the boys' seats, with a line of pierced **quatrefoils** below them. Over the priest's door is a large monument for Paul d'Ewes who died in 1624 and his two wives. It is made the more interesting because details of the contract between the parish and the (otherwise unknown) stone-cutter Jan Jansen are recorded. He agreed to:

> finish and set up...one tomb...in the chancel in Stowlangtoft Church...three pictures statues kneeling, a full yard high, cutt graven and coloured to the life, the man to be in a gowne, the two women in vailes...also fower pictures in the base, whereof one is of a man, the second of a boy fower yeares old kneelinge, and two other being dead - whereof one of the dead was a maide of tenne yeares old, the other a boy of two yeares old, and fower pictures more of women on the other. The oldest is married and to bee made with a vaile, the two others maidens of eighteen yeare, the fowerth a child of seven yeares.

And all this for £16 10s (a low price even for those days) to be paid in the church porch. You may see for yourself how well Jansen carried out his brief. The small organ is a prime piece of Victoriana made by Gray & Davison and exhibited at the Great Exhibition of 1851. The ranks of pipes are painted in peacock colours, and 'Gloria in excelsis' is inlaid in marquetry below them, with the sacred monogram and an overall dot pattern (also in marquetry) on the case. Close by, a **ledgerstone** once bore the brass figures of Robert and Alice Ashfield who died in 1550, but only the indents remain, as well as two shields. The church's other brass is an inscription in the floor of the **sanctuary** n. of the **altar** for Paul d'Ewes who died in 1630. On the s. side is a vestige of the earlier

church - the drain and part of an attached column of a C13 piscina. Alongside are two **dropped-sill sedilia**, with a third under its own cusped ogee arch. To its r. is a lovely little **Jacobean** bench, just the right height for children, with vine trails on the back rail and eight carved **baluster** legs. The C19 **reredos** is a relief carving in marble of the Last Supper with, as a variation, Christ standing in front of the table; the heavy and rather overblown canopy is worked in mottled marble. Above it, the 1854 e. window glass has 15 scenes from the life of Our Lord. Carried out in clear colours with very little shading, they show sensitive grouping of figures with a medieval feel about them, and may be the work of Alexander Gibbs. Three of the side windows contain glass by A.L. Moore of 1906 - figures symbolising the virtues of Love, Loyalty, Courage, and Humility. They have heavy **tabernacle work** above and below and are rich in detail (even if they are not inspired). Until 1977, the e. wall of the sanctuary was graced by an outstanding series of C16 carved Flemish panels given to the church in the 1870s, but they were wickedly stolen. Although recovered in Amsterdam, by 1986 the parish had still not been able to get them back despite all its efforts. Let us hope that persistance will prevail - as it deserves.

Stradishall, St Margaret (B6): A small-scale church, with **aisles** and **clerestoried nave**, set in a bosky churchyard. The tower dates from about 1300, with later brick battlements, and the line of an earlier and higher nave roof shows on the e. face. The s. aisle was added and the **chancel** adapted in the C14, leaving the trace of an earlier **lancet** in the n. wall. A **Tudor** brick **rood stair** lies in the corner between the chancel and the s. aisle and there is a **priest's door** on that side. The s. **porch** is very attractive, with an openwork timber frame standing on a high brick base, and part of the original C14 timber entrance arch survives. The inner C14 doorway has worn **headstops** and there is ancient ironwork on the door - three long strap hinges with floriated ends. Within is a small C14 three-bay **arcade** with octagonal **piers** and floors of honest brick. The nave **roof**, with cambered **tie-beams**, is almost flat and between the clerestory windows on the n. side there are remains of an early C17 text which had a broad painted border. The fragment of medieval painting to the r. of the n. door, mainly in red, was probably a figure of **St Christopher**. The early C15 **font** unfortunately has no step, but there is very varied **tracery** in the bowl panels and the shaft with its line of **quatrefoils** at the bottom. The **Royal Arms** over the tower arch are too dark to be identified with certainty but could be **Stuart**. The **capitals** of the **Early English** chancel arch were chopped back when the **rood loft** was fitted. The loft stair, with its modern door, turns out to be quite roomy, with a small window to the outside. The base of the C15 **rood screen**, to the r. of the chancel entrance, has **elevation squints** bored below the tracery in the panels (the n. side is a C19 replacement). In front stands a small **Jacobean** chest, with lozenge patterns carved in the panels. The plain late C17 pulpit stands on a coved stem and on the wall behind the lectern there is a framed section of C15 tracery which possibly belonged to the screen or loft. Some **balusters** from a set of C17 **communion rails** have been applied rather strangely to the front of the n. choir stalls and there are instructive traces of C13 wall paintings in the chancel - a band of decoration in red ties in with the lancet, and a matching section opposite has part of a larger scheme below. The e. window, with its attractive **reticulated** tracery, is filled with the sickly obscured glass that was so popular in the C19. Below the sill of the side window there is a **piscina** with a wide **cusped** arch. There are two pairs of de Carle tablets and those for William Rayner and his wife Frances on the s. wall are particularly nice - ovals set on mottled marble, with shapely little urns; all against contoured black backs.

Sudbury, All Saints (D7): To the s.w. of the town towards the river, the church stands at the angle of the street with the **chancel** hard up against the pavement. During the war with the Dutch in the 1660s the church was used as a prison and was somewhat damaged as a result. With the exception of the **Decorated** chancel, the whole building was reconstructed rebuilt in the C15 and the tower has a stair turret at the s.e. corner not unlike Sudbury, St. Gregory. There was once a spire but it was removed in 1822. There are large, three-**light** tran-**somed** bell openings and a **string course** with **paterae** runs below the stepped battlements. The w. doorway has worn **headstops** below the square **label** and the medieval door is trace-**ried**. Close to the tower on the n. side is a gravestone carved with the sun, moon, and carpenters' and masons' tools. The traceried n. door is also original and has a vine trail round the edge. Further along, the **priest's door** has good C19 carving. The two-storied n.e. **sacristy** has barred windows and is built level with the e. end of the chancel. The **aisle** battlements are set with shields and although there were once n. and s. **porches**, entry is now directly into the s. aisle.

The interior is wide and open and the **nave arcades** are unusually decorated with shields and paterae in the mouldings. Above the tall, three-light **clerestory** windows there is a fine cambered **tie-beam roof**, with large paterae on the **wall plates**; there are traces of colour overall. The wide n. aisle was rebuilt about 1460 and the cambered tie-beams have large centre **bosses**. In the n.w. corner stands the figure of a **woodwose**taken from the top of the tower. The C15 octagonal **font** has shields and **quatrefoils** in the bowl panels and a deeply traceried stem. The pews were installed as part of a restoration in 1850. The **poppyheads** are excellent work by Thomas Elliston, a local craftsman; they have great variety and those near the s. door are carved with bells showing that they were reserved for the ringers. The **rood stair** on the n. side of the chancel arch is blocked but the upper doorway is plain. Below it stands one of the best examples we have of a pre-**Reformation** pulpit. Made in 1490, it rises from a tall stem, beautifully proportioned and richly carved, with paterae below the **castellated** rim. It is in perfect condition and this is largely because it was boarded up and plastered, thus escaping mutilation and the accidental damage of the years. Uncovered by chance in 1850, it was restored by **Henry Ringham**; the plinth, monogram and steps are modern. Ringham may well have made the reading desks designed by C.F. Sprague which incorporate panels from the old **screen**. The oak lectern is in the form of a well-carved standing angel with uplifted arms and is a memorial to the men of the parish who fell in World War I. There is a **stoup** by the s. door and the remains of a **piscina** by the entrance to the s. aisle chapel. This was originally a **chantry chapel** founded by the Felton family in the C15 and its **parclose screens** are similar to those at St Peter's, Sudbury; they are tall, with **cusped** and **crocketted** arches and dense tracery above, topped by a vine trail and cresting. The chapel piscina has carving in the **spandrels** of the arch. The C14 chancel clerestory windows are blocked and the **high altar** is a **Stuart Holy table**. On the s. wall is a monument for Thomas Fenn (1818) and his family by **John Bacon the Younger** and Samuel Manning, redeemed from mediocrity by a bas relief roundel of the Good Samaritan at the bottom. The n. aisle chapel was probably rebuilt at the same time as the aisle and was the chapel first of the Waldegrave family and then of the Edens. Thomas Eden became patron of the living at the Dissolution and was Clerk of the Star Chamber in 1551. Suffolk and n. Essex were Puritan strongholds and the Burkitt family, who had a vault here, were kin to Cromwell and entertained John Bunyan when he visited Sudbury. Although most of the chapel is now taken up by the organ, there is an interesting painted genealogy of the Eden family on the e. wall dating from 1622. It spans five generations and, while the names have faded away, many of the shields of arms remain. Returning to the w. end, the tower arch is wide and open and the 1880s screen incorporates two more panels from the base of the old rood screen. The glass in the w. window is one of the few Suffolk examples of the work of **Walter Tower**, successor to Charles **Kempe**, and was installed in 1927.

Sudbury, St Gregory (D7): Sudbury's most handsome and important church stands in a spacious churchyard beyond a triangular green on the w. side of the town. The tower is solidly impressive, with a prominent stair turret rising above the battlements at the s.e. corner. The diagonal buttresses have five **set-offs** and are linked by well-defined **string courses**. **Put-log holes** show up plainly in the walls. A tomb at the base of the turret was moved from within the church, probably during the Commonwealth, and it is possible that it was once used as an **Easter sepulchre** in the **sanctuary**. The chest is decorated with shields within lozenges, and below the **traceried** hood of the shallow canopy there are indents showing that it originally carried **brasses** of two figures and an inscription (of whom, we have no means of telling). The **priest's door** on the s. of the **chancel** has leaf carvings in the **spandrels** and the square **label** drops to worn **headstops**. Nearby, the pin-

Sudbury, St Gregory: font cover

holes of two **scratch dials** survive in a buttress. The red brick n.e. **vestry** dates from the early C16 and there is a deep band of chequer **flushwork** under the n. **aisle** windows. There is a large niche which has lost its **dripstone** by the side of the s. aisle w. window. The s. **porch** is interesting because the small chapel on the e. side is combined with it in a unified design rather than being added as an afterthought. They lie beneath a common gable with a medieval cross at the centre and there is an ancient sundial below it. The C15 entrance doors have attractive tracery in the heads and a very decorative band of carving outlines the edges.

The internal tower buttresses and the line of an old **roof** indicate that the earlier building had no **clerestory** and was probably without aisles. The n. **arcade** dates from about 1370, while that to the s. was built about 100 years later, and both have unusually heavy **piers** for the period. Simon Teobald, or Simon of Sudbury, was born in 1317 and became powerful in the service of church and state. He was appointed Papal Nuncio to Edward III in 1356 and became Archbishop of Canterbury in 1375. In 1380, as Chancellor of England, he imposed the poll tax which, necessary though it may have been, was one of the oppressive acts of government that kindled the Peasants' Revolt. Refuge with King Richard II in the Tower did not save him from the mob that beheaded him messily on Tower Hill on 14 June, 1381. Meanwhile, however, he had been making significant changes at St Gregory's. With his brother, he founded a college of canons in 1375 (of which only the gateway remains w. of the church) and built an extended chancel for their use. The n. aisle of the 1370s was also his work and a chapel dedicated to All Souls in memory of his parents now houses the organ. Just within the church stands a fine mahogany chest, with a brass plate on top bearing the arms of the borough incorporating Simon's own heraldic **talbot** badge, and engraved with the names of the churchwardens for 1785. Beyond is the lovely mid-C15 **font** cover; telescopic and raised by a counter- balance, the bottom has canopied niches, and the upper range is set back with pierced **ogee** arches. It has been beautifully restored in recent years in blue, red and gold. The shaft columns of the font curve out to meet the shallow, traceried bowl. Within the tower, sections of C18 roof lead with wardens' names are displayed on the wall. The spandrels and main timbers of the cambered **roof** are picked out in colour and the easternmost bay is a painted **celure**, bright in blue, red and gold. Thoughtful restoration went on here for 20 years in the mid-C19 under **William Butterfield**. The work included the aisle roofs, new seating, decorative tiling, and very elegant wrought-iron lighting brackets on the arcade piers, made for gas by Corders of Ipswich and converted to electricity in 1973. The flushwork on the outside of the n. aisle was also part of this work. The oak pulpit, designed by Paul Earee and made by E.W. Beckwith of Coggeshall, replaced a C19 stone predecessor in 1925. The chapel of **St Anne** by the s. porch was once a place of pilgrimage and may have been dedicated to the **Blessed Virgin** originally. Within is a large monument to Thomas Carter, a town benefactor who died in 1706. The rear tablet is a combined epitaph and charity list and fat cherubs recline on the **pediment**. There is a Latin epitaph within an oval on the side of the tomb:

> Traveller, I will tell a wondrous thing. On the day on which Thomas Carter breathed his last a Sudbury camel passed through the eye of a needle. If thou art wealthy go and do likewise.

In the e. wall there are three tall, shallow niches, with an **angle piscina** in the corner, indicating that there was once an **altar** here.

There is another piscina in the s. aisle under a simple arch and the first window on that side has glass by **Heaton, Butler & Bayne**, with figures of **Saints Patrick**, **George** and **Andrew**. In the s.e. corner of the aisle is a late C13 slab which is the grave of Segeyna, wife of Robert de Quintin, a local wool merchant. Below the e. window is the stone of William Wood, college warden and founder of the town's grammar school who died in 1491. A window in the n. aisle in typical **Kempe & Co** style contains figures of **St Augustine**, **St Gregory** and the Venerable Bede, with vignettes from their lives below. There is now no **rood screen**, although one panel with a painting of **Sir John Schorne** survives in Gainsborough's house. A pity that it could not stay in the church where it belongs and has relevance. The early C16 chancel roof is flat with angular panelling that marks the move away from Gothic forms. It was beautifully restored in 1966 following the original colour scheme - a blue background patterned with stars, the ribs in red and gold. The **wall plate** carries lovely demi-angels bearing **Passion emblems**. A reminder of Simon of Sudbury's college is the fine range of stalls with **misericords** in the chancel. His talbot badge may be found on the first stall on the s. side and there is a particularly good head midway along the n. side. A **consecration cross** is painted on the wall by the vestry door, and if there is anybody in attendance you may care to ask for a view of Simon's skull (parted from his body which is buried at Canterbury) and kept in a recess in the vestry wall - a grisly relic decently concealed behind a little green door. I wonder how many choir boys have been petrified by that little surprise. The chancel e. window is high and short, and there is a small **aumbry** in the wall below. There is a larger version next to the piscina and there are traces of colour below the sills. The lower panels of the s. chancel windows are blanked off and contain figures of **Saints Peter**, **Paul**, **John** (see the poisoned chalice at his feet), **John the Baptist**, Elijah and Moses. They were painted by T.L. Green, brother of a late C19 rector; it is said that he used the parson as his model. There is no medieval glass in the church and for that we can blame **Dowsing** who, in January 1643, 'brake down ten mighty great angels in glass'. We may mourn, understandably, but the Puritan temper of Sudbury may well have been in sympathy with image breakers and government policy.

Sudbury, St Peter (D7): The church stands close to the bustle of the market place, with the statue of Gainsborough, the town's most famous son, to the w., while traffic laps the other three sides. It was a chapel of ease within the parish of St Gregory until the C16 when it acquired separate status. It was declared redundant in 1972 and four years later was vested in the **Redundant Churches Fund**. It is used for a variety of community purposes and when I visited the building was crammed with model railway enthusiasts, extensive layouts and stalls; the scent of hot dogs lay heavy on the air. Despite a credit card sellotaped to the **font** cover, it remains a consecrated building and a number of services are held there every year, both by Anglicans and Roman Catholics. There was a complete rebuilding in the late C15 and the style is therefore homogeneous **Perpendicular**. During the Middle Ages other buildings abutted and this probably accounts for its slight irregularity and the weeping of the **chancel** to the s. The **aisles** lap the tower on both sides, with internal arches to n. and s., and there is attractive matching **tracery** in all the w. windows. There are narrow, **transomed** bell openings and stone figures on the tower corners. The tall s. **porch** has an upper room and there was obviously a **groined roof** in prospect. There is no n. porch and the buttresses each side

of the door have niches. Both n. and s. doors have worn tracery. Entry now is by way of the w. door, and to the l. is a showcase containing lovely banners of St Peter's and St Gregory's, together with mayoral and mace-bearer's robes. In the intervals of completing his showpiece, All Saints, Margaret Street in London, **William Butterfield** carried out a sensitive restoration here in the 1850s. He replaced pews with chairs, designed choir stalls, and painted the roofs. There was a restoration in 1964 and the **nave** roof, rebuilt in 1689, is beautifully tricked out - panelled and coved in pale green, with gilded **bosses**. Over the chancel arch is a structural **celure** which has been renovated and repaired more than once but which is still more or less in its original form of a canopy for the old **rood**. There are traceried **spandrels** and centre bosses in the **aisle** roofs, and in the s. aisle one of the main timbers was used with its natural curve unchanged. It is quite unlike the rest, a variation that one would not expect in a church of this quality. The bowl of the mid-C15 **font** was taken by the Commonwealth mayor John Cooke to use as a horse trough but his horses refused to drink from it so he used it for pigs instead! Subsequently restored to the church, it is carved with shallow crosses. Nearby stand sections of the old **rood screen**. There are paintings of Moses and Aaron over the n. and s. doors and these were originally parts of a **reredos** which was removed during the 1850s restoration. They were painted in the 1730s by Robert Cardenall, a local artist who had studied under Kneller. There is a **piscina** at the e. end of the s. aisle and the s. aisle chapel is separated from the chancel by a beautiful **parclose screen**; it is tall, with **cusped** and **crocketted ogee** arches, with dense **tracery** above and delicate cresting. The complementary screen on the n. side fronts the organ. The **altar** in the s. chapel is a heavily carved piece of 1907; the **retable** under heavy canopy work is a deep bas relief based on da Vinci's Last Supper, flanked by **St Peter**, **St Gregory** and the **Four Evangelists**. The front panel carving is a Nativity, with angels and Old Testament prophets on either side. There is a piscina in the corner. The chancel arch is Victorianised and painted, and the almost flat roof is splendid in green and gold, with a red and white **celure**; there are large leaf bosses and a line of angel bosses up the centre. The **reredos** was designed by **George F. Bodley** in 1898. It is tall, and contained within a richly carved vine border; the crucified Christ occupies the centre, flanked by the **Blessed Virgin** and **St John** in niches; there are pairs of angels below, with an **Annunciation** in the centre, a splendid thing in which dull gold and plum red predominate. On each side there are deep curtains hung from hinged filigree brackets. The 1856 e. window was designed by **John Hardman Powell** (**Hardman's** nephew) for Butterfield.

Thelnetham, St Nicholas (F3): This church has a lovely setting in park-like surroundings on the edge of the village. The building dates from the early C14 and, like nearby Rickinghall Inferior, its s. **aisle** is gabled and sits alongside the **nave**. Its heavy corner buttresses have hoods and the window **tracery** is **Decorated**, with carved **spandrels** in the case of the s.e. window - an unusual feature which, again, can be seen at Rickinghall. There is a **priest's door** in the s. wall of the **chancel** and another is blocked on the n. side. The five-**light** e. window is remarkably wide for its height and, at the top, the intersecting tracery is contained within an outer band of oddly shaped **mouchettes** and **trefoils**. The nave n. windows also have Decorated tracery. The small tower w. window is **Perpendicular**, with a deep **label**, and above it is a niche with a **crocketted ogee** arch. The bell openings have Decorated

tracery and the **sound holes** are tiny **quatrefoils**. The battlemented **porch** is modest; its little side windows have sharply pointed arches and, inside, the s. door displays plain convex mouldings and leafy **headstops** with a niche overhead. Just within the door is a plain C14 **font** and beyond, an equally plain tower arch with no **imposts**. This style is to be seen again in the **arcade** between the aisle and the nave, resting on octagonal **piers**. Edmund Gonville, the founder of Gonville Hall (Gonville & Caius College), Cambridge, was a rector here in the C14 and the s. aisle was built in his time. There are fragments of the original glass in the heads of the **lancets** of the e. window, with pairs of pheasants in the centre and winged grotesques at the sides. Below the sill there was once an elaborately carved **retable** but only remnants remain. The **angle piscina** in the corner has been subjected to over-elaborate and heavy-handed reconstruction, probably by **R.M. Phipson** when he carried out the general restoration in 1872, or possibly in the 1850s because it has much in common with the one at Rickinghall Inferior. On the s. wall nearby is a monument to Sir Henry Bokenham and his wife. He was High Sheriff of the county in 1630 and died in 1648. In alabaster, and still showing traces of colour, it has busts of the couple within a curtained niche, with figures of their two children in oval recesses below. Overhead is a broken **pediment** enclosed in a **cartouche** of arms with a double crest, and the frame is garlanded at the bottom - a handsome memorial for a family that were Lords of the Manor from the C14 to the C18. By the n. door in the nave there is a **stoup**, and further e. hangs an attractive C18 roundel carved in walnut of the Flight into Egypt. Probably of Italian origin, it was given to the church by a former rector in 1946. A section of stone moulding with the figure of an angel stands on a window ledge by the C19 pulpit, and one wonders whether it once formed part of

the s. chapel retable. The chancel **screen** was installed in 1907 but the stairs leading to the old **rood loft** remain on the n. side (note that the bottom doorway is C14 but the upper one is **Tudor**). The chancel was restored in 1895 and given a new **roof** of Spanish chestnut. Apart from the fact that it has **king posts**, it is the same design as that in the nave which was probably put up in 1872. The whole of the chancel is tiled and there is a C14 angle piscina in the **sanctuary**, the larger arch trefoiled and an ogee head to the opening at the side. A large **squint** cuts through the wall between the s. aisle chapel and the e. end of the nave, no doubt to give a view of another **altar** (the church had three **guilds** before the **Reformation**). Below the squint is the church's only **brass**, a simple gothic letter inscription asking us to pray for the soul of Anne, the wife of John Caley, who died about 1500. Nearby, a section of medieval **tabernacle work** is fixed to the wall and may have formed part of the rood loft. Two pre-Reformation **mensa slabs** were uncovered in the churchyard in the C19. They both measure some 8 ft by 4 ft and, with their **consecration crosses** re-cut, they have been replaced on modern altars in the chancel and the s. aisle chapel. In the churchyard, e. of the chancel, lies John Middleton Murray, who died in 1957. He was one of the most controversial figures in C20 English letters and was editor of The *Athenaeum* in its last and most brilliant phase, and of The *Adelphi* in the 1920s. Husband of Katherine Mansfield, intimate of D.H. Lawrence, he was the foremost critic of his day. The severely simple stone, designed by his brother, describes him as 'author and farmer' and adds a quotation from King Lear: 'ripeness is all'. He is perhaps better remembered in the parish for his barbed and thinly disguised portraits of local characters in his book *Community Farm*.

Thelnetham, St Nicholas

Thorpe Morieux, St Mary (E6): In a pleasant setting off the main road, with fields around and a lake glimpsed from the churchyard to the s., the church is largely late C13 and early C14. The handsome tower has **Decorated** bell openings with a later **Perpendicular** w. window, **gargoyles** below the battlements, and a heavy stair turret on the s. With the exception of one **lancet** on the n. side the **nave** windows are Decorated and the V-shaped buttresses are unusual. So too are the angle buttresses to the **chancel**, with their long, steeply angled tops. A fragment of masonry on the n. side shows where the **rood stair** turret once was and there is a **priest's door** on the s. side of the chancel. The stone and flint base of the **porch** has been renewed but the open framework of wood is early C15 and is very attractive, with its pierced barge boards and open **tracery** above the **mullions** in the sides. The medieval doors have a border of **quatrefoils** cut in the solid and the w. door carries the same style of decoration. Down three steps into the nave is a C13 **font** standing on five columns, unadorned except for a band of cross-hatching at the bottom of the square bowl. On the n. wall is a plain 1840s tablet by Watts of Colchester for the Rev Hezekiah Harrison (prompting the thought that Christian names are not what they were). In the centre of the s. wall is a splendid C15 image bracket that was found within the **piscina** further along when it was uncovered during a restoration. It is large, with a vine trail carved below a battlemented cresting and its original location is unknown; however, there were **altars** dedicated to the **Blessed Virgin** and **St Nicholas** in the church and it is likely to have been used near one or the other. The large C14 piscina itself has attached shafts with ring **capitals** and there are traces of **cusping** in the arch. Close by is a bronze tablet for Lieut Cornwallis John Warner who was killed in 1915; it has his arms in enamelled colour, with replicas of his four medals and there is a duplicate at Brettenham. On the n. side the doorways and two steps of the **rood loft** stair remain in the wall. The chancel arch is sharply pointed with no capitals, and there are **hatchments** on either side; to the l., for John Haynes Harrison who died in 1839 and to the r., a modern example of 1934 for Sir Thomas Courtenay Theydon Warner. The C13 chancel is very wide and on the n. wall is a beautifully proportioned monument in grey and white of 1764 for John Fiske. The central florid **cartouche** with his arms in colour contrasts nicely with the plain background; there are small gilded torches on the **pediment**, and the lower panels carry well-lettered inscriptions for members of the family up to 1778. Opposite is a tall, tapering tablet of 1839 for Sarah and John Harrison, with the names of their children added for another 40 years; it has reversed torches each side, a torch urn on top, and is by John Soward of London - like most of his work, it is competent but rather dull. The C13 angle piscina in the **sanctuary** has **trefoil** arches with typically nubbly leaf cusps matching the foliage round the capital of the shaft, and to the r. are **dropped-sill sedilia**. The large slab of stone resting against the n. wall of the sanctuary has a bevelled edge and would appear to be the original **mensa**; measuring 5 ft 6 in by 3 ft 6 in., it has lost a corner and was presumably buried and rediscovered.

Thurston, St Peter (E4): A thorough restoration was begun in 1857, but in 1860 the tower collapsed onto the **nave**, taking with it nearly everything w. of the **chancel** arch; the side walls gave way when attempts were made to salvage the windows. There was no alternative but to rebuild the body of the church and, in keeping with the spirit of the age, the work was finished within a year. The architect was **E.C. Hakewill** and, although he followed the design of the original, using all of the old materials that

could be saved, the new church is 7 ft higher than it was, and the nave roof is more steeply pitched. The **Perpendicular** chancel, too, was extensively restored and given a new waggon roof. All this should not deter the visitor, for there is much of beauty and interest to see.

The interior is very tall, and above the re-used Perpendicular **arcades**, Hakewill substituted **quatrefoils** for the former two-**light** windows in the **clerestory** - not an improvement. He reproduced the blind arcading on the **aisle** walls, but the sills of the windows are a good deal higher than they were. The C14 **font** survived and has a reeded shaft like the one at Stowlangtoft, and six of the panels of the deep octagonal bowl are carved with large leaf patterns. The remaining two (e. and s.) have **green man** masks at their centres, and another green man hides in the **poppyhead** of a medieval bench end in the **vestry** space at the w. end of the s. aisle. The **finial** on the other end of that particular bench has the figures of two women back to back, kneeling in prayer, and there is a duplicate of this lovely little carving on the bench end in the s.w. corner. The finial next to it is yet another green man, an excellent one this time, rising from between two birds with vicious beaks. The bench to the r. of the s. door has a wide **traceried** end, with more tracery on the back, and another like it stands by the n. door. By the tower arch hangs the tattered battle ensign of **H.M.S. Wren** that was flown in the 1940 Narvik action, and over the n. door are the **Royal Arms** of Elizabeth II. The nave benches were designed by Hakewill and excellently carved by Farrow of Bury with varied poppyheads. The s. aisle e. window is a memorial to an infant who died in 1842, but the original glass was blown out during the war and the present design is by **Powell & Sons** - a compact group of the Virgin and Child with the Wise Men, set in striated glass with scattered symbols. Sir Walter Greene (appropriately enough, in view of the number of green men lurking about) not only restored the chancel but furnished it, and provided all the fittings. The pulpit is a very fine piece of work in oak - openwork panels with canopies and, within them, 2 ft figures of **Saints Andrew, James, Peter** and **John**; the bookrest is laid upon the spread wings of a charming little angel and two more stand at the foot of the steps. Opposite is a large oaken eagle lectern on a heavy turned stem that was apparently intended for Bombay cathedral but is not out of scale here. In front of the chancel steps is a **brass** inscription for two Thomas Brights who died in 1727 and 1736 - rarely does one see C18 brasses. The tall **screen**, with its light and lacy tracery, marked Queen Victoria's Diamond Jubilee, and beyond, the stalls incorporate medieval ends, their lozenge-shaped finials carved with foliage. Four panels on the n. and five on the s. fronts of the stalls are C15 and there is good small-scale carving in the **spandrels**; look particularly on the n. side for the man in bed, opposite a woman who may be pounding something in a mortar, and on the s. side for two bats. The window on the s. side nearest the screen has beautiful painterly glass of 1895 by **Ward & Hughes** which was copied from a Norwegian church. It depicts the angel and the three Maries at the tomb, with a brilliant sunrise showing up the Calvary crosses in the distance. The window on the s. of the sanctuary is also Ward & Hughes, but designed by **T.F. Curtis** in 1912 and in quite different style. The theme is 'Come unto me all ye that are heavy laden...' and Christ sits enthroned among the deaf, the blind and the crippled, in company with a Red Indian chief and a Chinaman - a sensitive grouping of figures below the curved and jagged rim of heaven. Opposite is another T.F. Curtis window of 1922, but nowhere near as good. The **reredos**, like all the C19 woodwork, is of high quality, richly canopied and crested. Standing

angels hold the **instruments of the Passion** (including the dice), and the centre panel is an **Annunciation** scene. All the figures are carved in limewood, stained to match the oak of the frame. To the r. is a good late C14 double **piscina** under **cinquefoiled** arches, with a heavy stone **credence shelf** half way up. The tops of the stepped **sedilia** have been restored. Thomas Gaffin cut the memorial for Admiral Sir William Hall Gage on the s. wall in 1864, and the epitaph was so long it had to go on a separate tablet underneath. Nearby is a pretty pair of ovals commemorating Robert and John Stedman (1809 and 1814). Gill Stedman, Gent, was provided with a plain and decent tablet by Thomas Farrow of Diss in 1852. Before leaving the chancel, use binoculars if possible to look at the tops of the windows nearest the screen; on the n. there are two bishops, with 'Scs Jeromus a doctor' (**St Jerome**, Doctor of the church) in C15 script above them; on the s. there are two angels bearing scrolls: 'Deo Date Gloriam' (To God give the glory), another angel and a mitred bishop. On your way out, study the medieval glass in the s. aisle w. window. Set in patterned Victorian **quarries**, you will see four good heads in the r. hand panel and a lovely head of Christ to the l., just above a naked wanton with long, auburn hair.

Timworth, St Andrew (D4): Timworth is a tiny hamlet, with the church quite isolated from it, and there is some reason to believe that this division dates from the **Black Death** or a subsequent fire. A narrow track winds round the edge of a field to a peaceful churchyard girt by mature trees and backed by pine forest. There was a major rebuilding here in 1868, but much of the material from the old church was re-used. In particular, the C14 tower with its **Decorated** bell openings is largely original and stands on the s. side, acting as a rather splendid **porch**. The stair turret is tucked into the n.w. angle and overlaps the **nave roof**. There is a variety of C19 windows, including one with very brash **tracery** in the w. wall, and the **priest's door** has an oddly decorated arch. The unusual thing to note on the outside is that a **scratch dial** is incised on a special block let into the angle of the s.e. buttress of the tower, about 12 ft up and aligned to face due s. Through a nice early C14 doorway into a largely Victorian interior, although the small **lancets** on the n. side of the **chancel** are reminders of its C13 origin. The **font** could also be C13, or else a very restrained Victorian copy. On the s. wall there is a large set of William III **Royal Arms** painted on boards, and the pulpit is an interesting mixture. The base, with nice cherub heads at the angles, is C18, as is the **acanthus** moulding of the rim, but the panels are some 200 years older. It apparently came from St James' at Bury, and the **communion rails** may well have done so too. They have delicate twisted **balusters**, with groups of four at the ends and as supports for the central gates. There are infill panels each side which add weight to the theory that the set was designed for elsewhere.

Tostock, St Andrew: cockatrice

Tostock, St Andrew (E4): Set a little apart from the e. end of the village, the church stands in a graveyard where a commendable balance is kept between manicured grass verges and natural growth with plenty of wild flowers. The **Decorated** tower has **flushwork** panelling on the buttresses and closely spaced **string courses** in the upper stages. There is an C18 or early C19 lean-to **vestry** to the n. of the late C13 **chancel** and the **nave** e. walls have wide, late **Perpendicular** recesses, presumably for statuary. The C14 s. **porch** has most unusual windows which, though largely blocked, retain their **tracery**, a large **reticulation** shape with a pair of **mouchettes** above and below. Within,

the impression is spacious, largely because there are no **aisles** and a single **roof** spans the whole width of nearly 30 ft. It is a fine late C15 example, with **arch-braces** alternating with double **hammerbeams** whose posts continue down in the bottom range to form pendants. These have figures set within canopies, there is varied tracery above the lower hammers, and the **spandrels** are all carved (look also for the little animal on one of the arch-braces). **William Dowsing** was here in 1643, and although his journal mentions only 'superstitious pictures', he may well have been responsible for chopping off the heads of the canopied figures and removing the angels from the ends of the upper hammers. The early C14 **font** stands on a reeded shaft and the panels of the heavy bowl are carved with a variety of leaf forms. The one on the n. side, however, is different - a pagan **green man** with tendrils curling from his mouth. There is continuous seating along the side walls and the lovely medieval benches stand clear, showing them off to good advantage. They have nicely traceried backs and there are two with traceried ends, as well as two more against the side walls. The buttressed armrests carry an interesting selection of grotesques, including a **unicorn** (third from the w. on the s. side of the centre aisle), a **pelican** in her piety (e. end of the s. wall bench), and a rare **cockatrice** (fourth from the door on the s. side). The four front ranges of benches are good modern copies and were no doubt added during the 1872 or 1889 restoration. The stair to the old **rood loft** rises on the s. side and, although the bottom door is blocked, one can see through the top opening to the little window that gave light from the outside. By the entrance is a small **aumbry**, and to the r. of the chancel arch is a plain recess that was probably associated with a **guild altar** (there were medieval guilds here dedicated to **Saints Andrew**, **Peter**, and **John the Baptist**. It now houses a 1914-19 war memorial. Above the pulpit is a strange tablet by Gaffin for George Brown, who died in 1857; it carries a plain cross with one long scroll looped round it and another beneath. It was thought well enough of to be copied for another member of the family in 1905. The chancel arch is C13 and the attached columns on the e. side have been cut away. The mid-C17 **communion rails** have pleasing **balusters** with acorn tops and the C13 **piscina**, on the s. side of the **sanctuary**, has an **ogee** arch. The e. window tracery contains fragments of C15 glass which include, on the r., a lovely little group of animals round a tree - a stag, sheep, pig, and an owl perched in the branches.

Troston, St Mary (D3): There are sound arguments for and against clearing graveyards of their stones, but there is no doubt that the church here is set off very well by the swathe of grass on the s. side. The path leads up to a fine C15 **porch**, with three canopied niches set above the arch with its foliage and blank shields in the **spandrels**. The front is faced with **flushwork** panels and there are carved stone panels in the **base course**. The battlements are decorated in flushwork and display 'M' and 'Maria' for the dedication, while the entrance arch has **fleurons** in the mouldings, both inside and out. The rather gaunt tower was built about 1300 - witness the 'Y' **tracery** in the w. window and in the bell openings. The oldest part of the building, however, is the **chancel**. Dating from the C13, it has small **lancets** in the side walls and an e. window formed of three stepped lancets. A most unusual feature of the **nave** is the way in which the roof timbers that project under the eaves have been roughly shaped and decorated with carving, a probable C17 addition. The C14 doorway into the church has holes in the inner **jambs** for a drawbar, and one passes into a nave that was built about 1320. The window tracery employs the four-petalled flower design which was a favourite in the **Decorated** period. The sharply pointed tower arch fades into the **imposts**, and above is a **sanctus-bell window** almost hidden in the roof timbers. The **font** is a plain octagon on a cylindrical shaft and is probably C13; the cover is crude C17 work. There are some medieval bench ends at the w. end with mutilated grotesques on the elbows, but most of the benches in the nave were carved by Robert Emelyn Lofft when he had the church restored in 1869, and they are unique in their weird ugliness. There are some fine medieval paintings on the n. wall: from the w., a large-scale C15 **St George** slaying the dragon (very attractive in pale red and white); a huge C15 **St Christopher**

beyond the unused n. door; an earlier and much smaller mid-C13 St George in silhouette; a C14 martyrdom of **St Edmund** which shows the king, an archer drawing a bow, and another figure beyond. Over the chancel arch are the faint remains of a painted **Doom**, and one can just make out the figure of Christ in the centre. On the s. wall of the nave is a small set of **Royal Arms** painted on board. They have been overpainted with 'G.R.' for one of the Georges, but the arms are those of James I, with the inscription 'Exurgat Deus dissipentur inimici' (Let God arise and let his enemies be scattered) - not at all common. The two-decker pulpit is a large and very odd combination. The pulpit itself is **Jacobean**, with typical panel decoration and canted reading ledge, but a massive reading desk was added to the front which has marquetry panels and heavily scrolled pilasters - possibly C17 Dutch. A low doorway leading to the **rood stair** is blanked off behind the pulpit and the upper opening will be seen above. On the s. side, the priest's stall incorporates medieval bench ends and panelling. At the e. end of the nave on the s. side is a **piscina** with pierced tracery in the arch, and on the wall nearby is a tablet to the memory of Capel Lofft who died in Italy in 1824. Barrister, reformer, and man of letters, it was he who encouraged the local poet Robert Bloomfield, whose poem The Farmer's Boy had such a phenomenal success in the early 1800s. In this corner of the nave there are two **consecration crosses** and two more are on the n. wall just above the panelling. The tracery of the windows on the n. side of the nave contains many fragments of medieval glass, including some quite exotic little buildings. The mid-C15 **screen**, with its bulky sill across the entrance, has been crudely repainted but the arches of the main **lights** have attractive **crocketted** and **cusped ogee** arches; the cornice and cross are modern. There are some medieval bench ends in the chancel

which were originally in the nave and the panelling on the walls was part of a set of C17 **box pews**. Windows in the C13 were seldom draught-proof and here one can see that the jambs of the lancets are rebated for shutters, and some of the hinge hooks remain. Another very rare survival is the original wooden shutter on the inside of the **low side window**. The iron hooks in the walls above the **sanctuary** steps supported the **Lenten veil** before the **Reformation**. The **Stuart communion rails** have simple turned **balusters**, with a scroll-carved top rail, and the riddell posts in green and gold that surround the altar were made by the Warham guild in 1947. Behind the **altar** is a most interesting length of panelling; 4 ft high, it has crude and varying apertures cut in it, and is likely to have been the eastern front of the **rood loft**. The western front, facing the congregation, would have been as ornate as the screen below, but this would not have been thought necessary for the other side. The late C13 double piscina on the s. side of the sanctuary has two **trefoil**-headed lancets, with a **quatrefoil** above them, and behind the pierced tracery is an original wooden **credence shelf** in an unusually high position. The e. window has glass of 1964 by Hugh Easton; in the centre is Christ at the table, with a disciple on either side. The dominant colours are a rich red, yellow, and deep blue and the composition is set in clear glass. On the n. wall of the chancel there are interminable epitaphs for Fane Walker (1790) and Mrs Anne Lofft (1801); between them, an oval medallion for Henry Capel Lofft, a lieutenant in the 18th Regiment of Foot who fell at Albuera in 1811.

Tuddenham, St Mary (B3): This is a handsome building in a quiet way. The early C14 tower has an attractive combination of **ogee**-headed niches flanking a **quatrefoiled** round window like the one at Icklingham, All Saints. There is a vestige of another niche or window just above and the bell openings have cusped 'Y' **tracery** through which one can see the medieval bellframe. The rest of the building is mainly C14 and notice how the **Decorated** tracery varies in the windows on the n. side. The e. window, with its pair of **headstops**, has **reticulated** tracery of the same period and there is an interesting variation at the top a circle enclosing **cusped** triangles. There are C15 windows on the s. side of the **chancel**, one in the s. **aisle**, and the **clerestory** is late C14, probably designed to allow for a n. aisle that was never built. By the mid-C19 the church was in a very poor state and in the 1870s there was a major restoration. The floor of Minton tiles, the serviceable pitch-pine pews, renewed **chancel** arch and pine chancel **roof** are familiar evidence of a restoration, but the roofs of the **nave** and aisle were rebuilt extremely well on the old plan and much of the C15 timber was incorporated, together with a number of angels on the **wall posts** and **hammerbeams**. The plain C14 square **font** with heavy chamfers stands on a base with **colonnettes** at the corners which does not match it and may be C19, as is the wooden cover. A small plaque on the n. door commemorates the crew of a Stirling bomber lost over Kiel: 'Went the day well? We died and never knew...'. There is a tomb recess in the n. wall under a sharply pointed arch which may be the resting place of Richard de Freville who died in 1325. The **Jacobean** pulpit stands on a modern base and is very plain but it does have a nice pair of brass **Ecclesiological Society** design candle holders. There is no longer a chancel **screen** but the **rood stairs** still go part way up in the wall on the s. side. By the s. aisle e. window is a niche for an image, with a Decorated **piscina** in the corner. There were four village **guilds** in the C15 and this will have been the chapel for one of them. The **vestry** is a C19

replacement but its door in the chancel n. wall is medieval, with **linenfold** carving and original ironwork. The C19 **altar rails** are an unusual combination of brass and oak and the **altar** itself is a plain **Stuart** table (although the top has been renewed). The e. end looks even more handsome inside because it has fine and large niches on either side of the window. Carefully restored, they have the same flattened cusping under **crocketted** ogee arches that can be seen over the niches on the w. face of the tower. On the s. side is a C14 piscina under a **cinquefoiled** arch, together with **dropped- sill sedilia**. As you leave, note the **stoup** to the l. of the door and the door itself whose strap hinges have been renewed while the rest is medieval. This makes four doors in the church that have survived for over 400 years.

Walsham-le-Willows, St Mary (E3): This is a large and handsome church for the size of the village, probably because the C11 Lord of the Manor gave the living, together with land to support it, to the Augustinian priory at Ixworth which he founded. Before the **Reformation** it was served by the canons from the priory. The building has many points of detail in common with Ixworth and it is likely that the same masons worked on both buildings. The style throughout is **Perpendicular** and the tower has well defined **drip courses** and corner pinnacles to the battlements. Most of the decoration is concentrated on the n. side facing the centre of the village and the tall **porch** is attractively chequered with **flushwork** in the style of Norwich guildhall, with a niche over the outer arch. The pattern of the **base course** continues along the length of the **nave**. The close-set windows of the **clerestory** have arches patterned with red brick and there is a line of square panels half way up decorated with crowned 'M's, Catherine wheels (there was a **guild** of **St Catherine**

Walsham-le-Willows, St Mary: the virgin's crant

here), the **sacred monogram**, and other devices. The **rood staircase** projects out of the angle between the **chancel** and the n. **aisle**, a mirror image of the arrangement at Ixworth. The s. side is much plainer and there is no porch there. Above the bench seats in the porch there is wooden panelling and the top rails are carved with: 'God's wyll be done in hevyn and erthe' on one side, and on the other: 'Ejus ne fueris curiosis MCCCCCXLI' (Thou shalt not be envious of him 1541).

The interior is spacious, attractive, and very well kept. Above the tall tower arch you will see a **sanctus-bell window**, and the tower w. window is filled with three panels of the Good Samaritan parable in deep, rich colour, with **tabernacle** work over them, probably by Taylor of Berners Street, London. The C14 **font** is beautifully chunky, and the bowl panels are carved with **crocketted** and **cusped ogee** arches, with leaves in the **spandrels** and pinnacles at the angles. There are worn heads beneath and the shaft has deeply cut **tracery** on all sides. An unusual feature is that crosses have been drilled at intervals around the rim. The octagonal pillars of the nave **arcades** have concave faces which are carved with ogee-shaped **trefoils** below the **capitals**, a feature repeated in the **jambs** of the outer porch arch. At the w. end of the s. aisle there is a range of oak panelling dated 1620, and over the s. door is a good set of George III **Royal Arms**. The C13 iron-bound parish chest, with its three locks and three old padlocks, stands nearby. There are medieval bench ends in the s. aisle and at the w. end of the nave which have **poppyheads**, but the figures or grotesques that were carved on the squared elbows have been cut away. At the w. end of the n. aisle, an **altar** is backed by a triptych in oils by Rosemary Rutherford, with the Last Supper flanked by Christ washing the disciples' feet and the vigil in Gethsemane. On the wall to the r. is an interesting old photograph of the wall paintings that were discovered and plastered over again in the C19 - a series of **Christ of the Trades**. The nave **roof** is perhaps the most splendid thing here. It has a flattish pitch and **hammerbeams** alternate with **arch-braced tiebeams**. Originally, the hammerbeams carried angels and the drilled tenons that held them can still be seen. They rose up to fit as braces into the timbers above, a most uncommon arrangement. The roof is a lovely pale golden colour and everywhere the faded vermillion painted decoration survives. Each spandrel above the long **wall posts** is carved with a sun in splendour and there is a double band of ornament on tie-beams, hammers, and on the **wall plate**. Hanging above the arcade on the s. side of the nave is a crant the virgin's garland - which is not uncommon in the south-west but unique in Suffolk. What remains here is the wooden disk carved with the name of Mary Boyce, a maiden who died aged 20 in 1685, they say of a broken heart. Below her name is a heart pierced by an arrow and on the anniversary of her death it was decorated with a wreath of flowers but the custom died out in the middle of the C18. In Shakespeare's *Hamlet*, the priest says over Ophelia's grave: 'Yet here she is allowed her virgin crants'.

The stair to the **rood loft** rises from a door at the e. end of the n. aisle and divides at the top to a doorway facing the nave and another facing the chancel. This suggests that the loft was wide enough to have a walkway back and front. There is an image stool above the lower door. The **screen** dates from the 1440s and the panels of the base have blind four-**light** tracery. The main lights have shapely, cusped and crocketted ogee tops and the remains of the vaulting, that rose to the underside of the loft, spring from delicate shafts above the buttresses. The entrance arch has a double ogee,

coming down to a reversed poppy-head of the sort so often seen on bench ends of the period, but I do not remember having seen one used like this before. The top of the screen and the cross are modern. In front is a good example of an **Ecclesiological Society** design brass lectern, and beyond the cumbersome and ugly C19 pulpit is the s. aisle chapel. It has a **piscina** with a trefoil ogee arch and there are **dropped-sill sedilia** alongside. The altar here is a nice C17 table, with a carved and moulded edge, rails and stretchers. The e. window and that to the s. have glass of the 1880s by W.C. Taylor of Berners Street. A little to the w. is an image niche which once had a canopy or hood; the stumps of iron supports can be seen in the stonework, and it probably contained a statue connected with one of the pre-Reformation guilds - the **Trinity**, **St John the Baptist** or **St Catherine**. In the base of the niche is a **cresset** that was found in a local garden. To the l. of the altar is a C13 grave slab and nearby a small patch of C14 tiles, two of which carry the profile of a man with an enormous nose. The window in the n. wall of the chancel is a memorial to Rosemary Rutherford, the stained glass artist, and is one of her own designs. The figure of the **Blessed Virgin** is surrounded by simple flower designs in a typically broad variety of pastel colours (a selection of Rutherford glass can be found at Hinderclay). There is a **priest's door** on this side and also the deeply recessed doorway to the medieval **vestry**. It is sheathed with leather, banded with iron, and has two locks. Churches were often used as safe deposits for their villages and you may have noticed that the vestry window outside is barred for extra security. The piscina in the **sanctuary** has been renewed, probably at the 1878 restoration when the chancel received a new **roof**. The terracotta **reredos** of 1883 is by George Tinworth (1843-1913). A craftsman of humble birth, he spent his whole working life with Doulton of Lambeth, and his talents were recognised by Ruskin, G.E. Street and others. His best known work is the reredos in St Stephen's chapel at York Minster, but all of it reflects his passionate sincerity and knowledge of the bible. Here we have a fairly conventional setting of the Last Supper, but the theme is 'Is it I?', and the figures of the disciples are full of urgency and puzzlement as they ask the question of the calm central figure. Only Judas turns away. As was his curious habit, Tinworth scratched in the names of all the figures and the relevant text reference in semi-illiterate lettering - strange contrast to the excellent modelling of the composition. The e. window contains fragments of medieval glass collected in a series of octagonal panels set in the main lights, and in the tracery there are angels and delicate designs in yellow stain. On the s. wall of the chancel is an elegant monument in marble to John Hunt who died in 1725. It has good lettering on the **touchstone** panel which is flanked by Ionic columns; a coloured **cartouche** of arms is on the **pediment** supported by delicate swags, and olive and palm fronds cross below within a curly frame. The chancel reading desk embodies two medieval bench ends and there are two more at the e. end of the choir stalls, as well as three panels of C15 work.

Wangford, St Denis (B2): Small and vulnerable in more ways than one, the church lies on the edge of Lakenheath air base, lonely among the heaths; a sure candidate for redundancy but for the fact that, by chance, it has fulfilled a need. It is now the Tabernacle Missionary Baptist church and is used regularly by a group of American Christians. It was originally **Norman** and both n. and s. doors are C12, with scalloped **capitals** on plain shafts and later arches. The C14 tower has angle buttresses to the w. and tall **Decorated** bell open-

ings. The **chancel** was pulled down in the C19 and subsequent restorations did not replace it. The e. window with its pretty C14 style **tracery** must, therefore, be modern. Inside, it is as plain and bare as any church could be and has a resigned dignity. The C19 pulpit and **altar** have been relegated to the tower and jostle the square C13 **font**, with its wide corner chamfers on bowl and shaft. A small niche by the n. door has an **ogee** arch and on the chancel n. wall there is a **brass** inscription for Dorothe Francklyn, with the shield of arms missing. She died in 1596 and was the sister of Sir Edward Coke, Queen Elizabeth's Attorney General. The e. wall carries early C19 boards with the Creed, **decalogue** and Lord's Prayer, and the modern **roof** has one set of **cusped arch-braces** on **colonnettes** to mark off part of the **nave** as a new chancel. Not an exciting building but be thankful that it is still used as the founders intended.

Wattisfield, St Margaret (F3): Judging by the shape of the small w. window and the interior arch, the tower must date from the end of the C13 or thereabouts. Unbuttressed, it has a **flush-work base course**, a large **Decorated** belfry window, and **Perpendicular** bell openings. There was a **scratch dial** on a **quoin** of the s.w. corner, just above the plinth, but little remains of it except the centre hole. The C15 s. **porch** (now the **vestry**) has a **knapped** flint face and the diagonal buttresses are decorated with crowned 'M's and monograms. The outer arch is picked out with thin red bricks and the top was extensively repaired in the C17 or C18 in brick. Above the arch a terracotta shield bearing remnants of the De La Pole coat of arms. Overhead is a stone sundial, unusually angled out from the wall. All the windows of the **nave** and **chancel** have Perpendicular **tracery** (much of it renewed), and you will see that the line of an earlier roof shows on the e. face of the tower. There is a **priest's door** on the n. side of the chancel. The n. porch is one of the few remaining examples in wood and probably dates from the C15 or early C16. The sides have been renewed in part, but the outer arch is formed from two large slabs of timber and simply moulded. Within the church, the tower arch is sharp and tall, with no **capitals**. The bowl of the C15 **font** carries blank shields and the shaft panels are decorated with window tracery. The C17 cover has a turned **finial** and the radiating ribs are carved with stylised eagle heads and scrolls. Both nave and chancel have modern, **scissors-braced** roofs and there is a heavy stone pulpit of 1888. The nearby window sill is lowered and may indicate that a side **altar** was positioned here before the **Reformation**. The stairs to the **rood loft** went up on the s. side of the nave and the doorway at the bottom still has its hinge pins. Parts of the old rood **screen** have been re-used in the front of the prayer desks and the lectern top. On the s. wall of the chancel, a memorial to Elizabeth Bury (d. 1746) has a graceful epitaph, typical of the 'age of elegance':

> ...Admit thee! to the chorus of the Blest,
> A willing traveller and a welcome Guest.

On the n. wall of the **sanctuary** is a small **touchstone** panel set in a plain alabaster frame. It is a C17 memorial to John Osborne, who sounds as though he was a local magistrate:

> A freind to vertue, A lover of learning,
> of prudence greate, of Justice a furtherer,
> Redress he did the wrongs of many a wight,
> Fatherless & widdowes by him possess their right,
> To search & trie each cause and end all strife
> With patience great he spent his mortal life.

> Whom blessed we accompt (as Scripture saith)
> Who peace did make & liv'd & died i'th' faith.

Westhorpe, St Margaret (F4): This small but interesting church stands attractively by the village street, with a yew tree close to the s. **porch**, and when I was there in the spring, primroses carpeted the churchyard. In 1419, Dame Elizabeth Elmham left money for work on the **aisles** and steeple. Like a number of others in the neighbourhood, two of the tower buttresses are at right angles, broadening the e. face; there are four **string courses** and one of them lifts up as a **label** over the **Perpendicular** w. window, while the parapet is set out in bold, flint and stone chequerwork. The n. aisle has Perpendicular windows and the C17 brick Barrow chapel projects on that side of the **chancel**; it has battlements, octagonal corner turrets, and the outline of a classical window in the e. wall. The chancel e. window has C19 **tracery**, and in the s. wall there is a **priest's door** and windows with **Decorated** tracery under deep labels. The window in the e. wall of the s. aisle is the same period but the design is unusually adventurous. The windows facing s. are Perpendicular, and when the porch was added in the C15, it was carelessly set out so that it encroaches on the window to the r. There is a niche over the outer arch and the early C14 entrance door has simple mouldings with **headstops**. To the r., a restored niche with a traceried head probably contained a **stoup**. The door itself is medieval, with surface tracery and closing ring.

Apart from work on the chancel in the 1890s, the interior was largely undisturbed in the C19 and has a homely intimacy. The floors are an attractively uneven mixture of bricks, medieval tiles and **ledger-stones**, and there is a C13 grave slab by the wall of the n. aisle, carved with the typical discoid cross and two omega signs.

By the tower arch is a C14 iron-bound chest with a domed lid, and propped up against the walls are C18 boards painted with the Lord's Prayer, Creed and **commandments**. The door to the tower stair is heavily banded with iron, a sign that the upper chamber was used as a secure store for village valuables. A small C17 **box pew**, whose only decoration is the turned corner **finials**, stands by the n. door, and on the n. wall is a set of **Royal Arms** that was re-used twice. They are lettered for George III and dated 1765, but cleaning has revealed the earlier initials of James II and Queen Anne. The plain octagonal **font** could be a C19 replacement but the cover is **Stuart**. The C15 **nave roof** is a lovely pale colour and the **tie-beams** alternate with **arch-braces** above a Perpendicular **clerestory** which has four windows each side. A large tablet is fixed to the **arcade** pillar opposite the door in memory of Nathaniel Fox, who died in 1679 - a plain **touchstone** epitaph within a marble frame, and a **cartouche** of arms at the top. Joined to it below is a smaller memorial for his sister Mary, who had died three years before. That has a marble skull and wreath underneath and there is a cherub head engraved on the panel, with this epitaph:

> Heavens Voyage Doth Not over hard appear,
> She tooke it in her Early Virgin year.

The pulpit warrants close attention because two of the panels contain Decorated tracery which make it, at least in part, one of the earliest in the county. The early C17 top cresting is in the style of chests of the period, and the rest is modern. To the r., a small door leads to the narrow **rood loft** stairs. The octagonal **piers** of the arcade originally had painted decoration and a section remains over the pulpit which shows a traceried and **crocketted** arch. There is also part of a C17 text above the s. door. In the wall of the s. aisle is a C14 recess which

has had a modern finial added to the arch. The grave slab below may well be that of Henry de Elmham who died in 1330. Beyond it is a fine example of a C14 **parclose screen**. The sturdy Decorated tracery is coloured green and red and consists of **mouchettes** within circles, resting on slender columns. Some of these are replacements but the originals are striped like barbers' poles in black and white. There are stencil patterns on the uprights, traces of colour on both sides of the base panels, and a **castellated** cornice to the w. The C14 **piscina** had its top entirely replaced in the C19 and two **screen** panels that hang on the e. wall were repainted with angels so that their original decoration is lost. In the n. aisle there is a board reminding us that it was to Westhorpe that Henry VIII's sister Mary Tudor came to live after she had married her second husband, Charles Brandon, Duke of Suffolk. She died at the manor house in 1533 but was buried in the abbey at Bury before resting finally in St Mary's church there. A piscina in the wall of the rood loft stairs shows that there was an **altar** at the e. end of the n. aisle but in the C17 the wall was removed to give access to the Barrow chapel. This has a heavy centre pendant to the roof timbers, and one of the original chancel windows remains unglazed on the r. There was an e. window initially but the space was taken up in 1666 by a large monument for Maurice Barrow. The back wall carries a Latin epitaph within a wreathed surround, with drapes held back by two overweight cherubs, while another pair support the family arms above a curved cornice. The object of it all reclines with fleshy head thrown back and hand to breast, and it is interesting that under the tasselled pillow there is the rolled straw mat that was a convention of monuments 100 years earlier. The whole thing was 'designed and begun by Maurice Shelton but he being sudanely snatched out of this world', it was finished by his brother Henry who was by that time Barrow's heir.

Moving into the chancel, note that the **capitals** of the arch were notched to hold the screen and that the stalls have their original front panelling and wide bookledges. On the n. wall is a small and late **brass** set in a wooden frame in memory of Richard Elcock, the 'pastor of the congregation', who died in 1630, and it has a pleasing epitaph in rhyme for 'This faithful, Learned, Humble Man of God...'. In the **sanctuary**, the altar carries a pre-**Reformation mensa**, complete with **consecration crosses**, and although the e. window is a replacement the shafts each side are original. To the l. is a fine monument for another member of the Barrow family, Sir William, who died in 1615. It has been well cleaned and his little alabaster figure dressed in armour has much of the original colour. He kneels opposite his two wives, Frances and Elizabeth, who are dressed in black and have curious flat headdresses that project beyond their foreheads. Their two children kneel behind and there are two tiny infants bearing skulls below the prayer desk (showing that they died early). On the s. side is an excellent C14 piscina with an **ogee trefoiled** arch and crocketted finial, and remains of arches either side of the **sedilia** show that they were once canopied. By the piscina on the e. wall is a small touchstone tablet framed in alabaster, with a coloured shield of arms for Maria Dandy who died in 1615.

Westley, St Mary (C4): A road swoops up the hill to the village from the s. and the little church from the top looks quite decorative from a distance. A very simple building, it was designed by William Ranger, the architect of Bury, St John. The **nave** has three stepped **lancets** at each end and the tower on the s.w. corner has **quatrefoils** in the middle stage lighting the **porch** within and pairs of lancets as bell openings. Ranger's eccentric

spire had to be removed in 1960 and was replaced by a red tile pyramid cap but a pencil drawing within shows what it was like. All the exterior was finished with Roman cement covered with **stucco** on which the various details were cast in imitation of stone, but this has weathered badly and is falling off in many places. The sandy-coloured interior is neat and simple and the boarded **roof** is supported by skeletal **arch-braces** rising to **king posts**, with open tracery. Under the ridge. They rest on little **hammerbeams** with octagonal pendants and are just the right weight for this size of building. Their apparent lightness is because they are cast iron - unusual material in a church but very popular in factory and railway architecture of the period. There is no **chancel** but the walls break back to form a shallow **sanctuary** at the e. end. On the w. wall is an uncoloured set of **Hanoverian Royal Arms** in plaster and a board states that the rebuilding provided an additional 75 seats, so the original must have been very small. The two-manual American organ is a nice period piece in good condition whose 'mouse-proof pedals', patented in 1887, are fascinating. Half way up the aisle is a large **ledger-stone** with a roundel of arms for William Brooks who died in 1795 and there are three more C18 stones in the **sanctuary**. These will have been transferred from the earlier church, like the boards painted with the **decalogue**, Creed and Lord's Prayer on the walls. The pulpit, more or less **Jacobean** in style, is a memorial for the two Westley men who died in World War I.

West Row: See Mildenhall, West Row (B3):

West Stow, St Mary (C4): This is a church that was heavily restored in the C19. It is beautifully situated in a churchyard that must be all of four acres and which is a nice conjunction of mown and wild areas. The C14 tower has chequerwork in the **base course** and on the buttresses, and the stair turret goes right to the top on the s. side. The windows on the s. side of the **nave** are Victorian, although the structure is basically C13. In the C14 **chancel**, a **string course** picks up the line of the window arches and continues round the corner buttresses. The four-**light** e. window has attractive **reticulated tracery** and there are C15 windows on the n. side of the nave, and one of the original C13 **lancets**. The **vestry** was added in 1903 to commemorate the reign of Queen Victoria, and if you look through the window you will be able to see the early **Norman** n. door, with the heavy roll moulding of its arch standing on rudimentary volute **capitals**. Through the C14 s. **porch**, and to the l. is the plain **font**, with blank shields in the panels. The cover is a very stolid Victorian design, with tall, gabled, blind windows giving the impression of an octagonal chapel topped by an over-large **finial**. The tower arch is tall and narrow and above it is a **sanctus-bell window**. There are fragments of medieval glass in the w. window, and high on the inner n. wall of the tower are two finely lettered tablets for a pair of John Edwardses who died in 1758 and 1775. I think it highly likely that they were cut by the same mason who provided the tablet for Robert Rushbrooke in Honington church. Roofs and fittings are all C19 but there is a **brass** placed in the most inconvenient position possible under the pulpit. It is a Latin inscription commemorating the priest William Boyce who died in 1591:

> ...born in Halifax, educated at Cambridge, preached in Suffolk. His heart stopped and now the grave holds his body and Christ his soul.

The Victorian chancel **roof** has rather fine and tall figures on the **wall posts**. They are a little difficult to see, but one angel on the s. side holds a chalice and one on the n. a ciborium. There is an **aumbry** with a modern door in the n. wall and opposite, a good C14 **angle piscina** with its gables and pinnacles heavily **crocketted**. The shallow stone **credence shelf** is unusual, having a band of leaf ornament under the edge, with a beast mask in the centre. The 1852 glass in the e. window is by **Ward & Hughes**; the four panels of Christ's miracles are brightly coloured but do not inspire.

Wetherden, St Mary (E5): This church is beautifully placed. A screen of huge limes laps the churchyard to the w. and s., while the land drops away at the e. end. The recently restored tower is early C14 and the w. door is flanked by **ogee**-headed niches under square **labels**, with a smaller version above the arch. There are **lancet**belfry windows, **Decorated tracery** in the bell openings, and the attractive w. window has three ogee-headed **lights** with a little **transom** over the centre one. The s. **aisle** is lavish and the w. end of it forms the **porch**. You will see that the fabric of the porch and the next bay differs from the rest in having a rough pattern of stone blocks. This shows that although the work was begun by Richard II's Chief Justice, Sir John Sulyard, in the 1480s, the w. end was completed by his widow's second husband Sir Thomas Bourchier, a fact confirmed by the central position of his arms over the s. door. The **base course** has a whole series of heraldic shields set in deep-cut tracery, the buttress to the r. of the doorway is carved with a pot of lilies in honour of the **Blessed Virgin**, and there is a well-defined **scratch dial** on a buttress further along. Like the tower, the **chancel** is in the Decorated style, with **reticulated** tracery in the e. window which has a little niche over it. The corner buttresses are angled and their gables are finely traceried.

Attached to the n. side of the chancel is a tiny **sacristy** under a lean-to roof and its miniscule lancet is a mere 2 in wide. A faint mark on the n. wall of the **nave** betrays the site of the **rood loft** stair and the sloping brick buttresses look like an C18 effort to combat structural weakness on that side.

Entry is via a low C14 doorway and within, the C15 **roofs** are outstanding. The nave has double **hammerbeams**, but note that the upper range is false and the stress is taken by **arch-braces** that rise from the back of the hammerbeams. The posts drop down to form pendants and carry finely carved C19 standing figures. This roof is rather dark but that in the s. aisle is both lighter in colour and better lit and is beautiful. The inner rafters are cranked to form a ceiling and a line of shields with the Sulyard arms forms **bosses** down the centre. All the main timbers are crested and carved in a variety of forms, and large demi-angels lift their wings at the base of the **wall posts**. The chapel at the e. end of the aisle is approached through an arch which has an angel **corbel** on the s. and a small human head on the n. A helm with a scrolled shield hangs nearby. Backing on to the chancel arch is the table tomb of Sir John Sulyard who died in 1574. His **achievement** is framed between alabaster **Corinthian** columns under a plain **pediment** and there is a line of four mutilated little figures kneeling above the heavy slab. Its bevelled edge has a finely cut inscription but note that the final words have been roughly chiselled away. They were 'Cujus animae misereatur Deus' (On whose soul may God have mercy) until **William Dowsing** came this way. He had a field day here on 5 February 1643 when he broke 100 'superstitious pictures' in this aisle alone - probably mainly stained glass in the windows. Having removed 'superstitious inscriptions' and 65 lbs of brass, he was short of time and left orders for 68 cherubim and 60 more idolatrous pictures to be removed and the steps

of the chancel to be levelled. He no doubt slept soundly, conscious of having done a good day's work. The C15 **font** has ogee arches in the bowl panels, within which are four large **paterae** and four shields - the crowns of East Anglia, a cross fleury, three small **Tudor roses**, and three scallop shells. There are large heads at the angles below the bowl and the **Jacobean** cover is a plain pyramid with a **castellated** rim. Overhead you will see a small and plain **sanctus-bell window** high in the tower wall. There is a good range of C15 benches on the n. side of the nave with **poppyheads** and traceried ends with grotesques on the elbows. N. of the font a bench has a **unicorn** at each end although they have lost their horns. Further e. there is a pair of squirrels eating nuts and by the wall a fox with a goose in his mouth. All the benches on the s. side, like the front four ranges on the n., are good C19 replicas. There are two suites of C18 painted deal **box pews** in the s. aisle and some more C19 benches. Although the pulpit is Victorian it incorporates medieval panelling with two ranges of tracery. The organ is at the w. end and this leaves the short chancel nicely uncluttered. An archway matching the **Perpendicular** nave **arcade** connects it with the s. aisle chapel. The roof is a hammerbeam again, with **king posts** above the arch-braces and standing figures under canopies on the wall posts. The stone corbels on which they stand are modern and one wonders whether the whole roof was reconstructed as part of the 1860s restoration. Beyond the door to the sacristy on the n. side of the **sanctuary** is an excellent example of a small **Easter sepulchre**, with a shallow, **cusped** ogee under a pointed arch. The e. window is flanked by a pair of image niches under **crocketted** ogee arches with **finials** and pinnacles. The sill of the window is lowered and no doubt contained a **retable** originally. The C14 **piscina** on the s. side has a large finial and there is one **headstop** on the cusped ogee arch.

Within it is an original wooden **credence shelf**, and to the r., **dropped-sill sedilia** with a single stone armrest. The 1860s e. window glass by **Henry Hughes** (of **Ward & Hughes**) is uninspired, with four large figures in the main lights, but in the tracery above there are some interesting medieval fragments. These include a large group of kneeling figures, two angels, and a C14 seated figure. The church's only remaining **brass** has been (I think) relaid in the centre of the chancel floor. It is for John Daniell (1584) and has four shields (his own, his wife's and for some odd reason those of his sons-in-law) and a rather good verse. There is more heraldry in the form of **hatchments**: s. aisle, w. wall bottom, Elizabeth Crawford (1828); w. wall, top, Dorothy Sulyard (1830); s. aisle, w. end, her husband Edward (1799); s. aisle, centre, their daughter Lucy Smythe (1830). So the family that built the aisle were still marking their presence there nearly 400 years later.

Whepstead, St Petronilla (C5): This church carries a unique dedication and brief details of the obscure Roman maiden **St Petronilla** will be found in the Glossary. A curving line of yews leads across to the late C15 tower which has a very odd shape. Its upper stage was taken down and awkwardly rebuilt a heavy stair turret is set in the angle of the s.e. buttress and the tower is cut short just above it, topped by later battlements. There are three small niches around the **Perpendicular** window above the w. door. A repair date of 1582 is cut high in the face of the s.e. buttress and until 1658 there was a spire, but it fell in the great storm on the night that Cromwell died. The **nave** and **chancel** are late C13, with windows using **plate** and 'Y' **tracery**, and an older and much higher roof line can be seen on the face of the tower. The chancel e. window has intersected 'Y' tracery, there is a **priest's door** to the s. with

one lion **headstop**, and in the C19 a **vestry** was built against the old n. door. Entry is via a C19 s. **porch** and the **dripstone** of the arch of the inner door has curled stops. To the r. is the remnant of a small **stoup**. Just inside is a small Victorian **font** and an open ringers' **gallery** is set within the tower. Beyond, the w. window is filled with striking glass by the **Powells** (about 1910?) - a dense design of interlaced panels illustrating the ark and its creatures, with a beautiful deep blue predominating. Like the benches, the roofs with their coved ceilings are modern, and in the chancel the ribs have been smartly picked out in red. As part of a C19 restoration the wide chancel arch was rebuilt in **Norman** fashion with bold **chevron moulding**, and this is in keeping with the **jambs** which are genuine Norman, their corners having small attached shafts on both sides. No **rood screen** remains but the steps leading to the vanished loft rise up steeply in the window embrasure in the s. wall and they continue through an archway to finish at a very small opening. Simple **piscinas** are sometimes found in window sills (there is one by the pulpit on the n. side) but to find one cut in a step of the rood stair, as here, is very unusual. Before the **Reformation** the church had a tabernacle of **St Thomas** and burned a light before a statue of **St Margaret** and the two piscinas are likely to have served **altars** dedicated to these saints. The pulpit is modern but it makes use of two late C16 panels. They have blind arches with better than average scroll carving, and marquetry is a feature of the **pilasters** and edging. The panels came from Plumpton House in the parish and may have formed part of an overmantel or the front of a chest. The window on the s. contains six C19 sets of arms with decorative mantling of local families including the Drurys. In the chancel on the n. side a window has 1924 glass by F.C. Eden with figures of St Petronilla and **St Peter** (there is more of his work at

Clare and Hengrave). The window opposite contains two tiny medieval heads at the top, three roundels with fragments, and a C17 continental roundel in yellow stain of **St Anthony**. On the s. wall there is a plain tablet flanked by **touchstone Corinthian** columns, with an **achievement of arms** above and stiff scroll and shell decoration below; it is by Matthew Wharton Johnson, whose rather undistinguished work is found in many churches. Here it commemorates General Sir Francis Hammond who died in 1850, having been George IV's first equerry and his Clerk Marshall of the Royal Stables, a resounding title if nothing else. The piscina in the **sanctuary** stands within a **Decorated** arch which has had its **cusping** cut away. The dado of blind arches on the walls is apparently C17 work. Above it on the n. wall is a touchstone and alabaster tablet for John Ryley (1672) whose inscription is a diverting mixture of wayward lettering styles. The 1908 glass in the e. window is by **James Powell & Sons** and it is a good Nativity scene spread across three **lights**. There are singing angels below the canopies and the colours are pleasing, but the vapid **Annunciation** in the bottom centre panel lets the rest down. As you leave, have a look at the C17 embroidered chalice veil framed on the s. wall of the nave and note how neatly the modern organ case has been placed over the n. door.

Wickhambrook, All Saints (B6): In a scattered village with a deceptive pattern of lanes, the church when found stands handsomely in a broad and open churchyard. Most of what can be seen is C14 but the n. **aisle** chapel that extends halfway along the **chancel** has flintwork in its e. wall that is apparently pre-Conquest, a sign that the first small building was sited there. Another clue to the church's antiquity is the little **Saxon** figure (now protected by a glass panel)

which was later built into the s.w. corner of the s. aisle. The tower has a deep **ashlar base course**, chequer battlements, a very tall and thin **Decorated** w. window, and a square turret to the s. The early C14 chancel windows have particularly attractive **tracery**, with a sexfoil in the head of the e. window and the four-petalled flower motif at the sides. There is a small **priest's door** to the s. and over the **Perpendicular** side windows of the s. aisle there are later brick battlements. The C14 n. **porch** is now plastered, and within is a very worn C13 doorway with deep mouldings edged with **dogtooth**. The side shafts have gone. Propped on the window ledge is a fine little tombstone of 1693 for Ruth Partridge, the vicar's daughter, who married a mercer - rustic swags down the sides and a curved, wavy-edged surface.

Passing the huge **stoup** by the door, one enters an interior that shows in many ways how the church was continuously altered during the C14 and C15. Although not large, it has a wide and open look, and on the n. side of the n. **arcade** there is the most curious beginning of a transverse arch. It has been suggested that this was planned as a new chancel arch on the axis of the first small building, but it may have been that a new n.e. chapel was planned but never completed when the **nave** arcades were built. The heavy C13 **font** on a modern shaft by the entrance was moved from the s. aisle in the 1950s and has a curious shape - octagonal, with triangular projections on four faces (**Cautley** thought that it had originally been square). In the n. chapel (connected by a low **Tudor** arch to the chancel) there is a lovely C13 **piscina**, its diminutive arch embellished with two bands of dogtooth, one inside and one outside the narrow moulding. The **rood stair** goes up from the chapel and note that there are two doorways at the top, showing that it led not only to the loft over the chancel **screen** but also to a **parclose screen** in the chapel. In the s. aisle at the e. end one can see where the piscina arch was lowered to allow the large C15 window to be inserted above it; the e. window here dates from about 1300. The tower arch is beautifully proportioned, tall and deeply moulded, and the arches of the nave arcade have rather unusual **hood moulds** on the n. side with mutilated stops. Overhead, the C14 **roof** was replaced by a late example of a **hammerbeam** design of the early C17. There is openwork arches above the hammers and **spandrels**, and it was stained black in an 1860s restoration - all of which gives it a leggy appearance against the white ceilings. Wickhambrook was an extreme example of C17 and C18 revolt against altar-centred worship; the parish placed a **three-decker pulpit** at the w. end and turned all the pews round so that the chancel was ignored. All was reversed in the 1860s and in 1886 came the splendidly uninhibited brass lectern. The chancel roof was heightened in the C18 and altered again later, so that the squared-off ceiling above the **archbraces** now makes the e. window look too small. There is no screen and it is a pleasant change to explore a chancel where the Victorians did not play around with the floor levels. The **sanctuary** has a set of C18 **communion rails** with close-set **balusters**, and on the n. wall is a small-scale and neatly executed 1630s monument in alabaster and veined marble for Mirable Cradock. In the s.e. corner is something much more grand - the tomb sculpted by **Nicholas Stone** for Sir Thomas Higham, with an alabaster reclining figure of the old man, noble in countenance, curly headed and with a spade beard. The epitaph on two large **touchstone** panels is a potted biography of this 'Gentillman of Ancient Desent' who fought under Essex for Queen Elizabeth at Rouen and slew Sir Edward Stanley in single combat in the Irish rebellion. He came back here to die in contented retirement in 1630. Further along in the s.

wall is a grilled recess which contains an excellent **brass** for Thomas Burrough, Elizabeth and Bridget his wives, and two groups of children behind their respective mothers. He died in 1597 and is soberly dressed, although the ladies display Paris caps and brocaded petticoats. One of the three shields has mantling and much of the original enamelling has survived.

Withersfield, St Mary (A6): Attractively sited in a village very close to the Cambridgeshire boundary, the church has a plain C15 tower with an octagonal turret at the s.e. corner. Its battlemented top rises above the parapet, a feature of a number of churches in this corner of the county. There is a yawning **gargoyle** on that side and the **Perpendicular** w. window has been renewed. The s. **aisle** with its **porch** was added in 1867 and the **chancel** rebuilt, so that the frontage to the road is very trim, with lots of **septaria** showing in the walls and heavy battlements to aisle and **nave**. The n. side has a much more subdued **stucco** finish and there is a blocked **Tudor** n. door. Within the porch, the large Tudor s. doorway (re-used at the rebuilding) is decorated with **fleurons** in the mouldings and has **tracery** in the **spandrels**; above it is a battered C14 niche. The door handle is a survivor from an earlier church C13, with a large pierced plate and an oval ring on which are riveted two lizards, those ancient symbols of good fortune that can also be found at Great Thurlow and Brockley. Just within is a **stoup** formed out of half of a **Decorated capital** that was probably saved from the original late C13 or early C14 **arcade**. There are pleasant brick and **pamment** floors and the **font** is an unusually late example from the C17, with three traceried panels and five shields of arms. The dark nave **roof** has false **hammerbeams** and bulky, roughly shaped **tie- beams** which conceal steelwork that was inserted in 1983 and which now takes the strain. Two of the hammers have the remains of small figures, and initials, together with the name of the firm that carried out the restoration, are carved on the n. **wall plate** above the **clerestory**. In contrast, the n. aisle roof is beautifully pale, with **archbraces** rising from **wall posts**, centre **bosses**, and heavily moulded timbers. Here again there was a total reconstruction in 1974 and it was excellently done. On the wall in the n.e. corner there is a **brass** inscription which asks us to pray for the soul of Robert Wyburgh who built the aisle in 1480. The 1970s glass in the aisle e. window is by Pippa Heskett - a figure of **St Cecilia**. The C15 n. arcade, with its **quatrefoil piers**, was faithfully copied on the s. side when the C19 aisle was added. In the n.e. clerestory window you will see a **Trinity** shield. There are two differing sets of medieval benches and those on the n. have square ends with shallow buttresses. The s. range is excellent, with **paterae** on the chamfers of the shaped ends and exceptionally large **poppyheads**. At the w. end **St Michael** is weighing souls, and an arm reaches up trying to redress the balance. At the e. end there is a very vigorous **St George** who is much smaller than the dragon he is trampling; and in between you will find a **pelican** and her young, two creatures rising from a mass of vine, a collared swan, and a long-haired mermaid with her scaly bottom half just visible. The early C17 pulpit has two ranks of blind arches with coarse, shallow carving and stands on a wooden base. **Dowsing** was here in January 1643: 'we brake down a crucifix and sixty superstitious pictures' is the quote from his journal and he was probably referring to the **rood** and stained glass. The blocked C14 door to the **rood loft** is at the end of the s. aisle, and above the remains of a Decorated niche to the r. of the **screen** there is a fragment of what was the upper door. The C15 screen, with its original heavy doors, has deep, Per-

Withersfield, St Mary: St George and the dragon

pendicular tracery and a double-**ogee** centre arch. The panel spandrels are carved with hogs, bearded heads in curly caps, birds and fish. It is a nice piece, despite a modern recolouring that ignored the basic medieval rules, and despite the addition of non-period frontal decoration, **cusps** and **crockets**. Nearby in the nave is the church's second brass - a shield and inscription for Joan Bury who died in 1579.

Wixoe, St Leonard (B7): This small church was heavily restored in the late C19, but is not without interest. The doorways and the coursed flintwork in the walls show that the building is **Norman** and originally there was an **apse** at the e. end. The plain n. door is blocked and a n.e. **vestry** was added by the Victorians, together with two prominent chimneys on that

224 THE POPULAR GUIDE

side and the s. porch. The large, weatherboarded bell turret is in the Essex tradition, and there is a **priest's door** on the s. side of the **chancel**. The s. doorway is good Norman work - single shafts with scalloped **capitals**, and an arch decorated with a band of **chevrons** and bobbins. To the l. of the door within, there is a plain octagonal C14 **font** and a **stoup** to the r. The **nave roof** is open waggon construction with two **tie-beams** and **king posts**. Below, the C19 pews have small **poppyheads** and **linen-fold** on the ends. All the windows are replacements and the 1890s e. window glass is by Cakebread, Robey & Co of Stoke Newington - the only example of their work in West Suffolk. It is an Ascension, with musical angels in the **tracery** and although conventional, the grouping of figures and quality of colour is excellent. On the n. wall of the **sanctuary** is a memorial to Samuel Berkeley who died in 1764 - a plain tablet beneath a broken **pediment** and flanked by swags. To the w., Henry and Dorothy Berkeley have as their monument a flat obelisk against a grey background, with a **cartouche** and two flaming urns on top. A grisly winged skull is carved in the panel below, and in the centre of the chancel floor their vault is marked with curiously precise dimensions. On the s. chancel wall is a plain little tablet by Denman of Regent Street for Josias Nottidge (1844) and the memorial for William and Elizabeth Payne (1843 and 1881) on the s. wall of the nave is by Harding of Ballingdon - plain, with a mushily draped urn on top.

Woolpit, St Mary (E5): This relatively small church is rich in ornament and was highly favoured by the abbey of St Edmundsbury in whose hands it was from before the Norman Conquest until the dissolution of the monasteries. There is no trace of the earlier buildings and the s. **aisle** is early C14 with a later brick parapet. The battlemented **chancel** is of the

same period and the **priest's door** on the s. side has shafts with round **capitals**. The corner buttresses have large niches with **ogee** tops, the e. window tracery is **reticulated**, and there is an C18 lean-to vestry on the n. side. The **nave** is mid-C15 and has a lavish **clerestory**, with panel tracery in the two-**light** windows, linked by bands of **flushwork** emblems and monograms. The n. aisle is simpler and was built in the early years of the C16. In 1702 a gale brought down much of the C14 tower and spire and it was repaired only to be devastated by lightning in 1852. This time a completely new one was designed by **R.M. Phipson** in the Fenland **Perpendicular** style and it is interesting to compare it with the Great Finborough tower and spire not far away that he built 20 years later. Below the deep openwork parapet is a boldly lettered text, and from behind tall corner pinnacles delicately curved and pierced flying buttresses support the stone spire which is set well back and provided with two ranges of windows. The stone s. **porch** is glorious, and of all the C15 examples in the county **Cautley** thought it was the best, and went so far as to say that its proportions and detail surpassed Northleach in Gloucestershire, making it the finest of its type in England. It towers above the s. aisle and the s. face is panelled throughout in **ashlar**. The mouldings of the outer arch are enriched by lion masks with leaves rather than tongues lolling from their mouths, and above shields bearing the three crowns of East Anglia there are triple niches flanked by another, larger pair with flattened pinnacles above double ogee arches. These once housed statues of Henry VI and his tigress of a queen. The angle buttresses are unusually distinguished by having image stools set on the gables at three levels and the openwork parapet is reminiscent of Pulham, St Mary, in Norfolk. The side windows match the

Woolpit, St Mary, porch

Woolpit, St Mary: double hammerbeam roof and celure

entrance arch and the whole of the e. wall is faced with high quality chequerwork in flint and stone. The inside of the porch is equally impressive and the vaulting **bosses** are carved with an angel, masks, and foliage. The inner doorway has a **crocketted** ogee arch, its mouldings enriched to match the entrance. The porch was a long time in the building (from 1430 to 1473 when the images were provided for the niches) and it is worth searching for the merchant's marks of three men who helped to pay for it: John Turnour's is scratched on the stone just inside the entrance arch on the r., John Stevyenson's is in the corner to the r. of the inner door, and Johannes Regnold's is to be found in the l. hand moulding of the inner doorway and has a heart at the bottom containing his initials.

After such an introduction the church's interior is no anti-climax, for it has an outstanding double **hammerbeam roof** built in 1440-1450, pale in colour and with a profusion of decoration that makes it very lively. There are deep **wall posts** with crocketted and pinnacled canopies over figures of bishops, kings and saints; below them are demi-angels bearing emblems and there are more on the ends of the hammers. All the main timbers are crested, tiny angels perch above the collar beams under the ridge, and the deep, double **wall-plates** are studded with yet more of them. Woolpit was Suffolk's C19 master woodworker **Henry Ringham's** first important commission; in 1844 he completely restored this roof and carved new angels to replace those destroyed by **Dowsing's** deputy in 1644. With the exception of the one holding an organ at the w. end, I think they are all Ringham's work and he replaced some of the heads of the standing figures. There is a three-light window in the e. gable and below it is a very intriguing construction. It con-

sists of five bays of delicately ribbed coving on shafts that rise from minia-ture demi-angels. The cornice is neat-ly mitred into the hammerbeams each side and Cautley was convinced that it was an integral part of the C15 design, forming a **canopy of honour** over the rood. Another authority believed it to be a portion of the old **rood loft**, but it was apparently installed in the 1870s and is likely to have come from another church. The C19 texts and sharp blue background colour are not congenial and tend to emphasize its alien nature. The **arch-braces** of the aisle roofs come down to wall posts on each side bearing fig-ures in the canopied niches. Ringham carved angels for them which match those in the nave and at this level they seem overlarge. The centre rafters between the arch-braces are carved with pairs of recumbent angels, head to head with wings folded - a beauti-ful concept. The wall plates and cen-tre beams are richly crested. The narrow aisles were designed as proc-essional ways and the fine medieval benches were arranged in two main blocks reaching just beyond the **arcades**. They have **poppyheads**, tra-ceried ends, carved backs, and gro-tesques on the elbows. On the n. side at the w. end is a pair of **ibex**, further along are dogs with geese in their mouths, and a pair of **griffins**. On the s. side at the w. end there is a chained monkey and another dressed as a seated monk. Ringham carved the front six rows and in doing so dupli-cated some of the original animals. He presumably also carved the fine pulp-it on its tall granite pedestal.

In the Middle Ages there were **guilds** of the **Holy Trinity** and the Nativity of the Virgin, and a shrine dedicated to 'Our Lady of Woolpit' attracted many pilgrims. It is possible that this was in the s. aisle where there is a very open C14 **piscina** under a **cinquefoiled** arch across the angle of the window embrasure. On the ledge of the **sedilia** next to it there stands part of the square shaft of a preaching cross, with remains of figures on three sides and a recognisable Calvary on the fourth. To the l., the outline of the rood loft stairs can be seen, with a little **quatrefoil** window half way up, and the bottom doorway is around the corner by the **screen**. Just in front of it stands the handsome, C16 lectern with that buttery texture and patina that brass achieves with age. Traditionally supposed to have been the gift of Queen Elizabeth when she visited the church, the base is supported on three dumpy lions and, as is often the case, the eagle's claws are missing. Others like it may be found at Cavendish, Upwell in Norfolk, and Corpus Christi College in Oxford. The main lights of the C15 rood screen have **cusped** and crocketted ogee arches with open tracery above them and there are patches of the original **gesso** decoration on the **mullions**. The bottom panels were repainted in the C19 and from l. to r. the figures are: **Saints Withberga, Felix, Mary Magdalene, Peter, Paul,** the **Blessed Virgin** and Child, **St Edmund** and **St Etheldreda**. All repeat the original subjects except St Felix who supplanted **St John the Baptist**. The entrance gates are early C17 and have a line of shaped splats below turned **balusters**, with damaged strapwork cresting the top rails. The top of the screen was altered and dated in 1750. The benches in the chancel are unlike those in the nave and have quite massive ends which are over 4 in thick. There are **green man** masks worked into the carving of three of the poppyheads and there is a seated figure on a buttress of the priest's stall. There is a collared ibex on the n. side and at the e. end of the s. range is a very interesting group of figures. Although the main figure is headless, a pot of lilies identifies her as the Blessed Virgin and there are two more women in the background. In the **sanctuary** the late C13 or early C14 double piscina is set within rough twin **lancets** and has a stone **credence shelf**. The e. window has

shafts each side and note that although one capital is conventionally carved with stiff leaf, the other has two little crawling beasts. The glass was restored and rearranged in the 1970s and there is a fine Virgin and Child panel in the centre, with modern roundels and shields in the rest of the main lights. The tracery contains a lovely set of medieval **Evangelistic symbols**, two angels blowing long trumpets, and three more standing on wheels. There are C15 fragments in the s. chancel windows and in the top of the n. window are four small early C19 figures of **Saints Andrew**, Paul, **John** and **Luke**. On your way out, pause to examine the remains of a stone **woodwose** on the window sill in the n. aisle and note that the unusual C14 circular **sanctus-bell window** was re-set in the tower wall.

Wordwell, All Saints (C3): With only a house and a farm for company, this little church lies by the side of the Bury to Elveden road and is now in the care of the **Redundant Churches Fund**. Prior to a restoration in 1827 it had been used as a granary, and in 1857 **Samuel Saunders Teulon** directed another refurbishment, but with the declared intention of saving all features of interest; twin buttresses were placed against the w. face of the **nave**, flanking a narrow **lancet**, and a double bellcote was added. Further work was done in 1866 with less consideration and a C17 pulpit was removed amongst other things. The building is basically early C12, as indicated by the regular coursing of the rubble walls on the n. side, where there is an unrestored doorway with plain arch and volute **capitals** to the columns. The **chancel** windows are C19 and the e. window has curious decoration round the arch, alternating triangles of dressed flint and **ashlar**. There is a **priest's door** on the s. side and the vestige of a **scratch dial** can just be seen on the s.e. angle of the nave. The wooden **porch**, designed

Wordwell, All Saints: bench back

by Teulon, stands on a flint and stone base. The **Norman** entrance doorway has a fine, unrestored **tympanum** carved with the Tree of Life, whose branches divide in the centre and become an interlace design; two hounds bay at the base of the tree, and their tails intertwine with the foliage. At the top of the r. hand **jamb** is a tiny carved figure of a man with his arms raised and, on entering, you will see that there is a larger version of him in the tympanum which, for some reason, faces inwards over the blocked n. door. There, the figure is accompanied by another holding a ring. The carving is much more primitive than the Tree of Life design and it may be pagan. Its meaning is a matter for conjecture, although the Sacrament of Marriage or Christ giving benediction to someone holding the crown of thorns have been suggested. The early C12 **font** is a simple, plain drum rest-

ing on a central shaft and three rough supports, with worn heads below the bowl. The benches in the nave have large, nicely varied **poppyheads** and good blank **tracery** on the ends. Some of the grotesques on the elbows are in good condition (the one nearest the pulpit, for example) but there are replacements at the w. end on the n. side - the dog and the whole of the next bench end. The best piece of carving is on the back of the bench by the door where there are three dragons, a jester emerging from a conch shell, and an animal with a bearded human head. The small bench below the w. window incorporates an end which dates from about 1400, and there is a nicely carved dog with its head down on the elbow - another like it can be seen on a similar bench by the n. door. The prayer desk by the chancel arch is of the same period; one of its poppyheads is in the form of a bird and there is another example in the chancel where the stalls have some medieval tracery with birds in the **spandrels**. The C19 semi-circular stone replacement pulpit is quite awful, but the Norman chancel arch has a big roll moulding on the w. side, volute capitals matching the doors, and chip-carved **imposts**. Either side are large early C14 niches which will have had **altars** below them, and the simple double **piscina** for the altar on the s. side may be found in the window sill nearby.

Worlington, All Saints (B3): Church Lane is a cul-de-sac and the church is at the far end, n. of the village street. The base of the tower is C13, judging by the **quoins**, but the rest is C14, with **ogee**-headed niches either side of a deeply moulded w. door. The w. window has pleasing **Decorated** flowing **tracery** and above it, a small **quatrefoil** belfry window, as at nearby Tuddenham and Icklingham, All Saints. On the n. side of the tower the filled-in **put-log holes** show up clearly. Although the C15 **nave** has a **clerestory** on both sides, there was evidently no call for a n. **aisle**. The C13 n. door was blocked up early this century and the westernmost nave window is modern, probably part of the 1897 restoration. The whole of the n. nave has recently been brutally cement rendered, with the added blemish of a crudely executed signature and date. There is a **sanctus-bell turret** on the nave gable, although its bell is now in the museum at Bury. The iron stay and ring fixed to the wall below can only have been a rope guide and, as such, is a most unusual survival which may have been associated with the use of the blocked double **low side window** to the l. of the **priest's door** in the s. wall of the late C13 **chancel**. That can be seen from inside the church and was an extension below the window as it exists now. The priest's door was renewed in the C19 and the niche below the corner of the nave roof looks like new work, although it may have replaced some-

thing similar. There are good C18 gravestones on this side of the church, and under the holly bush by the path to the priest's door is the base and socket of a medieval **preaching cross**. At some time a **scratch dial** has been re-used as a quoin on the s.e. corner of the aisle (upside down and about 8 ft from the ground). The C18 **porch** in yellow brick is plain except for a stylish variation on the w. side where there are blind circular and arched recesses, one of which has been used for a memorial tablet. Inside the porch to the r. of the C13 doorway is a deep niche with three very worn heads underneath, and the stone seat is cut away below leaving a space where the **stoup** stood. Apart from a new applied frame, the door is medieval and retains its original closing ring.

Though small, the interior is pleasing and full of interest. The early C14 octagonal **arcade piers**, standing on earlier bases, have concave sides with **trefoil** decoration at the top (like Walsham-le-Willows). They warrant a closer look because they carry medieval graffiti of exceptional importance. Apart from compass exercises and initials of all periods, on the pillar nearest the door there are three shields clearly incised. The largest is 9 in tall and has a lion rampant within a border. It is a very early example of an armorial shield and may have been borne by a member of the Gourney family who held **Norman** manors in Norfolk and Suffolk. The other two shields are similar and are versions of the arms of the Crusaders' kingdom of Jerusalem. In addition, there is a cross with a sharpened base which may represent the wooden cross that Crusaders carried and thrust into the ground wherever they stopped. Taken together, these faint outlines could be a villager's memory of his own journeying on crusade, but it is at least possible that this small church was the meeting place of a group of knights before they set out to join Richard the Lionheart on the Third

Crusade in 1190. If so, the stones will have been salvaged from the original arcade and used again. In the s.w. corner, the **vestry** is formed as a continuation of the s. aisle (an unusual position) and, judging by the slit windows, it was originally two-storied. The door is medieval and among the graffiti on the r. hand **jamb** the name of the C15 rector Simon Bagot can just be discerned. Another rector's name was more widely known in the late C17; Erasmus Warren published at least eight books. These included the texts of sermons he preached in Norwich cathedral in 1684 under the titles *Divine Rules* and *The End of Christ's Advent*. The **font** is probably early and appears to have been reshaped, with rudimentary columns cut on the corner chamfers matching four shafts below. Its base is attached to the arcade pier and there is an interesting survival built into the arch above - a pulley block carved in the shape of a hand to house the rope used for raising the cover. The present oak cover is modern.

An unusual addition to the church furniture is an **Act of Parliament clock** on the w. wall, given in the 1920s by a local landlord. The C14 bench ends in the s. aisle are square topped, with simple designs carved in the solid, three stepped **lancets** on some and large roses on others. The s. aisle chapel **altar** is a simple C17 table with carved top rail, and to the r., a very plain little **piscina**. The nave roof was restored in 1926 to the original C15 design and much of the old timber was retained. It has plain **hammerbeams** alternating with **tie-beams** which each support six tall posts, giving the whole a very open appearance. When **roods** were banned in the C16, both loft and beam were generally removed, but here the beam remains, set across the chancel arch. It is cambered and deeply moulded, and the rood, with its attendant figures and backing, will have taken up the whole of the top of the arch. Since 1973 the beam has carried a small

misshapen cross carved from bog oak which might well have deep significance but which is quite wrong and out of scale in its present position. The accompanying loft has gone but the access doorway and stairs were rediscovered in the n. wall in 1901. Opposite, on the s. aisle, the **capitals** and arch of the arcade have been deeply notched and there is likely to have been a **parclose screen** round the s. aisle chapel. The C17 octagonal pulpit, complete with stem, has simple gouge carving in the small upper panels. The short **Early English** chancel still has its battlemented **wallplates** but the ceiling was plastered, probably in the C18. There is a lancet in the n. wall set in a deep splay, and roundels and fragments of C14 glass are set in **quarries** decorated with cross motifs. The window just beyond the chancel arch on the s. side has curiously crushed Decorated tracery, and the form of the low side window can be seen at the bottom. The Early English e. window of three stepped lancets within one arch has 1909 glass by J. Dudley Forsyth. He was an apprentice of **Henry Holiday** and other work by him can be found at Mildenhall, West Row and Culford. This is a 'Suffer little children...' composition in dark and rather muddy colours, with grey flesh tints and steely canopy work. On the n. wall of the **sanctuary** is a plain tablet, white on grey, by Robert de Carle of Bury for James Gibson, aged 33 and rector here until 1850. How much nicer is the petite and elegant memorial opposite of 1738 to Martha Sankey - a shaped tablet with pendant pomegranate, and a pyramid over and flaming torch on top. Back in the nave, note the fragments of C14 wall paintings; above the pulpit there is a band of alternating **Tudor roses** and **sacred monograms**, and in a n. window embrasure, a **crocketted finial** in dark red and black. Nearby is a **brass** inscription for John Mortlock who, in 1620, bequeathed 30 shillings a year to the poor of the parish. To the w., the 1830s memorial to the Rev Sir William Henry Cooper is by Humphrey Hopper, a very competent London sculptor, particularly on small designs. This, in white marble on black, has a book, palm and cross above the tablet, an enamelled heraldic **achievement** on a roundel, and excellent lettering. To the e. is a good but unsigned monument for James Rice (1822) - a broad obelisk backs a well-modelled mourning woman draped over an urn in bas relief, knotted sheaves of palms above and a colourful shield of arms at the top. On the s. side, above the arcade, is a repainted benefactions board which mentions 'in-bread'. This refers to the thirteenth, or 'vantage loaf' - that part of the baker's dozen which was included to avoid the heavy penalties for giving short weight. As you leave you will see the **Royal Arms** of George III in a gilt embellished frame.

Wortham, St Mary (F3): The church stands by the side of the minor road that runs from Palgrave to Redgrave and is over a mile to the n. of Wortham itself. Its ruined round tower is the largest in England, being 29 ft across, with walls over 4 ft thick. **Cautley** was of the opinion that it was **Saxon**, dating from the early C11, and that it was built originally as a watch tower and for defence. What is known as the 'Sacred Stone' lies nearby - a glacial boulder that was probably the object of pagan veneration, and which may have prompted the building of the church here in order that Christanity might overlay the old religion. The tower roof and upper floors collapsed in 1789 and it now stands open to the sky, a most impressive ruin. A **Norman** church was added to it in the middle of the C12 and the foundations of its walls were found within the present **nave** when the floor was relaid. There was a major rebuilding in the middle of the C14 when the **aisles** were added; they are tall and relatively narrow, with large

Perpendicular windows. In the early C15, a fine **clerestory** was added which has a band of **flushwork** emblems between the windows on both sides including, on the s. side, the **sacred monogram** and the letters 'S', 'T', 'S', 'M', standing for 'Sancta Trinitas Sancta Maria'. The **chancel**, with its Perpendicular windows, is of the same date, but you will see that an earlier **Decorated priest's door** was re-used, with a stooled niche over it. Continuing round the outside, there is a two-storied **vestry** on the n. side of the chancel with a neat little pair of gables, and the n. door has been blocked and faced with excellent flushwork. The bells having fallen with the tower, an C18 boarded bellcote with a lead cupola and weathervane now stands at the w. end of the nave roof. There is a C13 grave slab clamped to the w. side of the tower, and over the entrance to the C14 **porch** is a sundial, with a very small niche above the inner doorway. Note as you enter that there are deep holes each side in the **jambs** to take a wooden bar for security.

Inside the door is the C14 **font** with a **castellated** rim; the panels have **crocketted** gables with fine **tracery** backing them and worn heads project at the angles below the bowl. Beyond the font are two more C13 grave slabs bearing three floriated crosses. The tower arch has been blocked up and the organ now stands in front of it. On the wall by the s. door is a very fine set of Charles I **Royal Arms** carved in wood and set in an oval frame. This is quite unusual, but there is another like it in the neighbouring church of Redgrave; they were probably carved by the same man. Above the C14 **arcades**, the nave **roof** has **arch-braces** alternating with **hammerbeams** and the ceiling has been plastered between the principals. The aisle roofs were rebuilt with local oak in the 1890s, and at that time new benches were made by Albert Bar-

trum of Wortham, who modelled them on the old ones and incorporated a number of the original bench ends. The excellent carvings on the elbows illustrate psalm 104 and were carried out by a Mr Groom of Ipswich. Each stands on a heavy block bearing the relevant text, and one can find a tortoise, owl, walrus, bear, lion, and among the figures, a man going forth to his labour. There are also blacksmith's tools carved on a bench end by the s. door. Two **hatchments** hang in the s. aisle; the one furthest e. was probably used for both Philip Vincent and his second wife Elizabeth (who died in 1724 and 1728 respectively); the other hatchment was for the Rev George Betts, rector of Overstrand in Norfolk, who died in 1822. The window in the wall of the s. aisle at the e. end contains ornamental glass of 1820-1830, some of it painted by **Robert Allen** of Lowestoft, and probably installed by Yarington of Norwich. The s. aisle chapel has a **piscina** with a **trefoil** arch and the window over the **altar** is a memorial for two men of the Suffolk Regiment who fell at Passchendaele and the Somme, with figures of **St George** and the archangel **Michael**. To the l. is a niche with a **cinquefoiled** head. The n. aisle chapel has a similar piscina and image niche and the altar there is a nice melon- legged C17 table. There is no **screen** and the chancel is very wide, with an arch-braced roof of 1904, resting on worn, heavy head **corbels**. The front of the **high altar** incorporates panels from the old **rood screen**, and round the walls of the **sanctuary** is a low range of blank arches with steep gables and tracery derived from the designs on the font. The e. wall has heavily carved stone panels, with vine trails and wheat, as well as verses from the Gospels, all dating from 1856. The C14 piscina has a **cusped** and crocketted arch, to which C19 grapevine **stops** have been added. Heavy C19 stone **decalogue** tablets flank the fine e. window, in which you will see the fragments of medie-

val glass, including a small scroll inscribed 'Caterrina' carried by an eagle. There may be some connection between this and the Catherine wheel emblem to be found on the n. clerestory outside. Near the lectern is a memorial to Richard Cobbold who was rector here from 1824 to 1877. He was the author of the novel *Margaret Catchpole* but, more importantly, he also chronicled the lives of the ordinary humble people of his parish in illustrated diaries that are a fascinating and poignant social record. Ronald Fletcher tells the rector's story in his book *In a Country Churchyard*.

Wyverstone, St George (F4): Like a number of churches in the area, the C14 tower has one pair of buttresses at right angles, thus extending the e. face, while the heavy w. counterparts are set diagonally. The small **Decorated** w. window matches the bell openings on the s. and w. but the other two sides have pretty, and quite individual elongated **quatrefoils**. The chequerwork battlements sport fine **gargoyles**. All other windows are **Perpendicular** and there is a **clerestory**, although no **aisles** were added to give it point. As at Hinderclay, the church has a wooden **porch** and the timbers of the outer arch are probably C14, set in a renewed frame. For some reason the porch is not centred on the C14 doorway, with its remains of head **corbels**. Within, there is a beautifully compact William and Mary **Royal Arms** on the w. wall, excellently carved in deep relief and cut to the outline of the **achievement**. Another set hangs on the n. wall, this time **Hanoverian** and dated 1812. The bowl panels of the early C15 **font** are carved alternately with roses in quatrefoils and shields in roundels, one of which carries a possible merchant's mark. Some of the bench ends at the w. end bear **poppyheads** and there is one C17 example on the n. side which is carved with churchwardens' initials and has a scrolled top. There is not much left of the church's medieval glass but, among the fragments, look for a tiny head of Christ at the very top of the westernmost window on the n. side. In the C15 **roof, arch-braces** alternate with **hammerbeams** which, like the **wall-plates**, are embattled. The entrance to the **rood loft** stair is in the n. wall and, unusually, there is a socket in the **jamb** for a lock. Nearby stands an iron-bound chest, the sides have been renewed but the rounded top is C14. Opposite is a deep C16 pulpit with **linen-fold panelling**. Overhead, centred on one of the main roof timbers is a rare survival, the pulley block from which was hung the rowell, a ring of lights that used to hang in front of the rood before the **Reformation**. Equally interesting is the **screen**. Although the pillars of the chancel arch are drilled for supports, only the base survives but this is one of only two in Suffolk (Gislingham is the other) where the panels contain carvings rather than paintings - very rare. They were badly mutilated in the C17 but the remnants can be identified. On the n. side, from l. to r.; **St Gabriel**, with the front of his body missing; the **Blessed Virgin**, minus her head (the two panels forming an **Annunciation** group); the Nativity, with all destroyed except one sheep and a wattle hurdle at the bottom; the Wise Men, with two heads missing. On the s. side, l. to r.: a rare scene of the mass of **St Gregory**, again, the fronts of the figures have been sheered off but the picture is clear; the saint kneels before an **altar** and raises the chalice, with the figure of Christ above and a woman to the r. The story is that, in order to sustain the faith of a sceptic, the sacred elements were transformed into a vision of the risen Christ as the pope celebrated mass. The remaining panel is carved with the **Visitation** scene from St Luke's Gospel - **St Elizabeth** with the Blessed Virgin (both obviously pregnant and one touching the other's body). The bottom of the panels are filled with quatrefoils and the heavy Perpendicular tracery was originally **crocketted**. In the **chancel** there are early C17 **communion rails** with turned **finials** on the posts. The floor levels were raised in the 1900 restoration and the **piscina** is now awkwardly low in the wall. The three-**light** e. window contains glass by 1926 by William Glasby - the risen Christ with angels above a panorama of Jerusalem, against a low line of purple hills.

GLOSSARY OF TERMS

Abacus (plural, abaci): A flat stone slab set on top of a pillar or **pier** to take the thrust of an arch springing from it. Most often seen in **Norman** and **Early English** architecture. (Compare with **impost** and **capital**.)

Acanthus: A stylised form of leaf decoration based on a family of plants which include Bears' Breech. Used originally by the Greeks, it became very popular in the C17 and C18, particularly for use on mouldings and scrolls.

Achievement of Arms: Heraldic arms in their full form with all or most of the following: shield of arms, crest, helm and mantling (its ornamental drapery), supporters (animals or humans), motto - as opposed to a plain shield of arms.

Act of Parliament clock: In 1797, Pitt's government levied an annual tax on all clocks and watches which so reduced the number in use that inn-keepers began to provide cheap wall clocks in their public rooms, particularly if stage-coaches called. The Act was repealed the following year but the clocks were common until 1830. They normally have a large wooden painted dial, black with gold numerals, and a short case to house the pendulum. Some have found their way into churches and there are

examples at Long Melford and Worlington.

Agnus Dei (The Lamb of God.): When **St John the Baptist** saw Jesus coming he said, 'Behold the Lamb of God who takes away the sin of the world'. The words were used in the mass as early as the C5 and by the C9 wax medallions were being made on Holy Saturday from remnants of the previous year's paschal candle. In the Middle Ages, the lamb bearing a cross or flag was widely used in painting and sculpture as a symbol of Our Lord.

Aisles: The parts of the church to the n. and s. of the **nave**, and sometimes of the **chancel**, under sloping **roofs** which give the impression of extensions to the main building. Which indeed, they often were, being added to accommodate side **altars**, (see **chantry chapels** and **guild altars**), as well as larger congregations, and to provide processional ways - an important requirement before the **Reformation**. These are not to be confused with the 'aisle' down which the bride steps which is the centre gangway of the **nave**.

Allen, Robert (1745-1835): Stained glass worker. He began as a porcelain painter when the Lowestoft factory opened and was works manager when they closed in 1802. He began painting on glass as a hobby while still at work and built his own kiln on retirement. His major work was the e. window of St Margaret's, Lowestoft, done in 1819 as a gift to the church when he was 74. It is a mixture of scriptural figures, heraldry, texts and 'fanciful ornaments'. It was removed in 1891 but some panels survive in a s. **chancel** window. More of his glass can be seen at Herringfleet, Wortham, and the Norfolk churches of Langley, Thurton and Little Plumstead.

Altar: The table used for the celebration of the Eucharist (Holy communion or mass) and to be found within the **sanctuary** at the e. end of the **chancel**. Originally of wood, but stone altars (see **mensa**) became common in the early church. When the practice of celebrating private masses became common in the Middle Ages, altars were set up elsewhere in the church (see **guilds** and **chantry chapels**) and the original altar became known as the **high altar**. At the **Reformation** there was controversy over the use of stone altars; more followed in Elizabeth's reign and in the C17 over the positioning of what was then called 'the Holy table' (see also **Laudian**. In recent years the practice has grown of siting an altar at the e. end of the **nave** to emphasise corporate worship.

Altar rails: See **communion rails**.

Anchorite/anchoress(female)/**anchorite's cell:** An anchorite - the word being derived from the Greek 'anakhoreo', retire - was a religious recluse who chose to be walled up for life in a cell attached to the church, in order to devote his or her mortal existence to prayer, meditation and piety. A small outer window gave light and a way for food to be passed in - and for people to receive wise advice from the recluse. Another small window, or **squint**, gave a direct view of the **altar** so that

the anchorite could watch the celebration of mass. (An example of such a cell is at Moulton.)

Angle piscina: See **piscina**.

Anglo-Saxon: The Anglo-Saxons were the Teutonic invaders who overran Britain in the Dark Ages. Between the C5 and C7 Norfolk and Suffolk were overrun and were settled by the Angles, who gave their name to East Anglia. **Saxon** architecture, distinctive in its simplicity, existed until it was superseded by **Norman** building following the Conquest of 1066 (see **Styles of Architecture**).

Annunciation: Annunciation representations are a regular subject for stained glass scenes, as well as wood and stone carvings - the Archangel Gabriel bringing news to Mary of the Incarnation, that she would conceive a child of the Holy Ghost (Luke 1: 26-38). The Feast of the Annunciation is 25 March, otherwise known as Lady Day, an important date too in the rural calendar, when tenant farmers' rents were due, and new tenancies were granted. Examples may be found in many churches.

Apse/apsidal: Rounded end of a building, usually the **chancel** at the e. end in churches. Derived from Romanesque architecture, semi-circular in shape, or consisting of five sides of an octagon, and often dome-roofed or vaulted; generally associated in Britain with **Norman** churches. It is said that the apse represents the raised platform of the secular 'basilica' or public hall which in Roman times was used as law court and treasury as well as meeting hall; though another theory is that it is borrowed from the platform of the meeting rooms of early Christian **guilds**.

Arcades: A series of arches, ie, those

down each side of the **nave** of an ais-
led church - supported by pillars.
Sometimes arcades are 'closed',
'blind' or 'blank' - a decorative outline on a wall or tomb or furnishing;
or when, as may often be found, an
aisle has been demolished and the
arcade bricked up, but leaving its pillars and arches outlined.

Arch-braced roofs: A roof carried on
a simple, braced arch. (See **roofs**, fig 4
for full description.)

Art Nouveau: An ornamental style
that flourished throughout Europe
during 1890 to 1910, characterised by
long sinuous lines mainly derived
from naturalistic forms, particularly
the lily, rose, and peacock. Sometimes occurring in church furniture
and fittings of wood and metal (as at
Horringer and Rattlesden), but more
often seen as an influence in the
stained glass of the period.

Arts and Crafts Movement: A movement active in the late C19 and early
C20 which opposed the shoddy
results of mass production and
emphasised the value of hand crafts.
One of the guiding principles was
that the artist should be involved in
every process, from initial design to
finished work. Selwyn Image, W.R.
Lethaby, **Christopher Whall**, Walter
Crane and Charles Rennie Mackin-
tosh were among the leading figures.
The movement's influence in church
art is mainly to be seen in stained
glass of the period (as at
Herringswell).

Ashlar: Square hewn stone, often
used as facing for brick or rubble
walls.

Assumption of the Virgin: The translation of the Virgin Mary, body and

soul, into heaven - a theme often represented by medieval artists in painting and sculpture. The Feast of the
Assumption is 15 August, a festival
first initiated in the year 582 by the
Roman Emperor Maurice. The Eastern Orthodox Church, with a poetic
touch, celebrates the Assumption as
'The Feast of the Falling Asleep of
Our Lady'. (See Nowton, C17 Flemish
glass.)

Aumbry: A small cupboard or recess
in which were stored the Holy oils
used in baptism, confirmation and
extreme unction (anointing of the
dying person by the priest); also the
sacred vessels/plate used for mass or
communion. Sometimes the aumbry
held the Reserved Sacrament - the
consecrated bread, 'reserved' from a
mass (see also **Easter sepulchre**). The
aumbry is generally found on the n.
side of the **chancel** (opinions vary
about medieval usage), but sometimes near the **piscina** - which is
almost always on the s. side - and in a
few cases may be near the **font**. Originally, very few parish churches had
sacristies for storing the plate and
valuables. The priest robed at the
altar, his vestments meantime being
kept in a parish chest, the vessels for
altar and font being placed in the
aumbry. Thus chest plus aumbry
equals the later **vestries**. Occasionally
the aumbry was used in the C15 as a
safe for documents, not only belonging to the church, but to parishioners.
as it would be secured by door and
lock. Very few of these wooden doors
remain today, though the hinge and
latch marks in the stone can often be
made out. The aumbry at Icklingham,
St James still has its door and there is
an excellent C14 example at
Rattlesden.

Bacon, John (1740-1799): A mainly
self-taught sculptor who first learned
his skills in a porcelain factory and
later worked for Wedgwood. Shortly

after he was elected to the Royal Academy in 1770, he modelled a bust of George III for Christ Church, Oxford which so impressed the king that Bacon received the commission for Chatham's gargantuan monument in Westminster Abbey. Singularly apt in recognising what the public wanted, his was a career of great prosperity and his output prolific. Examples of his work may be seen at Ampton, Finningham and Hawstead.

Bacon, John the Younger (1777-1859): Son of John Bacon, trained by him, and something of a child prodigy, he was sculpting figures at the age of 11. Extraordinarily prolific and successful, monuments by him are legion, but he was not the equal of his father. Examples of his work may be seen at Assington, Edwardstone, Hawstead, Market Weston, Mildenhall, Nowton and Stoke-by-Nayland.

Ball flower: An early C14 decorative ornament in sculpture. See **Decorated** under **Styles of Architecture**.

Baluster: A short, decorative column, often slightly pear-shaped, ie, bulging at the middle and tapering at top and bottom.

Banner-stave lockers: In the late medieval period, parish **guilds** proliferated and all had their banners to be carried in the processions which in medieval times were an important part of services on Sundays and Feast Days (see also **galilee porches**). Between times, the banners would be placed in the guild chapels, and the staves in their lockers, which explains the long, narrow upright niches in the walls of some churches which can seem so puzzling.

Barrel organ: A mechanised organ

played by turning a handle which revolves a cylinder, 'set' with several tunes. In the public mind, associated with Italian organ grinders and liveried monkeys, but in fact a regular part of the fittings at one time of many rural churches. Now these delightful curiosities, complete with several cylinders of good old hymn tunes, are few and far between, but there is an example at Shelland.

Bar tracery: Tracery in the heads of windows, constructed in separate pieces, as distinct from **plate tracery**, where the pattern is cut directly through the masonry. See **Early English** under **Styles of Architecture**.

Base course: A horizontal layer of masonry, decorative in character, usually at the base of towers. See **courses**.

Bestiary: A medieval collection of stories, each based on a description of certain qualities of an animal or plant. The stories all derive from the 'Physiologus', a C2 Greek text in which each creature is linked to a biblical text. Extremely popular in the Middle Ages, the bestiaries presented Christian allegories for moral and religious instruction, and many are illustrated, thus providing prototypes for many imaginative carvings.

Biers: Some churches - and particularly, for obvious reasons, those with a long path between **lych-gate** and church - have a platform to carry the coffin to and from the funeral service. These curious conveyances can often be seen, discreetly tucked away at the back of the **nave** or in a side **aisle**. Most of them are Victorian but there are interesting C17 examples at Little Saxham, Dalham and Kedington, with an unusual C19 version at Acton.

Billet: Billet moulding or decoration was particularly used in **Norman** work. It was formed by cutting notches in two parallel and continuous rounded mouldings in a regular, alternating pattern.

Black Death: Some time in the 1340s a horrific epidemic of bubonic plague ('The Black Death' is a modern expression coined in the C19) began, possibly in China, and by 1348 it had reached the south of France where it devastated the papal city of Avignon. By the end of the year it had crossed the Channel and begun the ravages which, in twelve months, would leave between a third and a half of the nation's population dead. It cut off in its prime the greatest flowering of English architectural beauty (see **Decorated** under **Styles of Architecture**). On 1 January 1349 the king, Edward III, issued a proclamation postponing Parliament because 'a sudden visitation of deadly pestilence' had broken out in and around Westminster, and by June the full fury of the plague had reached East Anglia. In the dreadful year ending 1350, it has been estimated that at least half, and probably more, of the population of Norfolk and Suffolk were swept away. Plague broke out again at intervals over the next three centuries until the last major outbreak, culminating in the Great Plague of London in 1665, when a quarter of the inhabitants died. What is remarkable, in considering the Black Death in relation to our churches, is that it was followed by one of the greatest ages of church building.

Blank/blind arcading: See **arcades**.

Blessed Virgin: See **Mary the Blessed Virgin** under **Saints**.

Blomfield, Sir Arthur William (1829-99): Son of the bishop of London and one of the successful architects of the Victorian era. He established his own practice in 1856 and was President of the Architectural Association in 1861. He carried out important cathedral restorations at Canterbury, Salisbury, Lincoln and Chichester, and designed many churches in England and abroad. Culford is his completely and he restored/rebuilt at Herringswell, Rattlesden, Fornham All Saints, Beyton and Dalham.

Bodley, George Frederick (1827-1907): Church architect and decorative designer, Bodley was **Sir George Gilbert Scott's** first pupil in the 1840s and established his own practice in 1860. From 1869 to 1897 he was in partnership with Thomas Garner and much of their work is indistinguishable. Bodley excelled in the use of late Gothic forms, and in furnishings his preference for rich colour enhanced by gilding shows in the many designs he provided for Watts & Co. He was also the first to commission stained glass from **Morris & Co.** Examples of his work are to be found at Long Melford, Barton Mills and Sudbury (St Peter).

Bosses: A boss is the carved ornamentation seen at the intersections of roof beams or of the ribs in vaulted (see **groining**) ceilings. Usually they represent foliage or grotesque animals or figures, but may often be intricately worked with biblical scenes, with portraits, heraldic arms and symbols.

Box pew: Large pews panelled to waist height or higher, often with seats on three sides, and entered by a door from the **aisle**. Nicknamed 'box pews' from their similarity to horse-boxes or stalls. They came into favour in the late C17 and early C18 and were often embellished with curtains, cushions and carpets. Most disappeared in the wave of C19 restorations. There are good examples at Kedington, Kentford and Shelland. See also **Prayer book churches**.

Brasses: Brasses are incised memorial portraits and inscriptions, usually found set into the floor or on top of tombs, although some may be seen fixed to walls and furnishings. Brasses are made in an alloy called latten, a mixture of copper and zinc. This was chiefly manufactured at Cologne, where it was beaten into rectangular plates for export to Britain, the Low Countries and elsewhere. Such memorials were for long favoured by a wide range of classes, from the nobility, through the priesthood, scholars and monks, to merchants and families of local standing. The earliest brass to be seen in England is said to be that of Sir John d'Abernon at Stoke d'Abernon in Surrey, dated 1277 in the reign of Edward I. It was not until the first half of the C17 that the fashion petered out. In the 1830s, interest stirred again, and in the 1840s **Pugin** combined with **Hardman** to design and produce brasses in the medieval manner. Effigies and inscriptions became popular, and although Hardmans were by far the major suppliers, many firms were at work. Very few were produced after the spate of war memorials in the 1920s. Suffolk is rich in medieval brasses, with particularly fine examples at Acton, Hawstead, Long Melford and Redgrave, and there are interesting modern brasses at Clare and Lavenham. But brasses are more than memorials: they are remarkable, pictorial commentaries on four centuries of our history, martial armour, manners, customs, dress and fashion. See also **chalice brass**.

Burlison & Grylls: A firm of stained glass manufacturers founded by John Burlison and Thomas Grylls in 1868. They had trained with **Clayton & Bell** and had close links with **Sir George Gilbert Scott** and **G. F. Bodley**, for whom much of their earliest and best glass was done. Its accomplished drawing followed C15 and C16 precedents and the work was of a high technical standard. The firm closed in 1953. Examples may be seen at Ampton, Gazeley and Great Whelnetham.

Burse: A stiffened fabric envelope designed to contain the linen cloth on which the chalice and paten are placed during the Eucharist. A rare medieval burse belonging to Hessett is now in the British Museum.

Butterfield, William (1814-1900): The architect and decorative designer who will always be remembered for two London churches at least - All Saints, Margaret Street, and St Matthias, Stoke Newington. His was a highly individual interpretation of the Gothic style, often characterised by structural polychromy - bands and patterns of bricks in contrasting colours, and his strong sense of craftsmanship may have stemmed from his apprenticeship in the building trade. He was a staunch Tractarian and for many years directed the **Ecclesiological Society's** scheme for the design of church furnishings. He directed restoration and rebuilding at Sudbury (St Gregory and St Peter), Lawshall and Bacton.

Butterfly head-dress: 'Butterfly' is a name given in the C16, and used ever since, for a style fashionable in the previous century, from about 1450 to 1485. Its high fashion status is indicated by its appearance on effigies of the period in brass and stone. The head-dress consisted of a wire frame, fixed to a close-fitting ornamented cap, supporting a gauze veil spreading out above the head on each side like a pair of diaphanous butterfly wings.

Cambridge Camden Society: See **Ecclesiological Society**.

Canopy of honour: See **celure**.

Capital: The usually decorated and ornamented top of a column/pillar, from which springs the arch which the pillar supports. (Compare with **impost** and **abacus**.)

Cartouche: Latin, 'carta', paper. Sculptural representation of a curling sheet of paper.

Castellated: Decorated with miniature battlements like a castle.

Cautley, Henry Munro (1875-1959): Diocesan Surveyor from 1914 to 1947 and authority on church architecture and fittings. His only complete church in the county is Ipswich, St Augustine, built in 1926, but many others bear witness to his work. His *Suffolk Churches and their Treasures* was first published in 1937 and is still essential reading for those interested in the county's medieval heritage. The fourth edition was supplemented in 1982 by Anne Riches' *Victorian Church Building and Restoration in Suffolk*, a subject that Cautley resolutely refused to contemplate. His *Royal Arms and Commandments in our Churches* was one of the first monographs on the subject. A man of parts, he farmed at Butley, specialising in Red Poll cattle, and he enjoyed the gift of water divining. His father was rector of Westerfield and Cautley himself read the lessons there for over 60 years. The superb pews at Mildenhall are an enduring memorial to his love for ancient churches and to his generosity.

Celure: Otherwise known as a 'canopy of honour'. A panelled and painted section of the roof of a church, either over the **altar**, or at the eastern end of the **nave** over the position occupied by the **rood**. There are examples at Bury (St Mary), Stowlangtoft, Norton, Sudbury (St Peter), Sudbury (St Gregory), Monks Eleigh and Woolpit.

Censer: See **thurible**.

Chalice brasses: These are small memorial brasses, surmounted by a representation of the Chalice and Host. (Latin, 'hostia' - the bread which is The Body of Christ). There is an example at Gazeley. See also **brasses**.

Chancel: The e. end section of a church, containing the **altar** Before the **Reformation** the chancel was restricted to the clergy and the celebration of mass, the people occupying the **nave** Separating the two was a **screen** (thus the derivation of the word from the Latin cancellus - lattice). Traditionally, the parson was responsible for the repair and upkeep of the chancel while the parishioners cared for the rest, and this sometimes resulted in separate building programmes. In some cases it explains the difference in age and style between the two parts of the church. See **rood loft** and also note **weeping chancel**.

Chantry chapels: The most distinctive development in C14 and C15 church affairs was the growth of chantries. Instead of leaving money to monasteries or similar foundations, rich men began to favour their parish church and to endow priests to say daily masses for them and their families after their death. By the C15 all large, and many small, churches contained a number of such chantries - often with their own chapel or **altar** and furnished with vestments, ornaments and sacred vessels. They provided light, profitable work for a priest although the less well-endowed chantries had to make do with a part-time stipendiary chaplain. These priests were not under the jurisdiction of the incumbent and endless disputes and not a few abuses followed. For those who could not afford the luxury of a private chantry, membership of a local **guild** often offered a substitute. Chantries were abolished by Edward VI in 1547 ostensibly on religious grounds but really to meet an acute shortage in the Exchequer.

Chevron moulding: The chevron or zigzag is a characteristic decorative moulding of **Norman** architecture, its bold 'V' shapes being used from the early C12 around open arches and arches of windows and doors. See **Styles of Architecture**.

Christmas, John & Matthias: Sculptors and sons of Gerard Christmas, a carver of high reputation in the reign of James I. They succeeded him in the lucrative post of carver to the Royal Navy in 1634. Their masterpiece was the work on the royal ship *Sovereign of the Seas*, built for Charles I in 1637. Versatile and extremely competent, they were also pageant masters to the City of London. Examples of their work may be found at Ampton and Denham (St Mary), and one of their father's best works is at Hawstead.

Christ of the Trades: Medieval wall paintings occasionally included a figure of Christ surrounded by various tools, and interpretations of their significance vary. They may illustrate the sanctity of labour and Christ as the divine craftsman, but dice and cards are sometimes included so the theme is more likely to be the evil of Sabbath breaking, the Redeemer's wounds renewed by man's blasphemy and disregard. There are examples at Hessett and Risby and there is

evidence of one at Walsham-le-Willows.

Chrysom child: When a child was baptised, it was swaddled for the Christening service in the 'chrysom' cloth or sheet, which often belonged to the parish. If the child died before its mother had been churched (ie, had been to church after the birth to receive the priest's blessing and purification) it was then buried in the chrysom cloth, thus becoming a 'chrysom child'. In this form it was represented on tombs and brasses, as, for example, at Long Melford and Lavenham.

Churchyard cross: See **preaching cross**.

Cinquefoils: See **foils**.

Clayton & Bell: A firm of stained glass manufacturers founded by John Richard Clayton and Alfred Bell in 1855, and still continuing under Michael Bell. Their studio was one of the largest of the Victorian period and they were notable for the brilliance of their High Victorian designs and consistency in their use of colour. Their work of the early 1860s was of a particularly high standard. Examples at the cathedral, Bury (St Mary), Great Finborough, Higham, Rattlesden, Horringer, Barton Mills, Newmarket (St Agnes) and Lidgate.

Clerestory: An upper storey, standing clear of its adjacent roofs, and pierced with windows which usually correspond in number with the number of arches, or bays, in the **arcade** below. Its pronunciation - 'Clear-storey' - explains the clerestory's function, namely, clear glass windows letting in light on the large covered area below.

Clerk: See **parish clerk**.

Cockatrice: (Also known as a bas-
ilisk.) A fabulous reptile hatched by a
serpent from a cock's egg. Both its
breath and its look were supposed to
be fatal. In medieval imagery it takes
the form of a cock with a barbed serpent's tail. Examples on bench ends
can be found at Stowlangtoft, Tostock
and Denston and as a heraldic crest at
Long Melford.

Collar beam: See **roofs**.

Collar of SS or Esses: A decorative
collar of gold or silver composed of Ss
linked together. There are many theo-
ries concerning the origin of this mark
of honour and what the 'S' stood for
(Sovereign, Seneschal, etc). The earliest effigy shown wearing it in this
country dates from 1371 and so it cannot, as some have maintained, have
been introduced by Henry IV. He did,
however, issue a regulation in 1401
limiting its use to sons of the king,
dukes, earls and barons and to other
knights and esquires when in his
presence. During the reigns of Henry
IV, his son and grandson, it was a royal badge of the Lancastrian house,
with a white swan as pendant rather
than the more usual portcullis. It was
later restricted to the Lord Chief Justice, the Lord Mayor of London, the
Heralds and Kings of Arms and the
Serjeants at Arms. See Bury (St Mary).

Colonnette: A small column.

Commandment boards: See **decalogue boards**.

Communion rails: The rails against
which the congregation kneel to
receive communion (and no doubt
taking it for granted that this is and

always was their purpose) were originally installed for quite other reasons.
They were to protect the **altar** from
irreverent people and even less reverent dogs - and the **balusters** were to be
set close enough to ensure this. Before
the **Reformation** the **chancel** was
always closed off by a **screen (rood
loft/screen)** usually fitted with doors,
and the people normally never
entered it. At great festivals, they
watched through the screen as the
priests celebrated mass and parishioners received the sacrament. When
general participation in services and
the administration of the sacrament
to the people became the norm, different arrangements were needed. Archbishop **Laud** ordered that the altar
should be railed and not moved from
its n.s. position, and the rails often
enclosed the altar on three sides.
Whether there should be rails or no,
Richard Montague, Bishop of Norwich, made his position clear in a **Visitation** question in 1638: 'Is your
communion table enclosed, and ranged about with a rail of joiners and
turners work, close enough to keep
dogs from going in and profaning that
holy place, from pissing against it or
worse?' The Bishop further ordered
that 'the communicants being entered
into the chancel shall be disposed of
orderly in their several ranks, leaving
sufficient room for the priest or minister to go between them, by whom
they were to be communicated one
rank after another, until they had all
of them received.' This was to come
into conflict with the Puritan habit of
demanding that communion should
be received by the congregation seated in their pews. In 1643 communion
rails went the way of other 'monuments of superstition and idolatry',
but at the **Restoration** in 1660 old
habits were resumed and the taking of
communion at the sanctuary rail
became accepted practice. At that
time three-sided rails were popular
and examples can be found at Ixworth
Thorpe, Kedington, Brent Eleigh and
Great Livermere. Kedington also has

rare sets of communicants' pews. (See also **Prayer book churches** and **Housel bench**.

Comper, Sir Ninian (1864-1960): Distinguished and highly individual architect of the Gothic Revival, who in the course of 70 years built 15 churches, restored and decorated scores, and designed vestments, windows and banners for use literally all around the globe, from America to the Far East, for both the Roman and Anglican communions. He designed the furnishings in the Suffolk Regt. chapel, Bury (St Mary) and a grill at Kettlebaston.

Consecration crosses: Painted or carved, indicate the points at which the walls of the church, and the **altar** slab (the **mensa** were touched with Holy oil by the bishop at the consecration of the building. On the altar were incised five crosses - one at each corner and one in the middle - signifying the **five wounds of Christ**. Medieval practice varied but normally three crosses were marked on each of the four walls, both inside and out, and spikes bearing candles were inserted below them. The bishop's procession would circle the church before he knocked to be admitted by the single deacon within. The floor was marked from corner to corner with a cross of ashes in which the bishop would inscribe the Latin and Greek alphabets before anointing the rest of the crosses and the altar. In many cases a sacred relic would be sealed within or near the altar at the same time. Comparatively few consecration crosses survive but they can be found at Barton Mills, Bury (St Mary), Bardwell, Troston, Hessett, Sapiston, Gazeley, Great Livermere, Kettlebaston, Long Melford, Risby and Stansfield. There are external examples at Dalham, Buxhall and Monks Eleigh and on door **jambs** at Depden and Finningham.

Corbels: A highly practical item which often doubles as a very decorative one. This is the support, set firmly into the wall, to carry a weight from above (see **roofs**) and will usually be carved, either decoratively, or with heads which may be reverent or formalised, delightfully (and irreverently) portrait-like or entirely fanciful.

Corbel table: A continuous row of **corbels** set into a wall to support the eaves of a roof.

Corinthian: A column of one of the classical (Grecian) orders, comprising a cushioned base, the shaft or pillar itself (usually fluted), and a capital (ie, the head of the pillar) enriched with **acanthus** leaves.

Courses: A course is, in general terms, a horizontal layer of masonry. A **base course** will usually be at the base of the tower - a purely decorative course, a little above the ground, designed to set off the tower visually. In Suffolk, local flint is often used to great effect here, knapped and set flush into stone panelling (thus, **flushwork** to create a most attractive contrast, as well as a visual impression of upward, vertical thrust. A **string course** is a moulding whose purpose is to indicate the divisions of a tower into its several stages, though in some cases it is carried over the tower window(s) to create an impression of lightness and uplift. Finally, a **drip course** is, as its name indicates, a raised course doing the practical job of carrying off rain from the wall surface. See also **dripstone**

Credence/Credence shelf: This is a shelf on which the elements of the mass or communion are placed before consecration by the priest; usually found within the niche of the **piscina**

beside the **altar**, or the site of a former altar. Can sometimes occupy a niche of its own.

Cresset stone: A stone drilled with holes that were filled with oil on which a wick was floated, a primitive form of candle lighting. There is an example at Walsham-le-Willows.

Crockets/crocketting: This is an exuberant ornamentation of the **Decorated** period, in the first half of the C14, though it was to be carried through with enthusiasm into the later **Perpendicular** style (see **Styles of Architecture**). It is a little projecting sculpture in the form of leaves, flowers etc, used in profusion on pinnacles, spires, canopies and so on, both inside and outside the building.

Crossing/crossing tower: The crossing is the part of the church at the intersection of the cross shape of a church, where **chancel** and **nave** and n. and s. **transepts** meet. The crossing tower is the central tower built over this point.

Cusps/cusping: From the Latin 'cuspis', a point (of a spear). These are the little projecting points on the curves of window and **screen tracery**, arches etc, which give a foliated, leaf-like appearance.

Decalogue board: The decalogue (a word derived from the Greek) is the Ten Commandments collectively. The decalogue board, it follows, is a large board upon which the Commandments are written. These became a regular part of church furnishings in the reign of Elizabeth I, when it was state policy to clear churches of the decorations and adornments which were regarded as 'popish'. In 1560, Elizabeth ordered

Archbishop Parker to see 'that the tables of the Commandments be comely set or hung up in the east end of the **chancel**.The following year more explicit instructions were given: the boards were to be fixed to the e. wall over the communion table. The Creed and Lord's Prayer were not so ordered but were felt to be 'very fit companions' for the Commandments. Decalogues were also set up on the **tympanum** - panelling which filled the curve of the chancel arch to replace the discarded **rood loft** (see also **Royal Arms**). In most cases today, the decalogue boards have long since been moved from their position behind the **altar** but are usually displayed on a convenient wall of **nave**or **aisles**.

Decorated: This was the high point of ornamented Gothic architecture in the first half of the C14. See **Styles of Architecture**.

Dogtooth decoration: An ornamental carving of the **Early English** period (see **Styles of Architecture** in the C12/C13 which looks like a four-leafed flower. One suggestion is that it is based on the dog's tooth violet.

Doom: A picture of the Last Judgement, normally found painted over the **chancel** arch (which symbolically separated earthly from heavenly things). Christ is often represented seated on a rainbow, with souls being weighed below before being despatched to join the blessed on His right hand or the damned on His left. There are examples at Bacton, Cowlinge, Stanningfield, Stoke-by- Clare, Chelsworth and Troston.

Dowsing, William (1596?-1679?): In August 1643 Parliament ordered a general destruction of **altars**, pictures and images in all churches, and the

Earl of Manchester, as general of the eastern counties, appointed William Dowsing as his visitor in Suffolk to carry out the work. Dowsing had been born at Laxfield and later lived at Coddenham and Eye. He toured the county between January and October 1644 and is the best known of the despoilers simply because he kept a diary. The original manuscript has vanished but a transcript was made in the early C18 and it was first published in 1786 (C.H.E. White edited the best edition in 1885). Dowsing employed deputies but took a personal delight in wreaking vengeance on all that he considered 'popish', often exceeding his brief in digging up floors and disturbing tombs. An eyewitness of his work in Cambridgeshire said: 'he goes about the Country like a Bedlam breaking glasse windowes, having battered and beaten downe all our painted glasse... and compelled us by armed soldiers to pay... for not mending what he had spoyled and defaced, or forthwith to go to prison'. It should not be assumed that all congregations and ministers in this strongly Puritan area were averse to the purge, but some churches saved their particular treasures by guile or obstinacy. Nevertheless, Dowsing exacted a terrible reckoning. At Clare: 'we broke down 1000 Pictures superstitious; I broke down 200; 3 of God the Father and 3 of Christ and the Holy Lamb, and 3 of the Holy Ghost like a Dove with wings; and the 12 Apostles were carved in Wood, on the top of the Roof, which we gave order to take down; and 20 cherubims to be taken down; and the Sun and Moon in the East window, by the King's Arms, to be taken down'. His work done, he seems to have returned to obscurity and one of his name was buried at Laxfield in 1679. His was a very personal interpretation of the psalmist's: 'Let the righteous put their hand unto wickedness'.

Drip course: See **courses**.

Dripstone: A projecting ledge or moulding over the heads of doorways, windows etc, serving the practical purpose of carrying off the rain. When the same architectural addition is used inside a building, as a decorative feature, it is called a **hood mould**.

Dropped-sill sedilia/window: See **sedilia**.

Early English: This is the style development of the mid-C12 which heralded the arrival of Gothic, or pointed architecture in Britain - as well as the birth of a truly native style. See under **Styles of Architecture**.

Easter sepulchre: Immediately to the n. of the **high altar** a recess in the wall, ranging from the plain to the richly canopied, housed the Easter sepulchre. In some cases the top of a table tomb in the same area was used, and occasionally it was designed for this purpose. The sepulchre itself was normally a temporary structure of wood and a fragment of such a frame exists at Barningham. On Maundy Thursday, a Host was consecrated (Latin, 'hostia', victim - the bread which is the Body of Christ) and placed in the Easter sepulchre, to be consumed at the following day's Good Friday mass. This practice still continues in the Roman Catholic and some Anglican churches today, the Host being 'borne in solemn procession ... to the altar of repose', to be processed back to the high altar the following day. Until the **Reformation**, the sepulchre would be watched over from Good Friday to Easter Day partly from a belief that the final appearance of Christ would be early one Easter morning. Sometimes the watchers were paid. The sepulchre was often the setting for a dramatisation of the Resurrection.

Ecclesiological Society, The: The Cambridge Camden Society, later to become the Ecclesiological Society, was founded by J.M. Neale, B. Webb, and others in 1839, and lasted until 1868. During that time it exerted an extraordinarily powerful influence on churchmen, architects and laymen in laying down what it believed to be correct principles for church design, building and ornament. Its activities coincided with the great wave of church building and restoration during the mid-C19 and much of what we see now is a direct result of its activities. The preferred style was **Decorated**; anything earlier was tolerated but **Perpendicular** was stigmatised as 'debased' and classical architecture was anathema. Its critics have claimed that it destroyed more than all the Puritan iconoclasts put together, but the enthusiasm it engendered probably saved many medieval buildings that would otherwise have been lost.

Edward the Confessor: See under **Saints**.

Elevation squint: Central to the Eucharist (mass) is the consecration of the bread and wine. During the Middle Ages, the standard practice was for the priest to raise the wafer of bread and the cup to symbolise the offering and for adoration by the people. Those kneeling close to the **chancel screen** could not gain a clear view, and the more determined sometimes bored a hole in the panel in front of their accustomed place so that they need not rise from their knees. These apertures have become known as elevation squints, and examples may be found at Icklingham (All Saints), Santon Downham, Hessett, Dalham, Cowlinge, Brent Eleigh, Stradishall and Lavenham. See also **squint**.

Emblems of the Trinity: Used extensively in wood, stone and glass to represent the idea of the three persons of the Godhead: Father, Son and Holy Spirit. The forms vary and include the equilateral triangle, the **trefoil**, three interlocking circles and a widely used 'Trinity shield' which bears three inscribed and linked circles. Sometimes the image is pictorial with God the Father holding a miniature Christ between His knees, with a dove superimposed. There are interesting examples at Nowton (Flemish glass), Bardwell (C15 glass) and Haughley (**font** carving).

Encaustic tiles: The Victorians invented the process of burning- in different coloured clays onto tile and brick, to produce a stencil-like effect. In churches built during the C19 and in others 'restored' and 'improved' these tiles were freely used on floors and walls.

Evangelistic symbols: On **fonts** and **screens**, in stained glass etc, the symbols of the **Evangelists** are represented as man, eagle, lion and ox, all winged. The biblical source is the four all- seeing, never-sleeping creatures around the throne of God, in the vision of **St John the Divine**:

> The first living creature was like a lion, the second was like an ox, the third had a face like a man, the fourth was like a flying eagle...
> (Revelations 4:7). The Evangelists

associated with the symbols are **John**, eagle; **Luke**, ox; **Matthew**, man; and **Mark**, lion.

Evangelists: See **Evangelistic symbols**.

Fan vault: A C15 architectural development in which the ribs of a vaulted roof were arranged in a fan pattern, rising in a trumpet shape from the walls and meeting at a **boss** or pendant; the spaces between the ribs were panelled and the effect is opulent. Seldom seen in parish churches but there are examples at Mildenhall, Denston, Long Melford and Lavenham. See also **groining**.

Finial: A carved or moulded ornament, often in foliage or floral form, or as a particularly decorative **crocket**, completing the points of arches, pinnacles or gables. Any finishing in this sense, no matter how plain or simple, is still technically a finial.

Five wounds of Christ, The: On fonts and elsewhere, the five wounds of Christ are often represented. They are, of course, the wounds of the Crucifixion - to hands, feet and side, recalling doubting Thomas':

> Except I shall... put my finger into the print of the nails, and thrust my hand into his side, I will not believe (John, 20:25).

See also the **instruments of the Passion**, which often accompany representations of the wounds.

Fleuron: A flower-shaped ornament used to decorate mouldings both in wood and stone.

Flint-knapping: Flint split across the middle, with craftsmanly skill, to achieve a shell-like fracture, and a lustrous, flat surface. See **flushwork**.

Flushwork: This is the use of **knapped** flints, set flush into panelled patterns in brick or stone, a combination which adds visual beauty and striking impact to so many Suffolk and Norfolk churches.

Foils: From the C12, foils were a much used adornment in Gothic architecture. The **Early English** style produced the graceful **trefoil**, or three-leafed shape: it is said that this was intended to represent the **Trinity** - three in one and one in three - and that **St Patrick**, in C5 Ireland, so the story goes, put together three leaves of shamrock to illustrate to his converts in a visual way that profound mystery. Be that as it may, the trefoil was followed architecturally by the **quatrefoil** (four leaf), **cinquefoil** (five leaf), **sexfoil** (six leaf) and multi-foil.

Font: Receptacle for baptismal water, normally made of stone, but sometimes of wood or metal. The traditional place for the font is at the w. end of the church near to the main entrance, symbolising that baptism is the first stage in the Christian life. Medieval fonts were provided with a lockable cover to ensure the purity of the baptismal water and to guard against misuse or profanation. See also **Seven Sacrament Fonts**.

Four Evangelists: See **Evangelistic symbols**.

Four Latin Doctors: 'Doctor' here indicates one who is learned, a theologian. The Four Latin Doctors were the leading theologians of the early Christian Church in the west - **Ambrose, Augustine of Hippo, Jerome** and **Gregory** See **Saints**.

Gabriel: See **Saints**.

Galilee porches: The western porch of a church was often called the 'Galilee porch' because it was the final 'station' in the Sunday procession. The priest at the head of the procession symbolised Christ going before his disciples into Galilee after the Resurrection ... In medieval times these processions were an important part of the Sunday and Feast day services and must have made an impressive sight with the colours of robes and banners. (See also **banner-stave lockers**.)

Galleries: Have a fascinating pedigree in churches. Before the **Reformation**, when every church had its **rood loft** in the **chancel** arch, singers might use the loft as a gallery, the singing being accompanied by a simple organ. In the couple of centuries that followed the Reformation and the destruction of the old rood lofts, galleries - usually at the w. end of the **nave** - became a common feature. There was housed the village orchestra (the enthusiastic, if not always entirely harmonious sounds, of clarinet, flute, bass fiddle, bassoon and hautboy - predecessor of the modern oboe). Village choirs were common, although the robed and surpliced variety were a mid-Victorian innovation. When organs again became popular they were sometimes placed in a western gallery, and there they can still occasionally be found. Many more galleries were inserted in the C19 to accommodate the larger congregations of the period.

Gargoyles: Quite simply, a spout jutting outwards from a wall so as to throw rainwater well away from the building. But there is much more to them than that. Almost always in ancient churches they are grotesquely carved in all manner of fanciful forms of weird beasts and dragons and devils and representations of human vices like the **Seven Deadly Sins**. This choice of subjects has a very positive aspect to it: if there is good in this world, there is assuredly evil; so also in the world of the spirit; so equally in the sphere of those forces 'beyond the normal' which the modern mind is again coming to examine and accept. To appreciate goodness and beauty, it is necessary to recognise the face of

evil and ugliness - and this medieval man knew and practised. As his mixture of reverence and superstition also inclined to the view that dragons and demons were always prowling evilly round his church, what better way of keeping them at bay than putting their own kind on guard, on the basis, presumably, of 'it takes a devil to catch a devil'.

Gesso: This is a system of coating a base, usually wood, with a thick layer of plaster of Paris, or with gypsum (one of the powdered minerals used to make up plaster of Paris). When it is hard, the artist/sculptor carves into it his chosen design, to produce an incised effect which is then painted and, in church art, almost always gilded.

Gibbons, Grinling (1648-1721): An interior decorator, wood carver and sculptor of genius, who worked for Charles II, was master carver to George I, collaborated with Sir Christopher Wren at St Paul's, and was the chosen instrument of the noblest in the land to beautify their country mansions (Petworth and Burghley, for example). He was especially known for the beauty and delicacy of his carvings of birds, flowers and foliage.

Green man: The green man is a foliate mask, often of demoniacal appearance, probably representing the spirit of fertility and often having living vines issuing from its mouth, and as such, an occasional device in wood and stone carving - a touch of persistent paganism in Christian art. Interesting examples can be found at Mildenhall (roof), Thurston (**font** and bench ends), Tostock (font), Woolpit (stalls), and Cavendish (roof **boss**).

Griffin: Traditionally the guardian of

treasure - but also used in church sculpture, carvings and paintings. The griffin, or gryphon, is a mythical monster with an eagle's head, wings and fore-legs; and the body, tail and hind-legs of a lion. Heraldry uses this fabulous creature too. There is a griffin on the arms of the City of London, for example. In Oriental folklore, a couple of griffins pulled Alexander the Great in a magic chariot up to heaven, while he was still alive that is, just to have a look around. See Mildenhall, Norton, Risby, Lakenheath and Woolpit.

Groining: This is the creation of a vaulted ceiling, divided into segments by raised, intersecting lines - these lines, between the angled surfaces, being the actual 'groins'. Found in carved canopies, as well as in **roofs**.

Guilds/guild altars: In corners of churches, in the e. ends of **aisles** etc, may often be seen **piscinas**, and occasionally **squints** which, as is frequently repeated in the body of this book, indicate the presence of a guild or **chantry altar** in pre-**Reformation** times. Indeed, English guilds, according to one authority, 'are older than any kings of England'. They were associations of those living in the same neighbourhood who remembered that they had, as neighbours, common obligations - an obligation to put into practice the commandment to 'love thy neighbour'. Their religious commitment would often be shown by having their own altar in their parish church, served by a priest whom they maintained. There were two main divisions: craft or trade guilds, whose purpose was the protection of particular work, trade or handicraft; and religious societies or, as they are sometimes called, 'social guilds'. The split was one of convenience rather than a real distinction. All had the same general character-

istic, the principle of brotherly love and social charity, and none was divorced from the ordinary religious observances daily practised in pre-Reformation England. Broadly speaking, they were the benefit societies and provident associations of the Middle Ages - a helping hand as ready to help the sick or look after poor children as to lodge pilgrims cheaply. Dr Augustus Jessop, canon of Norwich cathedral, headmaster of Norwich school, and local historian around the turn of this century, wrote descriptively of:

> ...small associations called guilds, the members of which were bound to devote a certain portion of their time and money and their energies to keep up the special commemoration and the special worship of some Saint's chapel or shrine which was sometimes kept up in a corner of the church, and provided with an altar of its own, and served by a chaplain who was actually paid by the subscriptions or free-will offerings of the members of the guild whose servant he was.

Nearly everyone was a member of one fraternity or another. One distinct help to the parish was the provision of additional priests for the services of the church. Beccles guild of the Holy Ghost, for example, had a priest 'to celebrate in the church'. Beccles being 'a great and populous town of 800 **houseling** people... the said priest is aiding unto the curate there, who without help is not able to discharge the said cure'. See also **chantry chapels**.

Hakewill, Edward Charles (1812-1872): A church architect who was one of Philip Hardwick's pupils in the 1830s and District Surveyor for St Clement Danes and St Mary-le-Strand. In 1851 he published *The Temple: an Essay on the Ark, the Tabernacle and the Temples of Jerusalem*. He carried out restorations at Langham, Drinkstone and Elmswell, nd the major rebuilding at Thurston.

Bakewill, John Henry (1811-80): An architect who enjoyed an extensive practice mainly in Wiltshire, Suffolk and Essex, building many churches, schools and parsonages. He was one of the consulting architects for the Incorporated Church Building Society and designed Bury's St Peter.

Hammerbeam roofs: A brilliant conception, architecturally and artistically, of the late Gothic period, late C15-C16, in which the thrust of the roof's weight is taken on 'hammer' brackets. See **roofs**, figs 6, 7 and 8.

Hanoverian: The period during which the sovereigns were of the House of Hanover, from George I to Victoria.

Hardman, John & Co: The family were originally button makers in Birmingham but John Hardman (1811-67) met **Pugin** in 1837 and they became friends. The following year they were partners in a new metal-working business which set out to provide church fittings and accessories of all kinds, for which Pugin provided all the designs in medieval style. Starting with small projects, mainly in precious metals, the venture blossomed. As Hardman and Iliffe, the firm took part in the Great Exhibition in 1851 and the medieval court displayed an extraordinary range of Pugin's designs and Hardman's craftsmanship. The revival of memorial **brasses** was largely due to them and Hardmans became by far the largest suppliers, producing some notable designs. In the early days, Pugin's influence was pervasive and stained glass was added to the repertoire in 1845. He was the chief designer in this medium until his death in 1852 when the role passed to Hard-

man's nephew, John Hardman Powell who continued until 1895. The firm's early work set standards for the Gothic revival in stained glass, and despite the changes in taste that have until recently dismissed it as unworthy of serious attention, it is of high quality and beauty. Examples include Chelsworth, the cathedral, Freckenham, Fornham All Saints and Rattlesden.

Hatchments: Many churches display on their walls large, diamond-shaped boards, bearing a coat of arms and either the motto of the family whose coat it is, or the simple word - but perhaps ultimate expression of confident faith - 'Resurgam' (I shall rise again). Dating from the second half of the C17 through to the end of the C18, these boards were carried in procession at the burial of the holder of the arms. Afterwards for some months they adorned the dead man's house, and finally were transferred to the church. The composition of the boards followed a formalised pattern - the background is black on the l. hand side if the dead person was a husband, black on the r. if a wife; for a bachelor, widow or widower, the whole background would be black.

Headstops: The decorative **stops** at the ends of **dripstones** and **hood moulds** over arches, doors and windows.

Heart burial: If a person died away from home he sometimes requested that his heart be buried in his parish church. The chosen place was marked either by a miniature effigy or by a heart (sometimes cupped in hands). There are not many in East Anglia but there is a rare example of a double heart burial at Exning.

Heaton, Butler & Bayne: A firm of stained glass manufacturers founded by Clement Heaton and James Butler in 1855, joined by Robert Turnill Bayne in 1862. They took over the role of the most original Gothicists from **Clayton & Bell** and produced an impressively varied series of high quality windows in the 1860s which were fine examples of the High Victorian style at its most accomplished. There was significant collaboration with **Henry Holiday** and other artists of the aesthetic movement in the 1870s and the firm continued to produce glass until 1953. Their earliest surviving Suffolk window is at Hawstead and good examples at Burton Mills, Botesdale and Bury (St Mary).

Herringbone work: A technique of positioning stones, bricks or tiles in 'arrow formation', like the bones of a fish, with alternate courses in different directions, giving a zigzag effect. Not a decorative device, but a strengthening and supporting measure. The technique goes back to Roman times, but continued through the **Saxon** period and well into the **Norman** era.

High altar: See **altar**.

Holiday, Henry G.A. (1839-1927): Artist, writer and one of the key stained glass designers of the C19. When his friend Burne-Jones left the **Powells** in 1861 he became their chief designer, working in his highly individual version of the **pre-Raphaelite** style. He also accepted commissions from Shrigley & Hunt and Saunders. His earliest Suffolk work is at Shimpling and other windows may be found at Hawstead and Lackford.

Holy table: See **altar**.

Holy Trinity: See **emblems of the Trinity**.

Hood mould: See **dripstone**.

Hour-glasses/stands: There was a time when long sermons were the rule rather than the exception, particularly after the **Reformation**, in Cromwell's Puritan period in the mid-C17, and in the C18 when preachers were renowned for their long-windedness. For their own guidance preachers often had an hour-glass on or near the pulpit, to indicate the passing time (though when the hour was up it was not unknown for sermonisers to turn the glass over and start again). Before the Reformation hour-glasses were used, though less commonly, to time private meditations etc. Numerous hour-glass stands remain today in our churches - among Suffolk examples are those at Bradfield St George, Barnardiston and Kedington.

Housel bench/houseling people: 'Housel' was the medieval word for the Eucharist and the 'houseling people' were those parishioners who had received communion. Provision was sometimes made for the congregation to sit in the **chancel** when they came from the **nave** to receive communion and the 'housel benches' have survived at Shelland. The special pews at Kedington served the same purpose.

Howson, Joan: See **Townshend, Caroline & Joan Howson**.

Ibex: An animal with horns that curve back along the neck. According to the **bestiaries** it was able to throw itself over the precipices and land safely on its horns. There are examples at Woolpit, Hawstead and Hunston.

IHS: See **sacred monogram**.

Impost: A simple bracket or moulding set as a 'lip' in a wall to carry a springing arch. A typical attribute of plain and massive **Saxon** architecture, in which field it is almost exclusively used in this book. (Compare with **capital** and **abacus**.

Instruments of the Passion: Often used symbolically in carving and painting. They are: Christ's cross; the crown of thorns; the spear that was thrust into His side; the cup of vinegar; and the reed and sponge by which that vinegar was offered as Christ hung on the cross (John 19:28-9). The dice which were used to cast lots for His clothing and a ladder are additional symbols. Typical examples may be found at Bardwell (roof) and Thurston (**reredos**).

Jacobean: Style of architecture dating from early in the C17 with the reign, 1603-1625, of James I. See **Styles of Architecture**.

Jamb/jamb shaft: The upright of a doorway, or the side of a window opening: the 'shaft' is a decorative shaft or slim column at the angle of the window splay with the wall, and can often be used to remarkably beautiful and delicate effect.

Jesse tree: Isaiah prophesied: 'And there shall come forth a rod out of the stem of Jesse, and a Branch shall grow out of his roots'. This gave medieval artists a wonderful opportunity to illustrate the human genealogy of Christ as a tree (often a vine) springing up from the body of Jesse with each generation pictured as the fruits, with the **Blessed Virgin** and Christ child at the top. Occasionally, pagan figures, like Virgil and the sybils, slipped in. Versions may be found at the cathedral, in Bury, and at Ickworth.

Kempe & Co (Kempe & Tower): A firm of stained glass manufacturers founded by Charles Eamer Kempe in 1869, a designer who had worked for **Clayton & Bell**. His nephew, Walter Ernest Tower, took over in 1907 and continued until 1934. Their work is generally in C15 mode, intricate and often sentimental, with a distinctive colour range. Kempe was one of the most successful late Victorian designers and there was little change in the style he adopted, even in the C20. His windows are sometimes signed with a wheatsheaf emblem, while those of Tower often have a castle superimposed on the sheaf of corn. Typical examples can be found at Santon Downham, the cathedral, at Bury, Risby, Dalham and Hopton, with Tower's work at Newmarket (St Mary) and Sudbury (All Saints).

Kennel head-dress: A style of head-dress fashionable from about 1500 to 1540, but not in fact given its name as we know it until the C19. It appears distinctively on figures on **brasses** and tombs of the period, and on carved heads of **corbels** etc. The head-dress consisted of a hood wired up to form a pointed arch over the forehead, with borders framing the face to each side. The early kind hung in folds to the shoulders behind; but after 1525 the back drapery was replaced by two long pendant flaps which hung down in front on each side of the neck. Both kinds will be seen represented. Examples are at Euston, Denston, Long Melford and Hawkedon.

King-posts: An upright roof beam set between horizontal cross beams, or between cross beam and roof ridge, to prevent sag and give greater stability. See **roofs**, fig 3, for full description.

Knapped/knapping:
See **flint-knapping**.

Label: A **dripstone** carried over a door or window enclosing the top.

Lancet: The slim, pointed window which characterises the beginnings of **Early English** architecture from about 1200. See **Styles of Architecture**.

Laud: See **Laudian**.

Laudian: This refers to Archbishop William Laud, 1573-1644. His seven years as Archbishop of Canterbury, during which he tried to impose certain disciplines of worship on the English and Scottish churches, had far reaching effects, but for him resulted in his execution. Laud wanted to reform the English church in a way compatible with Protestantism, yet without giving way to the sweeping changes and austerities called for by the increasingly powerful Puritans. Brought down to its simplicities, he wanted a disciplined order and form of worship which centred on the **altar**, placed against the e. wall of the **chancel**, with an enclosing rail around it; and with the communicants kneeling within the chancel to receive the sacrament. But these were matters of bitter and violent debate. From Elizabeth I's reign, the altar often had been placed 'table-wise', ie, e. to w. at the **nave** end of the chancel; or a temporary table was set up in the nave - the intention being in each case for the communicants to be within sight and hearing of the priest at the altar. But there were those who refused to kneel, or even to enter the chancel, and who certainly would not tolerate, in the e. end altar, what smacked to them of a Popish **high altar**, divorced from the people. The impression which comes down to us of the Archbishop is of a man of honest intent - but whose every action seemed to turn people against him. He was accused of 'popery' and of warmth towards Rome; blamed for

the disastrous and ineffective moves against Scotland, both judicial and military, intended to make its churches conform with his ideas; then he issued 'canons' (ie, instructions) which appeared to many to enshrine the absolute rule and 'divine right' of King Charles I - whose position by now was already seriously threatened. In December 1640 Parliament impeached Laud for treason, and he was imprisoned in the Tower. But it was not until March 1644 that he was put on trial and then it was a complete mockery of justice, for the House of Lords had decided in advance that he was guilty of trying to alter the foundations of church and state. Nonetheless they hesitated to sentence him until the House of Commons threatened to set the mob on them if they didn't. On 10 January 1644, staunchly declaring his innocence and good intent, William Laud, at the venerable age of 72, died under the axe, Parliament having graciously agreed that he should be excused the usual traitor's punishment of being hung, drawn and quartered. The irony is that, by the end of the century, the forms of service which developed in the Anglican church were much in sympathy with the things for which Laud fought and died. See also **Prayer book churches, communion rails,** and **mensa slabs**.

Lavers & Barraud (Lavers & Westlake): Stained glass manufacturers. Founded by Nathaniel Wood Lavers in 1855; he was joined by Francis Philip Barraud in 1858, both men having been with **Powell & Sons** in the 1840s. Lavers was the craftsman and business head, relying on competent artists to design his windows, but Barraud was a prolific designer for the first decade of the partnership, specialising in small figure medallions. In the 1860s the firm was much favoured by the leaders of the **Ecclesiological Society**. From then on, major commissions were designed by Nathaniel H.J. Westlake and he became a partner in 1868, doing the majority of the figure work. At that time their colouring was light and sweet, with a wide range of tints, and the leading was meticulous. Towards the end of the century there was a steady deterioration in aesthetic standards, with mass production methods being used to meet the heavy demand. Westlake was head of the firm in 1880 and continued to his death in 1921. There are good examples of their work at Lavenham and Bradfield Combust, with others at Culford, Bury (St Mary), Chelsworth, Drinkstone, Elmswell and Rickinghall Inferior.

Ledger-stone: When the art and use of monumental **brasses** declined in the first half of the C17, sculpture in stone began to come into its own in our churches. But while those splendid, opulent examples which adorn wall or table tomb may be the first to catch the eye, it often pays to drop one's gaze to the ground to those dark, massive slabs in pavements of **chancel**, **nave** and **aisles**, incised with arms, crests and epitaphs. These are our ledger-stones, and a study in themselves, as many carry quite marvellous inscriptions which can so easily be overlooked.

Lenten veil: It was the custom in medieval times to 'curtain off' the **altar** during Lent with a Lenten veil. This was suspended from **corbels**, or hooks, of which a few examples remain in Suffolk churches set in the chancel walls - see Bury, St Mary (pulleys), Troston (hooks) and Norton (drilled block). Some churches echo the custom today by veiling the **reredos**.

Lights: A frequently used word in these volumes. Very simply, it is the space between the vertical divisions of a window or **screen**. So if a window

has just one centre **mullion**, it is a two-light window (not to be confused with an occasional usage of 'light' in the sense of candles or lamps kept burning before images, the **rood**, and tabernacles).

Linen-fold panelling: This was an innovation in wood carving of the C16 in the **Tudor** period - an elegant and beautifully restrained representation in wood of linen laid in crisp vertical folds. Seen on a range of church furnishings.

Lombardic script: This is a calligraphic form of writing which developed in Italy after the Roman and Byzantine periods. A variant of it was used for papal documents and for legal work in Rome until the early C13. From time to time it is used on tombs and memorials in English churches.

Long and short work: Distinctive of **Saxon** craftsmanship, upright stone alternating with flat slabs in the **quoins** at the corners of buildings. See **Styles of Architecture**.

Lonsdale, Horatio Walter (1844-1919): An artist in stained glass who designed much of the glass produced by W.G. Saunders, particularly for the architect William Burges. He later executed many windows of his own which illustrate the high quality of his draughtmanship, and some are extremely attractive, as at Freckenham.

Low side windows: Almost as much nonsense has been written about low side windows as about **weeping chancels**. These small, square or oblong windows were usually low down in the s. wall of the **chancel**, just e. of the chancel arch, and fitted with shutters so that the window could be opened. It has been suggested that these were 'leper windows' for these afflicted people to look in and thus share in the mass - a ridiculous assertion, since not even in medieval times would lepers have been allowed to roam at leisure. The actual use of these windows, most authorities agree, was so that, at the point in the mass at which the priest raises the cup and the consecrated bread for the people to see, a bell could be rung through the open window so that: 'people who have not leisure daily to be present at Mass may, wherever they are in houses or fields, bow their knees' (Archbishop Peckham, 1281). A hand bell may have been used but sometimes a bell was housed in a turret on the roof (see **sanctus-bell**). Sometimes the low side window was incorporated in a larger window but many of the separate ones have been blocked up. Interesting examples can be seen at Hopton (double), Great Livermore and Gazeley (both sides of chancel), Troston (original shutter), Little Whelnetham (original grill) and Stanningfield (**quatrefoil** shape).

Lowndes, Mary (1857-1929): Arts and Crafts stained glass worker. A pupil of **Henry Holiday**, she designed her first window in 1885 and soon after taught herself the techniques of glass painting. She worked with, and was influenced by, **Christopher Whall**, and in 1897 in partnership with A. J. Drury, she set up Lowndes & Drury. Known as 'The Glass House', their studio and workshop in Fulham became the focal point for workers in stained glass, and the staff were at the disposal of any artist who cared to employ them. Mary Lowndes designed and made many fine windows between 1890 and the 1920s but the only example of her work in Suffolk is at Snape.

Lych-gate: The word 'lych' is derived

from the **Anglo-Saxon** 'lic' or 'lich', and from the German 'leiche', all meaning corpse. The purpose of the lych-gate is to provide shelter and resting place for coffin bearers on the way to the church. In former times, the lych-gate would have seats and a coffin table, on which the coffin would be set. Poor people who could not afford a coffin might be placed, temporarily, in the parish coffin; but otherwise they would be wrapped in a sheet and placed straight onto the coffin table, where they would be received by the priest, who here speaks the first sentences of the burial service. Ancient lych-gates are rare, most being C19/C20.

Mason's marks: It was the practice of medieval masons to identify their work by cutting an individual symbol on selected blocks of stone. A fine and large example can be seen on the s.w. buttress of the tower at Rickinghall Superior.

Mass dials: See **scratch dials**.

Mensa slabs: In pre-**Reformation** times, the **high altar** and **altars** in **chantry chapels** were of stone, topped with a slab or 'mensa' (Latin for table). Each had five crosses carved upon it, one at each corner and one on the centre, representing the **five wounds of Christ**. After the suppression of the monasteries, begun in 1536 by Henry VIII, the chantries too were soon dissolved, and with them went their altars. But stone high altars remained, and in the reign of Henry's son, the boy-king Edward VI (a convinced Protestant) a movement was led by two of his bishops to have them removed and replaced by wooden tables. This was realised in 1550 when the king in Council commanded every bishop to order this change in all the churches in his diocese. Many more sweeping changes in church interiors and in forms of worship were to follow in this period, and much wanton destruction, as the demands of a new age were ruthlessly achieved. (See under **Prayer book churches** how these changes developed). There is a mensa dated 1420 at Mildenhall, a massive example at Cowlinge, and others at Thelnetham, Thorpe Morieux, Denston, Flempton, Little Whelnetham and Westhorpe. See also **consecration crosses**.

Misericords: In the **chancels** of many churches remain ancient stalls with hinged seats. Underneath, the tip-up seats are carved generally with very free expression and often with exuberant irreverence and humour: anything from the wildest caricatures to cartoonish domestic scenes and upsets. All are worth examining closely, wherever they are found. On the leading edge of these seats is usually a smooth, hollowed surface on which, during long services, the elderly, or just the plain sleepy, could lean and rest. Thus the name, from the Latin 'misericordia', pity, compassion. There are good examples at Stowlangtoft, Norton and Lavenham.

Morris, William & Co: Stained glass manufacturers. William Morris (1834-96) was a designer, poet, and prolific writer on artistic and other matters. In 1861, he drew together a group of artists which included Burne-Jones, Ford Madox Brown, Rossetti and Philip Webb, to found Morris, Marshall, Faulkner & Co. The firm revolutionised British taste in furnishing and interior decoration and, from the outset, stained glass was an important part of their activities. Morris assumed responsibility for colour, and all cartoons were by the partners themselves. Rossetti dropped out in 1865 and from 1869 Burne-Jones was much more active, becoming sole designer in 1875, after which Morris gave only occasional

attention to the work. Burne-Jones died two years after Morris in 1898 and thereafter John Henry Dearle was chief designer. He had worked with Morris for many years and echoed his style and that of Burne-Jones. Good design and technical excellence, combined with Morris' genius for colour, put their windows in a class apart, particularly between 1865 and 1875. Although Dearle followed them faithfully, re-using and adapting many of their designs, his work in the 1920s was an empty continuation of an outdated style. The firm closed in 1940. There are eight windows by Morris & Co in Suffolk - at Bacton, Freston, Great Barton, Hopton-on-Sea, Thornham Magna and Westerfield.

Mouchette: A **tracery** shape or motif, used principally during the **Decorated** period early in the C14. It is a curved dagger or spearhead shape, **cusped** and arched inside.

Mullion: Vertical bar dividing **lights** in a window.

Nave: The main 'body' of a church - from the Latin 'navis', a ship. Traditionally the nave was for the congregation, the **chancel** being for the clergy. Indeed, so much was it a preserve of the people that once services were over, it was used for parish meetings, as a courtroom and perhaps for the performance of mystery plays. Outside, meanwhile, the churchyard might be market place and fairground. See also **preaching crosses**.

Norman: The Romanesque form of architecture, with its distinctive rounded arches and massive round pillars, introduced to England following the **Norman** Conquest of 1066. See under **Styles of Architecture** for full description.

O'Connor, Arthur and William:
Stained glass artists whose father
Michael began in Dublin as an heraldic painter before moving to London
in 1823. He had studied with **Thomas
Willement** and worked with **Pugin**
and **Butterfield**. He took his sons into
partnership in the 1850s and when
Arthur died in 1873, William George
Taylor joined the firm and managed it
from 1877 onwards. Much of the
O'Connors' work is distinguished by
fine colour and an effective deployment of lead lines. Windows they
can be found at Hessett, Bardwell,
Brent Eleigh and Rickinghall
Superior.

Ogee: This is a lovely, flowing 'S'
shaped arch or moulding - a convex
curve flowing into a concave one.
Usually they are not very large
because, by their very nature, they
cannot carry heavy loads; but their
grace lends them to the heads of canopies, to **piscina**, **sedilia** and the like;
sometimes also to doorways, giving
them an engaging and curiously Oriental look; as well as in the **tracery** of
windows, **screens** etc. Adorned with
crocketting, ogee arches are still more
attractive. They came into general use
in the C14, playing an important role
in the development of the sumptuous
windows of the late **Decorated** period, with their flowing tracery of
which the ogee curve forms an integral part. See **Styles of Architecture**.

Pamment: An unglazed flooring tile
used widely in East Anglia; the average size is 9 in square, 2 in thick.

Parclose screen: The screens which
separate **chantry** or side chapels, and/
or **aisles**, from the main body of the
church. See also **rood loft/screen**.
There are C14 examples at Westhorpe
and Cowlinge and those at Lavenham
are exceptional C16 work.

Parish clerk: Not the 'clerk' to the
parish council of late Victorian, local
government invention. But a paid
office which was for centuries of central importance in church services. In
short, it was the job of the clerk to lead
the singing and the responses to the
prayers, and to voice a healthy
'Amen' both at the end of prayers and
of the sermon. Sometimes he filled
the role of choirmaster; certainly he
would 'give the notes' on a pitch pipe,
just as unaccompanied choirs today
are given on a pipe the four notes for
sopranos, altos, tenors and basses.
After the **Reformation** in the C16, the
clerk continued to exercise his role;
indeed, the replanning of church
interiors to meet the new Protestant
requirements gave him a special seat
in the **three-decker pulpits** which
appeared at this time (see **Prayer
book churches**). In the C17, under
James I and later Charles II, the parish
clerks, who had the dignity of being a
London Company, were given new
Charters which stipulated that:

> every person that is chosen Clerk
> of the Parish should first give sufficient proof of his abilities to sing at
> least the tunes which are used in
> the parish churches.

He sang on until soon after Victoria
ascended the throne, when most of
his duties were given to curates. Then
came the local government acts of the
late C19, which finally consigned
him to history and left only his seat at
the foot of the three-deckers to
remind us of a 700-year-old tradition.

Parish guilds: See **guilds/guild altars**.

Passion emblems: See **instruments of
the Passion**.

Paterae: Round ornaments in bas
relief, often used to enrich
mouldings.

Pediment: The low triangular gable used in classical building but often employed on classically styled monuments in churches.

Pelican: The pelican has long had a special place in religious symbolism and may often be seen as a device used in medieval carving and embellishment. There is a legend that the bird tore its own breast to feed its young upon its own blood - the source of the idea, it is suggested, being that the tip of the pelican's bill, which usually rests on this ungainly bird's chest, is touched with red. In medieval art the ungainliness is replaced by a dove-like representation and the legend transmuted into a symbolism of Man's fall and redemption through the Passion of Christ. Here we find that the parent bird was said to kill its young in a moment of irritation - then, 'on the third day', to restore them to life by tearing its breast and letting its own blood pour over them. The complete carving of the bird and its young is often referred to as 'the pelican in her piety'. In the C18 and early C19 a female figure with the pelican signified Benevolence (often used by the sculptor **John Bacon**). The **font** at Risby has a particularly good example and there is a modern realistic interpretation at Beyton.

Perpendicular: The great age of church building, in the second half of the C14 and through the C15, in the style characterised by soaring upward lines in great windows and majestic towers. See full description under **Styles of Architecture**.

Pevsner, Sir Nikolaus: Author of the monumental and remarkable undertaking. *The Buildings of England* series - 46 volumes, written between 1951 and 1974, meticulously recording the principal buildings - domestic, public and church (including the

detail and furnishings of the latter) of every county in England, and masterminded throughout by Pevsner himself. His volume on Suffolk appeared in 1961 and an edition, revised by Enid Radcliffe, was published in 1974.

Phipson, Richard Makilwaine (1827-84): As an architect he was not outstanding and sometimes verged on the incompetent, but he was very active in Norfolk and Suffolk from 1850 onwards. As joint diocesan surveyor from 1871 until his death, he had a hand in most of the restorations during that important period and by then had become well known, particularly for his work at St Mary le Tower, Ipswich and St Peter Mancroft, Norwich. He designed the replacement tower at Woolpit and the church at Great Finborough.

Pier: The architectural term for a column or pillar.

Pietà: A carving or painting of the **Blessed Virgin** as Our Lady of Sorrows, seated with the dead Christ laid across her knees. To be seen in C15 glass at Long Melford, in C17 continental glass at Nowton and Great Saxham, in glass at Bardwell, on a **reredos** at Cavendish, and in a C19 painting at Horringer.

Pilaster: A miniature pillar, rectangular in section, usually based in style on one of the classical orders of architecture, and normally applied to a wall.

Pillar piscina: See **piscina**.

Piscina/angle piscina/double piscina/pillar piscina: A stone basin near an **altar** (its presence today indicates that there was formerly an altar there), usually set into a niche in the wall below an arch or canopy, sometimes projecting outwards on a bowl, which in turn may be supported by a small pillar. Occasionally too a piscina may be found let into a pillar. The piscina was used for cleansing the communion vessels after mass, thus it has a drain hole in its basin, which allows the water used in the cleansing to run down into consecrated ground. It is obligatory that where water has been blessed, or has come into contact with anything consecrated, it must be returned to earth. Sometimes there is a small shelf in the piscina niche called a **credence shelf**. The angle piscina is one built into the angle of a window or **sedilia**, and opened out on two sides, often affording the opportunity for beautiful carving and design. Double piscinas (two side by side) may occasionally be found. These had but a short span of fashion in the late C13-early C14: one was used by the priest for the cleaning of the vessels, the other for washing of his own hands. A pillar piscina is not, as the name might imply, a piscina set into a pillar; but a piscina which protrudes from a wall, its bowl and drain standing on a miniature pillar, either attached to a or standing clear of the wall. A corbel piscina has, instead of a pillar, its bowl supported by a corbel or pendant.

Plate tracery: This is tracery in the heads of windows where the pattern is cut directly through the masonry; as distinct from bar tracery, which is constructed in separate pieces. See **Early English** under **Styles of Architecture**.

Poppyheads: The boldly carved floral ornament which graces the ends of bench pews, said to be derived from the French 'poupée', puppet, doll or figurehead. It was carved during the great age of C15 church building and

wood carving that poppyheads came into being and achieved their highest artistic expression. The carvers often seem to have been given a free hand, with diverse and interesting results including animals, grotesques, faces and so on.

Porches: It was not until the C14 that porches came to be regarded as an essential part of the church paln, so few are found from before that date. It explains of course why **scratch** dials will often be found beside the inner door, inside the porch, where the sun could not possibly reach them. Quite simply, the porch was a later addition. Having become established, the porch assumed a practical importenc4e in medieval times which we tend to forget today. Services of baptism began here; sentences were spoken from the burial service, after the first pause in the **lych-gate**; women were churched (i.e, purified and blessed) after the birth of a child; part of the wedding service was conducted here; in the porch the kneeling penitent received absolution; and the porch was one of the 'stations' in the regular Sunday and Feast Day processions. Not least, the porch was a convenient meeting ground for the carrying out of much civil and legal business. Some porches also have a second storey originally intended as a priest's room, but later much used as the first and only school in the parish. The n. porch at Mildenhall is the largest in Suffolk and the upper room there was a Lady chapel. The finest example is at Woolpit.

Powell, James & Sons: Stained glass manufacturers. Founded in 1844, the business had one of the longest histories in the trade and did not close until 1973. It was among the most important and progressive firms, making a significant contribution both in technology and in the art form. Many of their designs came from artists of the calibre of Burne-Jones, **Henry Holiday** and **Christopher Whall**. Examples may be found at Hepworth, Thurston, Newmarket (All Saints), Whepstead, Hawstead, Great Bradley, Shimpling and Ixworth.

Prayer book churches; A phrase used to describe those churches where the furnishings and layout still embody the geat shift of emphasis inchurch worship that came, first with the **Reformation** and then with the Puritans. The old, and strict, division of priest in **chancel** from people in **nave** was put away, and the English prayer book of 1549 required the laity to take part in all of the service; matins and evensong were to be conducted from the chancel and everybody had to hear the Lessons. The **altar** became 'the table' for the first time in the 1552 revision. After the Civil War, Sunday services (except on infrequent Sacrament Sundays) were conducted entirely from the reading desk, and soon the convenient reading desk cum pulpit became the rule (see **three-decker pulpits**). In the C18 virtually every church in the land had its pews (often enclosed for each family - see **box pews**) arranged to focus on the reading desk. Then, in the 1830s, a 'new wave' of churchmen were inspired by **Pugin** and John Newman's Oxford Movement, to sweep away these things. Their vision was to have truly Gothic churches again, and C18 domestic church interiors were anathema. Today, very few of the sensible and seemly furnishings of the Age of Reason are to be found, but there is a fine example at Shelland.

Preaching/churchyard crosses: In ancient times, when the churchyard was a gathering place, market and fairground, most churches had a preaching or churchyard cross, from which the resident priest, or wandering friars, might preach to the assembled people. The stumps of some of these crosses remain. There is the head of a C10 cross at Kedington and parts of others at Elmswell, Brockley, Hawstead, Hessett, Rickinghall Inferior and Woolpit.

Pre-Raphaelites: The pre-Raphaelite Brotherhood was a group of Victorian artists, much reviled in its day, who sought to go back to principles before the Italian master. Raphael (d. 1520) imposed his mark (one of the major figures in the world history of art, he was the painter of many celebrated works, including decorative work in the Vatican). The Brotherhood had only three members, Rossetti, Millais and Holman Hunt, and lasted only five years from its establishment in 1848. But, with its pre-occupation with biblical and literary subjects and the artists' urge for 'social realism', it had a great influence on several other artists of note, among them Burne-Jones. It was he who later, with **William Morris**, briefly tried to revive the Brotherhood. Inevitably the pre-Raphaelite movement left its impression on the church art of the period, as evidenced in Burne-Jones' work.

Priest's door: Most **chancels** have a small door, usually on the s. side, which was the priest's 'private entrance'. It fits into context when it is remembered that, in pre-**Reformation** times, the chancel was the priest's particular responsibility (only occasionally entered by the laity) while the parishioners looked after the **nave**.

Pugin, Augustus Welby Northmore (1812-52): English architect. He early became a Roman Catholic and some of his best plans were drawn from churches and cathedrals. He also had a large share in the designs and plans for the Houses of Parliament in 1836. Through pressure of work he went insane, and died at the age of only 40. However his influence on the interior furnishing of churches as we know them today was considerable.

Purbeck marble: References to purbeck marble are frequently in relation to **fonts**. The first wave of fonts in this material came during the **Norman** period, and it was used for long afterwards. The grey stone is not in fact marble at all, but a hard limestone full of shells. It comes from strata stretching from the Isle of Purbeck, the peninsula off s.e. Dorset (famous for its quarries for a thousand years) and northwards through to Aylesbury.

Purlin: The purlin is the main horizontal supporting beam of a roof See **roofs**, fig 4.

Put-log holes: The holes where the horizontal members of the (timber) scaffolding slotted into the walls during construction.

Putti (singular, putto): Little naked cherub boys first seen in that form in the work of **Renaissance** artists in Italy; and regularly in the work of C18/C19 sculptors in England in the adornment of monuments and tombs. It is possible that these cherubs have their origin in the naked Eros and Mercury representations of ancient classical, pagan belief, one of the many examples of 'Christianising' ancient deities, places and practices.

Pyx: This is the receptacle, suspended over the **altar**, in which the Host (the consecrated bread - the Body of Christ, Latin, 'hostia', victim) is 'reserved'. Note the story of **St Clare** under **Saints**. The pyx was sometimes veiled and Hessett's pyx cloth is now in the British Museum.

Quarry: A diamond-shaped pane of glass.

Quatrefoils: See **foils**.

Queen posts: Upright roof beams set in pairs on horizontal cross or **tie-beams** and thrusting up on each side to the main horizontal supporting beams, or **purlins**, of the roof. Designed, like the **king** post, to prevent sag and give greater stability. See **roofs**.

Quoins: Quite simply, the outside corner stones at the angles of buildings. See also **long and short work**.

Raphael: See **Saints**.

Rebus: A punning representation of a name or word by the use of symbols, normally in churches referring to the name of the place or the name of a donor.

Redundant Churches Fund: It having been recognised that church and state should share responsibility for churches no longer required for regular worship and for which no suitable alternative use could be found, the Fund was set up by law in 1969. Its declared aim is to preserve churches which are of architectural, historical or archaeological importance, and it is financed jointly by the Department of the Environment (60%) and the Church Commissioners (40%), plus contributions from the general public, local authorities and other organisations. The Fund was caring for 216 churches in 1986, of which 16 are in Suffolk, and many of them are used for occasional services.

Reformation: In particular terms, the

great religious movement in western Europe during the C16, founded on a return to biblical sources and their fresh interpretation, which led to the rejection of Roman and papal authority and the establishment of Protestant churches. In England the original motivations were more basic, being political and economic, rather than theological. Firstly, a ruthless, single minded, vastly vain and wholly autocratic monarch in Henry VIII, intent on putting away one wife and taking another by whom he could beget an heir. Secondly, his calculating eye on the wealth of the monasteries backed by his aristocracy and gentry, who could not wait to get their hands on the spoils. Even when he had broken with Rome, however, Henry did his best to minimise the impression of any break with the tradition begun in England by St Augustine a thousand years earlier. The true religious, reforming Reformation came with his son, the boy-king Edward VI, who though young, was a fanatical Protestant (see **Prayer book churches**).

Reliquary/reliquary chamber: A container for relics. The bodies of saints and martyrs were venerated by the early church and wherever possible an **altar** would contain, or have housed nearby, a portion of bone or object associated with a saint. Some became famous centres of pilgrimage and a source of revenue for the church. There is a reliquary chamber at Gedding.

Renaissance: A movement which began in Italy during the C14 in which there was a startling rebirth of culture, particularly in the arts and literature, which drew its inspiration from the classical models of Greece and Rome. It spread to the rest of Europe during the C16 and the style of architecture and decoration which originated in Florence in the early C15 gradually replaced the Gothic

tradition. See also **Styles of Architecture, Jacobean/Caroline**.

Reredos: A screening at the back of an **altar**, usually richly embellished in painting or carving. Few old examples remain, many having disappeared at the **Reformation** and in the century following. See also **decalogue boards**.

Respond: This is the half-pillar, attached to a wall, which supports an arch, most often seen at the ends of **arcades**.

Restoration: The period from 1660, following the restoration of the Monarchy after the Civil War and Cromwell's government, and the accession of Charles II.

Retable: A shelf or ledge at the back of an **altar** on which statues, lights or crosses could stand. The term can also apply to a painted or carved panel in the same position. See also **reredos**.

Reticulated: (Latin, 'rete' a net; 'reticulum', a bag of network - the link being that the tracery forms a net-like pattern.) A form of 'flowing' **tracery** in windows which was developed at the height of **Decorated** achievement during the first half of the C14 (see **Styles of Architecture**, fig 17).

Ringham, Henry (1806-1866): Master joiner and carver. During the C19, when so many churches were restored, the standard of craftsmanship was high and, because methods and tools had not changed significantly, many joiners and woodcarvers were able to match the work of their C15 predecessors. In this, no one excelled Henry Ringham. He came to

Ipswich from Lincolnshire as an unlettered teenager, and by a mixture of perseverance and native genius made himself the master of Gothic woodwork. He devoted his life to the restoration of churches, and in 1843 was entrusted with his first big commission at Woolpit. Roofs and benches were his speciality and before he died he had worked on 83 churches in the county, the last being Wherstead. His work can be identified at Lavenham, Sudbury, All Saints (pulpit), and the Drinkstone benches may well be his.

Rood screen/loft/beam/stair: The rood (Old English for wood) is the cross with the figure of the crucified Christ, the dominant symbol of atonement. Before the **Reformation** all churches were divided in two: the **chancel** for the clergy, the **nave** for the people. Between them was a wooden screen (often with a door) which stretched from pillar to pillar under the chancel arch, and in some cases right across the church. This screen is known as the rood screen because above it stood (or hung) the great crucifix, the rood itself. This sometimes stood on a separate beam (the rood beam) and was normally flanked by figures of the **Blessed Virgin** and **St John**. In many cases there was a loft built above the screen so that the images could be maintained (they sometimes had special clothes) and to carry **lights**. On occasion, the loft housed singers and during the mass the Gospel was read from there. Access to the loft was by stairs in one or both of the side walls. At the **Reformation** the rood and its images were almost universally torn down and destroyed in violent reaction against Rome and 'popery'. The fact that so many screens survive is due to Queen Elizabeth who, in a Royal Order of 1561, directed that while the great rood and its figures should go, the screens themselves should remain, and be topped with a suitable crest or

with the **Royal Arms**. Where screen as well as rood had already been destroyed, a new screen - or 'partition', as the wording had it - was to be constructed: for the Elizabethan view was quite clearly that the church should be partitioned into two distinct sections. The issue of screens and their role was to rumble on for another century. In 1638 Richard Montague, bishop of Norwich, was pointedly asking his clergy:

> Is your chancel divided from the nave or body of your church, with a partition of stone, boards, wainscot, grates or otherwise? Wherein is there a decent strong door to open and shut, (as occasion serveth) with lock and key, to keep out boys, girls, or irreverent men and women? And are dogs kept from coming to besoil or profane the Lord's table? While rood stairs

and screens are common, rood lofts are very rare but there is a section of the e. front of a loft at Troston and a very good reproduction of a complete loft at Rattlesden. Rood beams survive at Worlington, Hargrave, Denston, Onehouse and Rushbrooke. Above average screens are to be found at Lavenham, Barningham, Harleston and Kedington (post-Reformation).

Roofs: The development, structural variety and embellishment of church roofs is a fascinating field. Here is a potted guide to a richly complex subject. Coupled rafter roofs are a simple variety, which also serve to indicate the roof components (fig 1). The principal rafters, the feet of which are secured to a **wall plate**, have a collar beam to support them and to prevent sagging. More support is given by the collar braces, with struts lower down giving more strength. Another framing system is the scissor beam (fig 2), which can exist with the cross beams only, or with a supporting collar. As a precaution against spreading of the roof, a tie-beam was often added

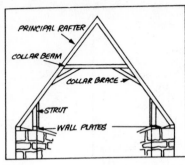

Fig 1.

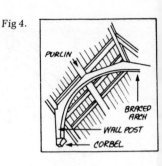

Fig 4.

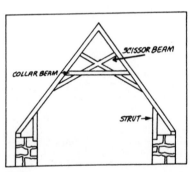

Fig 2.

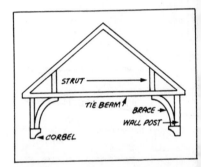

Fig 5.

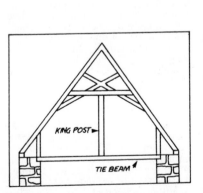

Fig 3.

between the wall plates (fig 3); but as tie-beams have a tendency to sag in the middle a central **king post** served to prevent this. The **arch-braced** construction is where the roof is carried on a braced arch which incorporates 'in one' the strut, collar brace and collar beam (fig 4). The function of the tie-beam has already been seen in fig 3. With a low-pitched roof, it is often used simply with struts upward to the principal rafters, and downward on brace and **wall post** to a **corbel** set into the wall (fig 5) well below the wall plates. With the advent of the **hammerbeam** development (fig 6), a new splendour was added to the roof builder's art. Instead of a tie-beam

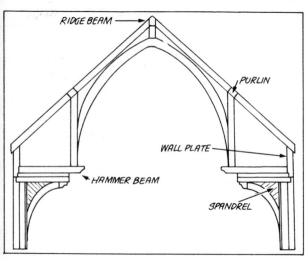

Fig 6.

Fig 7.

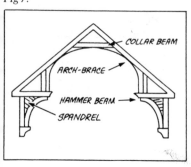

Fig 8.

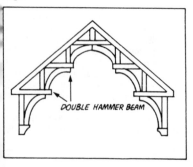

spanning wall to wall, there are hammerbeam brackets, from which spring a vertical strut, upward to the principal rafter at its intersection with the **purlin** (refer again to fig 4), the main horizontal supporting beam. Continuing upward, curved arch-like braces meet either at the ridge beam, or at a collar beam, set very high (fig 7). From there it was a natural development to the double hammerbeam. Fig 8 is self explanatory. The ends of the hammerbeams are often embellished with angels or decorative carvings. Roofs of exceptional quality may be seen at Mildenhall, Bury (St Mary), Palgrave, Walsham-le- Willows, Haughley, Wetherden and Rattlesden.

Rope, Margaret Agnes (1882-1953): Arts and Crafts stained glass worker. A Roman Catholic, she studied at Birmingham and her first commission in 1910 was the w. window of Shrewsbury Catholic cathedral. Moving to London and working in 'The Glass House' (see under **Lowndes, Mary**), she collaborated with her cousin **Margaret E. Aldrich Rope**. Their first work was a memorial window in Blaxhall church in 1911. In 1923 she entered the Carmelite monastery at Woodbridge, but was able to continue with her work on stained glass. She later moved to the monastery at Quidenham in Norfolk but illness prevented much further work. Apart from the Blaxhall window, examples of her craftsmanship may be seen in the former Franciscan convent chapel at East Bergholt and in the Roman Catholic church at Kesgrave.

Rope, Margaret E. Aldrich: Arts and Crafts stained glass worker. Born of an artistic family at Leiston, she spent her childhood at Blaxhall and studied stained glass under Alfred Drury at the Central School of Arts and Crafts. She assisted her cousin **Margaret Rope** at 'The Glass House' in making the Rope memorial window at Blaxhall in 1911, and after the war she returned to Fulham and began securing independent commissions. She continued to produce work of high quality until her retirement in the 1960s. Windows by her may be found at Barnby, Little Glemham, Leiston, and Kesgrave Roman Catholic church.

Royal Arms: Many churches display Royal coats of arms, usually square and framed, painted on wood or canvas; though they may also be found in carved wood or stone, cast in plaster, or set in stained glass. Occasionally the arms set up and painted in a lozenge shape, like a **hatchment**, but this is unusual. It was only during the reign of Henry VIII, when he assumed complete control of the English church, that Royal Arms began to come into regular use. Catholic Queen Mary was later to order their removal, and the replacement of the old **rood lofts**. But with Elizabeth's accession, they began to reappear;

indeed Elizabeth directed their use and indicated that the **tympanum** (the top part of the **chancel** arch, panelled in) was the place to display them. Inevitably many disappeared during Cromwell's Commonwealth, for in 1650 his Parliamentarians ordered 'the removal of the obnoxious Royal Arms from the churches'. The **Restoration** Parliament in 1660 made Royal Arms compulsory in all our churches, a practice continued generally until Victoria's accession, ordering that 'the Armes of the Commonwealth wherever they are standing be forthwith taken down, and the Kings Majesties armes be set up instead thereof'. Hosts of Royal Arms will be found throughout the county but the following are of particular interest: Rushbrooke (claimed as earliest but suspect), Preston (Elizabethan), Mildenhall (largest), Redgrave and Wortham (oval), Troston (James I), Dalham (**Hanoverian**), Long Melford and Acton (quality carving).

Sacred monogram: The two names of Christ and Jesus, originally written in Greek, were often reduced to the first two letters, or the first, second and final, or the first and last; when written in Latin they became: IH-XP, IHC-XPC, or IC-XC. For centuries the symbol XP (known as the Chi Rho) was used in various forms. The name came to be written IHESUS in English and IHC became IHS. This was later taken to mean (conveniently but erroneously) 'Jesus Hominum Salvator', Jesus, Saviour of mankind.

Sacring bell: A small bell rung at that point in the mass when the priest holds up the Host above the **altar** (the action known as the Elevation). See Hawstead.

Sacristy: A room, often with specially strengthened doors and windows, where the vestments, church plate and other valuables were stored. There are examples at Rattlesden, Hessett and elsewhere.

Saints: 'For all the saints'.... On **rood screens**, on **fonts**, in woodwork and stained glass, a panoply of saints is represented in Suffolk churches. Almost all of them have some identifying emblem - which adds yet another element of interest for the church visitor. The following is a list of those to be found in the county, with emblems, brief story background and some representative locations.

Agatha: Represented either with pincers in her hand or with her severed breasts upon a dish, indicating the horrid nature of her martyrdom in C6 Sicily. She vowed her virginity to Christ and refused to yield to the lust of the local governor, who took ghastly revenge. She is invoked against fire (another of her tortures) and against diseases of the breasts. Agatha is also patron saint of bell founders. (She is represented at Nowton.)

Agnes: Her symbols are a sword, often thrust into her neck or bosom, and a lamb - Latin, 'agna', a pun on her name. Ancient Rome, about 300 AD. and 13-year-old Agnes refuses to marry the prefect's son. She was publicly stripped, but her hair miraculously grew long to cover her. They tried to burn her, but the flames declined to help. So at last she was stabbed. (Newmarket is the only Suffolk dedication and she is represented at Nowton.)

Alban: Often represented with a tall cross or a sword, he is credited with being Britain's earliest martyr. He was a Roman knight who had been converted to Christianity here in Britain in the C3. He was ordered by his superiors to sacrifice to pagan gods,

refused to do so, and was condemned to be executed at Verulamium, the city which became St Albans. He converted the first executioner who tried to despatch him. The second was more successful and beheaded the saint, whereupon the man's eyes dropped out! Alban is the only saint to have enjoyed a continuous cult in England from Roman times. (He is represented at Kettlebaston.)

Ambrose: One of the **Four Latin Doctors**. Usually represented with a beehive - allusion to intriguing story of swarm of bees which settled on the baby Ambrose's cradle. Also seen wearing his bishop's robes and holding whip or scourge, recalling penance he imposed on all-powerful Roman Emperor Theodosius to atone for a frightful massacre carried out at his order. Ambrose became Bishop of Milan in 374. Central figure in the early church with powerful influence on the Roman emperors. (He is represented at Dalham.)

Andrew: The saltire (X-shaped cross, Scotland's part of Union Jack) and fishing net are his symbols. One of the Twelve, he was a fisherman before he became a disciple. Legends of his later life are legion, including one that he visited Scotland, thus becoming its patron saint. Martyred by crucifixion, it is said, upon an X-shaped cross. The locations where he is represented are too many to list but note the C17 stained glass figure at Hawkedon and the **misericord** carving of his martyrdom at Norton.

Anne: According to the apocryphal Gospel of St **James**, Anne was the mother of the **Blessed Virgin** who, after years of childlessness was told by an angel that she would bear a daughter who would become world famous. She vowed that the child would be devoted to the Lord and presented

Mary to the temple at the age of three. Another tradition identifies her with the widowed prophetess Anna who was in the temple when Jesus was received (Luke 2: 36-8). She is usually represented teaching the Virgin to read. (She is represented at Mildenhall, Cockfield, Sudbury (St Gregory) and Long Melford.)

Anthony of Egypt: Pigs and bells are this austere saint's peculiar symbols, and occasionally an Egyptian cross like the letter 'T'. Born about 251 in Egypt, he lived in the desert as a hermit, where he was duly and thoroughly tempted by the devil. He bestirred himself however to found a monastery, return to civilisation to refute heresies, work miracles and write letters which are still quoted. The **reliquary** for his bones in Alexandria was looked after by Hospitallers who attracted alms by ringing little bells. The pigs? For reasons unknown, the Hospitallers' porkers were allowed to roam freely in the streets! (He is represented at Whepstead, Nowton and Cavendish.)

Apostles: The twelve chief disciples of Christ (the lists of names vary slightly, probably becaused the same person was known by more than one name). They were: **Peter, Andrew, James the Great, John, Philip, Thomas, Bartholomew, Matthew, James the Less, Simon, Jude** (Thaddaeus/Judas son of James), Judas. After the suicide of Judas Iscariot, his place was taken by Matthias. Both **Paul** and Barnabas are referred to as apostles in the Acts of the Apostles.

Appollonia: This poor saint is most often seen having her teeth forcibly removed with huge pincers or herself holding aloft a tooth representing the torture which preceded the martyrdom by fire of this aged and pious deaconess in Egypt in 249. Not sur-

prisingly, she is invoked against jaw and tooth-ache. (She is represented at Coney Weston, Norton, Gazeley and Long Melford.)

Audry: An alternative name for **Etheldreda**.

Augustine of Hippo: One of the **Four Latin Doctors** of the early church; a profound and sustaining influence through the centuries on the church's thought and teaching. Often represented holding a flaming heart in his hand or; in his bishop's robes (he was bishop of Hippo in N. Africa for 35 years to his death in 430) and carrying a pastoral staff. His saintly adulthood followed a dissolute youth, from which he was rescued by **St Ambrose**. Augustine, a man of flesh as well as spirit, is credited with the memorable prayer 'O Lord, make me chaste ... but not yet'. (He is represented at Sudbury (St Gregory).)

Barbara: A tower, and a chalice with the Host (the consecrated bread) above it are her emblems. This lady, goes the story, was an early Christian convert in godless Italy, to the fury of her pagan father, who shut her up in a high tower. When she tried to escape he beat her up then handed her over to a judge who condemned her to death. She was tortured and decapitated, whereupon, very properly, both father and judge were consumed by bolts of lightning. Barbara is thus patroness of architects and firearms, and also protectress from thunderbolts and lightning or any form of explosion. (She is represented at Coney Weston, Hessett and Nowton.)

Bartholomew: One of the Twelve, his emblem is the butcher's flaying knife for thus, it is said, he was martyred somewhere along the Caspian Sea, being first flayed alive and then beheaded. More gruesomely, he is sometimes seen in medieval art carrying the skin of a man, with the face still attached to it. It follows that he is the patron saint of tanners. (He is represented at Coney Weston, Haverhill and Rattlesden.)

Blaise: During the horrific persecution of Christians around the year 300 by the Roman Emperor Diocletian, innumerable martyrs died various and nasty deaths. Blaise, bishop of Sebaste, in Armenia, was first torn with iron combs, and then beheaded. A large comb is thus his symbol in medieval art and it also conveniently made him patron saint of wool combers! Interesting to note that Parson Woodforde, in his celebrated diary, describes a solemn procession in the saint's honour in Norwich in March, 1783. (He is represented at Lavenham.)

Botolph: No definite symbol, though he is properly represented as an abbot, occasionally holding a church in his hand. Many churches are dedicated to him, including the famous Boston Stump church in Lincolnshire where in the C7 he was abbot of a monastery founded by himself; though one source says that he 'dwelt in a dismal hut amidst the swamps of the fenland rivers'. There are five churches dedicated to the saint in Suffolk, including Botesdale (Botolph's Dale).

Catherine of Alexandria: The emblem of this saint is a wheel of the devilish variety, set with spikes and knives, on which she is said to have been martyred in C4 Egypt, and which in turn inspired the spinning firework the Catherine wheel. The wheel, however, flew to pieces as she was spun on it, the knives etc skewering her persecutors. Her head was then cut off and from the wound flowed milk, not blood, which could explain why she is patroness of nurses. The number of representations of her is too numerous to list here, but Lavenham and Stowlangtoft have interesting examples.

Cecilia: Daughter of a C3 noble Roman family, she refused to worship idols and was beheaded. Her many converts to Christianity included her husband Valerian (with whom she lived in virginal wedlock) and one of her symbols is a garland of roses or lilies because an angel is said to have brought them one each from Paradise. When she heard the organ playing at her wedding she 'sang in her heart' to God and dedicated herself to His service. Thus she is the patron saint of music and her common emblem is a harp or an organ, although this was never used in English pre- **Reformation** pictures. (She is represented at Mildenhall, Nowton, Great Thurlow, Withersfield and Hopton.)

Christopher: Patron saint of travellers pictured on many a dashboard medallion, he was probably a C3 martyr in Asia Minor. Legend describes him as a giant who wished to serve the greatest king in the world. A hermit preached the Gospel to him and suggested that he live by a dangerous river nearby and help wayfarers across. As he carried a child over one day, the waters rose and he seemed to bear the weight of the whole world on his shoulders. When they reached the other side, the child was revealed as Christ himself. The saint is invariably represented as a giant holding a huge staff as he fords the river with the Christ-child on his shoulder. He was so popular that nearly every church had a statue or painting of him. It was normally placed opposite the main door so that passersby could see it easily, for it was believed that:

> If thou the face of Christopher on
> any morn shalt see,

Throughout the day from sudden death thou shalt preserved be.
Examples are common but the wall painting at Bradfield Combust is particularly good and so is the glass at Norton. Nowton has the scene of his torture.

Clare: Clare's emblem is a **pyx** (the receptacle in which the reserved sacrament, the consecrated bread, is contained, and suspended over the **altar**). This is the Clare of Assisi, spiritually beloved and influenced by **St Francis**, who founded the Order of Poor Clares, vowed to a life of absolute poverty. She spent her life as abbess of her convent at Assisi and never left the town. When she was old and sick, Assisi was threatened by the Saracens of the invading German Emperor Barbarosa's army. Clare was carried before him, deep in prayer and carrying a pyx containing the Blessed sacrament whereupon the invaders fled. Bradfield, St Clare is uniquely dedicated to her.

Dominic: Born of a noble Spanish family in 1170, he pursued a conventional clerical career until he became convinced of the need to reform the church in southern France. In 1218 the pope gave him authority to establish his Order of Friars Preachers and his zealous missioners became known as the Black Friars by the colour of their robes, reaching England in 1221. Illustrations of the saint are rare but a C17 Flemish roundel at Nowton shows his vision of the **Blessed Virgin**.

Dorothy: Usually shown holding a spray of flowers and/or a basket of fruit. During the persecution of the Emperor Diocletian in the early C4, she was threatened with terrible tortures unless she rejected her Christianity and married the prefect. Her reply, it is said, was:

Do to me what torment thou wilt, for I am ready to suffer it for the love of my spouse, Jesu Christ, in whose garden full of delights I have gathered roses, spices and apples.
On her way to execution, she was mocked by a young lawyer who scornfully asked her to send him some of those roses and apples. After she had been beheaded, an angel appeared to the lawyer, bringing from Dorothy in Paradise the requested gift, whereupon he was converted and followed the saint to martyrdom. (She is represented at Hawkedon.)

Edmund, king and martyr: King of East Anglia from 855 until 870 when the Danes defeated him in battle and took him prisoner. He refused to renounce his faith and they tied him to a tree, shot him with arrows, and finally beheaded him. His murderers left his head in a wood to rot, but those that sought it were guided by its ability to cry 'Here! Here!'. They found it guarded by a great grey wolf; the wolf followed the cortège to Bury and then returned to the wood. The great abbey church was dedicated to St Edmund and his shrine became a principal place of pilgrimage. Hoxne is the traditional site of the martyrdom although one school of thought prefers Hellesdon near Norwich. The saint's usual emblem is an arrow or arrows but the wolf's head is sometimes seen - as at Hawstead. Representations are naturally plentiful but note the C14 glass at Barton Mills, a wall painting at Troston, a modern bronze at Little Thurlow, and the martyrdom carved on a **misericord** at Norton.

Edward the Confessor: Usually seen in kingly crown, and holding aloft a ring. This deeply pious king of England, immediately before the **Norman** Conquest of 1066, built Westminster Abbey - the price for not having kept his vow to make a pilgrimage to the Holy Land. Confronted once by a beggar asking for alms, the king, having no money, slipped a ring from his finger and gave it to him. The beggar, it seems, was really **St John the Evangelist**, who returned the ring to English pilgrims in Palestine and foretold the king's imminent death. (He is represented at Coney Weston and Hessett.)

Eligius, or Eloy: Patron saint of farriers, his symbol is a blacksmith's hammer and tongs and occasionally a severed horse's leg. Eligius was a charitable and devoted bishop in C6 France and Flanders, much given to good works. His most famous exploit was to lop the leg off a difficult horse which was refusing to be shod, fix the shoe to the offending limb then put the leg back again and make the sign of the cross, whereupon the again-complete beast trotted happily away. (He is represented at Freckenham.)

Elizabeth: No distinguishing symbol, but usually represented at the moment of the **Visitation**, when the Virgin Mary came to tell her of the visit of the angel to announce Christ's birth, Elizabeth already being near her time with the child who would be **John the Baptist**. (She is represented at Stanton, Great Thurlow, Ingham, Newmarket (St Mary) and Wyverstone.)

Elizabeth of Hungary: Rarely represented. Daughter of a C13 king of Hungary, she married a prince and lived in great happiness with him until, to her great grief, he died on his way to the Crusades in the Holy Land. Always a woman of immense charity and kindness, she now took to a life of poverty and severe personal austerity, and to nursing and tending the sick. She died at the age of just 24, in 1231, worn out by her labours, and

was canonised four years later by Gregory XI. (She is represented at Nowton.)

Ethelbert: He was king of East Anglia in the late C8, and was executed by King Offa of Mercia for 'political offences', say some sources; through the machinations of King Offa's wife, goes a more likely story. Handsome Ethelbert arrived to seek the hand of Offa's daughter, who was much smitten by him but so was her mother who, in jealousy, persuaded her husband to lop off the visitor's head. Rarely represented but four Suffolk churches are dedicated to him.

Etheldreda: No special emblem, but generally represented as a royally crowned abbess. Daughter of a C7 king of East Anglia and born at Exning, she was twice married before becoming a nun. She founded a nunnery at Ely, became its first abbess and was known for her deep devotion and piety. After death her body remained incorrupt and its miracle-working powers made Ely a great centre of pilgrimage. (She is represented at Mildenhall, Norton, Dalham, Horringer, Ampton, Newmarket (St Mary), Rattlesden and Woolpit.)

Faith: Her symbols are a palm branch and a grid-iron upon which latter object she was unpleasantly roasted to death in France about the year 287, just a few years after **St Laurence** suffered the same martyrdom in Rome, both for holding fast to their Christian beliefs. Legend has it that a thick fall of snow came down to veil her body during her suffering. Occasionally, as at Gazeley, her emblem is a saw.

Felix: Usually seen as a bishop. One of our East Anglian saints, who came here in the C7 from France to preach the Gospel, and in 630 became the first bishop of Dunwich. For the 17 years of life that remained to him, he worked steadfastly to establish the Church on the eastern seaboard, founded schools, and preached extensively, with the friendly support of the king of the East Angles. (He is represented at Kettlebaston and Woolpit.)

Francis of Assisi: Usually seen as a friar holding a cross, often accompanied by the animals and birds with whom he is always associated; sometimes also with the 'stigmata', the wounds of Christ in hands and feet and side. Oddly this much loved saint is only occasionally represented in medieval art, though his story is so well known - his birth in wealthy circumstances in C12 Italy; his decision as a young man to devote himself to poverty, prayer and charity; his establishment of the Franciscan Order; his healing powers; and not least, his rapport with wild animals. He died, aged only 45, in 1226, and was canonised two years later. (He is represented at Santon Downham, Flempton and Herringswell.)

Fursey: A C7 Irish abbot who became an East Anglian saint. He came to these shores about the year 630 and established himself at Burgh Castle, near Great Yarmouth. His mission was successful but the raids of the Mercians forced him to seek refuge in Gaul. There he founded the monastery of Lagny and a number of churches. He died about 650 and was buried at Peronne. (He is represented at Kettlebaston.)

Gabriel: One of the seven archangels mentioned in the Book of Daniel and in **St Luke's** Gospel. He is the archangel of the **Annunciation** and appears in many carvings and paintings with the **Blessed Virgin**.

Genevieve: Rarely seen, and her emblems vary - a spinner's wheel because some say that she was a shepherdess, a candle which burned throughout a night of wind and rain, or keys at her girdle to show that she is the patron saint of Paris. Born at Auxerre, she became a nun at 15 and devoted herself to a life of poverty and good works under the guidance of St German. Paris was spared the ravages of Attila the Hun in 451 through the efficacy of her prayers and, by her encouragement, the church of St Denis was built there. She died peacefully at a great age in 512. (She is represented at Barnham and Euston (dedication).)

George: The martial knight, armoured and mounted, and England's patron saint, famed for his exploits in rescuing the beautiful maiden from the terrible dragon, and then killing the fire- breathing beast. All this took place in Palestine, where subsequently George was horribly put to death for refusing to sacrific to idols. It was during the Crusades to Palestine that he was adopted as England's patron. King Richard Coeur-de-Lion is said to have had a vision of him, assuring him of safety and victory in a forthcoming battle against the Saracens. Commonly seen, but note the carving in Mildenhall n. aisle, good wall paintings at Troston and Bradfield Combust, and a bench end at Withersfield.

Gertrude: Brought up in the palace of the C7 Frankish King Dagobert I, Gertrude was resolute in her virginity and joined her mother St Iduberga in her monastery at Nivelles. She became abbess, renowned for piety, good works and deep learning. On the continent she was a popular patron saint of travellers as an alternative to **St Christopher**. (She is represented at Flempton.)

Géry or St Gaugericus: He was born in the diocese of Trèves in the late C6 and became a priest there. He was later consecrated bishop of the united dioceses of Cambrai and Arras and governed them for 40 years, eradicating paganism. The city of Brussels recognises him as its founder since the first settlement grew round the chapel he built there. Seldom seen in England, there is a modern figure of him in a window at Hawstead.

Giles: His emblems are a doe or hind at his side, sometimes an arrow piercing his hand or leg, he being dressed as a monk, or abbot with crozier (crook). He lived as a hermit in C8 France, with his doe for company. One day a king and his companions hunted the doe, which fled to the saint for protection. However, an arrow loosed off by the king by chance struck Giles. In penance the king built a monastery on that very site, Giles became the first abbot. About 150 churches are dedicated to him. (He is represented at Risby.)

Gregory (the Great): Represented as a pope, with a dove, and a roll of music in one hand. One of the **Four Latin Doctors**, he was born of noble Roman stock in 540. He became a monk and founded several monasteries, into one of which he retired. It was he who, seeing fair-haired British slaves in the Rome slave market, commented: 'Not Angles, but angels'. It is said he came briefly to Britain as a missionary but was recalled to be elected, much against his will, as pope. It was he who sent **St Augustine** to these islands and gave his name to Gregorian chants (thus the symbolic roll of music). One of the best known incidents in his life came to be called the mass of St Gregory. It is said that, in order to sustain the faith of a sceptic, the sacred elements of bread and wine were transformed on the **altar** into a vision of the risen Christ as the Pope celebrated mass. It is illustrated on a screen panel at Wyverstone. (He is represented at Barnham and Sudbury, St Gregory.)

Helen: Represented wearing a crown and holding a cross, sometimes an Egyptian cross, like a letter 'T'. Mother of Emperor Constantine the Great, but her own parentage is mysterious. One story says she was an inn-keeper's daughter. Another (much more colourfully) says she was the daughter of King Coel of Colchester, Old King Cole of the nursery rhyme. What is certain is that she married an emperor and bore another: and that as an old lady she set off on pilgrimage for the Holy Land, where she found fragments of the True Cross and brought them to Europe. (She is represented at Coney Weston.)

Hubert: Born into a noble family of C7 France, he was a great hunter until one day, during a chase, a stag appeared before him with a shining crucifix between his horns. Hubert prostrated himself upon the ground - and from that moment his way of life was changed. He went on a pilgrimage to Rome, was ordained, and thereupon consecrated by the pope as bishop of Liège. Legend says that **St Peter** appeared to Hubert and gave him a key which had the power to cure lunatics. Another version says that at his ordination the **Blessed Virgin** appeared to him and gave him a white silk stole with which he was able to cure hydrophobia. He is patron saint of huntsmen and hunting, and the subject of a fine **Arts and Crafts** window at Herringswell.

Hugh: A C13 Carthusian monk and bishop, born in France, but invited to this country by Henry II to become prior of a monastery in Somerset. The establishment flourished under his charge, so Henry chose him to be bishop of Lincoln. He is said to have been the most learned monk in the land. He rebuilt his cathedral, established schools, and was much called on for his wisdom as a judge. His reputation was for simplicity and kindness, yet of being wholly immovable on matters of truth, doctrine and principle. (He is represented at Coney Weston.)

James the Great: Usually seen with a sword, or with the pilgrimage necessities of staff, wallet and scallop shell. One of the **apostles** closest to Christ and subsequently one of the leaders of the church, he was executed by Herod Agrippa in 44 AD (Acts, 12: 2). Many traditions surround him; enough churches claim relics to make up half a dozen bodies. Strongest however is the belief that his body was put into a boat, without sails or rudder, which travelled unaided out of the Mediterranean, around Spain and fetched up at Compostella, on the northern coast, where James' shrine became throughout the medieval age one of the greatest places of pilgrimage. Representations of him are legion.

James the Less: His emblem is a fuller's club, a curved implement like a hockey stick, used by a fuller (a cloth cleanser) to beat cloth, with which he was killed by a blow on the head after he had survived either being stoned (one version) or being hurled from the pinnacle of the temple in Jerusalem by the Scribes and Pharisees. This occurred after James, one of the twelve, presided over the great Synod in Jerusalem which reached agreement on how far Gentile converts to Christianity should be made to observe Jewish rites and customs. Representations of him are very numerous but note the stained glass figure at Hessett which probably represents him as a child with his emblem of martyrdom.

Jerome: Usually seen with a cardinal's hat; sometimes with an inkhorn, and with a lion at his feet. One of the **Four Latin Doctors**, he became secretary of the Roman See about 381, after much travel and study. (From medieval times, this office was held by a cardinal, thus Jerome's representation.) Later he travelled again, coming at last to Bethlehem, where he founded a monastery and fulfilled his ambition of translating the Bible from its original languages, Hebrew and Greek, into Latin: the Vulgate of the Roman church (thus the inkhorn). There is a charming story that a lion came to his monastery with an injured paw. The saint healed it, and the animal stayed on as his faithful companion. (He is represented at Dalham, Nowton and Thurston.)

Joachim: Traditionally the husband of **St Anne** and father of the **Blessed Virgin**. Examples are rare, and although he is sometimes shown in company with the Virgin and his wife, in the medieval glass at the cathedral at Bury he stands alone, cradling a lamb, the symbol of purity and innocence.

John the Baptist: His story needs no telling in detail; this man who baptised Christ and 'led the way', and who died at a whim of Herod's daughter Salome. Examples are easy to find but note the C14 glass at Barton Mills, the Flemish glass at Nowton and the Hawstead **font**.

John the Divine/the Evangelist: As one of the **Four Evangelists** (see also **Evangelistic symbols**)his emblem is an eagle, but he is often shown with a cup or chalice from which a snake or devil is emerging. This is a reference to the story that he was offered poisoned drink but made it harmless by making the sign of the cross over it. John, 'the disciple whom Jesus loved', and whose figure normally stood on Christ's l. hand on the **rood**, was hurled into boiling oil in Rome but emerged unharmed. He was banished to Patmos and is said to have spent the closing years of his long life at Ephesus. He is represented in many churches.

John Lateran: The Lateran basilica is the cathedral church of Rome which, when it was rebuilt in 904, was dedicated to **St John the Baptist**, with a later association with **St John the Divine**. It became known as 'S. Giovanni in Laterano' and the title was occasionally used elsewhere, as at Hengrave.

Joseph: Little is said in the Gospels about St Joseph but stories abound in the literature of the early church. It is said that he was a widower chosen under divine guidance by the high priest as a husband for the **Blessed Virgin**. He continued as a carpenter until Christ saved his body from corruption at the age of 111 and entrusted his soul to the hosts of heaven. Joseph normally figures in Nativity scenes (as at Long Melford) and in the flight into Egypt, but a C15 glass panel at Hessett portrays him with the Virgin in front of the emperor.

Jude or Thaddaeus: Most often seen holding a boat, though sometimes with a club or carpenter's square. One of the Twelve, he is said to have preached in Mesopotamia, Russia and finally in Persia, where he was attacked and killed by pagan priests, says one tradition; another, that he was hung on a cross at Arat and pierced with javelins. (He is represented at Haverhill, Rattlesden and Lavenham.)

Laurence: He shares with **St Faith** the emblem of a grid-iron (both were mar-

tyred by being roasted on one). He is usually shown in the vestments of a deacon, an office he held under the martyred Pope Sixtus II. During the diabolical persecutions of the Emperor Valerian in the C3. Laurence was ordered to reveal the treasures of the church, whereupon he disappeared into the noisome alleys of Rome to return with a retinue of cripples and beggars. 'These are the church's treasures,' he declared. It was an answer which earned him an agonising death. There are nine churches dedicated to him in Suffolk, including Eriswell.

Leonard: His symbols are chains or fetters in his hands, his robes those of an abbot. This courtier turned monk was given land near Limoges in C5 France by King Clovis, at whose court he was brought up. There he founded the monastery of Noblac, of which he became first abbot. Legend has it that the king gave him the right also to release any prisoner whom he visited, and he is thus the patron saint of prisoners. (He is represented at Horringer.)

Louis: Louis XI was king of France in the mid-C13, a model Christian monarch noted for his piety and spartan way of life, his patronage of friars and building of churches. He twice went on Crusade to the Holy Land and died in Tunis in August 1270. He was canonised only seven years later. Representations usually show him as a king holding a crown of thorns and a cross of three nails, recalling the sacred relics he brought back to France and housed in the superb Sainte-Chapelle in Paris. (He is represented at Nowton.)

Luke: One of the **Four Evangelists**, his special symbol is an ox (see **Evangelistic symbols**), probably a reference to the sacrifice in the temple at the beginning of his Gospel, while tying in neatly with Revelation (4: 7). **St Paul's** 'fellow worker', he was with him on his later journeys and referred to as 'the beloved physician', hence the tradition that he was a doctor. There is another story dating from the C6 that he was a painter who gained many converts by showing them portraits of Christ and the **Blessed Virgin** - the first icons. Thus he is also the patron saint of artists.

Margaret of Antioch: Her emblem is a writhing dragon, which she transfixes with a cross. Thrown into prison in Antioch for her Christian belief, this legendary lady was tempted by the devil in the guise of a terrible dragon. Some have it that the dragon was miraculously decapitated; others that he swallowed her but burst when her cross stuck in his throat; others still that she simply made the sign of the cross and he faded away. That she is guardian of women in childbirth presumably has something to do with her 'caesarian' irruption from the dragon. (She is represented at Coney Weston, Stanton, Nowton, Bury (St Mary), Norton and Stowlangtoft.)

Mark: One of the **Four Evangelists**, his symbol being the winged lion (see **Evangelistic symbols**). The significance of the lion is intriguing - it typified the Resurrection, based on the curious idea that the lion's young were dead for three days after birth, and were then brought to life by the roaring of their parents. In interesting parallel is the symbolism of the **pelican**. Mark's story as evangelist, and his missionary travels, thread through the New Testament. There is a tradition that later he went to Rome, then to Alexandria, where he became the city's first bishop, and was subsequently martyred during Nero's reign. What is certain is that in the C9 his relics were taken to Venice, whose patron saint he

became and has remained, and where his lion symbol is much in evidence.

Martin: Rarely represented despite the popularity of this figure who typified the saintly virtues of simplicity, piety, charity and concern for others. When he is portrayed, it is generally as a bishop offering alms to the needy. He was born in C4 Hungary and trained as a soldier, but after giving half his cloak to a beggar on whom he took pity, he dreamed that night that he saw Christ wearing the half of the garment he had given away, and was straight-away baptised. He founded a monastery, became known for his piety and, much against his own wishes, was made bishop of Tours. His reputation for miracles and healing, and his **St Francis**-like rapport with animals, grew from this time. Five churches in Suffolk are dedicated to him, including Exning and Fornham St Martin, where there is a **misericord** carved with the scene of his gift to the beggar. There is a C17 Flemish glass portrait at Nowton and a modern version at Long Melford.

Mary the Blessed Virgin: The mother of Christ, pre-eminent among the patron saints of the medieval church. Out of the 500 in Suffolk, over 150 are dedicated to the Virgin, and no other individual saint reaches a third of that. Originally, a number of them will have been associated with one of her specific feast days such as the **Assumption**, but it is now rare to find instances that can be substantiated. Acclaimed as 'the only bridge between God and man', she became the primal intercessor, 'Queen of Pity', and few churches will have been without at least an **altar**of Our Lady. The Assumption and **Annunciation**scenes were popular subjects for painting and carvings, and hers was the attendant figure on Christ's r. hand as part of the **rood** group. She figures also in some **Doom** paintings and is sometimes shown as a child being taught to read by her mother **St Anne**. The Blessed Virgin's usual emblem is a lily and her badge a crowned 'M' or 'MR' for 'Maria Regina', Queen of Heaven.

Mary Magdalene (Mary of Magdala): She was one of a number of women 'healed of evil spirits' mentioned in **St Luke's** Gospel, and was among those who stood watching the Crucifixion. Both **St Matthew** and **St John** tell how she came to the sepulchre on the first Easter day, heard from the angel that Christ was risen and hastened to tell the disciples. The first appearance of the resurrected Christ was to her as she wept by the tomb. From the earliest times, some commentators have identified her with Mary of Bethany, sister of Lazarus, and also as the un-named woman who, as a sinner, washed Jesus' feet with her tears, dried them with her hair, and anointed them with ointment. Thus she has become the archetype of the Christian penitent and her emblem is the pot of ointment. According to an early tradition she was martyred at Ephesus, but a livelier story was current by the C9. In it, her enemies cast her adrift with Lazarus and Martha in a rudderless ship that fetched up at Marseilles where Lazarus became a bishop and Magdalene preached the Gospel. According to this version she spent the last 30 years of her life as a contemplative near Aix-en-Provence. (She is represented at Barnham, Bardwell, Clare, Bury (St John), Risby, Woolpit and Lavenham.)

Matthew: According to his own Gospel, Matthew was a customs officer in the service of Herod Antipas when he was called by Jesus to become one of the twelve **apostles**. He was the Levi at whose feast Jesus and his disciples scandalised the Pharisees and an early tradition tells of him preaching to the Hebrews. His commonest symbol is the creature that 'had a face as of a man', one of the four mentioned in Revelation. (See **Evangelistic Symbols** He is said to have met his death by the sword for opposing a king's marriage to a consecrated virgin and so a sword is sometimes substituted. To confuse things further, he may carry an axe like St Matthias, or a carpenter's square. The commonest alternative is a money bag in reference to his early profession. He can be found in many churches but note the glass portraits at Hawkedon and Onehouse.

Michael: A very popular choice for medieval dedications. In the Old Testament, Michael was 'the great prince which standeth for the children of the people', the guardian angel of the Jews, and the relevation of **St John** portrays him leading the angelic host against the devil and all his works. And so he appears as a winged angel in shining armour striking down the dragon, but his role as the weigher of souls was a popular notion and he is often seen in **Doom** paintings with the scales of justice. (He is represented at Mildenhall, Great Thurlow, Withersfield, Brandon, Bury (St John and St Mary) and Newmarket (St Agnes).

Nicholas: Very few facts are known about this C4 bishop of Myra in Asia Minor, but the legends are spectacular, and he was a popular choice for dedications. There was once a famine in the land and an innkeeper, with nothing to set before his guests, cut up three boys and put them in a pickling tub. Along came the bishop and smartly restored them to life, providing a subject popular with medieval congregations and, incidentally assuming the role of the patron saint of children. The sign of the three golden balls is seldom seen now in city streets but they were another of St

Nicholas' symbols and he was the patron saint of pawnbrokers too. The balls stand for the bags of gold that he left secretly at the house of an improvished nobleman in order that his three daughters should not lack dowries. The Russian church called him 'Sant Niklaus', which came in time to be our own 'Santa Claus' that answer to an adman's prayer but still part of the children's magic. (He is represented at Hessett, Nowton, Denston, Chelsworth, Great Whelnetham and Ickworth.)

Patrick: Probably Scottish by birth, he was captured and enslaved by an early Irish chieftain in the early C5. He escaped to Gaul and studied under St Germanus before returning to Ireland as a courageous and successful missionary. He converted King Liogaire at the Hill of Slane and thereafter established churches throughout the land. He is credited with banishing snakes and poisonous animals from Ireland with the help of a staff that he claimed to have received from Christ. He died in 463 and was buried at Saul in County Down. Although he is a patron saint of Ireland, very few medieval churches are dedicated to him and he is rarely represented with his emblem of snakes. He shares the dedication at Elvedon with **St Andrew**, there is a mosaic at Newmarket (St Agnes) and glass at Sudbury (St Gregory) - all modern.

Paul: A sword is this apostle's symbol, usually pointing down With this weapon his head was struck off at the order of the Emperor Nero, about the year 66 in Rome, when his success in converting eminent people to Christianity (including one of Nero's concubines) became too much for the emperor to tolerate. Upon his beheading, it is said, milk flowed from the wound. Paul's life story is too well related in the Acts of the Apostles, and in his own Epistles, to need

retelling here. Representations of him are very numerous, but note the excellent C15 stained glass figure at Hessett and the **font**at Stowlangtoft.

Peter:

Thou art Peter, and upon this rock I will build my church . ... I will give unto thee the keys of the kingdom of heaven.

So Christ spoke to his beloved apostle. And so, always, Peter's symbol is the keys. The Gospels tell his story during Christ's ministry on earth, but not his ending. He was crucified - upside down, at his request, as he did not consider himself worthy to die in the same way as his master - in Rome by the Emperor Nero, at about the same time that **Paul** was beheaded there. Examples of Peter and his crossed keys are legion.

Peter Martyr: A Dominican friar who was born at Verona in the early C13. His eloquence and reputation as a worker of miracles led to his appointment as inquisitor to rid northern Italy of heresy. He met his death at the hands of hired assassins who cleft his head with an axe and drove a knife into his heart, and so he is normally shown with a blade in his head. (He is represented at Long Melford.)

Petronilla: Known sometimes as St Pernel, she is identified only through an inscription that was found in a Christian cemetary in Rome. It gave her name as 'Aurelia Petronilla' but a mis-reading of this prompted the C5 legend that she was a daughter of **St Peter**. He was supposed to have been rebuked for not using his power to cure her paralysis but he said that it was for her own good and that she would recover to wait upon them - and she did. Thus she is sometimes shown as a serving maid holding a key (for St Peter). The dedication to her at Whepstead is unique in this country.

Philip: One of the Twelve, Philip is seen either with a cross, for like his Lord, he was to suffer crucifixion, at the hands of pagans in Asia Minor; or with a basket of loaves and fishes, recording his connection with the universally known biblical story of Christ's feeding of the 5,000.

Raphael: One of the seven archangels. He is described in the Book of Tobit as the angel who hears the prayers of holy men and brings them before God; in the Book of Enoch, he is said to have healed the earth defiled by the sins of the fallen angels. (He is represented at Newmarket (St Agnes).)

Roche: He was a popular saint in the Middle Ages but the stories of his life can only be found in the fanciful *Golden Legend*. There he is described as a young man of Montpellier who, in response to his father's dying wish, used all that he had to succour the poor and went on pilgrimage to Italy. Having arrived, he caused plague epidemics to cease in various places, including Rome, but was infected himself. He retired to a lonely forest hut, and until he recovered, a dog brought him a daily loaf of bread from his master's table. He is shown as a pilgrim with the marks of the plague on him. Examples are rare in England but his figure is carved on a continental **reredos** at Cavendish, accompanied by the helpful dog.

Simon (the Zealot): He is named as one of the twelve **apostles** in the bible but no other details are given. All stories about him come from the *Golden Legend* and he is supposed to have preached in Egypt and gone with **St Jerome** to Persia. Once there, his mir-

acles so discredited the pagan idols that he was hacked to pieces. Later, he was identified with Simon the 'brother of the Lord' (ie son of Cleopas and Christ's cousin). His usual emblem is a fish to show that he was a fisherman, but confusing alternatives crop up: an oar, an axe, or a saw. (He is represented at Finningham, Haverhill, Lavenham and Rattlesden.)

Sir John Schorne: Rector of a Buckinghamshire parish around 1300, he is said to have wiled the devil into a boot and there kept him prisoner. Never formally canonised, Sir John was honoured for his piety and for his working of miracles. Sudbury (St Gregory) had a painting of him which is now in Gainsborough's house.

Stephen: Shown always with a heap of stones in his hands, or on a platter or book. The first Christian martyr, he was stoned to death by the Jews of Jerusalem, when he fearlessly answered their charges of blasphemy (Acts, 6 and 7). The church tests the faithful by celebrating his martyrdom on 26 December. (He is represented at Higham, Hessett and Lavenham.)

Thomas: The **apostle** who is chiefly remembered for refusing to believe that the other disciples had seen the risen Lord, the original 'doubting Thomas', and for whom Jesus reappeared that he might be 'not faithless but believing'. The C3 Acts of Thomas record that he was taken to India to be a carpenter for King Gundaphorus, but he spent his time preaching and working miracles, which all led to his being arrested and run through with spears. His emblem is normally a spear but it can also be a carpenter's square, and he is the patron saint of builders and masons. (He is represented at Brettenham and Rattlesden.)

Thomas of Canterbury (Thomas Becket): Represented always as an archbishop. Occasionally he may have a sword or an axe, a reference to his famous martyrdom at the hands of four of Henry II's knights in Canterbury cathedral at Christmas 1170. Thomas' shrine became a place of veneration and miracles. Four centuries later, Henry VIII branded him traitor, rather than saint, which is why representations of him are often defaced with particular savagery and thoroughness. (He is represented at Risby(?), Fornham St Martin (the martyrdom itself), Kettlebaston and Lavenham.)

Uriel: In Jewish apocryphal texts he is one of the four chief archangels who stand in the presence of God. (He is represented at Newmarket (St Agnes).)

Veronica: Traditionally identified as the woman who was cured by touching Jesus' robe (Matthew, 9: 20), she figures in the medieval *Golden Legend* as having wiped Christ's face as he carried the cross. The handkerchief or head-cloth was imprinted with his features and a portrait professing to be the original imprint has been in Rome since the C8 and at St Peter's since 1297. Competing claims are made by Genoa and Milan. Pictures of Christ's face on linen, communion plates, etc, became known as vernicles. There is a C17 Flemish roundel at Nowton illustrating the story and another at Depden.

Walstan of Bawburgh: Norfolk's own farmer-saint, patron saint of farm workers, usually shown crowned (denoting his royal blood) and holding a scythe. The son of a prince, he chose a life of poverty, taking a job as a farm-worker at Taverham near Norwich. After his many years of faithful labour, Walstan's master wanted to make him his heir. But Walstan declined and asked instead for a cart and a cow in calf. She produced two fine young bulls which he trained to pull his cart. In his old age, Walstan received a divine visitation foretelling his death, which came as he worked out in the fields. His body was placed on his cart and, unguided, his bulls set out. They paused at Costessey, where a spring sprang up and continued to give water until the C18. At last they came to the saint's birthplace at Bawburgh, passing clean through the solid wall of the church, and leaving behind them yet another spring, which as St Walstan's well was famous for centuries. His shrine here attracted many pilgrims until it was destroyed at the **Reformation**. (He is represented at Bury (St Mary).)

Withberga: She was a daughter of Anna, king of East Anglia, and sister of **St Etheldreda** and St Sexburga. After education at Holkham on the north Norfolk coast, she founded a nunnery at East Dereham and was its abbess for many years. The small community lived simply, and it is said that when they were reduced to poverty, two does appeared and provided enough milk to save the nuns from starvation. She is always shown as a crowned abbess, sometimes in company with the two does. (She is represented at Woolpit.)

Sanctuary: That part of the church containing the **altar** (or, if there is more than one altar, the **high altar**. It is normally bounded by the **communion rails**.

Sanctus-bell/turret/window: At the point in the mass at which the priest raises the consecrated bread and the chalice of wine for the people to see, a bell was rung (and sometimes still is) so that 'people who have not leisure daily to be present at Mass may, wherever they are in houses or fields, bow their knees' - the words of Archbishop Peckham in 1281. Some churches have a small turret on the e. gable of the **nave** to house the bell used for this purpose. Examples can be found at Worlington, Haughley, and Bacton. In other cases, a sanctus-bell window is to be found in the interior wall between tower and nave, placed so that it has a clear view of the **altar**. Such an arrangement allows a ringer to use one of the tower bells for the same purpose. See also **low side windows**.

Saxon: The period, with its distinctive architecture, preceding the **Norman** Conquest of 1066, a vital era in the general establishment of Christianity in these islands. See also **Anglo-Saxon**; and **Saxon** under **Styles of Architecture**.

Schorne, Sir John: See under **Saints**.

Scissors-braced roofs: A roof in which the beams are crossed and interlocked diagonally in the shape of an opened pair of scissors. See **roofs**, figs 2 and 3.

Scott, Sir George Gilbert (1811-78): One of the leading architects of the Gothic revival in England and one of the great names of the Victorian era. Stimulated by **Pugin's** enthusiasm, he designed the Martyr's Memorial in Oxford, one of the early key works of the new movement. Prolific and successful, he worked on hundreds of churches, either as designer or restorer, and subsequently much of his work attracted bitter criticism. Westminster Abbey, Ely, Salisbury and Lichfield cathedrals all bear his mark, not to mention the Albert Memorial and St Pancras station. His one complete church in Suffolk is at Higham, and his most extensive restoration

and rebuilding was Bury, St James, before it was promoted to a cathedral.

Scratch dials: On or near the s. doorways of many old churches may be seen circles incised in the stone, usually about 6 in across, with lines radiating down from a centre hole. A wooden or metal peg was put in the hole and its shadow marked the time of day, a primitive sundial, but one with a specific purpose. The marks related to the times for morning mass, noon and vespers (evensong) to assist the punctuality of both priest and people in the days before clocks and watches. Sometimes the dials were divided into four 'tides' of three hours and, occasionally, the line for mass is thicker or identified with a short cross bar. There are cases where lines have been added to the top half of the circle, no doubt by mischievous young hands, and the dial at Barnardiston is unusual in having numbers. (Examples can be seen at Barton Mills, Sapiston, Worlington, Ousden, Wetherden, Cowlinge, Kettlebaston and Kedington.)

Screen: See **rood screen**.

Sedilia: These are seats (usually made into decorative and archectural features, with miniature columns, arches and canopies, and detailed carvings) on the s. side of the **chancel**. Generally there are three seats. These can be all on the same level; or 'stepped', ie, on descending levels; and/or 'graduated', ie, under separate arches but contained within a composite pattern, frieze or frame. In many cases, a simple seat is created by building a low window sill, called **dropped-sill sedilia**. The three seats were specifically for the priest, the deacon (who read the Gospel), and the sub-deacon (who read the Epistle). Though three seats are the norm, numbers can vary between one and eight, and they may be found beside subsidiary **altars** as well as the **high altar**. In places where the seats seem impractically low, it may well be that the floor levels have been raised as part of reconstruction or restoration (the Gothic revivalists were particularly keen on the ritual significance of steps leading up to the **sanctuary** and **altar**, and these were often not there originally).

Septaria: Nodules of limestone or ironstone which contain other minerals, frequently used as a building material in the s.w. of the county.

Set-offs: The sloped, angled surfaces on buttresses at the points where the buttress 'sets-off' another stage further out from the wall it is supporting.

Seven Deadly Sins: Pride, Covetousness, Lust, Envy, Gluttony, Anger, Sloth. Pride was always pre-eminent and the others encompassed other human failings; drinking went with Gluttony, suicide was linked with Anger, and spiritual idleness was seen as a form of Sloth. Pictures of them were often placed close to the **Seven Works of Mercy** to give them greater emphasis (as at (Dalham), and they were occasionally used to decorate bench ends - as with the Gluttony subject at Finningham. (An example can be seen at Hessett.)

Seven Sacrament Fonts: The finest and most interesting series of late C15 **fonts**. They total 38, of which 13 are in Suffolk, 23 in Norfolk and one each in Kent and Somerset. All are octagonal and seven of the bowl panels are carved with representations of the sacraments: baptism, confirmation, mass (holy communion), penance, ordination to the priesthood, marriage, extreme unction (anointing of the dying); the eighth panel varies

and includes baptism of Christ at Badingham, Laxfield, Westhall and Weston; crucifixion at Cratfield, Great Glemham, Woodbridge, Monk Soham and Denston; martyrdom of **St Andrew** at Melton; the panels are so defaced at Blythburgh, Southwold and Wenhaston that the subject cannot be identified. All suffered mutilation to some degree, but the font at Cratfield is arguably the finest of all.

Seven Works of Mercy: Sometimes called the Corporal Works of Mercy, are: to feed the hungry, to give drink to the thirsty, to welcome strangers, to clothe the naked, to visit the sick and to visit prisoners. Derived from **St Matthew's** Gospel (25: 34-9), the six works are normally augmented by a seventh, the burial of the dead. There is an incomplete version at Dalham.

Sound holes: Instead of windows at the first floor level, some towers have square, oblong or shaped openings, often treated very decoratively. These are very common in Norfolk and their purpose is not, as might be supposed from the name, to let the sound of the bells out (the bell openings higher up do that) but to light the ringing chamber and allow the ringers to hear the bells. (Examples can be seen at Hepworth, Thelnetham and Long Melford.)

Spandrels: The triangular space between the curve of an arch or the supporting braces of a roof, the wall or upright brace, and the horizontal line above. Often filled in with rich and delicate tracery (see **roofs**).

Squint (or hagioscope): An opening cut obliquely through a wall or pillar to give a view of the **high altar** from side chapels and **aisles**. During the mass, the squint made it possible for the act of consecration by a priest at a side altar to be coordinated with the celebration at the high altar. This was necessary because **chantry** and **guild** masses were not allowed to take precedence over the parish mass. Where there is a squint in the outer wall of a church it may point to the existence of a former chapel or, much more rarely, an **anchorite's** cell. The idea still persists that squints were provided so that lepers could watch the mass, but there is no basis for this at all. It is sometimes possible to determine the original site of the high altar by taking a line through a squint, useful in those cases where the **chancel** has been shortened or lengthened. Examples are easy to find but the squint that passes through two walls and the intervening corner of a chapel at Long Melford is of more than usual interest. See also **low side windows** and **elevation squints**.

Stone, Nicholas (1586-1647): Greatest sculptor of his century, he was born the son of a quarryman in Devon, but soon moved to London, then to Holland, to gain greater experience. In Holland he apprenticed himself to Hendrik de Keyser, a famous Dutch master mason. The story has it that one piece of work he carried out so delighted his master that Stone was given the hand of de Keyser's daughter in marriage. By 1614, Stone was back in London as mason and statuary; and quickly gained such a reputation that he was employed by the king on the royal palaces and on great buildings in London. Only five years after his return from Holland, he was made master mason to James I, and in 1626 Charles I confirmed him in that appointment. His earliest work in Suffolk is at Hawstead, and there are other fine pieces at Ampton, Redgrave, Hessett and Wickhambrook.

Stops: See **headstops**.

Stoup: In the porches of many churches, or just inside the main door, there are basins, usually recessed into the wall. More often than not they are very plain, but where there was once ornament or decoration it has usually been defaced because they were one of the targets of the Puritans. This was because the stoups held holy water which was mixed once a week before mass. On entering the church, worshippers dipped their fingers into the water and crossed themselves as a reminder of their baptismal vows. To prepare the water, salt was first exorcised and then blessed; the water itself was then exorcised and blessed, the salt was sprinkled over it in the form of a cross, and then a final blessing given to the mixture.

Street, George Edmund (1824-81): One of the leading C19 architects in the field of church building and restoration, he worked for **Sir George Gilbert Scott** for five years before beginning his own practice in 1849. C13 Gothic was his favourite medium, although he was not content to copy slavishly. Of the hundreds of churches he was concerned with, St Philip and St James, Oxford (1862) was the test-piece for the High Victorian 'vigorous' architecture. It was admired and loathed in equal measure. One of his best known works is the Law Courts in the Strand, unfinished at his death. (An example of his work can be seen at Freckenham.)

String course: See **courses**.

Stuart: The Royal House of Stuart, which inherited the Scottish throne in 1371 and the English throne, on the accession of James I, in 1603. The Stuart period is taken to be their years of English kingship: James I, Charles I, Charles II, James II, William and Mary, and finally Anne, who reigned

1702-14. After the death of Anne, George I, the non-English-speaking German from Hanover, succeeded to the English crown and the Stuart day was over, its last fling being the '45 Rebellion of Bonnie Prince Charlie, 'The Young Pretender'.

Stucco: A fine plaster which, when it contains gypsum and pulverised marble, is known as 'stucco douro'. It was introduced into England at Nonesuch Palace in the reign of Henry VIII and can be boldly modelled and undercut. A fine example of its use can be seen at Euston.

Styles of Architecture: From the days of the Saxons, before the **Norman-**Conquest of 1066, through to the Georgians in the C18, architecture both sacred and secular has passed through many developments and details, fads and fancies, inspirations and inventions. The names we use so easily to describe those phases - **Early English, Decorated** etc - interestingly were coined only in the last century, and given convenient, even precise dates. But such dating can be more than misleading. Just as fashions in costume took time to filter through from city or court to provincial outposts, so changes in architectural ideas were only gradually assimilated. For example, there are those instances of the lush shapes of the Decorated style still appearing after the **Black Death**, well into the 1360s and 1370s where, presumably, masons with the old skills had survived the pestilence. Window shapes and **tracery** offer the clearest guide to individual styles and are normally the most helpful features for the layman.

Saxon: From the C7 to the Conquest. Characterised by roughness of construction, crudely rounded arches and triangular-headed window open-

ings (see figs 9 and 10). Equally distinctive of the period is their **long and short work** at corner angles of buildings. This is where upright stones are alternated with flat slabs, often re-using Roman tiles and other materials, salvaged from local remains. (Examples are found at Little Wratting, Onehouse, Risby, Wordwell, Beyton, Fakenham, Hengrave and Little Bradley.)

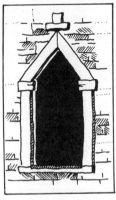

Fig 9. Saxon triangular-headed form.

Fig 10. Typical Saxon round-headed window with crude arch.

Norman: From the Conquest to about 1200, including the **Transitional** phase, spanning the reigns of William I and II, Henry I, Stephen, Henry II and Richard I. Massive walls and pillars are typical features, mighty rounded arches and still, small round-headed windows, though they might be used in groups, with heavy pillar-like **mullions** between them. But after the **Saxon** crudity, here is growing craftsmanship and artistry, with rich, bold ornamentation. The small windows of the period are usually deeply splayed (see figs 11 and 12). These would originally have been filled with parchment or oiled linen - glass came later. (Examples are found at Ousden, Moulton, Little Saxham, Pakenham, Wordwell, Harleston, Great Bradley etc.)

Fig 11. Norman slit window – interior view of typical deep 'arrow slit' embrasure.

Transitional: This is the phase of the changeover from the rounded, Romanesque architecture of the Normans to the Gothic movement in England - the triumph of the pointed arch and, as it seemed then, a new age of learning and faith. It took three or four decades, to about 1200, for the changeover to take full effect. Massive pillars during this time became slimmer and lighter, and might sometimes bear a pointed arch, carved in **Norman** character. These attractive, slimmed down columns would also be used in clusters, and would continue to be so used during the full flowering of **Early English**. (Examples are found at Chevington and Kettlebaston.)

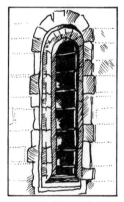

Fig 12. Norman slit window – exterior view.

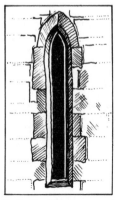

Fig 13. Early English lancet – the first arrival in England of pointed Gothic.

Early English: Gothic has now fully arrived, and with it the first really native English architectural style. It spans roughly the 100-year period from the end of the reign of Richard, through John and Henry II, and into the time of Edward II, to about 1300. The simple, elegant **lancet** made its appearance, first used singly (see fig 13) then in groups.

As ideas developed, the space between the heads of two lancets placed together was pierced with an open pattern, cut directly through the masonry: this is known as **plate tracery** (see fig 16). From there it was but a step to fining down the tracery by constructing it in separated pieces, that is, **bar tracery**. In the **Decorated** style which followed, this technique reached a wonderful zenith. Intermediate, however, about the year 1300 (and a most useful dating device) came a most distinctive phase, the 'Y' traceried window. (Fig 14 is self-explanatory.) A development of this was the extension of the Ys through three or four **lights** producing the simplest interlocking tracery with slim and graceful pointed heads. Everything at this time became finer in conception: bold buttresses, effortlessly

Fig 15. *Early English lancets composed in a group.*

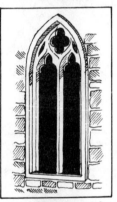

Fig 16. *Simple geometric 'plate' tracery.*

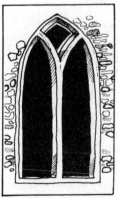

Fig 14. *The typical 'Y' traceried window of around 1300.*

thrusting arches, beautiful foliage carving and, most distinctive of this period, the **trefoil**, or three-leaf decoration. (See also **emblems of the Trinity** and **foils**.) This was much used in window tracery and in decorative carving. Also popular was the **dogtooth** moulding, which looks like a square, four-leafed flower, said to be based on the dog's tooth violet. (Examples can be found at Cavenham, Chevington, Clare, Great Barton and Lidgate.)

290 SUFFOLK CHURCHES

Decorated: This supreme time of architectural achievement and marvellous confidence in the use of shape and decoration had but a half-century of full life - during the reigns of the first three Edwards - before the catastrophe of the **Black Death** struck Europe in 1349-1350. In East Anglia, it has been estimated that half the population died. This was then, the high point of ornamented Gothic. Windows grew larger, **tracery** became progressively more flowing

Fig 17. The flowing beauty of the Decorated style's 'reticulated' form.

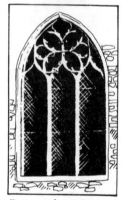

Fig 18. Decorated artistry in imaginative flow – the butterfly motif.

and adventurous: from the 'geometrical', with circles, **trefoils**, **quatrefoils**, lozenges etc (see **foils**) dominating the tracery, it burgeoned ultimately to the virtuosity of **reticulated** or net-like tracery (see fig 17) and the creative beauty of form as seen in fig 18. Rich ornamentation and carving abounded, including the distinctive **ball flower**, a little globule whose carved petals enclose a tiny ball; and also a sculptural explosion of pinnacles and **crocketting**, both inside and outside the church, from gable ends to tombs. Of many examples in Suffolk of Decorated work, the following come to mind: Rickinghall Inferior, Buxhall, Haughley and Redgrave.

Perpendicular: This style takes us from the aftermath of the **Black Death**, through Richard II's reign, and successively those of Henry IV, V and VI, Edward IV and Richard III to the time of Henry VII, until around 1500, when the **Tudor** adaptation took place. The Perpendicular style, as its name implies, is one of soaring upward lines, drawn in great windows by vertical **mullions** (see fig 19), by majestic, clean-lined towers; and by meticulously panelled buttresses and parapets and the ornamented bases of walls (see also **flushwork**). Rich decoration is typical, though it usually has more of the grandly formal than of a purely aesthetic beauty. The majority of churches embody something of the style, even if it is only a window or two, but Lavenham, Long Melford, Mildenhall and Bury (St Mary) are tremendous Perpendicular showpieces. Among the smaller churches, Denston, Walsham-le-Willows, Hessett and Stowlangtoft are outstanding.

Tudor: Here we are talking of roughly the century to 1600 spanned by Henry VIII, the boy-king Edward VI, Mary and Elizabeth. Not so much a style as

Fig 19. The classic Perpendicular window, its mullions thrusting to the head of the arch.

an adaptation, in that the Tudor mode, as far as churches are concerned, is basically the flattening of the **Perpendicular** arch, while otherwise retaining the same features (see fig 20). Decoration had become stereotyped, with interminable repetitions of the royal badges, the rose and the portcullis, and family heraldry followed the trend so that badges and shields of national magnates and county gentry are to be found carved in wood and stone. Red brick had become a fashionable alternative to stone, and in some cases it displaced the local flint as a basic material which could be laid quickly and produced locally. Hargrave tower is one example, and brick was a popular choice for **porches**, some of which are most attractive, as at Great Bradley, Fornham St Martin and Ixworth Thorpe.

Jacobean/Caroline: From the early C17 with the reign - 1603-25 - of James I (Latin, Jacobus), and continuing with the reigns of Charles I and II (Latin, Carolus). It was during James' reign that a stirring towards a **Renaissance** expression of architecture truly

began in England. It was a style, and a movement, which employed the principles of the ancient Greek classical building concepts, much classical detail and ornamentation, and as in the Elizabethan period, a copious use of bricks. This stylised approach found expression in furniture too, as will be found in many examples in churches. During James' reign, the Renaissance movement found its resident genius in Inigo Jones (d. 1652) whom James appointed Surveyor General of the Works. After Jones came another genius, Sir Christopher Wren. And if his masterpiece, St Paul's cathedral, remains one of our greatest Renaissance buildings, it was nonetheless in country houses and grand mansions that the Renaissance spirit was most evidenced. In our churches, the Jacobean title applies as often as not to wood carving, pulpits, typically high bench backs etc, and to aristocratic monuments.

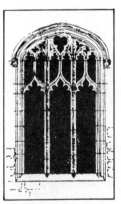

Fig 20. The Tudor contribution – a flattening of the arch over a Perpendicular window.

Symbols of the Evangelists: See **Evangelistic symbols**.

Tabernacle work: Representations of

canopied stalls, niches and pinnacles, particularly in stained glass and wall paintings.

Talbot: An heraldic hound or hunting dog, seen in the arms of a number of families, but particularly associated with the Talbots, Earls of Shrewsbury.

Tester: Flat canopy above a pulpit, acting as a sounding board.

Teulon, Samuel Saunders (1812-73): An architect of the High Victorian period, whose churches and large houses are remarkable for their eccentricity and panache. His compositions are often irregular and characterised by harsh, spiky detailing, combined with polychromy. Although his work has acquired a reputation for extreme ugliness it does not always deserve it and his restorations were sometimes quite restrained, as at Ampton, Pakenham and Wordwell.

Three-Decker Pulpits: After the Civil War, the normal Sunday service was conducted entirely from the reading desk, and only on the infrequent Sacrament Sundays would minister and people move to the **altar**. Convenience demanded that pews be grouped round a focal point, and the C17/C18 solution was a three-decker pulpit. The service was read from the second tier, and the minister climbed to the pulpit above to deliver his sermon (if the curate took the service, the rector would sit in the pulpit until sermon time). The **parish clerk** led the responses, and conducted the singing from his special pew below, and the three compartments were combined in a number of ways, often ingeniously. Some churches made do with two-deckers wherein the reading desk and pulpit were planned as a

unit, or separate accommodation was found for the clerk, but such arrangements are occasionally the result of later alterations to suit changing needs or parsons' predilections. For decades the three-decker was the focus of congregational worship (with spasmodic acknowledgement of the altar's pre-eminence), and it gathered to itself cushions for the ledges, candlesticks, **hour-glass**, wig-stand, and the odd hat peg. West Suffolk has some fine specimens - Shelland, Great Livermere, Ickworth and the splendid example at Kedington. See also **Prayer book churches**.

Three Living and Three Dead: An intriguing allegorical theme that was popular with medieval artists, although very few examples survive with enough detail to give an idea of its importance. Based, it is said, on a C13 French poem, the 'story in pictures' tells of three spirited young courtiers (always represented in English examples, for some reason, in royal and hunting guise, though the poem indicates neither) who encounter three Deaths in the form of skeletons. The first young blade flees, as the first skeleton dolorously tells him that 'As I am so shall you be'. The second young courtier, though he greets the skeletons as heaven sent, is rewarded with the levelling observation that 'Rich and poor come to the same end'. Courtier number three is inspired to expound philosophically on mortality confirmed by his skeleton's 'No-one escapes'. (Examples can be seen at Kentford and Great Livermere.)

Thurible: Known also as a censer, it is a pierced metal container used for the ceremonial burning of incense. The incense is burned on charcoal and the thurible is usually suspended on chains so that it can be swung in the hand of the thurifer as he censes the **altar**, the priest or the congregation, thus fanning the charcoal and directing the smoke at will. The thurifer is sometimes attended by a boy bearing a boat-shaped vessel containing incense for replenishing the thurible.

Tie-beam: The wall-to-wall cross beam or truss supporting a roof. (See **roofs**.)

Touchstone: A smooth, fine-grained black stone (jasper, black marble or similar) widely used in C16-C18 for funeral monuments.

Townshend, Caroline (1878-1944) and Joan Howson (1885-1964): Arts and Crafts stained glass workers. Caroline Townshend studied at the Slade and then became a pupil of **Christopher Whall** in 1900. Her first commission was in 1903 and she was one of the original tenants of 'The Glass House' (see **Lowndes**). Joan Howson had studied stained glass at Liverpool and became her apprentice before World War I. They became partners in 1920, with Townshend designing and Howson collaborating in the making and specialising in the repair of medieval glass. Miss Townshend died in 1944 but Joan Howson continued to work, mainly on restorations. (An example of their work is at Pettaugh.)

Tracery: Ornamental open-work in wood or stone, especially in the upper parts of windows and screens; the term also aplies to similar patterns on solid panels.

Transepts: Projecting 'arms' of a church, built out to n. and s. from the point where **nave** and **chancel** meet, to form a cross shaped or cruciform ground plan.

Transitional: Though 'transitional' can refer loosely to any change from one phase of architecture to another, it is particularly applied to the transition from the 'rounded' Norman to the 'pointed' Gothic, in the second half of the C12. (See under **Styles of Architecture**.)

Transoms: The horizontal crosspieces in window **tracery**, most noticeable in **Perpendicular** windows.

Trefoil: See **foils**.

Trinity: See **emblems of the Trinity**.

Tudor: The dynasty founded by Henry Tudor, victor of Bosworth Field against Richard III (My kingdom for a horse . . .). He was crowned Henry VII in 1485; Henry VIII followed, then Edward VI, Mary I (Bloody Mary) and finally Elizabeth I, who died on 24 March 1603, 'the last of the Tudors and the greatest of Queens'. For the church, it was a cataclysmic time. Various aspects of this are dealt with under the headings **communion rails; Laud; mensa slabs; Prayer book churches; Rood Screen**; and **Royal Arms**. If the interiors of churches were changed beyond recognition during this era, the Tudor influence upon church architecture as such was negligible. (See under **Styles of Architecture**.)

Tudor roses: A typical flower decoration of the period. (See **Tudor** under **Styles of Architecture**.)

Tympanum: Space over head of door, or in head of filled-in arch, plain or carved. See also **Royal Arms** for special connection. (A **Norman** example is found at Wordwell.)

294

Unicorn: A swift and fierce little animal from the **bestiary**, with the well-known single horn on its forehead. The only way to catch it was to lay a trap with a virgin. The beast was so attracted by her purity that it would run up, lay its head in her lap, and fall asleep. Thus it became the symbol of purity and feminine chastity, and for the **Blessed Virgin** in particular. There are unicorns on bench ends at Lakenheath, Ixworth Thorpe and Wetherden, on **fonts** at Norton and Pakenham, on the **screen** at Hargrave and in glass at Rushbrooke.

Uriel: See under **Saints**.

Vestry: That part of the church in which the vestments are kept and where the clergy robe for services. It sometimes doubles as a **sacristy** and occasionally as a choir robing area.

Virgin Mary: See **Mary the Blessed Virgin** under **Saints**.

Visitation, the: Having been told by the archangel Gabriel that she would bear a son, whose name would be Jesus and whose kingdom would have no end (Luke, 1) the Virgin Mary hurried to tell the news to her cousin Elizabeth, already near her time with the child who would be **John the Baptist**. This meeting is commemorated on 2 July as the Visitation.

Wall plate: See **roofs**.

Wall post: See **roofs**.

Ward & Hughes: Firm of stained glass manufacturers founded by Thomas Ward and James Henry Nixon in 1836. They traded as Ward & Nixon until 1850 when Henry Hughes

became chief designer. After Hughes' death in 1883, the firm continued under Thomas Curtis until the 1920s and some later windows are signed by him. They were the largest suppliers to Norfolk and Suffolk in the C19, and their 1850s-1860s High Victorian work was well drawn and often pleasing in design and colour. In 1870, their massive production was rationalised and was often dull, repetitive, and poorly designed thereafter. Good examples are at Barton Mills, Bury (St Mary), Thurston, Long Melford and Hopton.

Warrington, William (1833-66): He described himself as 'artist in stained glass, heraldic and decorative painter, plumber, glazier and paperhanger'. He designed in medieval styles and some of his detailing was distinctly fanciful. The firm continued under his son James until 1875. (Examples of his work can be found at Hessett and Shimpling.)

Weeping chancels: Much nonsense has been written (and is still being perpetuated in some church guide books today) about chancels which incline away from the rectangle formed with the **nave**. The popular fallacy is that this is intended to indicate the drooping of Christ's head on the cross onto His right shoulder, as He is always shown in medieval representations of the Crucifixion. As **Cautley** put it with splendid acidity, the idea is 'too absurd to be credited by any thinking person'. In any event, it should be noted that there are as many chancels which 'weep' left as right. The explanation, quite simply, is that mathematical accuracy was not the forte of medieval masons, and the chancel being 'out of true' with the nave was straight-forwardly a result of ground-plan inaccuracy or expediency. It was often the result of a rebuilding which affected only the chancel or the nave. (An example of this can be found at Sudbury (St Peter).)

Westmacott, Sir Richard (1775-1856): Sculptor. In 1793 he went to study in Rome, where he quickly established himself in the artistic world of Italy. He returned home in 1797 and set up his own studio, which within six years was handling in one year commissions worth the then staggering sum of £16,000. Chimney pieces for the great and titled appear to have been Sir Richard's specialities. However, carvings from his hand, lauding Nelson and the Duke of Wellington, are placed over the grand entrance to Buckingham Palace. The famous Waterloo vase which now stands in the palace gardens is also his work, as is the group of sculptures in the **pediment** of the British Museum. (Examples of his work can be found at Great Finborough and Shimpling.)

Whall, Christopher (1849-1924): Arts and Crafts stained glass worker. For ten years he designed for the firms of Saunders, **Hardman**, and the **Powells**, but became disenchanted with their mass production approach and the lack of opportunity to control the whole process, from cartoon to installing the window. He was fortunate in his contacts with leading architects and was able to influence others through teaching, while his high standards of craftsmanship and insistence on continous involvement made him a leader in the movement. His book *Stained Glass Work* is still one of the best handbooks on the subject. His finest work is in Gloucester cathedral but there are lovely windows at Herringswell and Sproughton in this county.

Willement, Thomas (1786-l871): Leading glazier of the early C19 when the art was at a low ebb. Much of his early work was heraldic and there are fine examples in St George's chapel, Windsor. He advertised himself as 'stained glass artist to Queen Victoria' and was in business from 1812 to 1865. There is a **St Edmund** window by him in Bury (St Mary) and a good piece of work at Dalham.

William and Mary: The 'joint' reign of William III (1688-1702) and Mary II (1688-94), he a Dutch Protestant, she the daughter of the deposed Catholic James II. Architecturally, a period of gracious houses and fine furniture.

Woodwose: A wild man of the woods, bearded and hairy and usually carrying a club, as he can be seen in some churches in carvings on **fonts** and on woodwork. In **bestiaries** he is frequently found fighting with lions, and these scenes alternate round the bases of many East Anglian fonts. One medieval text describes the woodwoses as wild men of India who fought the Sagittarii - were naked until they had slain a lion, after which they wore its skin. The Sagittarius represented man's body and the woodwose his soul; as the lion was slain, so the soul overcame the vanities of the world, and this was used as an appropriate theme for a baptismal homily, with the figures round the font or in the roof overhead as illustrations. (Examples can be found at Mildenhall, Freckenham, Norton, Haughley, Sudbury (All Saints) and Woolpit.)

Wooldridge, Harry Ellis (1845-1917): Stained glass designer. As a painter, musican and critic, he had a wide influence on the educated taste of his time. He was a friend of Burne-Jones and designed many windows for the **Powells**. He worked in the **Renaissance** manner, with correct drawing and pre-determined colours. He contributed two volumes to the *Oxford*

History of Music and was co-editor, with the Poet Laureate, of the *Yatten-don Hymnal.*

Wyatt, John Drayton (1820-91): An architect who joined **Sir George Gilbert Scott** in 1841 and became one of his principal assistants. Although he set up his own practice in 1856, he continued to collaborate with Scott for many years as a draughtsman and detail designer. In 1867 he was appointed diocesan architect to Bath & Wells but our interest lies in his work as consulting architect to the archdeaconry of Sudbury. He was active in many churches, including Rickinghall Inferior, Sudbury (St Gregory), Brandon, Mildenhall, Clare, Hartest, Freckenham, Higham, Thorpe Morieux and the cathedral.

Wyvern: A mythical winged dragon with two eagle's feet and a snake-like barbed tail. (Examples can be seen at Mildenhall, Hargrave and Honington.)

NOTES

NOTES

NOTES

NOTES

NOTES

NOTES

NOTES

NOTES

NOTES

NOTES

NOTES

NOTES